WITNESS INTIMIDATION

Recent Titles from QUORUM BOOKS

The Adversary Economy: Business Responses to Changing Government Requirements
Alfred A. Marcus

Microeconomic Concepts for Attorneys: A Reference Guide
Wayne C. Curtis

Beyond Dumping: New Strategies for Controlling Toxic Contamination
Bruce Piasecki, Editor

Payments in the Financial Services Industry of the 1980s: Conference Proceedings
Federal Reserve Bank of Atlanta, Sponsor

Japanese Business Law and the Legal System
Elliott J. Hahn

YOUTHJOBS: Toward a Private/Public Partnership
David Bresnick

State Government Export Promotion: An Exporter's Guide
Alan R. Posner

Principles for Electric Power Policy
Technology Futures, Inc., and Scientific Foresight, Inc.

The Debt Dilemma of Developing Nations: Issues and Cases
Chris C. Carvounis

Business and Technological Dynamics in Newly Industrializing Asia
Wenlee Ting

Employee Development Programs: An Organizational Approach
Bobby C. Vaught, Frank Hoy, and W. Wray Buchanan

International Accounting: Issues and Solutions
Ahmed Belkaoui

WITNESS INTIMIDATION

The Law's Response

Michael H. Graham

Q

Quorum Books
Westport, Connecticut • London, England

Library of Congress Cataloging in Publication Data

Graham, Michael H.
Witness intimidation.

Bibliography: p.
Includes index.
1. Witnesses—United States. 2. Admissions (Law)—United States. 3. Evidence, Hearsay—United States. 4. Intimidation. I. Title.
KF9672.G7 1985 347.73'66 84-11780
ISBN 0-89930-104-5 (lib. bdg.) 347.30766

Library of Congress Catalog Card Number: 84-11780
ISBN: 0-89930-104-5

First published in 1985 by Quorum Books

Greenwood Press
A division of Congressional Information Service, Inc.
88 Post Road West, Westport, Connecticut 06881

Printed in the United States of America

10 9 8 7 6 5 4 3 2 1

To my Aunt Ida Russo and my Aunt Rose Silverman

Contents

Preface xi

Chapter 1. Introduction 3

A. The Problem and Its Extent 3

B. Legislative, Judicial, Prosecutorial, and Societal Response 8
  1. Preventive, Deterrent, and Remedial Action 8
  2. Admissibility of Prior Statements 11

C. The Approach 11

Chapter 2. Preventive Initiatives 16

A. The Fair Treatment of Victims and Witnesses 16
  1. American Bar Association Recommendations 16
    (a) Law Enforcement 17
    (b) Prosecution 18
    (c) Courts 19
    (d) Community Groups/Private Sector 20
    (e) Organized Bar 20
  2. Victim and Witness Protection Act of 1982 21
  3. President's Task Force on Victims of Crime 29
  4. National Judicial College Recommended Practices 30

B. Discovery of Prosecution Witnesses 34
  1. The Common Law 34
  2. Early Statutory Development 35
  3. Federal Rule of Criminal Procedure 16 37
  4. Jencks v. United States 38

5. Amended Federal Rule of Criminal Procedure 16 39
6. American Bar Association Standards 41
7. Uniform Rules of Criminal Procedure 44
8. Proposed Amendment to Federal Rule of Criminal Procedure 16 46
9. Revised American Bar Association Standards 50
10. Prospective 51

C. Material Witness Statutes 56

D. Depositions to Perpetuate Testimony 59
1. The Hearsay Rule 59
2. The Confrontation Clause 61
3. Early Statutory Development 65
4. Federal Rule of Criminal Procedure 15 67
5. Title VI of The Organized Crime Control Act of 1970 72
6. Amendment to Federal Rule of Criminal Procedure 15 74
7. Uniform Rules of Criminal Procedure 79
8. Evaluation 82

E. The Witness Protection Program 85

Chapter 3. Deterrent and Remedial Measures 103

A. The Crime of Intimidation 103

B. Restraining Order 112
1. Criminal 112
2. Civil 114

C. Monetary Recovery 116
1. Civil Tort Liability 116
2. Criminal Restitution 117
3. Victim Compensation Programs 121

Chapter 4. Substantive Admissibility of Prior Statements 125

A. The Problem 125

B. Former Testimony 127
1. Unavailability Requirement 128
2. Specified Criteria 130
(a) Same Party or, in Civil Action, Predecessor in Interest 130
(b) Similar Motive to Develop Testimony 131
(c) The Adequate Opportunity Dilemma 132

C. Prior Inconsistent Statements 133
1. Federal Rule of Evidence 801(d)(1)(A) 133
(a) The Orthodox Rule 133

(b) Advisory Committee's Proposal and Congressional Reaction 137
(c) An Assessment 141
2. The Requirement of Inconsistency 142
3. The Forgetful Witness 143
(a) True Lack of Recollection 143
(b) Feigned Lack of Recollection 144

D. Federal Rule of Evidence 803(24) 149

E. Federal Rule of Evidence 804(b)(5) 154

F. Prior Statement of Identification 160
1. The Prerequisites 160
2. Critique 162
3. Constitutional Considerations 163

G. Past Recollection Recorded 164

H. Confrontation Clause Issues 165
1. Available Declarant 165
2. Unavailable Declarant 168
3. Synopsis 173

I. The Waiver Doctrine 174
1. The Doctrine in Operation 174
2. Finding a Waiver 175
3. A Better Approach 177

J. Summary 181

Chapter 5. Refreshing Recollection 210

Chapter 6. Prior Inconsistent Statement Impeachment 215

A. The Prerequisites 216
1. Prior Disclosure of Content 216
2. Inconsistency 216
3. The Foundation 217
4. Good Faith Basis 220
5. Extrinsic Evidence 221
6. Limiting Instructions 221

B. The Voucher Rule 221
1. Surprise and Affirmative Damage 223
2. Federal Rule of Evidence 403 224
3. "Mere Subterfuge" or "Primary Purpose" 226

C. Lack of Recollection 226

D. Hostile Witnesses and Leading Questions 227

E. The Court's Witness Doctrine 232

F. Summary 233

Chapter 7. Expanding Substantive Admissibility 252

A. Prior Inconsistent Statements 254

B. Hearings and Depositions 259

C. Preservation Proceedings 263
1. The Components 265
(a) Noninvestigative Presiding Officer 265
(b) Facilitating Determining Trustworthiness 266
(c) Designated Counsel 268
(d) Procedure at Proceeding 271
2. Determining Admissibility 275
(a) Former Testimony 275
(b) Federal Rule of Evidence 804(b)(5) 276
(1) Unavailability Requirement 276
(2) Specified Criteria 278

Chapter 8. Conclusion 303

Bibliography 307

Index 315

Preface

In May 1982 I received a telephone call from Robert B. Lawler, Chief of the Appeals Division of the District Attorney's Office for Philadelphia, Pennsylvania. Lawler had read several of my writings in the field of evidence and thought I might be of some help in connection with an effort he was making to have the Supreme Court of Pennsylvania sanction the substantive admissibility of prior inconsistent statements.

The conversation quickly focused on a problem with which I was already familiar. The prosecution has in its possession a prior statement of a witness in which the witness implicates the defendant. However, by the time the witness is called at trial by the prosecution, the witness has been intimidated to testify in a manner different from what is reflected by the prior statement. The witness may claim lack of personal knowledge (I didn't see anything), lack of current recollection (I don't remember anything), or testify to facts that are either less helpful, neutral, or damaging to the prosecution (It definitely wasn't him) in comparison with the facts stated in the witness's prior statement. Such witnesses are commonly referred to as "turncoat" or "flipped" witnesses. Lawler advised that in Philadelphia they are said to have "gone south."

Lawler then relayed the facts from a recent trial to illustrate the injustice that may result when a witness has been successfully intimidated. The police responding to a radio call of a shooting found a man injured on the ground. The man told the officers that he had just jumped from an apartment window. On the window ledge of that apartment the police observed a woman hanging by her fingertips. Inside the apartment the police found two persons who had been shot to death and evidence indicating the earlier presence of narcotic drugs. The two witnesses gave statements to the police, one of the statements being tape recorded. Both witnesses named the killer, accused him of shooting at them as well, and admitted that they were associates of the killer in a drug ring. By trial both witnesses had "turned"; neither witness would testify in a manner consistent with their prior statements to the police. As with many witnesses who "turn," these witnesses had been intimidated by the defendant to change their testimony. Their prior statements, being hearsay, were not admitted at trial as substantive evidence. A guilty man went free.

Having been interested for some time in the subject of witnesses who have been intimidated to change their testimony or not to testify at all, the various maneuvers prosecutors have employed in court when faced with a "turncoat" witness, and the law's reaction to such maneuvers, I decided to attempt to describe in a book this unique area of the law in all of its many facets. As the law's response to attempts by prosecutors to place the prior statement of the witness before the jury by hook or by crook unfolded, problem areas surfaced and potential solutions came to mind. Although most, if not all, of these evidentiary problem areas had caught my eye before, I had never attempted to address them from the sole perspective of responding to the effects of witness intimidation. Having worked through the myriad of possibilities depending upon the actual testimony of the witness in court or the total absence of the witness's testimony, the circumstances surrounding the making of the prior statement, and the purpose for which the prior statement is offered at trial, I reached the conclusion that modification of existing evidence rules alone would provide an important but still inadequate response by the law to the problems caused by loss of in-court testimony due to witness intimidation. My solution, albeit only a partial solution, is to create a new hearing known as a "preservation proceeding."

During my investigation and research, I discovered, much to my surprise, that during the past few years persons involved in the criminal justice system had begun to react to the problem of witness intimidation from a viewpoint wholly apart form the admissibility of the prior statement of an intimidated witness at trial. Studies and hearings during the 1970's had confirmed the extraordinary breadth of the problem of witness intimidation. In response, the American Bar Association and Congress, among others, had acted to establish practices and procedures to insure, to the extent possible, the fair treatment of victims and witnesses. Measures were recommended to reduce the possibility of witnesses being intimidated and to respond if an attempt at intimidation was made. Moreover, proposals were set forth to address the day-to-day concerns of victims and witnesses caught up involuntarily in the criminal justice system.

Witness intimidation alters the lives of those intimidated and results in a refusal of the witness to testify or a change in what otherwise would have been the testimony of the witness. Examination of the law's response to reduce the opportunities for witness intimidation, to react when witness intimidation is attempted, to preserve testimony in anticipation of potential witness intimidation, and to determine admissibility of prior statements in the face of successful intimidation requires the exploration in relative detail of the many different aspects of practice, procedure, and the law of evidence bearing upon the problem as each operates alone and in conjunction with other aspects. Hopefully, this book meets the challenge.

I would like to thank Audrey Alterman, Kathy Kaplan, and Dewey Caton for their help in putting this book together.

WITNESS INTIMIDATION

Chapter 1

Introduction

A. THE PROBLEM AND ITS EXTENT

Vincent Pacilli was on trial on a narcotic charge. Vincent Pacilli discovered that Patsy Park had been subpoenaed to testify at this trial. Vincent Pacilli killed Patsy Park by slitting her throat and burning her body.[1]

An elderly man testified at a trial as an eyewitness to a furniture store holdup. On the afternoon that a new trial was granted, this elderly man and his wife were found seated in easy chairs in front of their television set—each had been shot in the back of the head at pointblank range.[2]

J. Edgar Hoover has described how mobsters hung a potential witness on a butchers hook for three days and tortured him until dead.[3]

Sam "Teetz" Battablia and "Joe Shine" Amabile, two high-ranking Chicago mobsters, threatened that witnesses in their extortion trial would be "beat into jelly with baseball bats."[4]

Two witnesses in a bank robbery conspiracy case were to testify against the leaders of a large bank robbery ring. One of the witnesses was taken for a ride and was pistol whipped. The wife of the other witness was severely beaten around the head, shoulders and stomach and a bottle was broken over her head. Both witnesses were told the beatings were a result of their upcoming testimony.[5]

During an investigation concerning racketeering and burglary several witnesses were threatened. As a warning of what would happen if he testified, one witness found a dead rat with an accompanying note at his bunkside.[6] Another witness was beaten and sexually molested in her home and was warned that she had better not testify. After she did she was murdered in an attack involving "dum-dum" bullets.[7] Still another witness confidentially told authorities that he had personally been present when other witnesses had been physically assaulted. After this witness' kneecaps were fractured he "felt it wise to abstain from testifying."[8]

A switchboard operator in an apartment building was an eyewitness to a robbery. The operator was repeatedly called at her switchboard only hours after the robbery and was informed that if she testified a bomb would be thrown in the lobby next to her switchboard. This eyewitness later told the police that she did not see anything.[9]

These reports are just only a few of thousands of examples of a serious problem facing the criminal justice system in this country—witness intimidation. *Witness intimidation* refers to threats made or actions taken by defendants or others acting on their behalf or independently to dissuade or prevent victims or eyewitnesses of crimes[10] from reporting those crimes, assisting in the investigation, or giving testimony at a hearing or trial. Witness intimidation is an extremely serious obstacle in the quest for law and order that is only now beginning to receive the attention it deserves.

Recent studies have unequivocally confirmed that witness intimidation is a pervasive problem. In 1973 the Institute for Law and Social Research examined witness cooperation. The study was based on 1,547 murder, rape, robbery, assault, and burglary cases originating in August-November 1972. The analysis revealed that about 23 percent of the 1,547 cases were not prosecuted because of what was classified as witness noncooperation.[11] A full 28 percent of all witnesses interviewed indicated that fear of reprisal by the defendant accounted for their noncooperation.[12] The greatest response given by witnesses when asked "What changes do you think would make witnesses more cooperative?" was "better protection of witnesses."[13] In 1976 New York's Victim Services Agency and the Vera Institute of Justice performed an extensive study on witness intimidation. The study discovered that 39 percent of the witnesses interviewed in Brooklyn Criminal Court were very much afraid of revenge by defendants and that 26 percent of the witnesses interviewed had actually been threatened at some time during the criminal process—21 percent by the defendant and 5 percent by the defendant's family or friends. The researchers concluded that as many as 7,500 witnesses are threatened each year in Brooklyn Criminal Court alone. Moreover, the study was limited to cases in which the crime was reported and an arrest was made. Thus excluded were the many cases in which, whether because of intimidation or other reasons, the crime was not reported to police or no arrest was made.[14]

There is also abundant anecdotal and impressionistic evidence of the magnitude of the witness intimidation problem. During the 1975 congressional hearings on proposed amendments to the Federal Rules of Criminal Procedure, the Department of Justice furnished the House Judiciary Committee with a list of more than 700 instances of witness intimidation ranging from assault to assassination arising in all manner of prosecutions.[15] In 1979 the Rape Prosecution Unit in Philadelphia advised that in 50 percent of reported rape cases, the rapist threatened the victim with violence or death if she reported the incident to the police or cooperated with the District Attorney.[16] Because of the increasing use of witness intimidation by criminals as an effective method of keeping victims or witnesses out of courtrooms, that same year a representative of the Chicago Police Department concluded that witness intimidation has even come to be viewed as an "innovative defense"—a certain means of securing an acquittal.[17]

Witness intimidation occurs in numerous contexts, in several general forms, and in an unlimited number of locations. The context in which witness intimidation is the most extensive is the world of organized crime. In fact, witness intimidation is one aspect of organized crime that characterizes it as a unique form of criminal activity and distinguishes it from ad hoc youth gangs, groups of pickpockets, and professional and occasional criminals in general.[18] Organized crime embodies witness intimidation in the position of the "enforcer." The enforcer's duty is to maintain the organization's integrity by arranging for the threatening, maiming, and killing of potential witnesses.[19] The Justice Department has indicated that 10 percent of all murders related to organized crime in a four-year period were of prosecution witnesses.[20] Very often, when a person would agree to testify against an individual connected to organized crime, whether the person was a member of the organization or a concerned citizen, they would either disappear, become involved in a fatal accident, or be murdered outright.[21] The Justice Department has also reported that more than 25 informants were murdered during an earlier four-year period.[22]

The violence and severity of organized crime's response to implicating witnesses has been attested repeatedly. Senator Tydings advised that scores of cases were lost because key witnesses turned up in rivers in concrete boots or were crushed—"James Bond-like"—along with their automobiles by hydraulic machines in syndicate-owned junkyards.[23] United States Attorney General Katzenbach stated that there are dozens of cases where witnesses have been beaten with baseball bats and tortured with acetylene torches, and there are even more cases of sudden unexplained silence by witnesses or potential witnesses.[24] More specifically, Vincent "Big Vinnie" Teresa, a mob hit-man, told how he and another "enforcer," Maurice "Pro" Lerner, were sent to an island to hit Joe Barboza, a mob killer who had become a federal witness.[25] They used a luxury yacht equipped with high-powered binoculars, high-powered telescoped rifles, explosives, and even wet suits and oxygen tanks for an underwater attack in order to try to silence Barboza.[26]

Although witness intimidation occurs frequently in the organized crime context, it is by no means limited to that situation. A great deal of witness intimidation takes place in a family or domestic setting. In New York a Domestic Violence Unit serviced approximately 450 victims in a six-month period.[27] Two-thirds of these victims did not press charges, and of those that did, 25 percent withdrew the charges later. Intimidation frequently accounts for the absence of charges being brought in domestic violence cases. The victim of domestic violence is often told by her abuser that she will be killed if she goes to the police or that her children will be harmed or taken away from her if she does not withdraw her charges.

Another context in which witness intimidation occurs is the prison system. The Assistant Director of the American Correctional Law Project stated:

> If victim/witness intimidation is a "persistent problem" in the free world, it is an epidemic in prison. It's one of the basic rules of the game for prison inmates. Intimidation is to be expected in virtually every case where an inmate may potentially be testifying against another inmate.[28]

He went on to describe a case of prison witness intimidation in which a "snitch" was stabbed by another inmate for no apparent reason. The attacker later stated that he did it as a matter of principle.

Intimidation can even occur in the context of a police station. In one case police officers brought the victim to the police station to identify the four men who had assaulted him earlier in the evening. During the identification, the officers left the assailants near the plaintiff. The four men attacked the victim a second time and inflicted serious injuries.[29]

Witness intimidation takes three general forms.[30] The first form is the traditional mode of an overt threat or actual use of force against the witness. The second form is family, community, or cultural intimidation. This occurs mostly in urban areas when the witness's family, neighbors, or friends exert pressure upon the witness not to testify or to aid authorities. The third form of intimidation is perceived or anticipated intimidation. This form of intimidation occurs when the victim or witness changes his or her testimony or does not testify for fear, however justified or unjustified, of reprisal by the perpetrator.

A 1981 Victims Services Agency study reported that 64 percent of intimidated witnesses surveyed were threatened by a direct verbal confrontation, such as "I'm going to get you," "You'll be sorry," or even "I'll kill you if you go to court."[31] The second most common form of intimidation, 23 percent, was a threat made by a telephone call to the witness. Half of such calls were anonymous. In some instances the defendant called the witness on the telephone to say hello, and although no overt threat was made, the mere sound of the defendant's voice was enough to prevent the witness from testifying. More than 7 percent of the witnesses interviewed reported that the intimidation was an actual physical attack, and another 6 percent of the witnesses were threatened with weapons, including guns, baseball bats, and even a sword. The witnesses' property was stolen, damaged, or destroyed in 17 percent of the cases. The Victims Services Agency study found in addition that there were indirect verbal threats (11 percent), such as threats conveyed through neighborhood rumors or through the witnesses' friends, and threats by looks or gestures (5 percent) and by notes (2 percent).[32] The Victims Services Agency study also indicated that 72 percent of threatened witnesses were both victim and eyewitness to the crime and that 47 percent knew the defendant before the crime.[33]

The intimidation of a witness often involves persons other than or in addition to the defendant. For example, when a woman charged a member of a family from whom she rented a trailer with rape, the defendant's family confiscated all of her belongings and told her they would not be returned until she dropped the charges. Another witness, a trainee in the Job Corps, was assaulted by one of her instructors, and when she reported the assault, she was dismissed from her training program for being a "troublemaker." One witness was sexually assaulted by her class instructor. When confronted by the witness, the instructor told her that if she reported the crime she would fail his class, that other instructors would fail her, that this would prevent her from transferring schools, and that he would use his influence to prevent her from being admitted to her chosen occupation.[34] Subtle and apparently innocent acts have been used by associates of the defendant to intimidate witnesses of gang-related crimes. In one instance gang members stood on the sidewalk in front of the witness's home and did nothing more than glare at the house. Another witness reported that after being raped by a motorcycle gang, several gang members not involved in the rape drove their motorcycles by her house.[35]

As indicated by the Victims Services Agency study, intimidation can and does occur anywhere and everywhere a witness can be found. Most threats, 42 percent, occurred in the witness's home or neighborhood. Another 20 percent of the witnesses reported that they were threatened at the scene of the crime, and 11 percent indicated they were threatened at the scene of the arrest. One witness even reported that he was threatened as he was riding to the precinct in the police car with the defendant. The telephone was used to threaten 23 percent of the intimidated witnesses. Fifteen percent of witnesses reported threats occurring in the court house, and still another 15 percent stated that they were threatened at school or at work.[36]

Regardless of the particular context, form, or location witness intimidation takes, witness intimidation constitutes an extremely pervasive and persistent problem. Witness intimidation is a crime that has two unique aspects—only unsuccessful attempts are ever reported and successful attempts thwart the criminal justice system from securing the convictions of the perpetrators of separate and distinct crimes. Witness intimidation has the devastating effect of undermining public confidence in the legal process. A criminal justice system that does not receive cooperation from witnesses will cease to function. Yet in Los Angeles, for example, as recently as 1978 the District Attorney's Office during a six-month period filed only five witness intimidation cases. Of these cases, it won three convictions. Two cases were dismissed. Two of those convicted were placed on probation, and the third was jailed on a misdemeanor count. Of the 20,000 persons in California's adult correctional system in 1979, only 11 were serving time for violation of the state's felony witness intimidation law.[37]

B. LEGISLATIVE, JUDICIAL, PROSECUTORIAL, AND SOCIETAL RESPONSE

1. Preventive, Deterrent, and Remedial Action

The traditional approach of the criminal justice system has been to focus solely upon the identification, apprehension, prosecution, punishment, and rehabilitation of offenders. Victims and witnesses to crimes have been considered only to the extent that they actually played a direct role in the identification and prosecution of offenders. Victims of crime were unlikely to obtain restitution from the convicted criminal and even less likely to receive any compensation for their losses from the government. Similarly, when it came to assisting victims and witnesses in overcoming the frustrations and economic sacrifices that reporting of criminal activity and involvement in criminal proceeding causes, the criminal justice system was virtually absent. Of more direct concern, the plight of the witness, whether or not also a victim, intimidated by the accused was almost totally ignored.

Although little concern was shown throughout the nation with the overall plight of the witness intimidated by the accused, this is not to say that with respect to the most severe threats to a witness's safety action was not taken. All of us have seen the old movies where the "material witness" was put up in an old hotel with a police guard. More sophisticated approaches involving the relocation of the witness and a change of identity have also been employed for some time. Most of the cases in which such drastic measures have been taken involve threats to a witness from members of organized crime. Formal recognition of the witness protection program of the federal government came in the Organized Crime Control Act of 1970.[38] The threat from organized crime members has also been a critical factor behind the absence of a rule requiring that the government in federal criminal prosecutions disclose in advance of trial the names of witnesses the government intends to call.[39] Moreover, when a witness involved in a federal or state prosecution indicated by action or conduct that he or she would not testify at trial, often but not always because of the threat of reprisal, the prosecution would frequently attempt to secure the witness's attendance by use of a material witness statute or secure the witness's testimony in advance of trial in the form of a deposition.[40]

Ironically, although the plight of the intimidated witness was generally being ignored, the importance of the assistance and cooperation of victims and witnesses was clearly recognized. Studies over the years have indicated two major reasons for victim noninvolvement or noncooperation. First, involvement in the operation of the criminal justice system often presents witnesses with so many major inconveniences and problems such as wasted time caused by trial delays, loss of income, and inappropriate physical accommodation at court that, all too frequently, even civic-minded, initially cooperative witnesses wish they had never stepped forward and vow never to do so again. Second, noninvolvement is often an initial predisposition that prevails over any thought of volunteering help. Such initial predisposition includes prejudices and attitudes toward personnel and agencies of the criminal justice system. Another aspect of predisposition fostering noncooperation takes the form of fear of reprisal. Although the fear of reprisal may occur spontaneously with an individual, more often it is brought about by physical threats or family, community, or cultural intimidation.[41]

During the late 1960's and early 1970's problems associated with being a victim or a witness to crime began to receive more attention. For example, the National Advisory Commission on Criminal Justice Standards and Goals referred to deficient "methods and procedures by which witnesses are used."[42] The commission observed, "Citizens—as victims, witnesses, defendants, or jurors—experience delay, inconvenience, and confusion."[43] After noting the need for greater citizen cooperation, "particularly as ready and willing witnesses," President Ford emphasized, "A lot of witnesses never show up, especially after the fourth or fifth continuance. . . . Even victims do not want to get involved with all the paperwork, interrogations, and repeated visits to the court house in a case that, after several continuances, may be dropped anyway. Sometimes the victim fears reprisal."[44] Several prosecutor's offices and police agencies began to initiate programs designed to improve the handling of witnesses.[45] The National District Attorneys Association established a commission on victim and witness assistance. The association's objective was "to develop a special capability on the part of the district attorneys to better serve the needs of victims of crime and witnesses to crime, and to thereby enhance the effectiveness of their prosecutive activities."[46] In addition, national and local groups sprang up to assist victims and witnesses.

In response to the increased awareness of the overall plight of victims and witnesses to crimes and the renewed appreciation of the importance of voluntary cooperation by such persons in the successful prosecution of offenders, recommendations for concrete action emerged. Some concrete action followed. Victim compensation programs were established in nearly three-fourths of the states.[47] Statutes providing for the availability of an order requiring the criminal defendant to make restitution as part of his or her sentence were enacted in several jurisdictions.[48] However, procedures with respect to witness notification, facilities, protection, and so on, designed to insure fair treatment and thus encourage full witness cooperation, were acted upon only in isolated instances throughout the country. Much remained to be done.

In the mid-1970's the American Bar Association turned its attention to the special needs and problems faced by crime victims. In 1976 the American Bar Association Criminal Justice Section created its Victims Committee. A major motivation for its creation was the recognition that the organized bar in concentrating its efforts for years on the rights of the accused had neglected the plight of crime victims and witnesses. The committee initially focused on improved treatment for victims by the criminal justice system. It suggested amendments to the American Bar Association's Criminal Justice Standards to reflect a concern for the fair treatment of victims and urged implementation of an American Bar Association policy supporting crime victim compensation legislation. The committee later turned its attention to the then largely unexamined problem of victim and witness intimidation. Its efforts eventually led in 1980 to recommendations for action by six segments of society: legislature, law enforcement, prosecution, courts, community groups/private sectors, and organized bar.[49] Spurred by the recommendations of the Victims Committee, Congress passed the Victim and Witness Protection Act of 1982.[50] The President's Task Force on Victims of Crime rendered its report during December of the same year.[51] Finally, exactly one year later the National Conference on the Judiciary on the Rights of Victims of Crime, held at the National Judicial College, Reno, Nevada, issued a similar call to action.[52] Included within the flurry of activity were recommendations to encourage the voluntary cooperation of victims and witnesses through adoption of practices and procedures designed in part to reduce the threat of intimidation.[53] The Victim and Witness Protection Act contains provisions making intimidation a separate criminal offense as well as providing for the availability of injunctive relief against anyone intimidating a witness.

The basic thrust of several of the recommendations put forth by the American Bar Association, the President's Task Force, and the National Conference on the Judiciary, as well as many of the provisions of the Victim and Witness Protection Act of 1982, directly address the problem of witness intimidation. Many others, such as providing for the prompt return of a victim's property, for notification to employers, and for federal funding of victim compensation programs, deal solely with additional concerns with the plight of victims of crime. With respect to the problem of witness intimidation, the thrust of each approach is the implementation of practices and procedures designed to prevent and discourage intimidation by reducing the opportunities for intimidation to occur, to respond quickly and thoroughly if an attempt at intimidation does occur, and to lend moral and financial support whenever feasible to victims of witness intimidation.

2. Admissibility of Prior Statements

The recommendations for action of the American Bar Association, the President's Task Force, and the National Conference on the Judiciary, as well as the statutory provisions of the Victim and Witness Protection of 1982, seek to prevent and discourage intimidation in the first instance and then seek to react appropriately to attempts at intimidation when it does occur. However, responding to an attempt at intimidation by means of police protection, a civil injunction, a criminal restraining order, or a criminal prosecution is available only if the intimidation is unsuccessful.

A witness who has been successfully intimidated will not come forward to seek protection of any kind or otherwise bring the action of the defendant to the attention of the authorities. A witness who has been successfully intimidated may be dead. A witness who has been successfully intimidated may refuse to appear voluntarily in court, may go into hiding to avoid the service of a subpoena, or may simply disregard a subpoena served upon him or her. A successfully intimidated witness who comes to court may feign a lack of recollection about the events relating to the crime for which the accused is on trial. Finally, a successfully intimidated witness who comes to court may "turn" or "flip" and tell a story completely different form the one related to prosecution authorities when first interviewed.

When a witness is successfully intimidated, the statement of fact he or she initially gave to prosecution authorities will not be forthcoming from the witness at trial. The question then becomes whether the government can introduce the prior out-of-court statement of the witness at trial and if so for what purposes under what circumstances. Resolution of the question of admissibility of the prior statement at trial raises issues concerning operation of the hearsay rule, the Confrontation Clause of the Sixth Amendment, as well as evidentiary principles governing the refreshing of a witness's recollection and those governing the impeachment of a witness called by a party by means of a prior inconsistent statement. Resolving questions of admissibility has been greatly affected by the enactment in 1975 of the Federal Rules of Evidence and the subsequent enactment by 27 states of rules of evidence modeled on the Federal Rules of Evidence.

C. THE APPROACH

The approach taken in this book to the law's response to the various aspects of the problem of witness intimidation can be summarized as one of description, analysis, critique, and proposal. The various practices, procedures, statutory schemes, and so on, developed to encourage the voluntary cooperation of witnesses, to shield witnesses from acts of intimidation, to respond to such acts when they occur, and to provide generally for the fair treatment of all victims and witnesses of crime are intermeshed. Each of the various components is described in Chapters 2 and 3, with greater emphasis being given to those aspects of the law's response bearing directly on the problem of witness intimidation. Chapters 4 through 6 examine in detail the admissibility of prior statements of a witness who has been successfully intimidated. Each of the many variations in fact pattern likely to arise is not only described and analyzed but critiqued as well. The framework for discussion is the Federal Rules of Evidence. The general common law of evidence is addressed to the extent necessary to place the description, analysis, and critique in both a historical and current day perspective.

Chapter 7 presents three recommendations for enhancing the likelihood that a witness's prior statement will be received as substantive evidence if the witness's testimony is lost to the trier of fact for any reason including witness intimidation. The first recommendation calls for an expansion of the breadth of prior inconsistent statements now substantively admissible. The second recommendation suggests enhanced employment of the preliminary hearing, other pretrial hearings, and the deposition in advance of trial to perpetuate the witness's testimony against loss by reason of intimadation. Finally, a proposal is made for the creation of a new hearing, referred to as a preservation proceedings, to further expand the possibility of substantive admissibility of the witness's prior testimony at trial. The thrust of the three recommendations is to provide for the admissibility at trial of prior statements of the witness whenever warranted by considerations of trustworthiness and at the same time hopefully to discourage attempts at witness intimidation. The final chapter, Chapter 8, contains a brief summary of the law's response, past, present, and future, to the problem of witness intimidation.

NOTES

1. *Federal Rules of Criminal Procedure Amendments Act of 1975*: Hearings Before the Senate Comm. on the Judiciary, 94th Cong., 1st Sess. 175 (1975) (statement of Paul Curran, U.S. Attorney for the Southern District of New York).

2. *Appendix to Compensating Crime Victims*: Hearings on H.R. 4257 and Related Bills Before the Subcomm. on Criminal Justice of the Comm. on the Judiciary, 96th Cong., 1st Sess. 175 (1979) (statement of William Heiman, Chief of the Rape Prosecution Unit, Philadelphia District Attorney's Office).

3. *Department of State, Justice, and Commerce, the Judiciary, and Related Agencies Appropriations for 1967*: Hearings Before a Subcomm. of the House Comm. on Appropriations, 89th Cong., 2d Sess. 272 (1966) (statement of J. Edgar Hoover, Director, Federal Bureau of Investigation).,

4. *Organized Crime Control Act of 1970*: Hearings on S. 30 and Related Proposals Before Subcomm. No. 5 of the House Comm. on the Judiciary, 91st Cong., 2d Sess. 114 (1970) (statement of Senator John McClellan).

5. *Federal Rules of Criminal Procedure Amendments Act of 1975, supra* note 1

at 177 (statement of John C. Keeney, Acting Assistant Attorney General, Criminal Division, Department of Justice).

6. *Id.* at 180.

7. *Id.*

8. *Id.*

9. *Id.* at 182.

10. As employed throughout this book, the term *witness* when used in conjunction with the term *victim* refers to nonvictim occurrence witnesses. As a matter of style the term *witness* will frequently be used singularly and as such is meant to refer to both nonvictim occurrence witnesses and victim occurrence witnesses.

11. F. Cannavale and W. Falcon, *Witness Cooperation* (Lexington, Mass.: D. C. Heath, 1976), p. 21.

12. *Id.* at 55.

13. *Id.*

14. R. Davis, V. Russell, and F. Kunreuther, *The Role of the Complaining Witness in the Urban Criminal Court* (New York: Victim Services Agency and the Vera Institute of Justice, 1980). See also E. Connick and R. Davis, *Examining the Problem of Witness Intimidation*, 66 Judicature 439, 440 (1983).

15. *Federal Rules of Criminal Procedure Amendments Act of 1975, supra* note 1 at 164 (statement of John C. Keeney, Acting Assistant Attorney General, Criminal Division, Department of Justice).

16. *Appendix to Compensating Crime Victims, supra* note 2 at 175 (statement of William Heiman, Chief of the Rape Prosecution Unit, Philadelphia District Attorney's Office).

17. *Id.* at 151 (statement Richard Brezeczek, Deputy Assistant to the Superintendent of the Chicago Police Department).

18. Senate Comm. on the Judiciary, Organized Crime Control Act of 1969, S. Rep. No. 617, 91st Congr., 1st Sess. 41 (1969).

19. *Id.*

20. *Oversight of the Witness Protection Program*: Hearings Before the Subcomm. on Administrative Practice and Procedure of the Senate Comm. on the Judiciary, 95th Cong., 2d Sess. 277 (1979). The report of the Witness Security Program Review Commission listed several typical recent cases involving the murder of witnesses:

> *Bompensiero, Frank*: Murdered February 22, 1977, while scheduled to appear before a Federal grand jury in Los Angeles concerning extortion in the pornography business.
>
> *Bowen, Harold*: Murdered February 22, 1977. It is believed that Bowen upset the organized crime community when he testified before a Federal grand jury on a theft charge which involved a member of a criminal organization.
>
> *Delia, Ellen*: Shot to death February 17, 1977, in Sacramento, California, where she had gone to give testimony concerning fraud and misuse of Federal and state funds in the operation of East Los Angeles Community Projects.
>
> *Delman, Gerald*: Shot by an unknown assailant two days after being subpoenaed and two weeks prior to scheduled testimony in a gambling case in Las Vegas, Nevada.
>
> *Ota, Stanley*: Shot to death November 17, 1976, in a public housing project. Two

months earlier, Ota had been arrested for the sale of one pound of heroin to undercover Federal agents. Shortly after his arrest, there were widespread rumors that the crime syndicate had ordered his death because of the possibility of his cooperation with government authorities.

Gretch, Anthony: Gunned down February 14, 1975. He had turned state's evidence in a gangland killing of Louis Mariani in 1963.

Giancana, Samuel: Murdered in his Oak Park, Illinois home on June 19, 1975, prior to a federal grand jury hearing.

Rand, Tamara: Shot in the head November 9, 1975. Rand was a San Diego realtor. After being cheated in several potentially lucrative real estate transactions, Rand began compiling evidence for a judicial retaliation.

Wellman, Alen E. and his wife Renate: Murdered December 15, 1974. He was scheduled to testify the following week against several organized crime figures.

Fucillo, Joseph: Shot and killed October 17, 1974. Fucillo had testified against two major organized crime figures.

Id. at 277-78.

21. *Id.* at 37 (statement of Thomas O'Connor, Executive Director, Prison Reform Task Force, New York Society for Ethical Culture, New York, N.Y.).

22. *Invasion of Privacy*: Hearings Before the Subcomm. on Administrative Practice and Procedure of the Sentate Comm. on the Judiciary, 89th Cong., 1st Sess. 1158 (1965) (statement of Nicholas deB. Katzenbach, United States Attorney General).

23. *Measures Relating to Organized Crime*: Hearings on S. 30, S. 974, S. 975, S. 976, S. 1623, S. 1624, S. 1861, S. 2022, and S. 2292 Before the Subcomm. on Criminal Laws and Procedures of the Senate Comm. on the Judiciary, 91st Cong., 1st Sess. 161 (1969) (statement of Senator Joseph Tydings).

24. Senate Comm. on the Judiciary, Obstruction of Criminal Investigations, S. Rep. No. 307, 90th Cong., 1st Sess. 3 (1967).

25. *Oversight of the Witness Protection Program, supra* note 20 at 144.

26. *Id.* at 144 (Exhibit 4).

27. *Appendix to Compensating Crime Victims, supra* note 2 at 198 (statement of Jeanine Pirro, Assistant District Attorney, Westchester County, N.Y.).

28. *Id.* at 167 (statement of David Rappaport, Assistant Director, American Correctional Association Correctional Law Project).

29. R. Goldstock and D. Coenen, *Controlling the Contemporary Loanshark: The Law of Illicit Lending and the Problem of Witness Fear*, 65 Cornell L. Rev. 127, 209 (1980).

30. American Bar Association, Criminal Justice Section, *Reducing Victim/Witness Intimidation: A Package* 1 (Washington, D.C., 1981).

31. E. Connick and R. Davis, *supra* note 14 at 442-43 (1983).

32. *Id.* The researchers explained that the figures total to more than 100 percent because several witnesses were threatened more than once.

33. *Id.* at 442.

34. *Appendix to Compensating Crime Victims, supra* note 2 at 6-7.

35. *Id.*

36. E. Connick and R. Davis, *supra* note 14 at 442. Once again, the figures total more than 100 percent because several witnesses were threatened more than once.

37. American Bar Association, Criminal Justice Section, *supra* note 30 at 1-3.

38. Pub. L. No. 91-452, §§ 501-04, 84 Stat. 922 (1970).

39. *See* Fed. R. Crim. P. 16.

40. *See* Chapter 2, Sections C and D *infra*.

41. *See* F. Cannavale and W. Falcon, *supra* note 11 at 9.

42. National Advisory Commission on Criminal Justice Standards and Goals, *A National Strategy to Reduce Crime* (Washington, D.C.: U.S. Government Printing Office, 1973), p. 108.

43. *Id.*

44. An address to the *Convention of the International Association of Chiefs of Police*, September 24, 1974, Washington, D.C.

45. Murray Teigh Bloom, *The Witness: Forgotten Men*, Reader's Digest, November 1974, p. 21. The article originally appeared in the *National Civil Review*, October 1974.

46. National District Attorney's document (undated) pertaining to the solicitation of proposals regarding evaluation of the Commission on Victim Witness Assistance, quoted in F. Cannavale and W. Falcon, *supra* note 11 at 15-16.

47. *See* Chapter 3, Section C3 *infra*.

48. *See* Chapter 3, Section C2 *infra*.

49. American Bar Association, Criminal Justice Section, *supra* note 30 at 9.

50. Pub. L. No. 97-291, 96 Stat. 1248 (1982). *See also* Chapter 2, Section A2 *infra*.

51. *See* Chapter 2, Section A3 *infra*.

52. *See* Chapter 2, Section A4 *infra*.

53. The responsibility of the judiciary to respect the interests of victims and witnesses was acknowledged by Chief Justice Burger in Morris v. Slappy, ____U.S. ____, ____, 103 S.Ct. 1610, 1617, 75 L.Ed.2d 610, 623 (1983):

> Of course, inconvenience and embarrassment to witnesses cannot justify failing to enforce constitutional rights of an accused. . . . But in the administration of criminal justice, courts may not ignore the concerns of victims. Apart from all other factors, such a course would hardly encourage victims to report violations to the proper authorities; this is especially so when the crime is one calling for public testimony about a humiliating and degrading experience.

Chapter **2**

Preventive Initiatives

A. THE FAIR TREATMENT OF VICTIMS AND WITNESSES

1. American Bar Association Recommendations

In 1977 the American Bar Association Criminal Justice Section focused its attention on developing a comprehensive approach to combat the problem of witness intimidation to recommend to the federal government and the states for implementation. To study witness intimidation and explore practical and realistic solutions, a Victims Committee established by the Criminal Justice Section drafted an initial package of proposals and scheduled public hearings.[1] The original draft package consisted of three sets of recommendations—proposed law enforcement and prosecutorial strategies and a proposed model state statute. It was printed in a brochure and disseminated to more than 2,000 judges, law enforcement officials, prosecutors, academics, criminal defense lawyers, state legislators, attorneys general, bar presidents, key congressional and executive branch personnel, directors of victim assistance projects, and members of groups such as the National Organization for Victim Assistance. Comments were sought to the recommendations and testimony solicited for the hearings. Some 80 requests to testify were received, along with dozens of letters commenting on the package.

The Victims Committee heard from 34 witnesses during its June 1979 hearings at the Mayflower Hotel in Washington, D.C.[2] More than 150 persons attended. The testimony and comments received on the package were fully analyzed. The final report emanating from the hearings consisted of six sets of recommendations. These recommendations were approved in August 1980 by the American Bar Association's policy-making House of

Delegates. The first set of recommendations, constituting the "Model Statute: Intimidation of Witnesses and Victims," is set forth in full in Chapter 3 as part of the discussion of the movement to make the intimidation of witnesses a distinct crime.[3] The remaining five sets of recommendations are reproduced below.[4]

(a) Law Enforcement

Recommendation 1.
Responsibility

Prevention of intimidation of victims and witnesses is a basic law enforcement responsibility which should be given high priority and a commitment of resources consistent therewith.

Recommendation 2.
The Victim/Witness Protection Unit

A victim/witness protection unit should be created, consisting of specially assigned and trained peace officers working under the command of a rank officer assigned full time to direct the unit. Adequate support services should be provided. The unit should be organizationally housed in a law enforcement agency whose jurisdiction is at least geographically coterminous with the district attorney's office and courts of general jurisdiction where the victims and witnesses to be served by the unit appear. The services provided by the unit should be available 24 hours a day through use of on-call designated officer during hours of low service demand.

Recommendation 3.
Referral

Victim/witness protection units should be referred those cases in which any significant potential for intimidation or retribution exists.

Recommendation 4.
Advice of Referral

Any individual victim or witness referred to the unit should be advised of the referral and contact methods.

Recommendation 5.
Persons Qualifying for Services

Crime victims, prosecution or defense witnesses, jurors and defendants should be eligible for service by the victim/witness protection unit.

Recommendation 6.
Underlying Charge

The type of underlying charge should not be a dispositive factor in determining eligibility for protection by the unit.

Recommendation 7.
Analysis of Security of Serviced Persons and Threat Posed

The officer assigned to assist a particular person to be served should conduct an analysis of the physical and emotional condition of the person, the person's relationship with the defendant or other threatener, the residential and employment status of the person, and that person's needs in terms of transportation and general security. The officer should also assess the actual or implied threats directed to the person to be served or that person's relatives, analyze the criminal background, record and prior relationships of the threatener to violent persons, maintain knowledge as to the bail status and location of the defendant (where he or she is related to the threat) and integrate such information in an appropriate security plan for the person to be served.

Recommendation 8.
Services to Be Provided

Actual law enforcement services should include telephone "hot line" setups, relocation capabilities, personal protection, increased patrol, transportation and investigation.

Recommendation 9.
Warnings

Direct contact with the defendant (with defense counsel present) prior to or following court appearances, can be used to advise the defendant of the victim/witness protection units's involvement in the case, and to warn the defendant concerning the statutory penalties involved in witness intimidation. The victim/witness protection unit should aggressively follow up alleged violations of the intimidation statute, collecting and presenting evidence to the district attorney for prosecutions of violations under that statute.

Recommendation 10.
Liaisons

To adequately effectuate its objectives, the victim/witness protection unit will need to maintain close liaison with the prosecutor's office, juvenile protective services, the United States marshal's office and other agencies.

(b) Prosecution

Recommendation 1.
Attitude

The prosecutor should recognize the adverse impact on the criminal justice system caused by intimidation of victims and witnesses and should lead in implementing programs to address this problem aggressively.

Recommendation 2.
Assignment and Processing

The prosecutor must advise law enforcement agencies of his keen desire to prosecute intimidation cases and should so assign such cases that the same prosecutor can aggressively and expeditiously move the case from issuance to sentencing.

Recommendation 3.
Courtroom Operations

The prosecutor should request as a condition of bond that the defendant neither directly nor indirectly intimidate a victim or witness, should refer those cases where intimidation is likely to the law enforcement victim/witness protection unit, should prevent the improvident release of information on the location of any victim or witness upon whom intimidation has been or is likely to be attempted, and should have a policy of demanding a speedy trial whenever threats occur.

Recommendation 4.
Warnings

The prosecutor by appropriate warnings to possible intimidators can often deter threats before, during or after trial.

Recommendation 5.
Post Trial Conduct

After trial, the prosecutor should continue to provide information for and urge law enforcement assistance to victims and witnesses who reasonably fear retribution.

(c) Courts

Recommendation 1.
Bench Measures

The trial judge should observe the behavior of persons in the courtroom to detect intimidating conduct. The judge, in his inherent power to maintain decorum in the courtroom, should address such conduct, depending on its gravity, by reprimand, removal from the courtroom, use of the contempt power and referral for prosecution.

Recommendation 2.
Motions to Dismiss

In those jurisdictions in which the court has the power to grant or deny motions to dismiss made by the prosecution when witnesses fail to appear, the court should assure itself that intimidation is not the cause of the nonappearance or that all appropriate investigations or countermeasures have been made.

Recommendation 3.
Continuances

If the court is provided with information giving it the basis for a finding that unavailability of a necessary witness may be due to intimidation, that should constitute good cause for granting a continuance, and such a continuance should be granted.

Recommendation 4.
Orders

The trial judge may, through his inherent powers to regulate the conduct of persons in the courtroom or over whom he has jurisdiction, order persons who appear to be engaging in intimidation to avoid contact with the apparent victims of that intimidation.

Recommendation 5.
Handbooks

Court systems should prepare and distribute victim/witness handbooks.

Recommendation 6.
Witness Facilities

Court should provide appropriate waiting facilities, with provisions for segregation, for witnesses.

(d) Community Groups/Private Sector

Recommendation 1.
"Friend in Court" Services

Community organizations should, in cooperation with courts, the bar and prosecutors' offices, establish "Victim Advocate" and/or "Friend in Court" systems.

Recommendation 2.
Victim Information Services

Community organizations should, in cooperation with law enforcement and prosecution agencies and the courts, establish victim/witness information centers to advise victims and prosecution and defense witnesses of the progress of cases concerning them.

Recommendation 3.
Witness Information Services

Community organizations should, in cooperation with the courts, prosecution agencies, and the bar, establish witness information systems in court buildings.

Recommendation 4.
Victim/Witness "Hotlines"

Community organizations should, in cooperation with law enforcement, establish victim/witness "hotlines."

Recommendation 5.
Post-Trial Victim/Witness Supportive Systems

Community organizations should, in cooperation with prosecution agencies and the courts, establish post-trial supportive systems for victims and witness.

(e) Organized Bar

Recommendation 1.
The Attorney as Prosecutor

The prosecutor should not harass or improperly intimidate any witness, and is, as a lawyer, subject to the standards of professional conduct and the state's mechanism for discipline. Complaints regarding intimidation of defense counsel, defense witnesses or defendants should be dealt with appropriately by lawyer disciplinary authorities.

Recommendation 2.
Defense Counsel

Defense counsel is not to harass or intimidate any victim or witness. Defense counsel is also to inform his client that the defendant is to have no contact with the victim and/or witness except through the offices of defense counsel.

Recommendation 3.
The Attorney as a Member of the Bar and Officer of the Court

Attorneys as officers of the court should be cognizant of the problem of victim/witness intimidation and, upon request, provide the intimidated victim/witness with legal advice and/or referrals to appropriate services.

Recommendation 4.
The Organized Bar

Recognizing their responsibility for the administration of justice, bar groups are highly appropriate "community organizations" to provide the services described in [the Community Groups/Private Sector Section] of this report.

Recommendation 5.
Creation of Bar Victim Committees

State and local bar associations should create victim committees to insure attention in their jurisdictions to problems faced by crime victims, and in particular to spotlight the problem of victim intimidation.

Recommendation 6.
Legislation

The bar should work to encourage passage in state legislatures of effective victim/witness intimidation statutes . . . and other legislation designed to minimize the pains of victimization.

2. Victim and Witness Protection Act of 1982

As a direct result of the efforts of the American Bar Association's Victims Committee in bringing to the forefront the importance of obtaining full cooperation of witnesses, the prevalence of witness intimidation, and the sad plight of the intimidated witness, Congress enacted the Victim and Witness Protection Act of 1982.[5] The purposes of the act, as set forth in Secton 2(b), are "(1) to enhance and protect the necessary role of crime victims and witnesses in the criminal justice process; (2) to ensure that the Federal Government does all that is possible within limits of available resources to assist victims and witnesses of crime without infringing on the constitutional rights of the defendant; and (3) to provide a model for legislation for State and local governments."[6] Section 2(a) states that Congress finds and declares that:[7]

(1) Without the cooperation of victims and witnesses, the criminal justice system would cease to function; yet with few exceptions these individuals are either ignored by the criminal justice system or simply used as tools to identify and punish offenders.

(2) All too often the victim of a serious crime is forced to suffer physical, psychological, or financial hardship first as a result of the criminal act and then as a result of contact with a criminal justice system unresponsive to the real needs of such victim.

(3) Although the majority of serious crime falls under the jurisdiction of State and local law enforcement agencies, the Federal government, and in particular the Attorney General, has an important leadership role to assume in ensuring that victims of crime, whether at the Federal, State, or local level, are given proper treatment by agencies administering the criminal justice system.

(4) Under current law, law enforcement agencies must have cooperation from a victim of crime and yet neither the agencies nor the legal system can offer adequate protection or assistance when the victim, as a result of such cooperation, is threatened or intimidated.

(5) While the defendant is provided with counsel who can explain both the criminal justice process and the rights of the defendant, the victim or witness has no counterpart and is usually not even notified when a defendant is released on bail, the case is dismissed, a plea to a lesser charge is accepted, or a court date is changed.

(6) The victim and witness who cooperate with the prosecutor often find that the transportation, parking facilities, and child care services at the court are unsatisfactory and they must often share the pretrial waiting room with the defendant or his family and friends.

(7) The victim may lose valuable property to a criminal only to lose it again for long periods of time to Federal law enforcement officials, until the trial and sometimes appeals are over; many times that property is damaged or lost, which is particularly stressful for the elderly or poor.

The need for the federal government to enact the Victims and Witness Protection Act of 1982[8] was addressed in 1981 by the Attorney General's Task Force on Violent Crime, which recommended that the Attorney General "should take a leadership role in ensuring that the victims of crime are accorded proper status by the criminal justice system" and by Chief Justice Warren Burger who, in a State of the Judiciary address, declared that the "rights of crime victims should be given equal time with the rights of the accused and convicted criminals."

The victim's interest in seeing that such changes occur was clearly articulated at the subcommittee hearing on the bill. "My life has been permanently changed," one witness told the subcommittee. "I will never forget being raped, kidnapped, and robbed at gunpoint." "However," she went on, "my sense of disillusionment with the judicial system is many times more painful. I could not in good faith urge anyone to participate in this hellish process." The witness then recited instances of being kept in the dark, of being treated insensitively, of having her trial given three last-minute postponements, of having her feelings discounted by the sentencing judge—and so on—a long and familiar litany of hurts that well-meaning public agencies so often inflict on victims. The fact that the process is often "hellish" for victims has outraged many in the criminal justice field, leading Attorney General Wiliam French Smith, for one, to say: "Some rights of law-abiding Americans are so fundamental as to cry out for protection. . . . They include the right to civilized and compassionate treatment when we have fallen victims to a law-breaker."

On the local level, an increasing number of individual law enforcement agencies, courts, prosecutors' offices, and correctional departments have taken it upon themselves to address victim and witness concerns. In addition, at least Washington, Oklahoma, Nebraska, and Wisconsin have passed "victims' bill of rights" legislation to encourage such activities. According to the American Bar Association Criminal Justice Section, the "basic" bill of rights that spurred subsequent legislation is Wisconsin's:

950.04 Basic bill of rights for victims and witnesses.

Victims and witnesses of crimes have the following rights:

(1) To be informed by local law enforcement agencies and the district attorney of the final disposition of the case. If the crime charged is a felony or is specified in ch. 940, the victim shall be notified whenever the defendant or perpetrator is released from custody.

(2) To be notified that a court proceeding to which they have been subpoenaed will not go on as scheduled, in order to save the person an unnecessary trip to court.

(3) To receive protection from harm and threats of harm arising out of their cooperation with law enforcement and prosecution efforts, and to be provided with information as to the level of protection available.

(4) To be informed of financial assistance and other social services available as a result of being a witness or a victim of crime, including information on how to apply for the assistance and services.

(5) To be informed of the procedure to be followed in order to apply for and receive any witness fee to which they are entitled.

(6) To be provided, whenever possible, a secure waiting area during court proceedings that does not require them to be in close proximity to defendants and families and friends of defendants.

(7) To have any stolen or other personal property expeditiously returned by law enforcement agencies when no longer needed as evidence. If feasible, all such property, except weapons, currency, contraband, property subject to evidentiary analysis and property the ownership of which is disputed, shall be returned to the person within 10 days of being taken.

(8) To be provided with appropriate employer intercession services to ensure that employers of victims and witnesses will cooperate with the criminal justice process in order to minimize an employee's loss of pay and other benefits resulting from court appearances.

(9) To be entitled to a speedy disposition of the case in which they are involved as a victim or witness in order to minimize the length of time they must endure the stress of their responsibilities in connection with the matter.

(10) To have the family members of all homicide victims afforded all of the rights under subs. (1) to (4) and (6) and (9) and analogous services under § 950.05, whether or not they are witness in any criminal proceedings.

Like Wisconsin's, the statutes of other states generally enumerate certain "rights" that victims and witnesses should be able to expect from the criminal justice system. In most instances, however, the statutes do not assign responsibilities for securing the rights, do not provide sanctions for failing to implement them, and do not create a cause of action by private citizens to have the rights enforced. Thus the "rights" are more properly called "guidelines" as they are termed in the Victim and Witness Protection Act of 1982. Nevertheless, experience has shown that the state guideline legislation on which Section 6 of the Victim and Witness Protection Act of 1982 is modeled has proved extremely helpful once enacted and that implementation of the guidelines is relatively routine.

In the federal criminal justice system, there had been little activity to improve the treatment of victims and witnesses before the Victims and Witness Protection Act of 1982. Despite the recommendations of the Attorney General's Task Force on Violent Crime, Congress had not previously given formal guidance or provided incentive to federal agencies to engage in such activities. Inactivity may be explained by the fact that Congress was well aware that the federal system processes relatively few cases involving the kind of personal crimes that inspired earlier state and local reform efforts. Nevertheless, such cases are not unheard of in the federal system. When squarely confronted with the plight of victims and witnesses to crimes in 1982, Congress responded by declaring that the victims and witnesses of federal crimes concerned deserve fair treatment as well. Moreover, Congress hoped that the Victims and Witness Protection Act of 1982 would serve as a model to encourage further state legislation and implementation in this area.

Congress mandated in Section 6 of the Victim and Witness Protection Act of 1982 that with respect to improving the relatively poor treatment being given to witness of crimes, whether or not victims:

(a) Within two hundred and seventy days after the date of enactment of this Act, the Attorney General shall develop and implement guidelines for the Department of

Justice consistent with the purposes of this Act. In preparing the guidelines the Attorney General shall consider the following objectives:

(1) Services to Victim of Crime.—Law enforcement personnel should ensure that victims routinely receive emergency social and medical services as soon as possible and are given information on the following—

(A) availability of crime victim compensation (where applicable):

(B) community-based treatment programs;

(C) the role of the victim in the criminal justice process, including what they can expect from the system as well as what the system expects of them; and

(D) stages in the criminal justice process of significance to a crime victim, and the manner in which information about such stages can be obtained.

(2) Notification of Availability of Protection.—A victim or witness should routinely receive information on steps that law enforcement officers and attorneys for the Government can take to protect victims and witnesses from intimidation.

(3) Scheduling Changes.—All victims and witnesses who have been scheduled to attend criminal justice proceedings should either be notified as soon as possible of any scheduling changes which will affect their appearances or have available a system for alerting witnesses promptly by telephone or otherwise.

(4) Prompt Notification to Victims of Major Series Crimes.—Victims, witnesses, relatives of those victims and witnesses who are minors, and relatives of homicide victims should, if such persons provide the appropriate official with a current address and telephone number, receive, prompt advance notification, if possible, of judicial proceedings relating to their case, including—

(A) the arrest of an accused;

(B) the initial appearance of an accused before a judicial officer;

(C) the release of the accused pending judicial proceedings; and

(D) proceedings in the prosecution of the accused (including entry of a plea of guilty, trial, sentencing, and where a term of imprisonment is imposed, the release of the accused from such imprisonment).

(5) Consultation with Victim.—The victim of a serious crime, or in the case of a minor child or a homicide, the family of the victim, should be consulted by the attorney for the Government in order to obtain the views of the victim or family about the disposition of any Federal criminal case brought as a result of such a crime, including the views of the victim or family about

(A) dismissal;

(B) release of the accused pending judicial proceedings;

(C) plea negotiations; and

(D) pretrial diversion program.

(6) Separate Waiting Area.—Victims and other prosecution witnesses should be provided prior to court appearance a waiting area that is separate from all other witnesses.

(7) Property Return.—Law enforcement agencies and prosecutor should promptly return victim's property held for evidentiary purposes unless there is compelling law enforcement reason for retaining it.

(8) Notification to Employer.—A victim or witness who so requests should be assisted by law enforcement agencies and attorneys for the Government in informing employers that the need for victim and witness cooperation in the prosecution of the case may necessitate absence of that victim or witness from work. A victim or witness who, as a direct result of a crime or of cooperation with law enforcement agencies or attorneys for the Government, is subjected to serious financial strains, should be assisted by such agencies and attorneys in explaining to creditors the reasons for such serious financial strain.

(9) Training by Federal Law Enforcement Training Facilities.—Victim assistance education and training should be offered to persons taking courses at Federal law enforcement training facilities and attorneys for the Government so that victims may be promptly, properly, and completely assisted.

(10) General Victim Assistance.—The guidelines should also ensure that any other important assistance to victims and witnesses, such as the adoption of transportation, parking, and translator services for victims in court be provided.

(b) Nothing in this title shall be construed as creating a cause of action against the United States.

(c) The Attorney General shall assure that all Federal law enforcement agencies outside of the Department of Justice adopt guidelines consistent with subsection (a) of this section.[9]

Section 6(a) of the act requires the Attorney General to develop guidelines addressing ten specified objectives and to assign responsibility for implementing them.[10] By this requirement Congress intended to recognize legislatively that many problems of crime victims and witnesses are caused by or are exacerbated by the criminal justice system itself and that the same system can and should be responsive to victim and witness needs, both as a matter of simple justice and because their cooperation is absolutely essential to a successful criminal justice system. Although Congress did not intend to limit the Attorney General to the ten objectives enumerated, it did require that the Attorney General address at least those ten, each of which had been successfully dealt with on the local level either as a result of state statute or policy directive. In some instances, traditional work patterns would have to be changed to comply with the guidelines. However, in no instance would the guidelines per se require the creation of new services beyond the various departments' budgetary capacity.

The objective of Subsection 6(a)(1) is to provide crime victims with services and information to minimize the effects of the crime itself and to provide realistic expectations regarding the victim's relationship to the criminal justice process. Under this subsection, law enforcement personnel are to insure that victims receive emergency social and medical services as soon as possible. They are also to provide victims with important information regarding victim compensation programs, community-based treatment programs, the role of the victim's participation in the criminal justice process, and the stages of the prosecution of significance to the victim. Section 6(a)(2) requires that victims be routinely advised about the steps that law enforcement can take to protect them from intimidation. Most of the information to be disseminated can be communicated in the form of printed material distributed by law enforcement officers to the victims.

Although Congress recognized that scheduling changes are necessary in many criminal cases, it also knew that the victim or witness is often the last to learn about such changes—not infrequently when he or she appears at the scheduled proceeding. Subsection 6(a)(3) sets out to avoid unnecessary, inconvenient, and often financially costly trips of victims and witnesses to proceedings by requiring that victims and witnesses be notified when proceedings have been postponed or cancelled. Congress also recognized that victims and witnesses of serious crimes have a legitimate interest in receiving advance notification of judicial proceedings in their cases. Accordingly, pursuant to Subsection 6(a)(4) victims and witnesses (and specified relatives, if the victim is a minor, or a homicide victim) who provide appropriate officials with a current address and telephone number are to receive prompt notification of judicial proceedings relating to their case.

Whereas Subsections 6(a)(1), (3), and (4) are concerned with giving victims and witnesses rudimentary, timely information about their cases, and Subsection 6(a)(2) seeks to make victims and witnesses aware of available protective measures against intimidation, the intent of Subsection 6(a)(5) is to permit victims to respond to certain information in ways that give them a sense of involvement in their cases. Subsection 6(a)(5) provides that in serious cases victims (or in the case of minors or homicide victims the victims' family) should be able to have their views heard by the prosecutor before certain key criminal justice decisions or recommendations are made in their case. The nonbinding consultation should precede recommendations on pretrial release, pretrial diversion, dismissal, and plea negotiations. American Bar Association Criminal Justice Standard 14-3.1 addresses plea negotiations, stating that "the prosecuting attorney should make every effort to remain advised of the attitudes and sentiments of victims . . . before reaching a plea agreement." In his testimony to the Senate subcommittee Ronald Zweibel, Chairman of the New York State Crime Victims Board, stated:

> In the past, the victim's place and interests in the system were much more central, but government gradually took over the prosecutorial role from the victim and relegated the crime victim to a mere informational source. By being treated as information sources, crime victims are often exposed to further hardships including: having to tell their story over and over again; appearing in court in anticipation of testifying; helping the police with identification; and a variety of other time-consuming, frustrating, and psychologically difficult activities.

Regardless of these hardships, the information provided by the victim is essential to the continued functioning of the system. In this vein, due process must be afforded to the victim which is readily provided to the offender. It must be acknowledged that the interests which the system has in the cooperation and assistance that the victim can provide is no greater than the interests victims have in being informed, notified, and in having their input considered in matters which so fundamentally affect their rights as people harmed by a society which failed to protect them.

The Attorney General, in framing appropriate guidelines under the act, was asked to consult eminent and responsible prosecutors who had experience in implementing similar guidelines locally. The three examples suggested were his Assistant Attorney General in charge of the Criminal Division, D. Lowell Jensen; a member of his Task Force on Violent Crime, David L. Armstrong; and a member of the President's Task Force on Victims of Crime, Robert J. Miller. Their experience, like that of others, is that the effect of eliciting victim views on discretionary decisions such as a negotiated plea is not to undermine prosecutorial discretion, to unduly burden the work load of assistant prosecutors, or to produce harsher punishments for offenders. Instead, in the vast majority of cases, the victim expresses confidence in the assistant prosecutor's recommendations but is grateful to have been consulted. Occasionally, however, the consulting process uncovers some facts about the case about which the prosecutor is grateful to learn and is influenced to handle the case in a more appropriate manner.

It is not uncommon for victims to be required to wait for long periods in the same courtroom areas as those who have been accused of the crime in question. In almost every case this is extremely uncomfortable for the victims and prosecution witnesses; not infrequently, it is intimidating as well. Subsection 6(a)(6) seeks to obviate this problem by requiring waiting facilities for victims and prosecution witnesses that are separate from those used by defendants.

Victims of property crimes are often astonished and disillusioned to learn that even though their property has been recovered by law enforcement officials, it is not returned to them for months or even years—if ever. Substituting well-documented photographs for the actual property has proven evidentially acceptable in California and several other states. This experience deserves replication whenever possible in the federal system, as set forth in Subsection 6(a)(7).

Cooperation with the criminal justice system often results in substantial financial hardship for witnesses whose employers either withhold their wages for the work time lost or fire them because of their absence. On the local level, when law enforcement officials have officially informed the witness's employer of the criminal justice obligations of the employee, the employer often agrees to forego such measures. Subsection 6(a)(8) encourages the federal system to use similar employer intercession methods and in cases of serious financial strain, resulting from the crime itself or subsequent participation in the criminal justice process, to notify creditors as well.

Congress recognized that training law enforcement officials concerning the various issues addressed by the Attorney General's guidelines is essential if the guidelines are to have the intended effect. For many years, the FBI Academy and other federal facilities have offered training courses to leaders of state and local law enforcement agencies, as well as to federal law enforcement officers and officials. Some of the new techniques in aiding crime victims have already found their way into the curricula of these professional training courses. Subsection 6(a)(9) encourages the Attorney General and other federal government officials to accelerate and institutionalize such efforts.

Subsection 6(a)(10) provides a final objective that other important means of assisting victims and witnesses be considered. This subsection is intended to promote a spirit of inquiry among those drafting, promulgating, and working within the guidelines to find techniques responsive to the needs of victims and witnesses, such as the adoption of transportation, parking, and translation services, that are not otherwise included within the ten specific objectives.

Subsection 6(b) expressly states that nothing in the act shall be construed as creating a cause of action against the United States. Congress expressed confidence that the Attorney General would promulgate realistic guidelines and assign responsibility for them so as to insure implementation to the maximum extent possible. When implementation is not possible for budgetary or other reasons, Congress, however, did not want to make the federal government liable. Since the Department of Justice is not solely responsible for all federal law enforcement, Subsection 6(c) requires other federal law enforcement agencies to develop their own guidelines consistent with the objectives set forth in Subsection 6(a).

3. President's Task Force on Victims of Crime

Two months after the enactment of the Victim and Witness Protection Act of 1982, the President's Task Force on Victims of Crime issued its final report.[11] Insofar as the Task Force speaks to the problem of witness intimidation, it speaks with the same mind as the American Bar Association and Congress. In brief, the Task Force recommends that legislation should be enacted by the states developing and implementing guidelines for the fair treatment of crime victims and witnesses. Such guidelines should seek to mitigate the problems that these citizens encounter in the criminal justice system by addressing nine specific objectives:

(1) The provision of services to victims of crime, including information on compensation for out-of-pocket losses, medical and psychological treatment programs, case status information, and protection from intimidation;

(2) Prompt notification to victims and witnesses of scheduling changes in court proceedings;
(3) Prompt notification to victims of violent crime concerning their cases, including the arrest and bond status of the defendant, and the eventual outcome of the case;
(4) Consultation with the victim during the various stages of the prosecution;
(5) Separate waiting areas for defense and prosecution witnesses awaiting court proceedings;
(6) Prompt return of property seized as evidence or recovered during an investigation;
(7) Contacting a victim's employer and creditors to seek their cooperation, by explaining the situation of the victim after the crime, the necessity of court appearances, and his temporary inability to meet outstanding debts . . . ;
(8) Training law enforcement personnel in victim assistance; and
(9) The provision of general victim assistance in a variety of areas, such as transportation, parking, and translators.

The Task Force also recommended that restitution be required by the court for property loss and personal injury, unless the court explicitly finds that restitution is not appropriate. Congress was asked (1) to enact legislation to provide federal funding to assist state crime victim compensation programs; (2) to enact legislation to provide federal funding, reasonably matched by local revenues, to assist in the operation of federal, state, local, and private nonprofit victim/witness assistance agencies that make comprehensive assistance available to all victims of crime; and (3) to establish a federally based resource center for victim and witness assistance. Prosecutors were asked to establish and maintain direct contact with victim/witness units and other service agencies. Finally, it was recommended that police officers should give a high priority to investigation of reports by witnesses of threats or intimidation and forward these reports to the appropriate prosecutor's office.

4. National Judicial College Recommended Practices

In the fall of 1982 the Judicial Administration Division of the American Bar Association provided a "seed money" grant to the National Conference of Special Court Judges. The National Judicial College was requested to design and plan for a national conference of state judges to examine victims' rights issues and to suggest guidelines with respect to them.[12] In view of the recommendations for the judiciary made in the report of the President's Task Force on Victims of Crime published in December 1982, the need for such a conference became ever more apparent. In April 1983 initial planning began to take shape, and in August the National Institute of Justice, Department of Justice, provided a substantial grant to fund the conference and the travel and lodging of two judges from each state, the

District of Columbia, and the Commonwealth of Puerto Rico. The National Conference of the Judiciary on the Rights of Victims of Crime met at the National Judicial College in Reno, Nevada, November 29 to December 2, 1983, and adopted in Plenary Session the following "Statement of Recommended Judicial Practices" concerning these rights.

I. FAIR TREATMENT OF VICTIMS AND WITNESSES

JUDGES SHOULD PLAY A LEADERSHIP ROLE IN ENSURING THAT VICTIMS AND WITNESSES ARE TREATED WITH COURTESY, RESPECT, AND FAIRNESS

A. INFORMATION ABOUT COURT PROCEDURES AND FACILITIES

ALL VICTIMS AND WITNESSES IN CRIMINAL CASES SHOULD BE PROVIDED ESSENTIAL INFORMATION ABOUT COURT PROCEDURES AND COURTHOUSE FACILITIES. JUDGES SHOULD ENCOURAGE THE FOLLOWING PRACTICES:

1. That victims and witnesses be provided with information regarding the rights and privileges available to victims and witnesses, and about the physical layout of the courthouse, parking areas, public transportation routes, witness fees, state compensation funds, and other available financial assistance;
2. That court administrators establish reception areas and provide victims and witnesses information about public and community services;
3. That prosecutors explain to victims the criminal justice system insofar as it relates to the victims' cases and what is expected of the victims in the prosecution of the cases.

B. NOTICE TO VICTIMS AND WITNESSES

VICTIMS AND WITNESSES SHOULD BE FULLY INFORMED ABOUT THE CRIMINAL JUSTICE PROCEEDINGS IN THEIR CASES. JUDGES SHOULD ENCOURAGE:

1. That the victims should be able to obtain from appropriate court personnel information concerning the status of their cases;
2. That, if requested, prosecutors inform victims of serious crimes that they may obtain, if possible, timely notice of all bail, pre-trial, trial and post-trial hearings, if the victims provide a current address or telephone number;
3. That if requested, appropriate officials, if possible, give timely notice to victims of serious crimes about the release of the defendant from custody, pre-trial and post-trial, if they provide a current address and phone number;
4. That victims be informed by prosecutors of the disposition of their cases.

C. SPECIAL SERVICES

JUDGES SHOULD RECOGNIZE THAT VICTIMS AND WITNESSES MAY REQUIRE SPECIAL SERVICES AND SUPPORT, BOTH MATERIAL AND PSYCHOLOGICAL. JUDGES SHOULD ENCOURAGE THE FOLLOWING PRACTICES:

1. Separate waiting areas for defense and prosecution witnesses;
2. Interpreter and translator services for victims and witnesses while they are in the courthouse;
3. An "on call" system to minimize unnecessary trips to court;
4. The expeditious return of evidence;
5. The availability of special transportation and protection to and from the courthouse when witnesses' safety is a consideration;
6. Informing the public generally of the importance of supporting the witnesses' participation in court proceedings and encouraging the adoption of legislation to accord witnesses the same protection from adverse actions by employers as are customarily given jurors and members of the National Guard;
7. Child care services for witnesses;
8. Crisis intervention, counseling and other support services for victims;
9. Ensuring the victim is not charged for rape examinations or other costs of collecting and preserving evidence;
10. Establishing fair and appropriate witness fees.

D. RESTITUTION

JUDGES SHOULD ORDER RESTITUTION IN ALL CASES UNLESS THERE IS AN ARTICULATED REASON FOR NOT DOING SO, WHETHER THE OFFENDER IS INCARCERATED OR PLACED ON PROBATION.

II. VICTIM PARTICIPATION

VICTIMS SHALL BE ALLOWED TO PARTICIPATE AND, WHERE APPROPRIATE, TO GIVE INPUT THROUGH THE PROSECUTOR OR TO TESTIFY IN ALL STAGES OF JUDICIAL PROCEEDINGS

A. PARTICIPATION MAY INCLUDE BUT IS NOT LIMITED TO THE FOLLOWING:

1. Pre-trial release or bail hearings;
2. The propriety and conditions of diversion;
3. The scheduling of court proceedings;
4. Continuances or delays; judges should state on the record the reason for granting a continuance;
5. Plea and sentence negotiations;
6. Sentencing;
7. Victim/offender mediation in non-violent cases, when appropriate.

B. TO ASSIST VICTIM PARTICIPATION:

1. A victim's advisor should be permitted to remain in the courtroom with the victim, but not participate in the judicial proceedings;

2. Victim impact statements prior to sentencing should be encouraged and considered;
3. The victim or the victim's family should be allowed to remain in the courtroom when permitted by law and when it will not interfere with the right of the defendant to a fair trial.

III. PROTECTION

JUDGES SHOULD USE THEIR JUDICIAL AUTHORITY TO PROTECT VICTIMS AND WITNESSES FROM HARASSMENT, THREATS, INTIMIDATION, AND HARM

A. THIS SHOULD INCLUDE;

1. Encouraging that separate waiting rooms be provided for defense and prosecution witnesses;
2. Requiring that bail be conditioned on the defendants having no access to victims or prosecution witnesses;
3. On showing of good cause, limiting access to the addresses of victims and witnesses;
4. Encouraging that victims and witnesses be advised that if they agree to be interviewed prior to trial by opposing counsel or investigators, they may insist that the interviews be conducted at neutral locations;
5. Encouraging legislation or rules which would require parole boards to advise the judge, the prosecutor, the public, and the victim where appropriate, prior to any hearing on the release of an offender convicted of a serious crime.

B. JUDGES IN PROTECTING SENSITIVE VICTIMS (MINORS, VICTIMS OF SEXUAL ABUSE, FAMILIES OF HOMICIDE VICTIMS, THE ELDERLY, AND THE HANDICAPPED) MAY CONSIDER THE FOLLOWING:

1. Expediting trials of cases involving sensitive victims;
2. Encouraging specially designed or equipped courtrooms to protect sensitive victims, provided that the right of confrontation is not abridged;
3. Permitting the use of videotaped depositions in cases involving sensitive victims, provided that the right of confrontation is not abridged;
4. Allowing sensitive victims to have an individual of their choice accompany them in closed juvenile proceedings, closed criminal proceedings, and in camera proceedings.

IV. JUDICIAL EDUCATION

JUDGES AT THE TRIAL AND APPELLATE LEVELS SHOULD BE ENCOURAGED TO PARTICIPATE IN TRAINING PROGRAMS DEALING WITH THE NEEDS, COMFORTS AND LEGAL INTERESTS OF CRIME VICTIMS

State, regional and national programs and conferences for judges and non-judges should be held on methods to improve the treatment of victims and witnesses and to develop solutions to the problems suggested.

V. ALL THESE RECOMMENDED JUDICIAL PRACTICES ARE SUBJECT TO EXISTING RULES OF COURT STATUTES AND CONSTITUTIONAL PROVISIONS.[13]

B. DISCOVERY OF PROSECUTION WITNESSES

1. The Common Law

At common law the defendant was allowed no discovery of the government's case. Courts professed a lack of power to compel production of evidence.[14] J. Wigmore asserted that this position developed, in part, from the permeation of the common law with instincts of sportsmanship.[15] One of the basic assumptions implicit in sports is that a contestant need not reveal his or her strengths or weaknesses. To require disclosure of evidence would be contrary to this principle. Thus neither party was required to give the other notice of its evidential resources, and surprise was not a valid objection. In 1895 Sir F. Pollack and F. Maitland reflected:[16]

> At one of these [extremes] the model is the conduct of the man of science who is making researches and will use all appropriate methods for the solution of problems and the discovery of truth. At the other stands the umpire of our English games, who is there, not in order that he may invent tests for the powers of the two sides, but merely to see that the rules of the game are observed. It is towards the second of these ideals that our English medieval procedure is strongly inclined. The judges sit in court, not in order that they may discover the truth, but in order that they may answer the question, "How's that?" This passive habit seems to grow upon them as time goes on. . . . Even in criminal cause, even when the King is prosecuting, the English judge will, if he can, play the umpire rather than inquisitor.

Sir James Arnould believed that this attitude resulted in an "English criminal procedure [which did] not so much seek the discovery of truth pure and simple, as the discovery of truth according to certain artificial rules."[17]

The refusal to allow discovery has also been explained as a reaction to the fear of abuse by unscrupulous opponents. Wigmore explained that unlike the modern concern for the innocent accused, early courts were more concerned with the dishonest defendant. If informed of prospective witnesses names and statements, the unscrupulous accused may attempt to tamper with the witnesses. If given notice of evidentiary facts to be offered at trial, he or she may prepare false evidence. In addition, because of the accused's privilege against self-incrimination, concern was expressed that discovery would be a one-way street.[18]

2. Early Statutory Development

As early as the mid-1600's Parliament heard complaints regarding this absolute denial of discovery. Objections by defendants, who were arrested without warrants, kept in custody until trial, and denied knowledge of the evidence against them, prompted Parliament to consider liberalizing the discovery process. The resultant modification of the common law,[19] however, was limited to defendants accused of treason. James Stephen reasoned:[20]

> It was a matter of direct personal interest to many members of Parliament that trials for political offenses should not be grossly unfair; but they were comparatively indifferent as to the fate of people accused of sheep-stealing or burglary or murder. . . . [The accused] was not allowed as a matter of right, but only as an exceptional favor . . . to see his [own] witnesses or put their evidence in order. When he came into Court, he was set to fight for his life with absolutely no knowledge of the evidence to be produced against him.

In the United States, neither party has a constitutional right to the discovery of its opponent's case, except in the limited instance where the prosecution's evidence will exculpate the defendant.[21] The early federal statutes on discovery followed the general flavor of the British treason statute while adding other capital cases to their coverage. These statutes of 1790, 1878, and 1926 provided that a list of "the witnesses to be produced on the trial for proving the indictment, stating the place of abode," was to be delivered "at least three entire days" before trial for treason and "at least two entire days" before trial for other capital offenses.[22]

During the early twentieth century, greater concern began to be exhibited for protecting the rights of the presumed innocent defendant. Accompanying this attitude was a greater disposition to extending assistance to the accused. Wigmore asserted:[23]

> The danger that, if guilty, he may be disposed and enabled to tamper with witnesses, to manufacture false evidence in defense, and otherwise to misuse the aid thus furnished,—this danger (unquestionably a real one) we ignore, or at least deliberately risk. The determination to protect the innocent accused has induced us to aid him, at any cost of accompanying dangers by giving him fair notice of the persons to be called against him as witnesses.

Following this sentiment, the American Law Institute's Code of Criminal Procedure recommended in 1930 that the permissible scope of the accused's discovery be broadened to furnish the defendants with the names of government witnesses.

Names of witnesses to be endorsed on indictment or information: When an indictment or information is filed, the names of all the witnesses or deponents on whose evidence the indictment or information was based shall be endorsed thereon before it is presented, and the prosecuting attorney shall endorse on the indictment or information at such time as the court may by rule or otherwise prescribe the names of such other witnesses as he purposes to call. A failure to so endorse the said names shall not affect the validity or sufficiency of the indictment or information, but the court in which the indictment or information was filed shall, upon application of the defendant, direct the names of such witnesses to be endorsed. No continuance shall be allowed because of the failure to endorse and of the said names unless such application was made at the earliest opportunity and then only if a continuance is necessary in the interest of justice.[24]

By 1930 many states had already statutorily liberalized the absolute common law denial of discovery. Fourteen states required the prosecuting attorney to endorse the names of witnesses to be called at trial known to him or her at the time of filing the information or indictment and to disclose the names of other witnesses as they became known.[25] Of these 14 jurisdictions, six states permitted the court to quash or set aside the indictment if the witnesses' names were not endorsed.[26] Twenty-eight states required the names of witnesses examined before the grand jury to be included on the indictment.[27] The Minnesota legislature further required that the court clerk furnish the accused with a copy of the witnesses' "depositions."[28] No other statute provided for production of any witness statements.

Although greater liberalization of discovery rules was the trend in most states in the early part of this century, the federal system was far more cautious. In the often quoted passage from United States v. Garsson,[29] Judge Cardozo in 1923 denied with sweeping language the accused's motion to inspect grand jury minutes:

It is said to lie in discretion, and perhaps it does, but no judge of this court has granted it, and I hope none ever will. Under our criminal procedure the accused has every advantage. While the prosecution is held rigidly to the charge, he need not disclose the barest outline of his defense. He is immune from question or comment on his silence; he cannot be convicted when there is the least faint doubt in the mind of any one of the twelve. Why in addition should he in advance have the whole of evidence against him to pick over at his leisure to make his defense fairly or foully, I have never been able to see. No doubt grand juries err and indictments are calamities to honest men, but we must work a price. Our dangers do not lie in too little tenderness to the accused. Our procedure has been always haunted by the ghost of the innocent man convicted. It is an unreal dream. What we need to fear is the archaic formalism and the watery sentiment that obstructs, delays and defeats the prosecution of crime.

The Advisory Committee Notes to the Federal Rules of Criminal Procedure promulgated in 1946 stated unequivocally that discovery was not a right then afforded the accused in a federal criminal prosecution.[30] In 1951 the Supreme Court also indicated that discovery in federal criminal cases did not exist before the Federal Rules of Criminal Procedure.[31] Commentators, however, have asserted that a limited right to pretrial discovery had been recognized in several earlier federal criminal cases. Subsequent to the adoption of the Federal Rules of Criminal Procedure, the First Assistant in the Criminal Division of the Justice Department rationalized providing limited disclosure to the accused: "later [pre-Rule] cases indicate rather strongly that the right of inspection does actually exist, and that this Rule does not create a departure from the law."[32] No cases, however, are cited. After making a detailed study of prerule federal cases, L. Orfield also arrived at the conclusion that several cases had indeed permitted limited discovery in criminal actions.[33] Orfield noted that as early as 1807 in United States v. Burr,[34] the court held that a letter written by the principal witness for the prosecution could be discovered by the defense before trial. Chief Justice Marshall, sitting as a Circuit Justice, stated that "if it be apparent that the papers are irrelative to the case, or that for stated reasons they cannot be introduced into the defense the subpoena duces tecum would be useless," otherwise the documents are subject to discovery. In the case at hand, however, Justice Marshall saw no reason to hesitate in granting the subpoena for discovery. Orfield's research disclosed that the next decision was not until 1917 when a federal court in Puerto Rico in dicta stated:

> What control has the court over the evidence before the evidence is offered? Has the court any right to make the government show its hand? The court undoubtedly has control over all the proceedings in a case, and it may be that if there is a showing that the evidence in the possession of the government must be exhibited to the defendant in order for him to properly prepare his case the court would exercise the power. . . . It may very well be that there is a power in the court to compel such production; there are no cases cited, but it would seem that there must in a clear case be such power in the court.[35]

3. Federal Rule of Criminal Procedure 16

Whatever the true state of the prior law, with the adoption of the Federal Rules of Criminal Procedure in 1946, the accused did have a limited right of discovery. The first draft of what later became Federal Rule of Criminal Procedure 16 resembled the very liberal discovery of documents and things contained in Rule 34 of the Federal Rules of Civil Procedure. Under the proposed rule, all relevant documents not subject to a privilege could be discovered. Several United States attorneys objected strenuously to the broadness of the draft proposal on the grounds that such liberality would lead to "fishing expeditions"[36] and result in the complete disclosure of the government's case.[37] These United States attorneys, among others, recommended that the rule should not include all documents and should specifically exclude witness statements.[38] The version of Federal Rule of Criminal Procedure 16 adopted in 1946 reflected the foregoing concerns.

Discovery and Inspection

Upon motion of a defendant at any time after the filing of the indictment or information, the court may order the attorney for the government to permit the defendant to inspect and copy or photograph designated books, papers, documents, or tangible objects, obtained from or belonging to the defendant or obtained from others by seizure or by process, upon a showing that the items sought may be material to preparation of his defense and that the request is reasonable. The order shall specify the time, place and manner of making the inspection and of taking the copies or photographs and may prescribe such terms and conditions as are just.

In the Advisory Committee Notes to Rule 16, the drafters indicated that the courts had previously made orders granting the defendant an opportunity to inspect impounded documents belonging to the defendant and that this rule simply restated this judicial trend. At the Institute Proceeding on the Federal Rules of Criminal Procedure, Aaron Youngquist stated that the purpose of Federal Rules of Criminal Procedure 16 was to protect "the right of the defendant to have access to his own papers, to his own property, as well as to the property seized from others by process, which may be material to his defense."[39] The rule makes no provision for producing witness statements or the names of potential witnesses or even the names of witnesses the prosecution intends to call. Instead, the rule focuses on materials to which the defendant ordinarily would have access, but because of activity by the prosecution, the material is no longer available. Thus what began as a liberal discovery rule was reduced to a very limited grant of discovery to the accused.

4. Jencks v. United States

In 1957 the United States Supreme Court in Jencks v. United States,[40] handed down a decision that ultimately led to a wrinkle being added to the discovery process in federal criminal cases. The court in *Jencks* held that the defendant is entitled to obtain for impeachment purposes documents containing relevant statements made by government witnesses touching the subject matter of their testimony at trial. A prior showing of inconsistency with regard to the statement need not be made by the accused to obtain disclosure. Although the *Jencks* decision was limited to disclosure of statements at trial and in no way contradicted Federal Rule of Criminal Procedure 16, the public widely misunderstood *Jencks* as providing the defendant far broader discovery rights. Criticism was directed at the Supreme Court particularly for what the public and the press perceived to be a disregard for national security and allowing unrestrained inspection of confidential records.[41] Moreover lower federal courts variously interpreted the scope of *Jencks*. Apparently, the confused interpretations arose from an uncertainty about when the statements of witnesses were to be produced and whether the statements should first be examined by the trial judge.[42] The Department of Justice, although accepting the principle of *Jencks*, stated that the "loose interpretation" of the decision by lower courts placed the department in a position in which it believed it was necessary to abandon meritorious cases. Attorney General Herbert Brownell opined that three main problems had developed: (1) insistence by some courts that the government turn over entire reports of the FBI even though only a small part of the report related to the testimony of the government witnesses; (2) orally made statements by witnesses contained in written government reports, not adopted by the witnesses, were required by some courts to be turned over to the defense; and (3) some courts interpreting the decision to require pretrial production of statements.[43] In response to public outrage and lower court confusion, Congress the very same year passed 18 U.S.C. § 3500,[44] the Jencks Act, for the purpose of clarifying *Jencks*.

The Jencks Act bars the court from compelling disclosure of statements made by a prospective government witness until *after* the witness has testified on direct examination in the trial. Only statements that can properly be called the witness's own statement[45] and only statements within the possession or control of the federal prosecutor are subject to production.[46] The Jencks Act did not conflict with any provisions of discovery under Rule 16. Rule 26.2 of the Federal Rules of Criminal Procedure now recapitulates 18 U.S.C. § 3500.[47] The Jencks Act merely states a rule of procedure governing trials before federal tribunals and does not apply in state criminal trials.

5. Amended Federal Rule of Criminal Procedure 16

During the two decades following adoption of the Federal Rules of Criminal Procedure, an even greater number of judges, attorneys, and commentators came to reject the "sporting game" notion still prevailing in federal pretrial discovery.[48] As a result Federal Rule of Criminal Procedure 16 was amended in 1966 to expand the scope of pretrial discovery available to the accused.

(a) *Defendant's Statements; Reports of Examinations and Tests; Defendant's Grand Jury Testimony*. Upon motion of a defendant the court may order the attorney for the government to permit the defendant to inspect and copy or photograph any relevant (1) written or recorded statements or confessions made by the defendant, or copies thereof, within the possession, custody or control of the government, the existence of which is known, or by the exercise of due diligence may become known, to the attorney for the government, (2) results or reports of physical or mental examinations, and of scientific tests or experiments made in connection with the particular case, or copies thereof, within the possession, custody or control of the government, the existence of which is known, or by the exercise of due diligence may become known, to the attorney for the government, and (3) recorded testimony of the defendant before a grand jury.

(b) *Other Books, Papers, Documents, Tangible Objects or Places.* Upon motion of the defendant the court may order the attorney for the government to permit the defendant to inspect and copy or photograph books, papers, documents, tangible objects, buildings or places, or copies or portions thereof, which are within the possession, custody or control of the government, upon a showing of materiality to the preparation of his defense and that the request is reasonable. Except as provided in subdivision (a)(2), this rule does not authorize the discovery or inspection of reports, memoranda, or other internal government documents made by government agents in connection with the investigation or prosecution of the case, or of statements made by government witnesses or prospective government witnesses (other than the defendant) to agents of the government except as provided in 18 U.S.C. § 3500.

(c) *Discovery by the Government.* If the court grants relief sought by the defendant under subdivision (a)(2) or subdivision (b) of this rule, it may, upon motion of the government, condition its order by requiring that the defendant permit the government to inspect and copy or photograph scientific or medical reports, books, papers, documents, tangible objects, or copies or portions thereof, which the defendant intends to produce at the trial and which are within his possession, custody or control, upon a showing of materiality to the preparation of the government's case and that the request is reasonable. Except as scientific or medical reports, this subdivision does not authorize the discovery or inspection of reports, memoranda, or other internal defense documents made by the defendant, or his attorneys or agents in connection with the investigation or defense of the case, or of statements made by the defendant, or by government or defense witnesses, or by prospective government or defense witnesses, to the defendant, his agents or attorneys.

(d) *Time, Place and Manner of Discovery and Inspection.* An order of the court granting relief under this rule shall specify the time, place and manner of making the discovery and inspection permitted and may prescribe such terms and conditions as are just.

(e) *Protective Orders.* Upon a sufficient showing the court may at any time order that the discovery or inspection be denied, restricted or deferred, or make such other order as is appropriate. Upon motion by the government the court may permit the government to make such showing, in whole or in part, in the form of a written statement to be inspected by the court in camera. If the court enters an order granting relief following a showing in camera, the entire text of the government's statement shall be sealed and preserved in the records of the court to be made available to the appellate court in the event of an appeal by the defendant.

(f) *Time of Motions.* A motion under this rule may be made only within 10 days after arraignment or at such reasonable later time as the court may permit. The motion shall include all relief sought under this rule. A subsequent motion may be made only upon a showing of cause why such motion would be in the interest of justice.

(g) *Continuing Duty to Disclose; Failure to Comply.* If subsequent to compliance with an order issued pursuant to this rule, and prior to or during trial, a party discovers additional material previously requested or ordered which is subject to discovery or inspection under the rule, he shall promptly notify the other party or his attorney or the court of the existence of the additional material. If at any time during the course of the proceedings it is brought to the attention of the court that a party has failed to comply with this rule or with an order issued pursuant to this rule, the court may order such party to permit the discovery or inspection of materials not previously disclosed, grant a continuance, or prohibit the party from introducing in evidence the material not disclosed, or it may enter such other order as it deems just under the circumstances.

The 1966 version of Federal Rule of Criminal Procedure 16 provided that the court may order the prosecution to permit the defendant to inspect and copy four types of materials: (1) relevant results or reports of physical examinations and of scientific tests or experiments made in connecton with the particular case; (2) relevant written or recorded statements or confessions made by the defendant; (3) relevant recorded testimony of a defendant before a grand jury; and (4) books, papers, documents, tangible objects, buildings, or places that are within the possession, custody, or control of the government. Federal Rule of Criminal Procedure 16 did not authorize the inspection of reports created by government agents in connection with the investigation or prosecution of the case, nor did it authorize discovery of oral, written, or recorded statements made by government witnesses to government agents. These statements are deemed to fall within the provisions of 18 U.S.C. § 3500. Statements that a third party tells a government agent were made by the defendant contained in the agent's report have also been held to be governed by the Jencks Act.[49]

The 1966 version of Federal Rule of Criminal Procedure 16 gives the court the power to issue protective orders. Subdivision (e) gives the court authority to deny, restrict, or defer discovery upon sufficient showing. The Advisory Committee saw the need for this section as a curb against abuses that may arise from the more liberal discovery procedure. Among the factors cited by the Advisory Committee to be taken into account when determining the necessity of a protective order are the safety of witnesses and others, the protection of information vital to national security, and the protection of businesses from economic reprisals.

6. American Bar Association Standards

In 1970 the American Bar Association adopted Standards for Criminal Justice relating to pretrial discovery and procedure in criminal proceedings. These standards were the result of a series of tentative drafts of minimum standards in the field of criminal justice that had begun in 1963. The Advisory Committee reappraised the traditional arguments against expanded discovery, observing that the advantage to the prosecution of surprise occurs only in a relatively few cases. Similarly, the Advisory Committee thought that the danger of perjury and witness intimidation exists in a minority of cases and could be dealt with on an individual case by case basis. The Advisory Committee sought to implement changes in pretrial procedures "to lend more finality to criminal dispositions, to speed up and simplify the process, and to make more economical use of resources."[50] Believing that the various pretrial discovery procedures at the time fell short of contemporary needs, the Advisory Committee drafted discovery practices that were more permissive than those of any jurisdiction.[51]

1.2 Scope of Discovery.

In order to provide adequate information for informed pleas, expedite trials, minimize surprise, afford opportunity for effective cross-examination, and meet the requirements of due process, discovery prior to trial should be as full and free as possible consistent with protection of persons, effective law enforcement, the adversary system, and national security.

Like the 1966 version of Federal Rule of Criminal Procedure 16, American Bar Assocation Standard for Discovery and Procedure Before Trial 2.1 set forth below speaks in terms of relevancy. Unlike the 1966 version of Federal Rule of Criminal Procedure 16, which is couched in language of discretion, *may*, Standard 2.1 employs the term *shall*, refers to disclosure as the "prosecutor's obligation," and stresses that disclosure is available as a matter of course—a motion to compel disclosure is not required. In practice, the greatest difference between Federal Rule of Criminal Procedure 16, as adopted in 1966, and the 1970 American Bar Association Standard 2.1 lies in the scope of discoverable materials.

2.1 Prosecutor's Obligations.

(a) Except as is otherwise provided as to matters not subject to disclosure (section 2.6) and protective orders (section 4.4), the prosecuting attorney shall disclose to defense counsel the following material and information within his possession or control:

(i) the names and addresses of persons whom the prosecuting attorney intends to call as witnesses at the hearing or trial, together with their relevant written or recorded statements;

(ii) any written or recorded statements and the substance of any oral statements made by the accused, or made by a codefendant if the trial is to be a joint one;

(iii) those portions of grand jury minutes containing testimony of the accused and relevant testimony of persons whom the prosecuting attorney intends to call as witnesses at the hearing or trial;

(iv) any reports or statements of experts, made in connection with the particular case, including results of physical or mental examinations and of scientific tests, experiments or comparisons;

(v) any books, papers, documents, photographs or tangible objects, which the prosecuting attorney intends to use in the hearing or trial or which were obtained from or belong to the accused; and

(vi) any record of prior criminal convictions of persons whom the prosecuting attorney intends to call as witnesses at the hearing or trial.

(b) The prosecuting attorney shall inform defense counsel:

(i) if he has any relevant material or information which has been provided by an informant;

(ii) if there is any relevant grand jury testimony which has not been transcribed; and

(iii) if there has been any electronic surveillance (including wiretapping) of conversations to which the accused was a party or of his premises.

(c) Except as is otherwise provided as to protective orders (section 4.4), the prosecuting attorney shall disclose to defense counsel any material or information within his possession or control which tends to negate the guilt of the accused as to the offense charged or would tend to reduce his punishment therefor.

(d) The prosecuting attorney's obligations under this section extent to material and information in the possession or control of members of his staff and of any others who have participated in the investigation or evaluation of the case and who either regularly report or with reference to the particular case have rep;orted to his office.

Most importantly, unlike the 1966 version of Federal Rule of Criminal Procedure 16, American Bar Association Standard 2.1 requires the prosecutor to disclose in advance of trial the names, addresses, and statements of witnesses to be called by the prosecution at trial. The Advisory Committee noted that 22 states by statute currently required that the accused be notified before trial of the witnesses to be called against him.[52] Although the Advisory Committee cited no state that required disclosure of witnesses' prior statements, the committee stated four reasons for furnishing the defense with such statements before trial:

(1) fairness requires that the statements be disclosed during trial in any event;
(2) if the disclosures are made prior to trial, the delays and attendant inconveniences occasioned by disclosures during trial will be avoided;
(3) for adequate preparation and to minimize surprise, disclosures should be made prior to trial; and
(4) any valid reasons for denying or delaying a given disclosure can be taken account of by the trial judge [as provided for in sections of protective orders (4.4) and work product, informants, and national security (2.6)].[53]

The American Bar Association Standards also provide for disclosure of grand jury minutes. The Advisory Committee noted that the majority of states at the time followed the traditional rule of nondisclosure of grand jury minutes but noted a trend toward liberalization. Five states, as well as Federal Rule of Criminal Procedure 16, provided for discretionary disclosure of transcripts.[54] Moreover, five states granted the defendant the absolute right to inspect relevant grand jury minutes.[55]

Like Federal Rule of Criminal Procedure 16, the American Bar Association Standards provide for pretrial discovery of tangible items, including documents and physical objects. Federal Rule of Criminal Procedure 16, however, makes the disclosure discretionary and requires a showing by the defendant that what he or she is seeking is material to the preparation of the defense and that the defendant's request is reasonable. The Advisory Committee of the American Bar Association rejected both of these prerequisites, reasoning that if such prerequisites were not construed liberally, it would be almost impossible for the defense to prove materiality without first inspecting the material.[56]

7. Uniform Rules of Criminal Procedure

In 1974 the National Conference of Commissioners on Uniform State Law proposed the Uniform Rules of Criminal Procedure.[57] In doing so, the commissioners drew heavily on the American Bar Association Standards and the Federal Rules of Criminal Procedure as well as the criminal procedure statutes of the several states. Among the objectives of the commissioners in drafting the Uniform Rules was to eliminate unnecessary use of the court's time and to provide broad discovery to both prosecution and defense. With respect to disclosure available to the accused, Uniform Rule 421(a) provides as follows:

> (a) Duty of prosecuting attorney. Upon the defendant's written request, the prosecuting attorney, except as provided in subdivision (b), shall allow access at any reasonable time to all matters within the prosecuting attorney's possession or control which relate in any way to the case, including statements, [portions of grand jury minutes or transcripts,] [law enforcement officer] reports, expert reports, reports on prospective jurors, papers, photographs, objects, and places. The prosecuting attorney's obligation extends to matters within the possession or control of any member of his staff and of any official or employee of this State who has participated in the investigation or evaluation of the case and who either regularly reports or with reference to the particular case has reported to his office. In affording this access, the prosecuting attorney shall allow the defendant at any reasonable time and in any reasonable manner to inspect, photograph, copy, or have reasonable tests made. If a scientific test or experiment of any matter may preclude or impair any further tests or experiments, the prosecuting attorney shall give the defendant and any person known or believed to have an interest in the matter reasonable notice and opportunity to be present and to have an expert observe or participate in the test or experiment.

Like the American Bar Association Standards, Uniform Rule 421(a) provides that the defendant is entitled to pretrial discovery without first seeking an order of the court. With respect to the breadth of such discovery, Uniform Rule 421(a) provides that the defendant must be permitted access to all matters within the prosecutor's possession or control that relate in any way to the case. As the Comment following Rule 421(a) notes, "[i]t seems that the only bases for giving the defendant less are adequately covered in the 'exceptions' specified in subdivision (b)."[58] This extensive scope of discovery allows access to witness names and statements, grand jury minutes, reports, papers, photographs, physical objects, and places. The exceptions to discovery are provided by Uniform Rule 421(b). Legal-work product is excluded as it is in civil litigation. The prosecutor may move for a protective order, and pending the making and the consideration of the motion, the prosecutor may deny access. If the court grants the protective order motion, the protective order will defer disclosure until the danger passes. A protective order may also be sought when earlier access to discoverable information will create substantial risk of harm, intimidation, or bribery. If only a part of the matter is legal-work product or would create a substantial risk of harm and so on, the remainder will be disclosed to the defendant. Uniform Rule 421(b) provides as follows:

(b) Exceptions.

(1) Legal work product. The prosecuting attorney need not allow access to:

(i) Legal research; or

(ii) Those portions of records, correspondence, reports, or memoranda which are only the opinions, theories, or conclusions of the prosecuting attorney or members of his legal staff.

(2) Pending motion for protective order. If upon the defendant's written request for access under subdivision (a) the prosecuting attorney informs the defendant that he intends to, and does in fact, move promptly and not later than [ten] days thereafter for a protective order, the prosecuting attorney may deny access, pending the court's ruling on the motion, to the extent that he reasonably believes the protective order will permit him to do so.

(3) Protective order.

(i) Risk of harm, intimidation, or bribery; continuing investigation. The court may permit the prosecuting attorney to defer access for a specified time to the extent that earlier access would create a substantial risk to any person of physical harm, intimidation, or bribery or to the extent justified by the need to protect the integrity of a continuing investigation. Deferral may not be permitted which prejudices a right of the defendant or which allows insufficient time before trial for the defendant to make beneficial use of the information sought, including any additional pretrial discovery thereby necessitated.

(ii) Protecting evidentiary value. The court may impose reasonable terms or conditions as to the manner of inspection, photographing, copying, or testing, to the extent necessary to protect the evidentiary value of any matter to which the defendant seeks access or the prosecuting attorney proposes to test.

(4) Excision. If only part of a matter is within an exception prescribed by this subdivision, the prosecuting attorney shall allow access to a copy of the matter form which the part within the exception has been excised in a manner showing that there has been excision.

Rule 422 of the Uniform Rules provides for the prosecution to inform the defendant of certain matters that the defendant may be unable to discover merely by using the access provided for in Rule 421. The provisions of Rule 422(a) relate primarily to what evidence the prosecution plans to introduce at trial. The prosecutor is required in part automatically to inform the defendant of his or her intent to use evidence that might be subject to a motion to suppress and of his or her intent to use the defendant's confession, admission, or statement at trial. Under Rule 422(b) the defendant may request the prosecuting attorney to file with the court a statement setting forth the name, address, and occupation of each person intended to be called as a witness against the defendant and, as far as it is ascertainable by the prosecuting attorney, any record of criminal convictions of the defendant.

8. Proposed Amendment to Federal Rule of Criminal Procedure 16

In 1974 additional amendments were considered to further broaden the defendant's right to pretrial discovery in the federal system under the Federal Rules of Criminal Procedure. The House Judiciary Committee's report noted that the most controversial proposed amendment was that addressed by Federal Rule of Criminal Procedure 16(a)(1)(E) providing for disclosure of a list of witnesses the government intended to call at trial.[59] The House Committee suggested that

> broader discovery by both the defense and the prosecution will contribute to the fair and efficient administration of criminal justice by aiding in informal plea negotiations, by minimizing the undesirable effect of surprise at trial, and by otherwise contribuitng to an accurate determination of the issue of guilt or innocence.[60]

The House Committee recognized that there might be a risk of danger to prosecution witnesses if their identities were disclosed before trial but believed that the risk was not as great as some prosecutors feared. Many states already had statutes or rules requiring the prosecution to notify the accused of the names of prosecution witnesses. The evidence before the House Committee did not in their opinion indicate untoward problems with witness intimidation. The Southern District of California was at that time following a broad pretrial discovery system like that proposed. The United States Attorney for the Southern District of California observed:

> Concerning the modification to Rule 16, we have followed these procedures informally in this district for a number of years. We were one of the districts selected for the pilot projects of the Omnibus Hearing in 1967 or 1968. We have found that the courts in our district will not require us to disclose the names of proposed witnesses when in our judgment to do so would not be advisable. Otherwise we routinely provide defense counsel with full discovery, including names and addresses of

witnesses. We have not had any untowards results by following this program, having in mind that the courts will, and have, excused us from discovery where the circumstances warrant.[61]

Moreover, proposed Federal Rule of Criminal Procedure 16(a)(1)(E) allowed the government two alternatives if it believed disclosure of a witness's name would create an undue risk of harm to the witness: the government could ask for a protective order, or the government could move the court to allow the perpetuation of a particular witness's testimony.

Regardless of the protections supposedly built into the proposed amendment, the Senate version of the proposed rule eliminated the provision of witness lists, making the names and addresses of government witnesses nondiscoverable. The conference adopted the Senate version believing that

It is not in the interest of the effective administration of criminal justice to require that the government or the defendant be forced to reveal the names and addresses of its witnesses before trial. Discouragement of witnesses and improper contact directed at influencing their testimony, were deemed paramount concerns in the formulation of this policy.[62]

Even though the conference rejected disclosure of witness lists, several other important liberalizations of discovery were incorporated into the 1975 amendments of Federal Rule of Criminal Procedure 16. The significance of the absence of disclosure of a list of government witnesses is in fact highlighted by the breadth of discovery otherwise made available to the accused. Federal Rule of Criminal Procedure 16, as amended, currently provides:

Discovery and Inspection.

(a) Disclosure of Evidence by Government.

(1) Information Subject to Disclosure.

(A) Statement of Defendant. Upon request of a defendant the government shall permit the defendant to inspect and copy or photograph: any relevant written or recorded statements made by the defendant, or copies thereof, within the possession, custody or control of the government, the existence of which is known, or by the exercise of due diligence may become known, to the attorney for the government; the substance of any oral statement which the government intends to offer in evidence at the trial made by the defendant whether before or after arrest in response to interrogation by any person then known to the defendant to be a government agent; and recorded testimony of the defendant before a grand jury which relates to the offense charged. Where the defendant is a corporation, partnership, association or labor union, the court may grant the defendant, upon its motion discovery of relevant recorded testimony of any witness before a grand jury who (1) was, at the time of his testimony, so situated as an officer or employee as to have been able legally to bind the defendant in respect to conduct constituting the offense, or (2) was, at the time of the offense, personally involved in the alleged conduct constituting the offense and so situated as an officer or employee as to have been able legally to bind the defendant in respect to that alleged conduct in which he was involved.

(B) Defendant's Prior Record. Upon request of the defendant, the government shall furnish to the defendant such copy of his prior criminal record, if any, as is within the possession, custody, or control of the government, the existence of which is known, or by the exercise of due diligence may become known, to the attorney for the government.

(C) Documents and Tangible Objects. Upon request of the defendant the government shall permit the defendant to inspect and copy or photograph books, papers, documents, photographs, tangible objects, buildings or places, or copies or portions thereof, which are within the possession, custody or control of the government, and which are material to the preparation of his defense or are intended for use by the government as evidence in chief at the trial, or were obtained from or belong to the defendant.

(D) Reports of Examinations and Tests. Upon request of a defendant the government shall permit the defendant to inspect and copy or photograph any results or reports of physical or mental examinations, and of scientific tests or experiments, or copies thereof, which are within the possession, custody, or control of the government, the existence of which is known, or by the exercise of due diligence may become known, to the attorney for the government, and which are material to the preparation of the defense or are intended for use by the government as evidence in chief at the trial.

(2) Information Not Subject to Disclosure. Except as provided in paragraphs (A), (B), and (D) of subdivision (a)(1), this rule does not authorize the discovery or inspection of reports, memoranda, or other internal government documents made by the attorney for the government or other government agents in connection with the investigation or prosecution of the case, or of statements made by government witnesses or prospective government witnesses except as provided in 18 U.S.C. § 3500.

(3) Grand Jury Transcripts. Except as provided in [Rules 6, 12i and 26.2,] and subdivision (a)(1)(A) of this rule, these rules do not relate to discovery or inspection of recorded proceedings of a grand jury.

(b) Disclosure of Evidence by Defendant.

(1) Information Subject to Disclosure.

(A) Documents and Tangible Objects. If the defendant requests disclosure under subdivision (a)(1)(C) or (D) of this rule, upon compliance with such request by the government, the defendant, on request of the government, shall permit the government to inspect and copy of photograph books, papers, documents, photographs, tangible objects, or copies or portions thereof, which are within the possession, custody or control of the defendant and which the defendant intends to introduce as evidence in chief at the trial.

(B) Reports or Examination and Test. If the defendant request disclosure under subdivision (a)(2)(C) or (D) or this rule, upon compliance with such request by the government, the defendant, on request of the government, shall permit the government to inspect and copy or photograph any results or reports of physical or mental examinations and of scientific tests or experiments made in connection with the particular case, or copies thereof, within the possession or control of the defendant, which the defendant intends to introduce as evidence in chief at the trial or which were prepared by a witness whom the defendant intends to call at the trial when the results or reports relate to his testimony.

(2) Information Not Subject to Disclosure. Except as to scientific or medical reports, this subdivision does not authorize the discovery or inspection of reports, memoranda, or other internal defense documents made by the defendant, or his attorneys or agents in connection with the investigation or defense of the case, or of statements made by the defendant, or by government or defense witnesses, or by prospective government or defense witnesses, to the defendant his agents or attorneys.

(c) Continuing Duty to Disclose. If, prior to or during trial, a party discovers additional evidence or material previously requested or ordered, which is subject to discovery or inspection under this rule, he shall promptly notify the other party or his attorney or the court of the existence of the additional evidence or material.

(d) Regulation of Discovery.

(1) Protective and Modifying Orders. Upon a sufficient showing the court may at any time order that the discovery or inspection be denied, restricted, or deferred, or make such other order as is appropriate. Upon motion by a party, the court may permit the party to make such showing, in whole or in part, in the form of a written statement to be inspected by the judge alone. If the court enters an order granting relief following such as ex parte showing, the entire extent of the party's statement shall be sealed and preserved in the records of the court to be made available to the appellate court in the event of an appeal.

(2) Failure to Comply with a Request. If at any time during the course of the proceedings it is brought to the attention of the court that a party has failed to comply with this rule, the court may order such party to permit the discovery or inspection, grant a continuance, or prohibit the party from introducing evidence not disclosed, or it may enter such other order as it deems just under the circumstances. The court may specify the time, place and manner of making the discovery and inspection and may prescribe such terms and conditions as are just.

(e) Alibi witness. Discovery of alibi witnesses is governed by Rule 12.1.

The 1975 version of Federal Rule of Criminal Procedure 16 also removes most discovery from formal motion practice and leaves it to informal compliance between prosecution and defense attorneys. This change in practice follows both the American Bar Association Standards and the Uniform Rules. The court will intervene only to resolve a dispute about whether something is discoverable or to issue a protective order.

Although Federal Rule of Criminal Procedure 16 does not require disclosure of the name and addresses of intended government witnesses, courts have nevertheless occasionally required that the names and addresses of intended witnesses be turned over by the government in advance of trial.[63] This may result from the fact that a great many federal prosecutors as a matter of practice voluntarily disclose the names, addresses, *and* statements of intended government witnesses in advance of trial, unless in the case at hand a risk of witness intimidation if disclosure is made is perceived.[64] Voluntary disclosure in advance of trial creates little if any additional risk of witness intimidation when the identity of the witness is already known to or easily discoverable by the defendant. Disclosure of names, addresses, and statements of intended witnesses under such circumstances saves time at trial and makes the trial more orderly. Moreover, the identity of any person, including an informer, may be discovered whenever the defendant's right to prepare his or her defense adequately outweighs the public interest in protecting the person from the threat of witness intimidation or preserving the flow of information from a confidential informant.[65]

9. Revised American Bar Association Standards

In 1978 the American Bar Association Standards for Criminal Justice proposed an open-file disclosure system.[66] The Task Force charged with redrafting Standards for Discovery and Procedure Before Trial recognized the traditional reasons for limiting trial discovery: subjecting victims and witnesses to threats or other abuse leading to the loss or destruction of physical evidence or otherwise adversely affecting the integrity of the case to be presented as trial.[67] The Task Force noted, however, that actual practice suggests that such problems do not arise in the majority of cases and that protective orders are an appropriate method of dealing with any problems that do arise.[68] Moreover, the American Bar Association Task Force thought that the attractiveness of the open-discovery system outweighed any potential problems resulting from its liberality. The Task Force concluded that open discovery expedites pretrial procedures to comply with speedy trial requirements and minimizes the need for judicial supervision of routine discovery. It also contributes to the effective exercise of the defendant's constitutional rights, particularly the right to confront witnesses against him. In addition, providing the defendant with access to information enhances the defendant's ability to exercise his or her right to compulsory process and to enter into meaningful plea bargaining. The Task Force further noted the likelihood of increased finality of convictions due to the reduction of error arising from inadequate information.

AMERICAN BAR ASSOCIATION
STANDARDS FOR CRIMINAL JUSTICE
DISCOVERY AND PROCEDURE BEFORE TRIAL

PART II. DISCLOSURE TO ACCUSED

Standard 11-2.1 Prosecutorial disclosure

(a) Upon the request of the defense, the prosecuting attorney shall disclose to defense counsel all of the material and information within the prosecutor's possession or control including but not limited to:

(i) the names and addresses of witnesses, together with their relevant written or recorded statements;

(ii) any written or recorded statements and the substance of any oral statements made by the accused or made by a codefendant;

(iii) those portions of grand jury minutes containing testimony of the accused and relevant testimony of witnesses;

(iv) any reports or statements made by experts in connection with the particular case, including results of physical or mental examinations and of scientific tests, experiments, or comparisons;

(v) any books, papers, documents, photographs, tangible objects, buildings, or places which the prosecuting attorney intends to use in the hearing or trial or which were obtained from or belong to the accused; and

(vi) any record of prior criminal convictions of the defendant or of any codefendant.

(b) When the information is within the prosecutor's possession or control, the prosecuting attorney shall inform defense counsel:

(i) if relevant recorded grand jury testimony has not been transcribed;

(ii) if the defendant's conversations or premises have been subjected to electronic surveillance (including wiretapping);

(iii) if the prosecutor intends to conduct scientific tests, experiments, or comparisons which may consume or destroy the subject of the test, or intends to dispose of relevant physical objects; and

(iv) if the prosecutor intends to offer (as part of the proof that the defendant committed the offense charged) evidence of other offenses.

(c) The prosecuting attorney shall disclose the defense counsel any material or information within the prosecutor's possession or control which tends to negate the guilt of the accused as to the offense charged or which would tend to reduce the punishment of the accused.

(d) The prosecuting attorney's obligations under this standard extend to material and information in the possession or control of members of the prosecutor's staff and of any others who have participated in the investigation or evaluation of the case and who either regularly report or, with reference to the particular case, have reported to the prosecutor's office.[69]

10. Prospective

As modern criminal procedure in advance of trial moved during the past 50 years from surprise pursuant to the sporting theory of justice toward the notion of justice enhanced by meaningful preparation in advance of trial, a clear split arose between the commentators, drafters of model statutes, and state legislatures on the one hand and Congress on the other hand. The split arose over disclosure of the names, addresses, and statements of witnesses the prosecution intends to call at trial. This split in approach involves an assessment of the risk that disclosure of a witness's name and address in advance of trial will lead to an unacceptable number of instances of physical harm, threats of physical harm, bribery, and so on—that is, witness intimidation.

Greater concern in Congress with the problem of witness intimidation arising from disclosure of the names of government witnesses in advance of trial, as evidenced by the Jencks Act and the refusal to enact proposed Federal Rule of Criminal Procedure 16(a)(1)(E), is a rational result of the difference in the nature of crime prosecuted in federal as compared to state court. Federal prosecutions are often against defendants associated with organized crime. Many organized crime prosecutions involve the use of informers. When an informer is involved, the defendant frequently will not know who it is who will be testifying against him or her, that is, the defendant does not already know the informer's identity. Given the association of many defendants in federal prosecutions with organized crime and given the large sums of money involved in many criminal activities triable in federal court, the defendant, if he or she learns of the identity of the witness against him or her, will have both the resources and contacts to intimidate the witness. A United States Justice Department report indicates that between 1974 and 1978, prosecution witnesses accounted for nearly 10 percent of all murders known to be attributable to organized crime.[70] Additional light on the breadth of the problem of witness intimidation in federal prosecutions is shed by a report by 95 United States district attorneys in 1975 detailing 700 cases of witness intimidation.[71]

The depth of concern generated for the safety of witnesses and the integrity of the prosecution of criminal cases in federal court surfaced fully in connection with the amendments proposed in 1974 to the Federal Rules of Criminal Procedure. As previously mentioned, proposed Federal Rule of Criminal Procedure 16(a)(1)(E) would have modified general practice under the Jencks Act to the extent of requiring pretrial disclosure to the defendant of the names and addresses of all government witnesses intended to be called at trial.[72] If the government believed that disclosure would create an unreasonable risk of harm, the government could either seek a protective order against disclosure under Federal Rule of Criminal Procedure 16(d)(1) or move to allow perpetuation of testimony under Federal Rule of Criminal Procedure 15. Disclosure of the contents of statements of the witness was not included. Although some district judges have as a matter of course or on occasion required such disclosure, and although prosecutors in the federal system have voluntarily disclosed the names of witnesses and prior statements as a matter of course or on occasion, Federal Rule of Criminal Procedure 16 had never so required.

In response to pressure from the Department of Justice and others, the House of Representatives amended proposed Federal Rule of Criminal Procedure 16(a)(1)(E) to require that pretrial disclosure of the names of witnesses should occur three days in advance of trial.[73] Proposed Federal

Rule of Criminal Procedure 16(d)(1) dealing with protective orders was amended as well to provide for "an order extending the three-day time limit of subdivision (a)(1)(E)," thus barring disclosure of the names of the government witness upon a proper showing of cause.[74] The House Committee on the Judiciary in its report supported proposed amended Federal Rule of Criminal Procedure 16(a)(1)(E) as follows:

> Perhaps the most controversial amendments to this rule were those dealing with witness lists. Under present law, the government must turn over a witness list *only* in capital cases. The defendant never needs to turn over a list of his witnesses. The proposed rule requires both the government and the defendant to turn over witness lists in every case, capital or noncapital. Moreover, the lists must be furnished to the adversary party upon that party's request.
>
> The Committee believes that it is desirable to promote greater pretrial discovery. As stated in the Advisory Committee Note,
>
>> broader discovery by both the defense and the prosecution will contribute to the fair and efficient administration of criminal justice by aiding in informed plea negotiations, by minimizing the undesirable effect of surprise at trial, and by otherwise contributing to an accurate determination of the issue of guilt or innocence. . . .
>
> The Committee, therefore, endorses the principle that witness lists are discoverable. However, the Committee has attempted to strike a balance between the narrow provisions of existing law and the broad provisions of the proposed rule.
>
> The Committee rule makes the procedures defendant-triggered. If the defendant asks for and receives a list of prosecution witnesses, then the prosecution may request a list of defense witnesses. The witness lists need not be turned over until 3 days before trial. The court can modify the terms of discovery upon a sufficient showing. Thus, the court can require disclosure of the witness lists earlier than 3 days before trial, or can permit a party not to disclose the identity of a witness before trial.
>
> The Committee provision promotes broader discovery and its attendant values—informed disposition of cases without trial, minimizing the undesirable effect of surprise, and helping insure that the issue of guilt or innocence is accurately determined. At the same time, it avoids the problems suggested by both the prosecutors and the defenders.
>
> The major argument advanced by prosecutors is the risk of danger to their witnesses if their identities are disclosed prior to trial. The Committee recognizes that there may be a risk but believes that the risk is not as great as some fear that it is. Numerous states require the prosecutor to provide the defendant with a list of prosecution witnesses prior to trial. The evidence before the Committee indicates that these states have not experienced unusual problems of witness intimidation.
>
> Some federal jurisdictions have adopted an omnibus pretrial discovery procedure that calls upon the prosecutor to give the defendant its witness lists. One such jurisdiction is the Southern District of California. The evidence before the Committee indicates that there has been no unusual problems with witness intimidation in that district. Charles Sevilla, Chief Trial Attorney for the Federal Defenders of San Diego, Inc., which operates in the Southern District of California, testified as follows:

> The Government in one of its statements to this committee indicated that providing the defense with witness lists will cause coerced witness perjury. This does not happen. We receive Government witness lists as a matter of course in the Southern District, and it's a rare occasion when there is any overture by a defense witness or by a defendant to a Government witness. It simply doesn't happen except on the rarest of occasions. When the Government has that fear it can resort to the protective order.

Mr. Sevilla's observations are corroborated by the views of the U.S. Attorney for the Southern District of California:

> Concerning the modifications to Rule 16, we have followed these procedures informally in this district for a number of years. We were one of the districts selected for the pilot projects of the Omnibus Hearing in 1967 or 1968. We have found that the courts in our district will not require us to disclose names of proposed witnesses when in our judgment to do so would not be advisable. Otherwise we routinely provide defense counsel with full discovery, including names and addresses of witnesses. We have not had any untowards results by following this program, having in mind that the courts will, and have, excused us from discovery where the circumstances warrant.

Much of the prosecutorial criticism of requiring the prosecution to give a list of its witnesses to the defendant reflects an unwillingness to trust judges to exercise sound judgment in the public interest. Prosecutors have stated that they frequently will open their files to defendants in order to induce pleas.

Prosecutors are willing to determine on their own when they can do this without jeopardizing the safety of witnesses. There is no reason why a judicial official cannot exercise the same discretion in the public interest.

The Committee is convinced that in the usual case there is no serious risk of danger to prosecution witnesses from pretrial disclosure of their identities. In exceptional instances, there may be a risk of danger. The Committee rule, however, is capable of dealing with those exceptional instances while still providing for disclosure of witnesses in the usual case.[75]

Fourteen members of the House Committee on the Judiciary disagreed:

Under the existing Rules regarding pretrial discovery, a defendant in a criminal case does not have the right to know the names of the witnesses that the government will call to testify against him until they take the witness stand.

The Supreme Court proposed that the defendant would take the right to the names and addresses of all witnesses the United States Attorney plans to call shortly after that defendant is indicted. The Department of Justice testified that, among other objections:

> The consequences of such a Rule are both dangerous and frightening in that government witnesses and their families will even be more exposed than they now are to threats, pressures, and physical harm.

The Committee has amended that proposal to provide that such names and addresses shall be given to the defendant "three days in advance of trial." While this modification makes subdivision (a)(1)(E) less onerous, it is still totally unacceptable in our opinion.

Those who support this Rule have apparently reached the remarkable conclusion that a defendant's right to expanded pretrial discovery is more important than the physical safety of witnesses to crimes.

In testimony before the Subcommittee a panel of United States Attorneys vigorously opposed the pretrial disclosure of witness lists on three basic grounds:

(1) They cited and documented hundreds of instances in virtually every judicial district in the United States where, under existing Rules, government witnesses are murdered, threatened or suborned to commit perjury.

(2) The prosecutors explained that many citizens are hesitant to come forward and report crime or testify at criminal trials because they fear retribution from the defendant. To identify them to criminal defendants before a trial will greatly enhance this climate of fear of reprisal. The U.S. Attorneys contend, and we agree, that to make this "fear of getting involved" worse, is not only unwise, it is unreasonable.

(3) Providing a defendant with a witness list, in addition to all of the other evidence he will receive pursuant to the new expanded right of discovery found in these proposals, will give him a reasonably clear understanding of the details of the government's case. A trial should be a search for truth and not a game. Unscrupulous defendants will use this information to shape their tactics and defenses to fit every configuration of the government's case. Unscrupulous defendants will forego certain defenses, gear their case to cultivating reasonable doubt, and will be generally safeguarded from tripping themselves up.

The Supreme Court recognizes the dangerousness of this Rule, but argues that, if the government believes a witness may be killed or intimidated, it can take that witness' sworn dispositon for use at trial. This is a hollow safeguard because, among other problems, depositions are taken only after notice. A defendant will have ample time to kill or intimidate the witness before the deposition can be taken. The Supreme Court also points out that, if the government fears for the safety of its witnesses, it can seek a protective order and if it is successful in obtaining it, not turn the names of witnesses over to the defendant. This provision will be unworkable in the great majority of cases because the government doesn't know until it is too late that a certain defendant was capable of murder or subornation of perjury.[76]

The Senate subsequently passed a version of Federal Rule of Criminal Procedure 16 eliminating subdivision (E). The Conference Committee concurred:

Rules 16 (a)(1)(E) and (b)(1)(C) (witness lists). The House version of the bill provides that each party, the government and the defendant, may discover the names and addresses of the other party's witnesses 3 days before trial. The Senate version of the bill eliminates these provisions, thereby making the names and addresses of a party's witnesses nondiscoverable. The Senate version also makes a conforming change in Rule 16(d)(1). The Conference adopts the Senate version.

A majority of the Conferees believe it is not in the interest of the effective administration of criminal justice to require that the government or the defendant be forced to reveal the names and addresses of its witnesses before trial. Discouragement of witnesses and improper contacts directed at influencing their testimony, were deemed paramount concerns in the formulation of this policy.[77]

The situation in state court is quantitatively and qualitatively different. Defendants in state court are less often connected with organized crime. Informers are less frequent. In many more cases the defendant already knows the names and addresses of witnesses against him or her or could easily find out by commonly available means such as the telephone book. In addition, more defendants in state court lack the resources, if not the contacts, to contract or otherwise cause a witness to be intimidated. Finally, although witness intimidation is a substantial problem in state court as well, the sense of the research and anecdotal reports is that threats and minor physical attacks characterize witness intimidation in state court, while severe physical attacks and death of witnesses is much more common occurrence in federal criminal prosecutions.[78]

C. MATERIAL WITNESS STATUTES

Charles Q. Stephens was a witness to the assassination of Martin Luther King.[79] He saw the killer running down the stairs of a Memphis rooming house soon after the fatal shots were fired. Stephens willingly agreed to stay in jail for his protection; he was free to come and go with a guard. The state, however, fearing for his safety, invoked its material witness statute. A criminal court judge set bail for Stephens at $10,000. Stephens, who could not meet his bail, was subsequently incarcerated in a county jail and confined without visitors for 31 days until his petition for habeas corpus was granted.[80]

Charles Q. Stephens is just one of many who have been jailed under a material witness statute. The federal government[81] and almost every[82] if not every[83] state has such a material witness statute on its books. These statutes can be traced to the Second Act of Philip and Mary enacted in 1555. Material witness statutes in this country originated in the 1880's.[84]

Material witness statutes are intended to secure a witness's appearance at a judicial proceeding when it is believed that the witness will not voluntarily appear to testify.[85] These statutes, although they are occasionally invoked for the protection of the witness, are really for the convenience of the litigation, usually the government. Because a material witness's testimony may be crucial to the government's successful prosecution of the case, material witness statutes were developed to insure the witness's presence at trial. Although material witness statutes were not enacted to reduce witness intimidation, they can help to prevent its effects, namely, the witness's physical unavailability to testify at trial.

State statutes generally require that a preliminary hearing on the witness's status in the case must be held. Typically, the prosecutor must allege on oath, usually by affidavit, facts and reasons that show that the witness is material and may be unavailable to testify at the required time. A witness is material if he or she has knowledge of facts closely connected to the crime or to the accused that are relevant and highly probative in a criminal action. A criminal action can include a grand jury proceeding or even a district attorney investigation. Usually, the crime involved must be a felony. A sufficient showing of probable unavailability at trial is often based upon allegations such as the witness's moving without having a forwarding address, the witness's not appearing when previously requested to do so, or an inability to serve, either easily or at all, a subpoena upon the witness on a prior occasion. Overall uncooperativeness and indications of the presence of witness intimidation are also relevant allegations. Although the judge or magistrate must make some inquiry concerning the materiality of the witness and his potential availability, the prosecutor's affidavit is usually held to be prima facie proof. The witness may challenge the prosecutor's affidavit, which then makes its allegations questions of fact. However, there are very few cases in which the witness is released due to insufficient evidence concerning the prosecutor's allegations.

If the court holds the witness to be material, it may require a personal recognizance or appearance bond of the witness in a set amount with or without solvent sureties to secure his attendance. Various factors must be considered by the court when it sets the amount of the bail. Some of the factors that the court will examine are the seriousness of the relevant crime, the character and health of the material witness, the need for protection of the witness, the relationship of the witness to the accused, the possibility of the witness's flight to avoid testifying, whether the witness has been difficult to locate, whether the witness has given conflicting statements to the police, the difficulty of procuring the witness's return to the jurisdiction if he or she leaves, whether the witness has an established residence in the state, and whether the witness is currently employed. If the material witness refuses or is unable to meet bail, he or she may be confined until having testified or until the case is dismissed. Some states impose the limitation that the length of the detention must be reasonable.

The federal material witness statute, U.S.C. § 3149,[86] is substantially similar to most state material witness statutes. An affidavit must be filed alleging that the witness is material in a criminal proceeding and that it may become impracticable to secure the witness's presence by subpoena.[87] If a judicial officer determines that the government has met the requirements of materiality and impracticability of securing attendance by subpoena, the witness will be released from custody pending the trial on his or her personal recognizance and upon the execution of an unsecured appearance bond in a set amount. If the judicial officer, however, determines that such a release will not reasonably insure the appearance of the witness as required, as a condition of release the judicial officer may place the witness in the custody of a designated person or organization that would supervise him or her; restrict the witness's travel, association, or place of abode; require an appearance or a bail bond with sufficient solvent sureties; or impose any condition reasonably necessary to insure the witness's appearance, including a requirement that the witness return to custody after specified hours.[88] No material witness may be detained because of an inability to comply with release conditions if the witness's testimony can be adequately secured by a deposition; a material witness may be detained for a reasonable time to take his or her deposition pursuant to Federal Rule of Criminal Procedure 15(a) of the Federal Rules of Criminal Procedure.

Both federal and state material witness statutes have been severely criticized on the ground that they punish innocent citizens because they happened to witness a crime. In fact, the ironic situation occasionally occurs when the accused is released on bail while the witness is incarcerated. Moreover, the witness is usually punished not for having done something, such as evading judicial process, but for something it appears the witness may do in the future. Commentators also allege that prosecutors abuse material witness statutes for purposes of detention. These statutes are susceptible to abuse because of the relatively easy-to-satisfy standards and requirements of proof involved. When prosecutors do not have sufficient proof to hold a criminal defendant, they often invoke the material witness statute to detain the suspect while a confession is obtained or more evidence is gathered.

Finally, there have been numerous constitutional attacks, albeit generally unsuccessful, upon material witness statutes. Material witness statutes have been challenged as violating equal protection under the Fourteenth Amendment, due process under the Fifth Amendment, the Eighth Amendment's prohibition of excessive fine, and the Fourth Amendment's prohibition of unreasonable seizures. Attacks have focused on the material witness's denial of right to counsel and right to a hearing, the paucity of witness fees, and the lack of procedural due process such as lack of notice or *Miranda* warnings.[89]

Material witness statutes have a role to play in combating the problem of witness intimidation. The role, however, is limited. There are some witnesses who, in the face of even the least threatening form of intimidation, will choose to opt out of having anything to do with the criminal justice system. Such a witness, once made the subject of a material witness order, may very well decide to appear at trial when requested to do so. On the other hand, it is most often not known in advance that a witness will not voluntarily appear. The material witness statute is of no help when a subpoena is returned to the prosecutor the day before trial because the server is unable to locate a witness who has decided not to testify. Moreover, even as to witnesses who come to court when they otherwise would not do so because of having been made subject to a material witness order, there is nothing that says that the witness will testify consistent with his or her prior statement.

D. DEPOSITIONS TO PERPETUATE TESTIMONY

The need for perpetuation of a witness's testimony by deposition in criminal cases is evidenced by the significant number of statutes authorizing the prosecution's taking of depositions for substantive admission at trial if the deposed witness's testimony proves unavailable.[90] Perhaps the greatest need for perpetuation of witness testimony by deposition or otherwise is under circumstances in which a witness may be intimidated into either not recalling or changing testimony at trial or in which the witness may be murdered, abducted, or simply scared off before trial. Obviously, the need to perpetuate testimony may arise under other circumstances as well, such as when the witness for reasons of health will most likely not be able to testify at trial.

1. The Hearsay Rule

Through the 1500's and until the mid-1600's, no firmly established hearsay rule existed in England. There was thus no bar to the substantive use of "deposition" evidence at a criminal defendant's trial. In ordinary felony trials[91] and treason trials,[92] admission of "depositions" as substantive evidence was the rule, rather than the exception. The term *deposition* as employed during this period referred to a written statement made *ex parte* signed by the witness under oath. Obviously, cross-examination of the witness was *not* part of the taking of the written statement.

Mr. Jardine, in his Criminal Trials, vol. 1, 514 says: "At the time of Raleigh's trial [2 How.St.Tr. 26 (1603)], most of the circumstances objected to by Sir John Hawles [under William 3, about 1696] were strictly legal and justifiable; for instance, at that time, the depositions of absent persons were read as the usual course of evidence which had prevailed for centuries in State prosecutions; this mode of proof constituted the general rule, and the oral examination of witnesses was the exception, which was in practice sometimes allowed, but was as often refused, and never permitted but by the consent of the counsel for the prosecution." He also asserts (Introd. vol. 1, 25) that "the ordinary mode of trying persons indicted for murder, robbery or theft'' forbade the use of depositions; but his only authority for this statement is Sir Thomas Smith's description of a trial, which does not sustain him; and the citations in the note above seem to disprove his belief.[93]

The hearsay rule began to take root in the middle 1600's, and by 1700 English courts recognized a definite rule that use of extrajudicial statements, even under oath, should not be made if the deponent could be produced to testify personally in court.[94] An ''exception'' to the rule, or at least an area in which the hearsay rule was not at first applied, was recognized where the sworn examination of a witness was conducted before a magistrate.[95] As the hearsay rule developed, it no longer was possible for the prosecution to rely upon a sworn out-of-court statement as sufficient evidence against an accused at trial. By the end of the 1700's it was generally recognized that even sworn ''depositions'' taken before a magistrate of a deponent unavailable at trial, could not be used as substantive evidence against an accused if the accused had not been afforded the opportunity of cross-examining the witness at the taking of his deposition:

On principle, as has often been pointed out, the question in all such cases depends simply upon whether there was an opportunity of cross-examination:

> *R. v. Paine*, 5 Mod. 163, 165 (1696): It was the opinion of both Courts [Kings Bench and Common Pleas], that the depositions should not be given in evidence, the defendant not being present when they were taken before the mayor and so had lost the benefit of a cross-examination.
>
> Richards, C. B. in *R. v. Smith*, Holt N.P. 614, 615 (1817) (having observed that the statute did not mention the prisoner's presence at all): Undoubtedly, however, the decisions established the point that the prisoner ought to be present that he might cross-examine. But here he had that advantage offered him and omitted to use it.
>
> Johnson, J. in *State v. Hill*, 20 S.C.L. (2 Hill) 607, 609, 611 (1835): If the accused is present and has an opportunity of cross-examining the witness, the depositions, according to the rule, are admissible. . . . We know, too, how necessary a cross-examination is to elicit the whole truth from even a willing witness; and to admit such evidence, without the means of applying the ordinary tests, would put in jeopardy the dearest interests of the community.[96]

Thus the doctrine became well settled under both English and American common law that for a ''deposition,'' as newly defined, to be received as substantive evidence at trial, it had to be taken before a person expressly authorized by law, whether a judge, a magistrate, or some other judicially authorized person, *and* the person against whom the sworn statement was offered must have had the opportunity to be present and to cross-examine the deponent. Additionally, a preliminary court order authorizing the taking of the deposition was needed. Such an order as provided by statute was ''usually obtainable only *upon certain conditions*—the illness or the impending departure of the deponent, and the like.''[97] Finally, the principle of confrontation required that the witness's personal attendance at trial be shown to be ''impracticable'' before a deposition could be used substantively.[98]

Impracticability of personal attendance created a necessity for the introduction of the witness's prior deposition. Such necessity was also found sufficient to warrant admission of a deposition when live testimony was unavailable for any reason whatsoever.[99] Specific cases of unavailability warranting use of a deposition included: (1) the death of the witness; (2) the witness's absence from the jurisdiction; (3) the disappearance of the witness and the proponent's inability to find the witness after diligent search; (4) the procurement of the witness's absence by the opponent; (5) the witness's inability to attend trial due to illness, infirmity, or age; (6) the witness's inability to attend because of imprisonment, official duty or privilege, or distance of travel; and (7) the witness's disqualification due to insanity, infamy, a subsequently acquired interest, or the exercise of a privilege.[100]

2. The Confrontation Clause

Wigmore stated that there has never been a distinction, on principle, as to the basic requirements for admissibility of deposition testimony between civil and criminal cases. Wigmore opined that the distinction once recognized in some jurisdictions could be chiefly accounted for by:

> (1) The constitutional provision requiring the confrontation of witnesses with the accused [was] regarded in a few jurisdictions as preventing any use, by the prosecution in criminal cases, of deposition and former testimony; (2) the statutory authorization for taking depositions has in some jurisdictions culpably failed to give the power on behalf of the prosecution in criminal cases; accordingly, if such a deposition [was] there offered, it [was] rejected for the simple reason that there never was authority in any officer to take it; the deposition is legally non-existent.[101]

In fact, doubt surfacing in the late 1800's about the constitutionality of permitting the use of depositions as substantive evidence against an accused by the prosecution under the Confrontation Clause of the Sixth Amendment hindered efforts for nearly 100 years to enact legislation authorizing the prosecution to take depositions for the purpose of perpetuating testimony.

> [E]arly doubt as to the constitutional propriety of allowing the prosecution to use depositions against the accused was widespread at the bar, a hundred years ago. The doubt showed itself in the legislature's *omission*, when providing authority for taking depositions generally, to include statutes *authorizing the taking of depositions on behalf of the prosecution*. This omission was almost universal in the several states. Hence, regardless of what the courts might have held if such depositions (as distinguished from testimony at a former trial) were sought to be used, there was little or no opportunity to present the question, for in practice they could not be taken, lacking the authority in any officer to take them.[102]

Such doubt about the constitutionality of using deposition evidence is curious. As Wigmore noted, countless American cases had previously allowed the use of former testimony, preliminary hearing testimony, and deposition evidence against an accused.[103] The only contrary precedent before 1886, not later overruled, appears to be that of Finn v. Commonwealth,[104] an 1827 Virginia case that decided the issue on English precedent, not on constitutional grounds. The *Finn* opinion relied on an English treatise[105] for the authority that deposition evidence cannot be admitted against an accused. That treatise, however, in turn had relied on Fenwick's Trial,[106] a 1696 decision actually to the opposite effect, that is, the deposition was admitted.[107] Nevertheless, the *Finn* decision "served to keep a doubt alive; and in the later generations a few ill-considered rulings in other jurisdictions have followed it."[108]

Not surprisingly, Supreme Court decisions of the same period lend support for the constitutionality of the use of prior testimony and deposition evidence against an accused. In 1895 the Supreme Court in Mattox v. United States,[109] found that there was "overwhelming" authority for the admission of this type of evidence under the Sixth Amendment, as long as the right of cross-examination was provided to the defendant on the prior occasion.

> Upon the other hand, the authority in favor of the admissibility of such testimony, where the defendant was present either at the examination of the deceased witness before a committing magistrate, or upon a former trial of the same case, is overwhelming. The question was carefully considered in its constitutional aspect by the supreme judicial court of Massachusetts in Commonwealth v. Richards, 18 Pick, 434, in which it was said that "that provision was made to exclude and evidence by deposition, which could be given orally in the presence of the accused, but was not intended to affect the question as to what was or was not competent evidence to be given face to face according to the settled rules of the common law." The subject was also treated at great length by Judge Drummond in United States v. Macomb, 5 McLean, 286, Fed. Cas. No. 15,702, and the substance of a deceased witness' testimony given at a preliminary examination held to be admissible. All the cases up to that time were cited in the opinion, and the decision put upon the ground that, the right of cross-examination having once been exercised, it was no hardship upon the defendant to allow the testimony of the deceased witness to be read. From the following list of cases it will be seen that the same doctrine prevails in more than a dozen States. Summons v. State, 5 Ohio 325; Brown v. Commonwealth, 73 Penn. St. 321: in both of which cases the question was elaborately considered. * * * While the precise question has never arisen in this court, we held in Reynolds v. United States, 98 U.S. 145, that if the witness is absent by the procurement or connivance of the defendant himself, he is in no condition to assert his constitutional immunity.[110]

Although the foregoing holding of *Mattox* would appear to resolve definitively the question of the admissibility of cross-examined deposition evidence, the court's less than enthusiastic language later in the opinion may very well have served to deter for many years the promulgation by Congress of a rule of criminal procedure permitting the prosecution to take the deposition of a witness for the purpose of perpetuating testimony.

The primary object of the constitutional provision in question was to prevent depositions or ex parte affidavits, such as were sometimes admitted in civil cases, being used against the prisoner in lieu of a personal examination and cross-examination of the witness, in which the accused has an opportunity, not only of testing the recollection and sifting the conscience of the witness, but of compelling him to stand face to face with the jury in order that they may look at him, and judge by his demeanor upon the stand and the manner in which he give his testimony whether he is worthy of belief. There is doubtless reason for saying that the accused should never lose the benefit of any of these safeguards even by the death of the witness; and that, if notes of his testimony are permitted to be read, he is deprived of the advantage of that personal presence of the witness before the jury which the law has designed for his protection. But general rules of law of this kind, however beneficient of their operation and valuable to the accused, must occasionally give way to considerations of public policy and the necessities of the case. To say that a criminal, after having once been convicted by the testimony of a certain witness should go scot free simply because death has closed the mouth of that witness, would be carrying his constitutional protection to an unwarrantable extent. The law in its wisdom declares that the rights of the public shall not be wholly sacrificed in order that an incidental benefit may be preserved to the accused.[111]

Nearly ten years later, the Supreme Court in West v. Louisiana[112] had occasion to address the introduction as substantive evidence in state court of a desposition of a witness at which the accused was present and had cross-examined. In *West* the Supreme Court refused to hold the Sixth Amendment of the United States Constitution applicable to the states. The court ruled that Louisiana law governed admissibility of such evidence and that it was bound by the decisions of the Supreme Court of Louisiana holding "[f]or many years . . . that upon such facts as were provided in this case it was proper to admit a deposition as evidence upon the trial of the accused; that in such circumstances he had been confronted with the witnesses within the meaning of the Constitution and laws of the State."[113] A federal constitutional question was raised by the introduction of the deposition testimony only to the extent of determining whether the defendant had been deprived of liberty without due process of law.[114] In this context the Supreme Court examined the state court's admission of the deposition to see if it comported with due process:

At common law, the right existed to read a deposition upon the trial of the defendant, if such deposition had been taken when the defendant was present and when the defendant's counsel had had an opportunity to cross-examine, upon proof being made to the satisfaction of the court that the witness was, at the time of the trial, dead, insane, too ill ever to be expected to attend the trial, or kept away by the connivance of the defendant. This much is conceded by counsel for plaintiffs in error, but they deny that the common law extended the right to so read a deposition upon proof merely of non-residence, permanent absence and inability to procure the evidence of the witness upon the trial.

There is some contrariety among the authorities and textwriters whether under the common law a deposition is admissible in such case. Assuming, however, that the state court erroneously held what the common law was on the subject, we must, in order to reverse this judgment, go further, and hold that a trial thus conducted and a deposition thus admitted did not furnish due process of law to the accused; in other words, that the refusal to exclude this deposition (an error regarding the admissibility of evidence) took away from plaintiffs in error a right of such an important and fundamental character as to deprive them of their liberty without due process of law.

The State of Louisiana had the right to alter the common law at any time, although it had theretofore adopted it with certain limitations. If, through its courts, it erred in deciding what the common law was, yet, if no fundamental and absolutely all-important right were thereby denied to an accused, he still had due process of law and could not complain to this court regarding the error, assuming, of course, that the decision did not conflict with some specific provisions of the Federal Constitution.[115]

The Supreme Court held that no federal right of the accused had been violated by the admission of the deposition, noting that the state court's action with respect to the grounds of unavailability was at most, if at all, but a slight extension of the common law rule. The Supreme Court emphasized that an opportunity to conduct cross-examination had been provided to the accused at the taking of the deposition:

Coming to a decision of the question before us, we are of opinion that no Federal right of the plaintiffs in error was violated by admitting this deposition in evidence. Its admission was but a slight extension of the rule of the common law, even as contended for by counsel. The extension is not of such a fundamental character as to deprive the accused of due process of law. It is neither so unreasonable nor improper as to substantially affect the rights of an accused party or to fundamentally impair those general rights which are secured to him by the 14th Amendment. The accused has, as held by the state court in such case, been once confronted with the witness, and has had opportunity to cross-examine him, and it seems reasonable that when the state cannot procure the attendance of the witness at the trial, and he is a non-resident and is permanently beyond the jurisdiction of the state, then his deposition might be read equally as well as when his attendance could not be enforced because of death or of illness, or his evidence given by reason of insanity.

We say this with reference to the question whether the admission of the deposition fails to give the accused "due process of law," as provided for in the 14th Amendment. As the 6th Amendment does not apply to the state courts, the question as to what is required under its provisions in order to preserve the right to be confronted with the witness is eliminated from any inquiry by this court in this case.[116]

The qualification by the Supreme Court that it was reserving ruling on whether an accused's Sixth Amendment right would have been violated had the prosecution occurred in a federal court once more left some room for doubt. Such doubts that did exist were not firmly laid to rest until much later. In 1965, in Pointer v. Texas,[117] the Confrontation Clause was held applicable to the states. Then in 1970, in California v. Green,[118] the Supreme Court emphasized that as long as the criminal defendant had been provided an effective opportunity for cross-examination of the witness at the time the prior testimony was taken, the prior testimony can be constitutionally admitted when the witness's testimony is found to be unavailable at trial.

3. Early Statutory Development

By the end of the nineteenth century, virtually all states had statutes providing for the taking of depositions, although not all statutes covered criminal trials.[119] A significant number of these statutes did authorize the prosecution to take and use depositions against an accused, although some required the consent of the defendant or provided for use only if the defendant sought to use deposition evidence.[120]

Section 30 of the Judiciary Act of 1789[121] was the first federal statute establishing the taking of depositions in the federal courts.[122] Two types of depositions were provided for: (1) depositions *de bene esse*, that is, an order for conditional taking; and (2) depositions *dedimus potestatem*, that is, a special commission. The original act of 1789 provided that notice and opportunity to cross-examine were not necessary for depositions *de bene esse* if either the opponent or his or her attorney was not within 100 miles of the taking of the deposition. This defect was remedied in Section 863 of the 1878 revised statute.

Section 863 of the revised statute continued to provide for depositions *de bene esse* but established that "reasonable notice must first be given in writing," and "whenever, by reason of that absence from the district and want of an attorney of record or other reason, the giving of the notice herein required shall be impracticable, it shall be lawful to take such depositions as there shall be urgent necessity for taking, upon such notice as any judge authorized to hold courts in such circuit or district shall think reasonable and direct."[123] Section 866 provided for depositions *dedimus potestatem* but stipulated that to prevent a failure or delay of justice, the provisions of Section 863 regarding notice would not apply.[124] The *dedimus potestatem* section also prescribed that "common usage" shall control the mode of taking and notice of such depositions. This "common usage" provision first was construed to permit the adoption of local statutory and common law modes,[125] but in 1884 the Supreme Court refused such a construction.[126] In 1892 this matter was cleared up by statute, and the lower federal courts were authorized to take, and presumably admit into evidence, the depositions according to the permissible method of the state in which the trial was conducted.[127]

Whether these statutes were meant to apply to defendants in criminal cases is unclear; it is even more uncertain whether the government had such a right. L. Orfield discussed the extremely sparse case law applying the foregoing statutes in his treatise on Criminal Procedure Under the Federal Rules:

> The first reported lower court federal case to allow a defendant to take depositions was decided in 1882. [United States v. Wilder, 14 F. 393 (C.C.S.D. Ga. 1882).] The defendant was charged in an information with smuggling. He submitted a petition and affidavit showing that he had witnesses residing abroad who were material to his defense. He asked a *dedimus potestatem* to take the depositions under section 866 of the Revised Statutes. The United States Attorney resisted the application on ground that it was unprecedented and without authority and on the ground that the deposition would not be admissible at the trial. The trial court granted the application for deposition by commission even though it was probably unprecedented in federal criminal cases. He pointed out that it was permitted in the state courts of Georgia, and allowed by statute in other states. The government would not be prejudiced as the taking would be at the expense of the defendant, and its admissibility would be determined on the trial. If it was rejected at the trial, the judge would, nevertheless, take account of it in imposing sentence.[128]

Orfield also discusses a district court decision, United States v. Cameron,[129] decided a year after *Wilder*, which construed Section 866 to apply to criminal defendants:

> The court referred to the language of the statute in effect since [1878] providing that "in any case where it is necessary, in order to prevent a failure of justice, any of the courts of the United States may grant a *dedimus potestatem* to take depositions according to common usage." This statute, in using the words "in any case," applied to criminal as well as to civil cases. The court pointed out that the statutory provision was originally enacted as a proviso to section 30 of the Judiciary Act of 1789 as follows: "Provided that nothing herein shall be construed to prevent any court of the United States from granting a *dedimus potestatem* to take depositions according to common usage when it maybe necessary to prevent a failure or delay of justice which power they shall severally possess." Possibly the act of 1789 did not cover criminal cases, but there is a strong argument that it did. The [1878] act definitely covered criminal cases. The [1878] provision appeared in a Chapter entitled "Evidence" which covered both civil and criminal cases. The words "common usage" in the [1878] act refer to the usage of the courts of the state in which the federal court sits, and not to the common law because when the statute was enacted it was common usage to take depositions under statutes. The 1789 act should be construed similarly. Missouri law had allowed such depositions for half a century. The defendant had shown necessity as the witness resided several hundred miles away and the defendant was unable to pay the cost of bringing him to the place of trial and the government could not pay such cost and the witness need not. The

court stated that it does "not say that all these facts must necessarily appear." Allowing depositions would prevent delay and continuances and a failure of justice. One need not fear perjury at the taking of the deposition as the government may cross-examine and later at the trial show the reputation for truth and veracity of the witness. If the witness commits perjury at the taking of the deposition he may be prosecuted for perjury as the court has authority of law to take testimony by deposition.[130]

In 1930 two federal circuit courts upheld lower court decisions denying defendants' requests for the taking of depositions. Both decisions recognized that the 1878 statute governed criminal trials. However, each limited application by insisting on strict application of notice, location, and other requirements relating to common usage.[131]

The 1878 statute had itself been revised and renumbered as 28 U.S.C. § 644 by the time of enactment of the Federal Rules of Criminal Procedure in 1945.[132] Section 644 was construed to be essentially the same as the earlier statute.[133] It was, however, extended by case law to provide the court with authority to assist a criminal defendant in securing the depositions of witnesses in foreign countries.[134] There appear to be no decisions under the 1789, 1878, or revised statute permitting the federal government to take depositions.

4. Federal Rule of Criminal Procedure 15

Rule 15 of the Federal Rules of Criminal Procedure, as adopted in 1945, allowed only the defendant in a criminal case to take depositions of prospective witnesses for possible substantive use at trial. At any time after the filing of an indictment or information and upon motion of the defendant and notice to the parties, the court could order that a deposition be taken if it appeared at the time of the motion that "a prospective witness may be unable to attend or prevented from attending a trial or hearing." Federal Rule of Criminal Procedure 15 provided as follows:

Fed. R. Crim. P. 15 (1945)

(a) When Taken. If it appears that a prospective witness may be unable to attend or prevented from attending a trial or hearing, that his testimony is material and that it is necessary to take his deposition in order to prevent a failure of justice, the court at any time after the filing of an indictment or information may upon motion of a defendant and notice to the parties order that his testimony be taken by deposition and that any designated books, paper, documents or tangible objects, not privileged, be produced at the same time and place. If a witness is committed for failure to give bail to appear to testify at a trial or hearing, the court on written motion of the witness and upon notice to the parties may direct that his deposition be taken. After the deposition has been subscribed the court may discharge the witness.

(b) Notice of Taking. The party at whose instance a deposition is to be taken shall give to every other party reasonable written notice of the time and place for taking the deposition. The notice shall state the name and address of each person to be examined. On motion of a party upon whom the notice is served, the court for cause shown may extend or shorten the time.

(c) Defendant's Counsel and Payment of Expenses. If a defendant is without counsel the court shall advise him of this right and assign counsel to represent him unless the defendant elects to proceed without counsel or is able to obtain counsel. If it appears that a defendant at whose instance a deposition is to be taken cannot bear the expense thereof, the court may direct that the expenses of travel and subsistence of the defendant's attorney for attendance at the examination shall be paid by the government. In that event the marshall shall make payment accordingly.

(d) How Taken. A deposition shall be taken in the manner provided in civil actions. The court at the request of a defendant may direct that a deposition be taken on written interrogatories in the manner provided in civil actions.

(e) Use. At the trial or upon any hearing, a part or all of a deposition, so far as otherwise admissible under the rules of evidence, may be used if it appears: That the witness is dead; or that the witness is out of the United States, unless it appears that the absence of the witness was procured by the party offering the deposition; or that the witness is unable to attend or testify because of sickness or infirmity; or that the party offering the deposition has been unable to procure the attendance of the witness by subpoena. Any deposition may also be used by any party for the purpose of contradicting or impeaching the testimony of the deponent as a witness. If only a part of a deposition is offered in evidence by a party, an adverse party may require him to offer all of it which is relevant to the part offered and any party may offer other parts.

(f) Objections to Admissibility. Objections to receiving in evidence a deposition or part thereof may be made as provided in civil actions.

The 1945 version of Federal Rule of Criminal Procedure 15 differed in several significant respects from the rules governing depositions in civil cases.[135] Depositions in a criminal case could not be taken by either party as a matter of right without court permission: a deposition in a criminal case could be had only by the defendant and then only pursuant to court order issued upon a specific showing relating to the prospect of the witness being unavailable at trial—an order within the court's discretion. Like the rules governing depositions in civil cases, Federal Rule of Criminal Procedure 15(e) provided for substantive admissibility of such depositions at a trial or hearing if (1) it appeared the witness was dead; (2) the witness was out of the United States; (3) the witness was unable to testify because of sickness or infirmity; or (4) the party offering the deposition was unable to procure the attendance of the witness by subpoena.

Federal Rule of Criminal Procedure 15 as finally adopted was substantially different from any of the preliminary drafts prepared by the Advisory

Committee. The preliminary drafts would have changed then existing law to allow the government, in addition to the defendant, to take depositions for the perpetuation of witness testimony.[136] Orfield, in commenting on an initial preliminary draft, noted in regard to what was then proposed rule 18:

> [Proposed] [r]ule 18(c) changes existing law by permitting the prosecution[115] as well as the defendant to take depositions. The rule provides a method for taking depositions instead of according to common usage. While the power of the court to direct the taking of depositions is enlarged, the exercise of such power is left within the court's discretion. To permit the indiscriminate taking of depositions would result in abuse and delay. It is more satisfactory to set up a procedure under which depositions may be taken only where the court is convinced that they are necessary. The *Federal Rules of Civil Procedure*, on the other hand, encourage depositions and permit them to be used as examinations before trial for the purpose of discovery as well as for the purpose of securing testimony. Civil procedure of course is not affected by any constitutional requirement of confrontation of witnesses.
>
> N. 115. Civil Rules 26 through 32 provide that in any case where it is necessary in order to prevent a failure or delay of justice the court may grant a *dedimus protestatem* to take depositions according to common usage. This statute has been held to authorize the courts in their discretion to grant commissions to criminal defendants to take depositions. United States v. Cameron, 15 Fed. 794 (C.C.E.D. Mo. 1883); Clymer v. United States, 38 F.2d 581 (C.C.A. 10th 1930).[137]

The Fifth Draft of this provision, then rule 20, dated June 1942, was submitted to the Supreme Court of the United States for comment. It was criticized by the Supreme Court, as well as across the nation, for permitting the government's use of depositions against an accused.[138] Although the grounds of the Supreme Court's criticism were never published, several commentators suggested that the Supreme Court's reasons were based on the "uncertain" constitutional status of the provision.[139]

Nevertheless, the Advisory Committee persisted in recommending a provision authorizing government-taken perpetuation depositions throughout the remainder of the preliminary drafts pointing out that 17 states had conferred the right by statute as of 1944.[140] The Advisory Committee's efforts were for naught. The Supreme Court rejected the final draft of this section in its entirety without comment and limited the taking of depositions to those sought by the defendant.[141] The deleted section provided as follows:

> The following additional requirement shall apply if the deposition is taken at the instance of the government or of a witness. The officer having custody of a defendant shall be notified of the time and place set for examination, and shall produce him at the examination and keep him in the presence of the witness during the examination. A defendant not in custody shall be given notice and shall have the right to be present at the examination. The government shall pay in advance to the

defendant's attorney and a defendant not in custody expenses of travel and subsistence for attendance at the examination.[142]

A member of the Advisory Committee made the following comments about the Supreme Court's rejection of the provision authorizing prosecution depositions:

> The recommendation was inspired by no desire to dispense with live witnesses who could be observed and cross-examined at the trial. The thought was simply that when it appeared in the preliminary stages of a proceeding that a material witness might later be unavailable, his deposition would in certain circumstances be useful. Just what uses the constitution and the judiciary would permit—given a deposition taken in the defendant's presence, as provided by the recommended rule—is a question which would have to be explored de novo. But it is not clear that the "right of confrontation" would preclude all use of depositions by the government, either at the trial or in preliminary and supplementary proceedings. After some early doubts, the familiar exceptions to the hearsay rule have become as accepted in criminal as in civil trials. The Court's action in eliminating depositions on behalf of the government may have been prompted by a feeling that the government could better afford to lose a few cases than make even a gesture which might be interpreted as favoring trial on a paper record.[143]

It must be remembered that in 1945, as previously discussed,[144] applicable doctrine consisted of the *Mattox*[145] and *West*[146] decisions. Thus there may still have been some doubt about the constitutionality of admitting depositions taken by the government. James Moore suggested that at that time "it had come to be believed by many that the constitutional requirement included the opportunity for the jury, as trier of facts, to see the witness while hearing his testimony against the defendant."[147]

Efforts to gain approval of the taking of perpetuation depositions by the prosecution were rekindled in the proposed amendments to the Federal Rules of Criminal Procedure in the early 1960's. The Preliminary Draft of Proposed Amendments to Rules of Criminal Procedure released by the Advisory Committee in December 1962 proposed that the 1945 version of Rule 15 be amended to strike the limitation "of a defendant" from the first sentence of Subsection (a), which then read that a prospective witness's deposition could be taken by court order "upon motion of a defendant." This elimination would then make a court-ordered deposition available "upon motion," that is, to any party so moving the court. Additionally, the first draft of the amendment sought to add a Subdivision "(g)," which was virtually identical to the subdivision of the final draft of the 1945 rules set deleted by the Supreme Court in the final version.[148] The recommendation to permit government perpetuation depositions was continued in the Second Preliminary Draft of proposed amendment to Rule 15 dated March 1964. However, several material additions were made to Subsection (g) including that the defendant's counsel was entitled to reasonable notice of the taking of the deposition, that a defendant might waive his or her right to be present at the taking without affecting the admissibility of the deposition at trial, and that the government was to produce any statements made by the witness for the defendant's examination and use at the deposition.[149]

Second Preliminary Draft of Proposed Amendments to Rules of Criminal Procedure (March 1964)

Rule 15

* * *

(g) The following additional requirements shall apply if the deposition is taken at the instance of the government or a witness. Both the defendant and his attorney shall be given reasonable advance notice of the time and place set for the examination. The officer having custody of a defendant shall be notified of the time and place set for the examination, and shall produce him at the examination and keep him in the presence of the witness during the examination. A defendant not in custody shall have the right to be present at the examination but his failure to appear after notice and tender of expenses shall constitute a waive of that right. The government shall pay to the defendant's attorney and to a defendant not in custody expenses of travel and subsistence of attendance at the examination. The government shall make available to the defendant for his examination and use at the taking of the deposition any statement of the witness being deposed which is in the possession of the government and which the government would be required to make available to the defendant if the witness were testifying at the trial.[150]

These proposed amendments to Federal Rule of Criminal Procedure 15 were both a reflection of the terms of then current state legislation and a response to the suggestions of several commentators who had argued that allowing depositions by the government would not violate the Confrontation Clause as long as the defendant and his or her counsel were permitted to be present and to cross-examine the deponent.[151] Additionally, Rule 27 of the Uniform Rules of Criminal Procedure, adopted by the National Conference on Commissioners on Uniform State Laws and approved by the American Bar Association in 1952, permitted the prosecution to take perpetuation depositions.[152]

The Standing Committee on Rules of Practice and Procedure nonetheless ignored this trend and rejected any proposed authorization of the taking of depositions by the government for substantive use at trial. There was thus no proposal for government depositions in the Report of the Judicial Conference on the 1966 amendments submitted to the Supreme Court for approval.[153] C. Wright suggested that "[t]he gingerly treatment of these proposals for government depositions was undoubtedly because of uncertainty whether these would be consistent with the Confrontation Clause of the Sixth Amendment. Until recently there were only a few old cases construing that provision, and these cases shed an uncertain light."[154] Hence Rule 15 went into the 1970's without amendment to provide for government depositions.

5. Title VI of The Organized Crime Control Act of 1970

The next attempt to enact federal deposition procedures for perpetuation of testimony and protection of witnesses on behalf of the government was a success, a success that later served as a springboard for a similar amendment to Federal Rule of Criminal Procedure 15. The Organized Crime Control Act of 1970,[155] introduced in the Senate as S.30 in 1969, contained a provision based upon then-existing Federal Rule of Criminal Procedure 15 expanded to authorize the taking of perpetuation depositions by the government as well as the defendant.

> The purpose of Title VI is to enable the Government to preserve testimony in a criminal proceeding, a right which now exists under Rule 15 of the Federal Rules of Criminal Procedure only for the defendant. The Title is designed to insure the availability of such testimony at the trial, even though the witness might be unavailable, and to eliminate the incentive to delaying tactics and underworld harassment and violence against prospective witnesses.[156]

Title VI, 18 U.S.C. § 3503, provides that depositions may be taken by the government to preserve testimony when "due to exceptional circumstance, it is in the interests of justice."[157] The provision, however, limits the authority of the government to take perpetuation depositions to those cases in which the Attorney General has certified that "the proceeding is against a person who is believed to have participated in an organized criminal activity."[158] This limitation was added by Congress to conform the provision to the sole purpose of the act, which was to deal with organized crime.[159] The statute does not provide a definition of the "exceptional circumstances" necessary to warrant the taking of a deposition for perpetuation of testimony, but the legislative commentary indicates certain situations meant to fall within the standard. They include "circumstances frequently encountered in organized crime prosecutions, where there are inherent risks that witnesses will be kidnapped, killed, or injured; will leave the jurisdiction or go into hiding; or will be subjected to offers or bribes or threats of physical retaliation."[160] The standards controlling the use of depositions at trial are the same as those in Federal Rule of Criminal Procedure 15(e) as enacted in 1945, with the exception that a deposition may additionally be used when "the witness refuses in the trial or hearing to testify concerning the subject of the deposition or the part offered."[161] When the government is the party taking the deposition, the defendant is entitled to receive notice to be present, to be tendered travel and other expenses, and to be represented by counsel of his or her choice or counsel appointed by the court.[162] The defendant is guaranteed a right of cross-examination, the scope of which "shall be such as would be allowed in the trial itself."[163] Section 3503 also provides, however, that the defendant's failure to attend the deposition, without good cause, will constitute a waiver of his or her right to be present.[164]

Title VI was enacted with the expectation that it would make a great contribution to the protection of witnesses and the perpetuation of their testimony in organized crime cases:

Use of violent and intimidating tactics against persons known or suspected of being potential government witnesses in organized crime cases is a matter of reported history. This provision for depositions to preserve the testimony of either defense or prosecution witnesses long has been needed. Too often charges or indictments initiated against organized crime individuals and activities have failed at the prosecutive level because essential witnesses have been killed, bribed or intimidated into forgetfulness.

Example—At the present time there is pending in the Eastern District of Louisiana the federal prosecution of State Attorney General Jack P. F. Gremillion, State Representative Salvadore Anzelmo, and others. They are charged with fraudulent acts contributing to the bankruptcy of Louisiana Loan and Thrift Company, which resulted in hundreds of people losing their savings. About one-third of the deposits had been loaned to, or through, organized crime enterprises. An important witness in this matter, secretary of the corporation, has died. S. 30 would have perpetuated his evidence, now lost.

On the night of December 16, 1967, Harry Bennett was murdered in Harrison County, Mississippi. Earlier that day he had indicated his intention of cooperating in a federal prosecution of various syndicate gamblers for interstate shipment of a crooked gambling device. Harry Bennett, a career professional gambler, was one of the co-defendants. He could have testified about meetings of defendants and counsel with Carlos Marcello. His lips were sealed for all time. If S. 30 had existed, this might not have been true.

Christian Faser, Jr. was indicted by a federal grand jury in New Orleans on March 28, 1969, charged with conspiracy and mail fraud in a scheme by which millions in state funds were deposited in the First National Bank of Jefferson Parish, in return for bribes. At the time of these alleged acts Faser was Executive Secretary to the then Governor of Louisiana, Jimmie Davis. Named with Faser as co-conspirators, but not indicted, were Numa P. Himbert, a former high official in the State Highway Department and State Commissioner of Administration; also State Senator E. W. "Kelly" Gravolet, who died prior to the indictment. After Faser's indictment, and with his trial pending, Himbert, a potentially significant witness, had also died. Title VI would have preserved his testimony.

In the Orleans Parish Civil District Court there was sworn testimony by an official of the Cresent City River Pilot's Association that a $50,000 bribe was paid to Christian Faser in 1960 for his assistance in influencing legislation. No State prosecution of Faser was undertaken.

Faser is now a State Representative from the Baton Rouge area. As a member of the Louisiana House Judiciary Committee, in recent weeks Faser helped defeat an attempt to introduce strong anti-gambling laws in Louisiana, modeled after effective federal statutes.

In the Federal Kansas City Mafia-Teamsters case referred to under Title V, above, one of the co-defendants was Floyd Hayes, who was convicted and then became a cooperative government witness. He made a series of statements to prosecutors about unsolved syndicate crimes which had extended over many years. Lacking the authority of Title VI, there was no incentive for preserving his testimony before his cooperation surfaced as a witness in a perjury trial. About six weeks later he was murdered. Five or more prosecutions died with him. S. 30 could save him—and them.[165]

[T]he leaders of organized crime have shown a great propensity to apply the techniques of intimidation and bribery with which they conduct their illegal businesses to their defense and criminal cases as well. As the distinguished senior Senator from Maryland, Mr. Tydings, testified before the Senate Subcommittee on Criminal Laws and Procedure:

> Unimplicated witnesses have been, and are now, regularly bribed, threatened or murdered. Scores of cases have been lost because key witnesses turned up in rivers, in concrete boots. Victims have been crushed—James Bond-like—along with their automobiles by hydraulic machines in syndicate-owned junkyards.

Title VI makes a two-pronged attack in that problem. First, it preserves the evidence which a witness has to give in a form which can be used at trial if the witness is unavailable at that time or has been suborned, but which is inadmissible if the witness appears at trial and offers the evidence in person. Second, by preserving the evidence which a witness can give, a deposition taken under Title VI largely eliminates the incentive which a defendant or his associates have to harm or kill the witness. Thus, Title VI reduces the chance of witnesses being harmed or bribed and at the same time provides an alternative way to present the testimony of witnesses who do become unavailable.

The utility of the deposition authority Title VI would confer, and the urgency of the need for its enactment, are illustrated by recent prosecution in Tucson of three reputed Mafia leaders. In that case, Joseph Bonnano, the alleged former boss of a New York "Cosa Nostra" family and Charles Battaglia and Peter Joseph Notaro, two alleged "Cosa Nostra" members, were charged with conspiracy to obstruct justice by obtaining false testimony from a former police sergeant.

All three defendants were, however, acquitted last March 4, because an essential but reluctant witness, who had corroborated the Government's case in testimony before the grand jury that returned the indictment, disappeared before the trial. The testimony of that witness, Floyd Max Shumway, obviously was in danger of loss before trial, and could have been preserved if Title VI had been law at the time. Since Congress had not yet enacted Title VI, no deposition could be taken, and the jury was needlessly deprived of the opportunity to hear crucial evidence.[166]

6. Amendment to Federal Rule of Criminal Procedure 15

In 1974 more than 30 years after the Advisory Committee's first attempt, Federal Rule of Criminal Procedure 15 was finally amended—virtually without comment—to permit either party to move the court for the taking of a perpetuation deposition.[167] The amended rule is modeled after Title VI of The Organized Crime Control Act of 1970 but is not limited, as is the latter, to proceedings against a person believed to have participated in organized criminal activity.

Federal Rule of Criminal Procedure 15 (1975)

(a) When Taken. Whenever due to exceptional circumstances of the case it is in the interest of justice that the testimony of a prospective witness of a party be taken and preserved for use at trial, the court may upon motion of such party and notice to the parties order that testimony of such witness be taken by deposition and that any designated book, paper, document, record, recording, or other material not privileged, be produced at the same time and place. If a witness is committed for failure to give bail to appear to testify at a trial or hearing, the court on written motion of the witness and upon notice to the parties may direct that his deposition be taken. After the deposition has been subscribed the court may discharge the witness.

(b) Notice of Taking. The party at whose instance a deposition is to be taken shall give to every party reasonable written notice of the time and place for taking the deposition. The notice shall state the name and address of each person to be examined. On motion of a party upon whom the notice is served, the court for cause shown may extend or shorten the time or change the place for taking the deposition. The officer having custody of a defendant shall be notified of the time and place set for the examination and shall, unless the defendant waives in writing the right to be present, produce him at the examination and keep him in the presence of the witness during the examination, unless, after being warned by the court that disruptive conduct will cause him to be removed from the place of the taking of the deposition, he persists in conduct which is such as to justify his being excluded from that place. A defendant not in custody shall have the right to be present at the examination upon request subject to such terms as may be fixed by the court, but his failure, absent good cause shown, to appear after notice and tender of expenses in accordance with subdivision (c) of this rule shall constitute a waiver of that right and of any objection to the taking and use of the deposition based upon that right.

(c) Payment of Expenses. Whenever a deposition is taken at the instance of the government, or whenever a deposition is taken at the instance of a defendant who is unable to bear the expenses of the taking of the deposition, the court may direct that the expense of travel and subsistence of the defendant and his attorney for attendance at the examination and the cost of the transcript of the deposition shall be paid by the government.

(d) How Taken. Subject to such additional conditions as the court shall provide, a deposition shall be taken and filed in the manner provided in civil actions except as otherwise provided in these rules, provided that (1) in no event shall a deposition be taken of a party defendant without his consent, and (2) the scope and manner of examination and cross-examination shall be such as would be allowed in the trial itself. The government shall make available to the defendant or his counsel for examination and use at the taking of the deposition any statement of the witness being deposed which is in the possession of the government and to which the defendant would be entitled at the trial.

(e) Use. At the trial or upon any hearing, a part or all of a deposition, so far as otherwise admissible under the rules of evidence, may be used as substantive evidence if the witness is unavailable, as unavailability is defined in Rule 804(a) of the Federal Rules of Evidence, or the witness gives testimony at the trial or hearing inconsistent with his deposition. Any deposition may also be used by any party for the purpose of contradicting or impeaching the testimony of the deponent as a witness. If only a part of a deposition is offered in evidence by a party, an adverse party may require him to offer all of it which is relevant to the part offered and any party may offer other parts.

(f) Objections to Depositon Testimony. Objections to deposition testimony or evidence or parts thereof and the grounds for the objection shall be stated at the time of the taking of the deposition.

(g) Deposition by Agreement Not Precluded. Nothing in this rule shall preclude the taking of a deposition, orally or upon written questions, or the use of a deposition, by agreement of the parties with the consent of the court.

The standard governing the court's grant or denial of a request to perpetuate testimony is whether "due to exceptional circumstances of the case it is in the interest of justice."[168] As proposed by the Advisory Committee and submitted by the Supreme Court, the rule provided for depositions in "special circumstances." The Advisory Committee Note's support of the proposed rule stated:

Subdivision (a) is revised to provide that the government as well as the defendant is entitled to take a deposition. The phrase "whenever due to special circumstances of the case it is in the interest of justice" is intended to make clear that the decision by the court as to whether to order the taking of a deposition shall be made in the context of the circumstances of the particular case. The principal objective is the preservation of evidence for use at trial. It is not to provide a method of pretrial discovery nor primarily for the purpose of obtaining a basis for later cross-examination of an adverse witness. Discovery is a matter dealt with in Rule 16. An obviously important factor is whether a deposition will expedite, rather than delay, the administration of criminal justice. Also important is the presence or absence of factors which determine the use of a deposition at the trial, such as the agreement of the parties to the use of the deposition; the possible unavailability of the witness; or the possibility that coercion may be used upon the witness to induce him to change his testimony or not to testify.[169]

Congress, however, preferred the language from Title VI of the Organized Crime Control Act of 1970, substituting "exceptional circumstances" as part of the 1974 amendment to Federal Rule of Criminal Procedure 15.[170] No guidelines were provided by Congress as to the categories of circumstances falling within the "exceptional circumstance" standard. Nor had the "exceptional circumstances" requirement been included in former Federal Rule of Criminal Procedure 15(a):

(a) When Taken. If it appears that a prospective witness may be unable to attend or prevented from attending a trial or hearing, that his testimony is material and that it is necessary to take his deposition in order to prevent a failure of justice, the court at any time after the filing of an indictment or information may upon motion of a defendant and notice to the parties order that his testimony be taken by deposition and that any designated books, paper documents or tangible objects not privileged, be produced at the same time and place.

However, commentators had suggested that the "assumption [in former rule 15 was] that they will be needed only in exceptional situations, since the ordinary witness subpoena in a federal criminal proceeding runs throughout the United States and not just within the district of issue or 100 miles from the place of trial as in a civil action,"[171] and that "[i]t was contemplated by the framers of [former Rule 15] that depositions would be used in criminal cases only in exceptional situations, as had been the practice therefore."[172]

Under Title VI and the 1974 amendment Federal Rule of Criminal Procedure 15, "materiality" was not included as a specific prerequisite to the taking of a perpetuation deposition in a criminal case.[173] Nevertheless, in United States v. Singleton,[174] the Second Circuit held that the "exceptional circumstances" of Title VI of the 1970 Act would be satisfied only when the standard of former Rule 15(a) was met, that is, "[i]f it appears that a prospective witness may be unable to attend or prevented from attending a trial or hearing that his testimony is material and that it is necessary to take his deposition in order to prevent a failure of justice." Moore has suggested that since the fulfillment of the unavailability, materiality, and necessity requirements of former Rule 15(a) meet the "exceptional circumstances" test of Title VI, from which the present Federal Rule of Criminal Procedure 15 was adapted, "past decisions concerning materiality would seem still relevant."[175]

A showing that the witness whose deposition is sought would tend to exonerate the defendant clearly satisfies the materiality requirement.[176] But to make this the *exclusive* test of materiality, when the deposition is sought by the defendant as the Second Circuit appears at one time to have done,[177] seems unduly restrictive. On the other hand, when the testimony sought is irrelevant or collateral on its face, the deposition motion should be denied.[178] A reduced showing of materiality was accepted as adequate in United States v. Steele, on the ground that the prosecution was not able to obtain voluntary access to the foreign deponent: "in the ordinary case where the witnesses reside in the United States, the witness who will be unavailable for trial will be available sometime prior to the deposition so that the parties will know with reasonable certainty the materiality of the proposed testimony.''[179] As the foregoing indicates, federal courts have enforced Federal Rule of Criminal Procedure 15's ''exceptional circumstance'' prerequisite in varying degrees when granting or denying requests for orders to take depositions. There appears to be no set formula for determining when the taking of a deposition will be allowed and when not allowed,[180] with the decision being highly influenced by the context and circumstances of the particular case.[181] It is clear, however, that the ''principal objective [of Federal Rule of Criminal Procedure 15] is the preservation of evidence for use at trial.''[182] Thus neither the defendant nor the government may take the deposition of an adverse witness.[183] In addition, depositions may not be taken for the purpose of providing discovery.[184]

Although affidavits in support of ''exceptional circumstances'' are ordinarily submitted by persons other than the defendant, a motion for a perpetuation deposition has been granted on the basis of defendant's affidavit alone.[185] When making the requisite showing would require the defendant to make significant admissions or disclose the theory of his or her defense in advance of trial, the court possesses discretionary power to provide for an *in camera* showing in the absence of the government.[186]

Federal Rule of Criminal Procedure 15(e) provides that a perpetuation deposition taken under Federal Rule of Criminal Procedure 15 may be employed as substantive evidence at trial, ''so far as otherwise admissible under the rules of evidence,'' if the witness proves unavailable at trial. Subsection (e) provides further that ''unavailability'' is to be determined in accordance with Rule 804(a) of the Federal Rules of Evidence:

Rule 804. Hearsay Exceptions; Declarant Unavailable

(a) Definition of unavailability. ''Unavailability as a witness'' includes situations in which the declarant—

(1) is exempted by ruling of the court on the ground of privilege from testifying concerning the subject matter of his statement; or

(2) persists in refusing to testify concerning the subject matter of his statement despite an order of the court to do so; or

(3) testifies to a lack of memory of the subject matter of his statement; or

(4) is unable to be present or to testify at the hearing because of death or then existing physical or mental illness or infirmity; or

(5) is absent from the hearing and the proponent of his statement has been unable to procure his attendance * * * by process or other reasonable means.

A declarant is not unavailable as a witness if his exemption, refusal, claim of lack of memory, inability, or absence is due to the procurement or wrong-doing of the proponent of his statement for the purpose of preventing the witness from attending or testifying.

Former Rule 15(e) provided that use of a deposition was permitted when the witness was dead, out of the United States, or unable to attend because of sickness of infirmity; or when the proponent could not procure the witness's attendance by subpoena.[187] Subdivision (e) thus extends substantive use to cases in which the witness is "unavailable" due to an exemption from testifying because of privilege, his refusal to testify despite court order, or where the witness asserts a lack of memory. On the other hand subdivision (e), through incorporation of Fed. R. Evid. 804(a), strengthens the efforts a proponent needs to make to procure a witness's testimony at trial from a mere subpoena to "process or other reasonable means."[188]

A Federal Rule of Criminal Procedure 15 perpetuation deposition may not be employed by the government as a means to clear the way for critical witnesses to leave the court's jurisdiction. In United States v. Mann,[189] the deponent was a juvenile Australian national, "a mere transient desirous of returning home."[190] She was, however, the government's crucial witness and had been illegally imprisoned after her apprehension and arrest at an airport for aiding a drug smuggler. The trial court sought to "ameliorate the injustice done her in the most expeditious manner possible,"[191] by allowing her to be deposed by the government and then to leave the jurisdiction to return to Australia. The First Circuit reversed declaring that the taking and introduction of the deposition at the defendant's trial for the purpose of allowing the critical witness to return home was improper. The defendant need not "bear the brunt" of the government's attempt to remedy the improper imprisonment of the witness.[192] "Reasonable means of procurement" of a witness's attendance at trial mandates that the government employ reasonable means to prevent a "present witness from becoming absent."[193]

7. Uniform Rules of Criminal Procedure

Uniform Rule of Criminal Procedure 431, approved in 1975, continues the authorization for the prosecution to take depositions to perpetuate testimony established by former Uniform Rule 27.[194] Uniform Rule 431 permits the taking of a person's deposition to perpetuate his or her testimony, with leave of court, at any time after the defendant has appeared.[195] A motion to perpetuate testimony "shall be granted . . . if it appears that the deponent may be able to give material testimony but may be unable to attend a trial or hearing."[196] Uniform Rule 431 provides as follows:

Rule 431: Depositions

(a) *When taken.* At any time after the defendant has appeared, any party may take the testimony of any person by deposition, except:

(1) The defendant may not be deposed unless he consents and his lawyer, if he has one, is present or his presence is waived;

(2) A discovery deposition may be taken after the time set by the court only with leave of court;

(3) A deposition to perpetuate testimony may be taken only with leave of court, which shall be granted upon motion of any party if it appears that the deponent may be able to give material testimony but may be unable to attend a trial or hearing; and

(4) Upon motion of a party or of the deponent and upon a showing that taking of the deposition does or will unreasonably annoy, embarrass, or oppress the deponent or a party, the court in which the prosecution is pending or the court of the [district] where the deposition is being taken may order that the deposition not be taken or continued or may limit the scope and manner of its taking. Upon demand of the objecting party or deponent, the taking of the deposition shall be suspended for the time necessary to make the motion.

Attendance of witnesses and production of documentary evidence and objects may be compelled by subpoena under Rule 731.

(b) *Witness who would not respond to subpoena.* If a party is granted leave to take a deposition to perpetuate testimony, the court, upon motion of the party and a showing of probable cause to believe that the deponent would not respond to a subpoena, by order shall direct a [law enforcement officer] to take the deponent into custody and hold him until the taking of the deposition commences but not to exceed [six] hours and to keep the deponent in custody during the taking of the deposition. If the motion is by the prosecuting attorney, the court upon further motion by the prosecuting attorney and a showing of probable cause to believe that the defendant would not otherwise attend the taking of the deposition, may make the same order as to the defendant.

(c) *Notice of taking.* The party at whose instance the deposition is to be taken shall give parties reasonable written notice of the name and address of each person to be examined, the time and place for the deposition, and the manner of recording. Upon motion of a party or of the deponent the court may change the time, place or manner of recording.

(d) *How taken.* The deposition shall be taken in the manner provided in civil actions, except:

(1) If the deposition is taken at a place over which this State lacks jurisdiction, it may be taken instead in the manner provided by the law of that place;

(2) It shall be recorded by the means specified in the notice; and

(3) Upon motion of a party and a showing that a party or the deponent is engaging in serious misconduct at the taking of a deposition, the court by order may direct that the deposition's taking be continued in the presence of a [judge], in which case the [judge] may preside over the remainder of the deposition's taking.

(e) *Place of taking.* The deposition shall be taken in a building where the trial may be held, at a place agreed upon by the parties, or at a place designated by special or general order of the court. If the defendant is in custody or subject to terms of release which prohibit leaving the state and does not appear before the court and understandingly and voluntarily waive the right to be present, a deposition to perpetuate testimony shall not be taken at a place which requires transporting the defendant within a jurisdiction which does not confer upon [law enforcement officers] of this State the right to transport prisoners within it.

(f) *Presence of defendant.*

(1) *At discovery deposition.* The defendant may be present at the taking of a discovery deposition, but if he is in custody he may be present only with leave of court.

(2) *At deposition to perpetuate testimony.* The defendant must be present at the taking of a deposition to perpetuate testimony, but if his counsel is present at the taking:

(i) The court may excuse the defendant from being present if he appears before the court and understandingly and voluntarily waives the right to be present;

(ii) The taking of the deposition may continue if the defendant, present when it commenced, thereafter voluntarily absents himself therefrom; or

(iii) If the deposition's taking is presided over by a [judge], the [judge] may direct that the deposition's taking or part thereof be conducted in the defendant's absence if the [judge] has justifiably excluded the defendant because of his disruptive conduct.

(3) *Unexcused absence.* If the defendant is not present at the commencement of the taking of a deposition to perpetuate testimony and his absence has not been excused:

(i) Its taking may proceed, in which case the deposition may be used only as a discovery deposition; or

(ii) If the deposition is taken at the instance of the State, the prosecuting attorney may direct that the commencement of its taking be postponed until the defendant's attendance can be obtained, and the court, upon application of the prosecuting attorney, by order may direct a [law enforcement officer] to take the defendant into custody and keep him in custody during the taking of the deposition.

(g) *Payment of expenses.* If the deposition is taken at the instance of the State, the court may, and in all cases where the defendant is unable to bear the expense the court shall, direct the State to pay the expense of taking the deposition, including the reasonable expenses of travel and subsistence of defense counsel and, if the deposition is to perpetuate testimony or if the court permits as to a discovery deposition, of the defendant in attending the deposition.

(h) *Substantive use on grounds of unavailability.* So far as otherwise admissible under the rules of evidence, a deposition to perpetuate testimony may be used as substantive evidence at the trial or upon any hearing if the deponent is unavailable [as defined in Rule 804(a) of the Uniform Rules of Evidence]. A discovery deposition then may be so used if the court determines that the use is fair in light of the nature and extent of the total examination at the taking thereof, but it may be offered by the State only if the defendant was present at its taking. [The deponent is unavailable for purposes of this subdivision if he:

(1) Is exempted by ruling of the court on the grounds of privilege from testifying concerning the subject matter of his statement;

(2) Persists in refusing to testify concerning the subject matter of his statement despite an order of the court to do so;

(3) Testififies to a lack of memory of the subject matter of his statement:

(4) Is unable to be present or to testify at the trial or hearing because of death or then existing physical or mental illness or infirmity; or

(5) Is absent from the trial or hearing and the proponent of his statement has been unable to procure his attendance by process or other reasonable means, unless his exemption, refusal, claim of lack of memory, inability, or absence is due to the procurement or wrongdoing of the proponent of his statement for the purpose of preventing the deponent from attending or testifying.] If only a part of a deposition is offered in evidence by a party, an adverse party may require him to offer or may himself offer all of it which is relevant to the part offered.

(j) *Deposition by agreement not precluded.* Nothing in this Rule precludes the taking of a deposition, orally or upon written questions, or the use of a deposition by agreement of the parties.

A defendant must be present at a deposition to perpetuate testimony, unless the defendant's counsel is present and either: (1) the court excused the defendant as having voluntarily waived his or her right to be present; (2) the defendant voluntarily absented himself or herself after the deposition was commenced; or (3) the presiding judicial official excluded the defendant because of his or her disruptive conduct.[197] If a defendant's absence from a perpetuation deposition was not excused in one of these manners, any deposition then completed may be used only as a discovery deposition.[198] A deposition to perpetuate testimony is admissible as substantive evidence at trial if otherwise admissible under the rules of evidence and the deponent is unavailable as *unavailability* is defined in Rule 804(a) of the Uniform Rules of Evidence.[199]

Uniform Rule 431 differs from Federal Rule of Criminal Procedure 15 in that the threshold standard for court approval of a perpetuation deposition appears more lenient. Under Uniform Rule 431, the government need show that (1) the deponent's testimony *may* be material, and (2) the deponent may be unable to attend trial. Federal Rule of Criminal Procedure 15, on the other hand, requires a showing of "exceptional circumstances," that is, (1) it appears that a prospective may be unable to attend or prevented from attending the trial, (2) his or her testimony *is* material, and (3) it is necessary to take his or her deposition to prevent a failure of justice.

8. Evaluation

Perpetuation depositions, as currently provided by statute, are clearly inadequate to protect against the loss of testimony by reason of physical injury, threat of physical injury, bribery, or other means of witness intimidation. Such statutes contain a critical restriction on the prosecution's taking of a perpetuation deposition—each requires that a defendant be given notice of the taking of the deposition and the opportunity to be present. These requirements in and of themselves restrict the taking of a deposition until an "advanced" stage in the investigation of the crime and the prosecution of the case. The prosecution must first discover, arrest, and formally charge the defendant. If the defendant already knows the identity of the witness and where he or she can be found, substantial opportunity for intimidation will exist before the taking of the perpetuation deposition. If the defendant did not already know the identity of the witness, notice of the deposition will disclose the witness's identity. A defendant must be given a period following notice of the perpetuation deposition in which to obtain the representation of counsel and prepare for the deposition. The time delay before and following notice of the perpetuation deposition incorporated into current perpetuation deposition statutes leaves witnesses terribly exposed to physical injury, threat of injury, bribery, and other means of witness intimidation.

The problem of witness vulnerability was recognized in the hearings before the Senate Committee on the Judiciary on the 1974 Amendment to Federal Rule of Criminal Procedure 16. In opposition to the proposed amendment to Rule 16 to require disclosure by the prosecution three days before trial of a list of witnesses anticipated to be called, John C. Keeney, Acting Assistant Attorney General, Criminal Division, argued:

> [U]nfortunately the three-day provision will not do what its proponents believed it would, i.e., minimize the exposure of the government's witnesses to possible intimidation. The Department of Justice recently polled all United States Attorneys across the country with regard to their views on the witness disclosure requirement as incorporated in H.R. 6799 as reported by the House Committee. All but one of approximately seventy who replied expressed strong opposition to the Rule. As they noted, the three-day provision adopted by the Committee is illusory. It only takes one day, or less, for a defendant or his friends to work an obstruction of justice or to intimidate a witness.[200]

The inherent vulnerability of witnesses once their identity is disclosed forms the crux of the problem of preserving untainted testimony and in protecting witnesses. Innocent members of the public are often forced into an unwanted spotlight by their happenstance witnessing of a crime. Once the witness's identity is disclosed, either as a result of the offense or incidental to the offense, through discovery, or by the media, a witness window of vulnerability is created. The House of Representative's version of Federal Rule of Criminal Procedure 16 providing for the perpetuation of a witness's testimony by deposition if the defendant seeks disclosure of a prospective witness's identity was thus not a satisfactory safeguard against witness intimidation.[201] "[N]otice must be given the opposing attorney and defendant before the deposition can be taken. If the defendant were going to 'coerce' or 'erase' the witness before trial, nothing would prevent his doing so before the deposition is taken."[202] The result of a motion for the taking of a perpetuation deposition is merely to start a race to be the first either to intimidate or to depose the witness. Notice to the defendant of intent to depose a witness identified by name and address at a reasonable time in the future most certainly reduces the prosecution's chance of winning the race.

Moreover, the standards governing a court's discretion to grant a motion for the taking of a deposition are not responsive to the problem of witness intimidation. Witness perpetuation statutes were not created with the realities of the witness intimidation problem firmly in mind. Rather, the statutes are constructed principally to obtain perpetuation depositions only after an "infirmity" threatens to incapacitate a witness placing his or her physical availability for trial in doubt. Accordingly, the criteria contained in perpetuation statutes require that the future unavailability of a potential witness be established as a prerequisite to the court's approving the taking of the witness's deposition. Although such a requirement is eminently sensible when "infirmity" is of concern, that is, when the witness is seriously ill, it is highly unsuited to responding to the problem of witness intimidation. Most acts of witness intimidation do not become apparent until *after* the fact—until *after* the damage has been completed. Hard evidence sufficient to establish to the satisfaction of the court that a prospective witness may be "prevented from attending court," that is, be intimidated, is simply lacking in the great majority of cases. Problems inherent in satisfying the court to permit a witness's testimony to be perpetuated on the basis of a likelihood that the witness will be prevented, that is, intimidated, from not testifying at trial were described in the debates on amending Federal Rule of Criminal Procedure 16 concerning disclosure of potential witness lists:

> Demonstrating that there has been a high incidence of violence and threats of violence in a range of federal criminal cases may seem a little beside the point. . . . [A] judge may want a reason peculiar to the case in front of him. The government cannot always be that specific. Our problem is with risks and probabilities, not near certainties. If we had particular reason to expect violence we could guard the witness or take other measures.[203]

Assuming *arguendo* that in a few cases there may be available sufficient evidence that a potential witness has been or may be intimidated to warrant a court-ordered perpetuation deposition, procedures associated with the perpetuation deposition itself may very well serve to aggravate rather than ameliorate the risk of witness intimidation. First, as previously mentioned, a knowledgeable defendant given notice of the deposition and the name and address of the witness would only intensify the defendant's wrongful efforts to guarantee that he or she be the first to reach the witness and ultimately be successful in suppressing the witness's testimony. Second, the presence of the accused and the accused's attorney, with the right to conduct cross-examination, may have an adverse affect on the witness's willingness at the perpetuation deposition to testify truthfully.

> To guard against witness intimidation, the amendment would also allow for the taking of depositions, to preserve testimony as security against a witness' being killed

or intimidated. However, the remedy is impractical. Defendants would be present, under Rule 15, at the taking of the deposition and would be entitled to cross-examine the witnesses. The process would be giving the defendant the most any defendant could desire in the way of pretrial discovery and place a premium upon inducing the witness, perhaps with more sophisticated measures than by violence, to give testimony at the deposition hearing that will destroy his effectiveness later.

There is another deficiency in the deposition concept. To a reluctant and frightened witness, it is another ordeal or source of worry. Then, too, what about the other government witnesses? Are they all to be deposed? Is a defendant to have a complete run-through of the case in advance of trial? Is he to have a crack at unnerving the witness at the deposition proceeding and then another crack at unnerving him at trial? As a tactical matter, the government would not be very much inclined to use the deposition provisions in the proposed amendment.[204]

E. THE WITNESS PROTECTION PROGRAM

In no single area of the criminal justice system is witness intimidation more prevalent than in the area of prosecutions directed against organized crime. Although instances of witness intimidation are not limited to the arena of organized crime, these criminals use fear "as a major linchpin to hold together their criminal activities."[205] Tampering with witnesses is one of organized crimes most effective counterweapons against the criminal justice system.[206] Ten percent of all organized crime-related murders in a four-year period were prosecution witnesses.[207] In fact, one aspect of organized crime that distinguishes it from other forms of criminal activities is the position of the "enforcer."[208] The duty of the "enforcer" is to maintain organization integrity by arranging the maiming and killing of potential witnesses.[209] The United States Attorney General has reported that after cases had been developed against racketeers, prosecution was forgone hundreds of times, because key witness would not testify for fear of being murdered.[210]

Congress responded to this obvious need for witness protection by formally authorizing a Witness Protection Program in The Organized Crime Act of 1970.[211] Title V of that act provides:

Sec. 501. The Attorney General of the United States is authorized to provide for the security of Government witnesses, potential Government witnesses, and the families of government witnesses and potential witnesses in legal proceedings against any person alleged to have participated in an organized criminal activity.

Sec. 502. The Attorney General of the United States is authorized to rent, purchase, modify or remodel protected housing facilities and to otherwise offer to provide for the health, safety and welfare of witnesses and persons intended to be called as Government witnesses, and the families of witnesses and persons intended to be called as government witnesses in legal proceedings instituted against any person alleged to have participated in an organized criminal activity whenever, in his judgment testimony from, or a willingness to testify by, such a witness would place his life or person or the life or person of a member of his family or household in jeopardy. Any person availing himself of such an offer by the Attorney General to use such facilities may continue to use such facilities for as long as the Attorney General determines the jeopardy to his life or person continues.

Sec. 503. As used in this title, "Government" means the United States, any State, the District of Columbia, the commonwealth of Puerto Rico, any territory or possession of the United States, any political subdivision or any department agency, or instrumentality thereof. The offer of facilities to witnesses may be conditioned by the Attorney General upon reimbursement in whole or in part to the United States by any State or any political subdivision or any department, agency, or instrumentality thereof the cost of maintaining and protecting such witnesses.

Sec. 504. There is hereby authorized to be appropriated from time to time such funds as are necessary to carry out the provisions of this title.

The purpose of the Witness Protection Program is to ensure the life and safety of witnesses and their families who were threatened on account of the witnesses' cooperation with United States government in prosecuting organized crime figures.[212]

The first section authorizes the Attorney General to provide for the security of actual and potential government witnesses and their families in organized crime proceedings, which do not have to be criminal proceedings. The next section confers broad authority on the Attorney General to determine the particular facilities to be afforded the witness and the length of time the facilities should be available. The Attorney General may rent, purchase, modify, or remodel protected housing facilities and otherwise provide for the health, safety, and welfare of government witnesses, their families, and members of their households. Protection of any of these persons may be made available whenever the witness's testimony places the life or person of the witness or members of the witness's family or household in danger. The protection is to continue for as long as the danger continues in the Attorney General's judgement. Additionally, the Witness Protection Program is available not only to federal but to state and local departments and agencies. The criminal proceeding concerning the witness must be a local or state police matter that is to be handled by those authorities. The Justice Department has provided procedures to establish a person as a protected witness in a nonfederal prosecution.[213]

The witness must meet three conditions as determined by the Assistant Attorney General. First, the person must be a qualifying witness in a specific case in process or during or after a grand jury proceeding. Second, there must be evidence that it would be advantageous to the federal interest for the Justice Department to protect the witness or members of the witness's family or household. Third, an additional condition may be imposed requiring reimbursement in whole or part by a state or local government for protection of its witness. If the witness meets the above conditions, a United States attorney, by an Assistant United States Attorney General through the United States attorney or by a division attorney, must submit a written request to the Assistant Attorney General. This request is marked "Confidential" and must contain the following information: the name, address, date, and place of birth, FBI or police numbers of the witness; the information or evidence to be supplied by the witness; the importance of the case and the names and importance of prospective defendants; any other federal or state cases in which the witness's testimony may be required; the names of persons connected with the case for whom witness protection has been previously approved and names of others connected with the case who are likely to be placed under the Witness Protection Program; a realistic estimate of the completion date of the trials; the degree of the threat made, the names of those who may threaten or harm the witness, including a report from an investigative agency substantiating the threat; the number of family or household members to be protected including their names, ages, and relationship to the witness; any medical problems of the witness; employment data concerning the witness; whether the witness is receiving or expecting to receive money from other state or federal agencies and how much; and, if the witness is incarcerated, when release can be reasonably anticipated. In the case of an emergency, the Assistant Attorney General is authorized orally to request protection for a witness for up to 72 hours. If this request is approved, the United States Marshals Service takes charge of the witness.

A security specialist of the Marshals Service will then contact the witness to inform him or her of the program's details and to interview the witness to obtain background information such as employment history, medical history, education, and other information necessary to provide protection. The security specialist then selects a relocation area and arranges for the transportation of the witness, his or her family, and all of the witness's belongings to the relocation area. If the witness needs immediate protection, the witness and the witness's family are temporarily relocated, usually in a hotel or motel, and personal belongings are placed in temporary storage, pending transportation to a permanent location area.

In the relocated area, the witness is assigned a deputy marshal who is the witness's contact and who provides the witness with local services, such as housing, routine medical care, and other services that the Marshals Service itself cannot provide. The witness and the witness's family are provided appropriate documentation, which includes legal name changes, driver's licenses, social security cards, professional licenses, birth certificates, school and medical records, passports, religious records, and other necessary records or documents. These documents are provided by legitimate sources and are not forgeries. The witness is given assistance in finding employment in the relocated area. The witness is also paid a monthly tax-free subsistence allowance, which is set depending on the number of dependents and the location in which the witness resides. This subsistence may be terminated 120 days after entry into the program or 60 days after the witness's last court appearance, whichever is later, or for various causes.

The Witness Protection Program has achieved significant results. Despite the fact that participation in the program requires a complete break with the past, including a change of identity and residence for the witness and the witness's immediate family, as of 1982 there were almost 4,000 active participants in the program.[214] The Justice Department has reported that no witness who has stayed in the program and maintained his or her cover has been killed as a result of being discovered.[215] The Marshals Service reports that 25 to 30 percent of witnesses in the program drop out. Ninety to 95 percent of witnesses participating in the program are persons who have themselves been convicted of crimes.[216] Thus most participants are organized crime members who want out. The remainder are innocent bystanders.[217]

Despite its accomplishments, the Witness Protection Program does not and cannot by itself effectively respond to the problem of witness intimidation. The program's authorizing statute, The Organized Crime Control Act of 1970, restricts its applications to witnesses involved in proceedings concerning organized crime. Although witness intimidation is extensive in the area of organized crime, it is clearly not the only setting in which intimidation occurs. Even within the scope of its mandate, the Witness Protection Program faces a major funding problem. The program is costly to maintain—it costs about $36,000 to set up and maintain an average family in the program. The program, faced with an increasing number of witnesses and budget cuts, has tightened standards to limit the number of participants.[218] Moreover, several operational problems with the Witness Protection Program were uncovered by a Senate subcommittee investigation and oversight hearing.[219] One of the most frequently cited problems was a lack of training of the United States marshals assigned to the Witness Protection Program. Special skills are absolutely essential to help relocated witnesses adjust to their new lives; yet the marshals have no training in this area. Another major problem of the program is numerous examples of delayed and inadequate documentation. Proper documentation is necessary for the witness to relocate properly and to acquire employment. Finally, the report uncovered many incidents of security breaches in the program. For example, there were allegations that marshals were on the payroll of organized crime, that marshals gambled with witnesses in mob-owned nightclubs, and that marshals are very loose with protected information on witnesses. These problems caused the chairman of the oversight committee to state, "You [the director of the United States Marshals Service] keep saying that you have been lucky so far, nobody has been killed. But that is what it amounts to—luck."[220]

Changing witness identity at great cost to the witness, the witness's family, and society is obviously a remedy to be employed as a last resort when the risk to the witness's safety is clear and present. Thus although the Witness Protection Program is of great help to a few potentially intimidated witnesses who find themselves in particularly threatening circumstances, it is of no help at all to the overwhelming majority of witnesses whose cooperation is essential to the day-to-day operations of the criminal justice system.[221]

NOTES

1. Funding for the project was obtained from the Florence V. Burden Foundation and from S. Shepherd Tate, then President of the American Bar Association.

2. The witness list included a congressman, the administrator of the Law Enforcement Assistance Association, a major city district attorney, two intimidated victims, academicians, criminal defense bar representatives, a state legislator, victim service agency officials, judges, and a major city police department representative. A substantial effort was made to hear witnesses whose positions were known in advance of the hearings to be contrary to the Victims Committee's draft package. The Victims Committee also heard from representatives of many agencies and criminal justice organizations. They included: National District Attorneys Association, American Correctional Association, American Psychological Association, United States Justice Department, National Association of Criminal Defense Lawyers, Pretrial Services Resource Center, American Probation and Parole Association, American Bar Association Litigation Section, Federal Bureau of Investigation, United States Marshals Service Witness Protection Program.

3. *See* Chapter 3, Section A *infra.*

4. American Bar Association, Criminal Justice Section, *Reducing Victim/ Witness Intimidation: A Package* 13-37 (Washington, D.C., 1981). *See also* American Bar Association, Criminal Justice Section, *Bar Leadership on Victim/ Witness Assistance* (Washington, D.C., 1980).

The Criminal Justice Section of the American Bar Association also published *Victim/Witness Legislation: Considerations for Policymakers* (Washington, D.C., 1981). The monograph described the more recent state victim/witness legislation as falling into four basic categories: (1) reforms that provide financial assistance to victims; (2) reforms that define or recognize rights of victims and witnesses; (3) special protections for certain classes of crime victims; and (4) institutionalizing and funding services for victims and witnesses. The purpose of the monograph was "not to advocate any specific type of law nor to serve as a comprehensive state-by-state index of existing statutes. Rather it [was] designed to inform lawmakers and others about legislative developments around the country and to point out some of the advantages and disadvantages of various approaches. Ultimately, of course, its authors [hope] that the monograph [will] be useful in promoting enactment of well-considered, practical and fair victim/witness legislation." *Id.* at vii-ix.

5. Pub. L. No. 97-291, 96 Stat. 1248 (1982).

6. Section 2(b) of the *Victim and Witness Protection Act of 1982* is presented as a note to 18 U.S.C. § 1512 (Supp. 1983).

7. Section 2(a) of the *Victim and Witness Protection Act of 1982* is presented as a note to 18 U.S.C. § 1512 (Supp. 1983).

8. The discussion in the text that follows relating to the *Victim and Witness Protection Act of 1982* reports the views expressed in and makes reference to authorities cited by the Report of the Senate Judiciary Committee, *The Omnibus Victims*

Protection Act of 1982, S. Rep. No. 532, 97th Cong., 2d Sess. 10, published at 3 U.S. Code Cong. & Ad. News 2515 (1982).

9. Section 6 of the *Victim and Witness Protection Act of 1982* is presented as a note to 18 U.S.C. § 1512 (Supp. 1983).

10. The guidelines that Section 6(a) requires the Attorney General to develop and implement are located at 48 F.R. 33774 (July 25, 1983).

11. Presidents' Task Force on Victims of Crime, *Final Report*, Washington, D.C., December 1982.

12. The "Preface" to the "Statement of Recommended Judicial Practices," *Participant's Manual for Judges on the Rights of Victims and Witnesses* (Reno: National Judicial College, 1984), states:

> Insufficient attention has been given to the role of victims and witnesses in the American system of criminal justice. This is traceable in part to our heritage in the common law with its sharp division between criminal actions. In legal theory, crime was a breach of the King's peace with the King, (the State), not the harmed individual, as the victim and proper party to bring the prosecution. This theory, combined with federal and state constitutional principles concerned with protecting an accused from an overreaching government, has caused the perception by some that criminals are protected with many procedural safeguards and rights while victims and witnesses are only necessary providers of evidence who must make themselves available whenever required by the system. The perception that our system of criminal justice has been callously indifferent to the financial and psychological interests of victims of and witnesses to crime has resulted in social action and legislation which insist that victims and witnesses be given the fair and considerate treatment that is their right.

13. *Id.* at 18-23. The "Conclusion" to the "Statement of Recommended Judicial Practices" states:

> Judges have a role in improving the treatment of victims and witnesses by reason of their position in the American Judicial system and their positions in their communities.
>
> Judges believe that fair treatment of victims and witnesses can, consistent with constitutional limitations, be brought about by changes in the law, rules of procedure and legislation. Judges believe that they can influence the acts of others, including officers of the court and public officials, in the treatment of witnesses and victims. Judges also can encourage community support for change in the treatment of witnesses and victims. By their attitude and the attitudes of their staff, judges can set examples in the treatment of witnesses and victims.
>
> We urge that our fellow judges exercise their leadership role in improving the treatment of victims and witnesses. Victims of crime should not be victims of the criminal justice system.

Id. at 23.

14. Rex v. Holland, 100 Eng. Rep. 1248 (1792).

15. 6 J. Wigmore, *Evidence* § 1845 at 486-91 (Chadbourn Rev. 1976).

16. 2 F. Pollock and F. Maitland, *The History of English Law* (1895), p. 667.

17. 2 J. Arnould, *The Life of Lord Denman* (1874), p. 92.

18. 6 J. Wigmore, *supra* note 15 at 490.

19. *See, e.g.*, 7 & 8 Will. 3, c.3 and 7 Anne, c.21 § 14.

20. 1 J. Stephen, *History of the Criminal Law of England* (1883), pp. 226, 398.

21. Brady v. Maryland, 373 U.S. 83 (1963).

22. *See, e.g.*, St. 1790, Apr. 30, § 29. The latest version of these statutes is 18 U.S.C. § 3432 adopted in 1948:

> Indictment and list of jurors and witnesses for prisoner in capital cases.
>
> A person charged with treason or other capital offense shall at least three entire days before commencement of trial be furnished with a copy of the indictment and a list of the veniremen, and of the witnesses to be produced on the trial for proving the indictment, stating the place of abode of each veniremen and witness.

23. 6 J. Wigmore, *supra* note 15 at 495-96.

24. American Law Institute, *Code of Criminal Procedure* § 194 at 85 (1930).

25. *Id.* at 608, Commentary to Section 194.

26. *Id.* at 609.

27. *Id.* at 607-8.

28. 1923 Minn. Gen. Stat. § 10631 ("Within two days after demand, the clerk shall furnish a copy of depositions to the defendant."). The term *deposition* in fact refers to a statement. *See* Chapter 2, Section D1 *infra.*

29. United States v. Garsson, 291 Fed. 646, 649 (S.D.N.Y. 1923).

30. Fed. R. Crim. P. 16, Advisory Committee Note (1946).

31. Bowman Dairy Co. v. United States, 341 U.S. 214, 219 (1951) (["Fed. R. Crim. Proc. 16] was a departure from what had heretofore been allowed in criminal cases.").

32. J. McInerney, *Proceedings Between Indictment and Trial*, 5 F.R.D. 156, 161 (1945).

33. 2 L. Orfield, *Criminal Procedure Under the Federal Rules* § 16.5 at 506-12 (Rochester: Lawyers Cooperative, 1966).

34. F. Cas. No. 14692d (C.C. Va. 1807).

35. United States v. Riera, 10 Puerto Rico F. 186, 188-89 (1917).

36. 1 Comments, Recommendations and Suggestions Received Concerning the Proposed Federal Rules of Criminal Procedure 128 (1943) (Joseph T. Vostava, U.S. Attorney for District of Nevada; Charles E. Kdierker, U.S. Attorney for Western District of Oklahoma; Walter C. Lindley, U.S. District Judge for Eastern District of Illinois; Victor E. Anderson, U.S. Attorney for District of Minnesota).

37. *Id.* at 129 (Thomas Morrisey, U.S. Attorney for District of Colorado).

38. *Id.* (Robert P. Butler, U.S. Attorney for District of Connecticut; Henry C. Blanton, U.S. Attorney for Eastern District of Missouri; Ralph F. Leseman, of Bar Committee for the 7th Cir.; Judicial Conference of 2d Cir.).

39. Address by Honorable G. Aaron Youngquist, Member of the Supreme Court Advisory Committee, Proceeding of the Institute on Federal Rules of Criminal Procedure (Feb. 16, 1946).

40. 353 U.S. 657 (1957).

41. Note, *The Jencks Legislation: Problems in Prospect*, 67 Yale L. J. 674 (1958).

42. S. Rep. No. 981, 85th Cong., 1st Sess. (1957).

43. H.R. Rep. No. 700, 85th Cong., 1st Sess. (1957).

44. 18 U.S.C. § 3500 (1957), the Jencks Act, provides as follows:

§ 3500. Demands for production of statements and reports of witnesses

(a) In any criminal prosecution brought by the United States, no statement or report of a witness or prospective witness (other than the defendant) which is in the possession of the United States shall be the subject of subpoena, or inspection, except as provided in paragraph (b) of this section.

(b) After a witness called by the United States has testified on direct examination, the court shall, on motion of the defendant, order the United States to produce any written statements previously made by the witness in the possession of the United States which are signed by the witness or otherwise adopted or approved by him, and any transcriptions or recording or oral statements made by the witness to a Federal law officer, relating to the subject matter as to which the witness has testified. If the entire contents of any such statements, transcriptions, or recordings relate to the subject matter of the testimony of the witness, the court shall order them delivered directly to the defendant for his examination and use. In the event that the United States claims that any statement, transcription, or recording ordered to be produced contains matter which does not relate to the subject matter of the testimony of the witness, the court shall order the United States to deliver such statement, transcription, or recording for the inspection of the court in camera. Upon such delivery the court shall excise the portions of said statement, transcription, or recording which do not relate to the subject matter of the testimony of the witness. With such material excised, the court shall then direct delivery of such statement, transcription or recording to the defendant for his use. If, pursuant to such procedure, any portion of such statement, transcription, or recording is withheld from the defendant, and the trial is continued to an adjudication of the guilt of the defendant the entire text of statement transcription or recording shall be preserved by the United States and, in the event the defendant shall appeal, shall be made available to the appellate court for the purpose of determining the correctness of the ruling of the trial judge.

(c) In the event that the United States elects not to comply with an order of the court under paragraph (b) hereof to deliver to the defendant any statement, transcription, or recording or such portion thereof as the court may direct, the court shall strike from the record the testimony of the witness and the trial shall proceed unless the court in its discretion shall determine that the interests of justice require that a mistrial be delared, or take such other action as the court deems appropriate.

45. Goldberg v. United States, 425 U.S. 94 (1976).

46. *See, e.g.*, United States v. Hutcher 622 F.2d 1083 (2nd Cir. 1980).

47. Fed. R. Crim. P. 26.2 provides as follows:

Production of Statements of Witnesses

(a) Motion for Production. After a witness other than the defendant has testified on direct examination, the court, on motion of a party who did not call the witness, shall order the attorney for the government or the defendant and his attorney, as the case may be to produce, for the examination and use of the moving party, any statement of the witness that is in their possession and that relates to the subject matter concerning which the witness has testified.

(b) Production of Entire Statement. If the entire contents of the statement relate to the subject matter concerning which the witness has testified, the court shall order that the statement be delivered to a moving party.

(c) Production of Excised Statement. If the other party claims that the statement contains matter that does not related to the subject matter concerning which the witness has testified, the court shall order that it be delivered to the court in camera. Upon inspection, the court shall excise the portions of the statements that do not relate to the subject matter concerning which the witness has testified, and shall order that the statement, with such material excised, be delivered to the moving party. Any portion of the statement that is withheld from the defendant over his objection of a conviction and an appeal by the defendant, shall be made available to the appellate court for the purpose of determining the correctness of the decision to excise the portion of the statement.

(d) Recess for Examination of Statement. Upon delivery of the statement to the moving party, the court, upon application of that party, may recess proceedings in the trial for the examination of such statement and for preparation for its use in the trial.

(e) Sanction for Failure to Produce statement. If the other party elects not to comply with an order to deliver a statement to the moving party, the court shall order that the testimony of the witness be stricken from the record and that the trial proceed or, if it is the attorney for the government who elects not to comply, shall declare a mistrial if required by the interest of justice.

(f) Definition. As used in this rule, a "statement" of a witness means:

(1) a written statement made by the witness that is signed or otherwise adopted or approved by him;

(2) a substantially verbatim recital of an oral statement made by the witness that is recorded contemporaneously with the making of the oral statement and that is contained in a stenographic, mechanical, electrical or other recording or a transcription thereof; or

(3) a statement, however, taken or recorded, or a transcription thereof, made by the witness to a grand jury.

48. *See, e.g.*, W. Brennan, *The Criminal Prosecution: Sporting Event or Quest for Truth*, 1963 Wash. U. L. Q. 279; D. Louisell, *Criminal Discovery: Dilemma Real or Apparent*, 49 Calif. L. Rev. 56 (1961); R. Traynor, *Ground Lost and Found in Criminal Discovery*, 39 N.Y.U. L. Rev. 228 (1964).

49. United States v. Dreitzler, 577 F.2d 539 (9th Cir. 1978).

50. American Bar Association, Standards for Criminal Justice, *Discovery and Procedure Before Trial* 2 (Washington, D.C., 1970).

51. *Id.*, § 1.2, Commentary at 34-46.

52. *Id.*, § 2.1, Commentary at 57.

53. *Id.* at 57-58.

54. *Id.* at 65.

55. *Id.*
56. *Id.* at 68.
57. Uniform Rules of Criminal Procedure, 10 U.L.A. 1-431 (1974).
58. *Id.* at 115, Comment to Rule 421(a).
59. *Federal Rules of Criminal Procedure Amendment Act of 1975*, Pub. L. No. 94-64, H.R. Rep. No. 94-247 at 2 U.S. Code Cong. & Ad. News 685 (1st Sess. 1975). Proposed Federal Rule of Criminal Procedure 16 did not provide for the disclosure of witness statements or even a list of all known witnesses. Only disclosure of the names and addresses of witnesses the government intended to call would have been required. Proposed Federal Rule of Criminal Procedure 16(a)(1)(E), 62 F.R.D. 271, 305 (1974) provided:

> (E) Government witnesses. Upon request of the defendant the government shall furnish to the defendant a written list of the names and addresses of all government witnesses which the attorney for the government intends to call in the presentation of the case in chief together with any record of prior felony convictions of any such witness which is within the knowledge of the attorney for the government. When a request for discovery of the names and addresses of witnesses has been made by a defendant, the government shall be allowed to perpetuate the testimony of such witnesses in accordance with the provisions of Rule 15.

60. *Id.*
61. *Id.* at 686.
62. *Federal Rules of Criminal Procedure Amendment Act of 1975*, Pub. L. No. 94-64, Conference Report 94-414 at 2 U.S. Code Cong. & Ad News 713, 716 (1st Sess. 1975).
63. *See, e.g.*, United States v. Opager, 589 F.2d 799 (5th Cir. 1979).
64. *See Discovery in Criminal Cases*, 33 F.R.D. 47, 114 (1964). *See also* text accompanying note 75 *infra*.
65. Brady v. Maryland, 373 U.S. 83 (1963).
66. American Bar Association, Standards for Criminal Justice, Chapter 11, *Discovery and Procedure Before Trial*, Standard 11-2.1 at 11-14 (2d ed. Washington, D.C., 1980).
67. *Id.*, Commentary at 11-16-11-17.
68. *Id.* at 11-17.
69. *Id.* at 11-17-11-18.
70. United States Department of Justice, *Report of the Witness Security Program, Review Committee* 8 (Draft, 1978), reprinted in *Witness Protection Program*: Hearings Before the Subcomm. on Administrative Practice and Procedure of the Senate Comm. on the Judiciary, 95th Cong., 2d Sess. 277 (1978).
71. *Federal Rules of Criminal Procedure Amendment Act of 1975*, Senate Conference Rep. No. 94-336, July 28, 1975, to accompany H.R. 6799 at 176.
72. Proposed Fed. R. Crim. P. 16(a)(1)(E), 62 F.R.D. 271, 305 (1974) is as set forth at note 59 *supra*.
73. Proposed amended Fed. R. Crim. P. 16(a)(1)(E), 2 U.S. Code and Cong. & Ad. News 701, 94th Congress (1st Sess. 1975), states as follows:

> (E) Government witnesses.—Upon request [of] by the defendant, *and subject to subdivision (d)(1), the attorney for* the government shall furnish to the defendant,

three days in advance of trial, a written list of the names and addresses of all *the* government witnesses [which] *whom* the attorney for the government intends to call in the presentation of the case in chief, together with any record of prior [felony] *criminal* convictions of any such witness which is within the [knowledge of] *possession, custody, or control of the government, the existence of which is known, or by the exercise of due diligence may become known, to* the attorney for the government. When a request for discovery of the names and addresses of witnesses has been made by a defendant, the government shall be allowed to perpetuate the testimony of such witnesses in accordance with the provisions of Rule 15.

74. Proposed amended Fed. R. Crim. P. 16(d)(1), *id.* at 703 provided as follows:

(1) Protective *and modifying* orders. Upon sufficient showing the court may at any time order that the discovery or inspection be denied, restricted or deferred, or make such other order as is appropriate, *including an order extending the three-day time limit of subdivision (a)(1)(E) or (b)(1)(C).* Upon request by a party, the court [shall] *may* permit the party to make such showing, in whole or in part, in the form of a written statement to be inspected by the judge alone. If the court enters an order granting relief following such [a] *an ex parte* showing, the entire text of the party's statement shall be sealed and preserved in the records of the court to be made available to the appellate court in the event of an appeal.

75. *Id.* at 685-87 (footnotes omitted).
76. *Id.* at 712-13.
77. *Id.* at 716.
78. *See* Chapter 1, Section A and notes 70 and 71 *supra.*
79. *Time*, Sept. 13, 1968, at 70-71.
80. State ex rel. Stephens v. Luttrell, No. 13997 R.D. (Cir. Ct. Shelby Cty., Tenn. Aug. 21, 1968).
81. 18 U.S.C. § 3149 (1976).
82. R. Carlson and M. Voelpel, *Material Witness and Material Injustice*, 58 Wash. U. L. Q. 1,2 (1980) (at least 45 states).
83. Comment, *The Plight of the Detained Material Witness*, 7 Cath. U. L. Rev. 37, 38 (1958) (every jurisdiction).
84. *Id.*
85. *See generally*, Comment, *Pretrial Detention of Witnesses*, 117 U. Pa. L. Rev. 700 (1969); Comment, *Witnesses—Imprisonment of the Material Witness for Failure to Give Bond*, 40 Neb. L. Rev. 503 (1961); Comment, *Confining Material Witnesses in Criminal Cases*, 20 Wash. & Lee L. Rev. 164 (1963); R. Carlson, *Jailing the Innocent: The Plight of the Material Witness*, 55 Iowa L. Rev. 1 (1969).
86. 18 U.S.C. § 3149 provides:

Release of material witnesses

If it appears by affidavit that the testimony of a person is material in any criminal proceeding, and if it is shown that it may become impracticable to secure his presence by subpoena, a judicial officer shall impose conditions of release pursuant to section 3146. No material witness shall be detained because of inability to comply with any condition of release if the testimony of such witness can adequately be secured by deposition, and further detention is not necessary to prevent a failure of justice. Release may be delayed for a reasonable period of time until the deposition of the witness can be taken pursuant to the Federal Rules of Criminal Procedure.

87. *See, e.g.*, United States v. Coldwell, 496 F. Sup. 305, 307 (E.D. Okla. 1979) (impracticable to secure witness's attendance when witness refused to cooperate with law enforcement officials, refused to testify unless impossible demands were met, witness's attorney indicated witness would not cooperate, and two attempts to serve subpoena on witness were unsuccessful); United States v. Feingold, 416 F. Supp. 627, 628 (E.D.N.Y. 1976) (impracticable to secure witness's attendance when attempts to serve subpoena on witness's attorney or on seven different days at witness's home were all unsuccessful).

88. 18 U.S.C. § 3146 sets forth the procedure for and conditions of release in noncapital cases before the trial.

89. *See* articles cited notes 82 and 85 *supra*.

90. *See* 5 J. Wigmore, *Evidence* § 1364 at 17 (Chadbourn. Rev. 1974).

91. Weston's Trial 2 How., St. Tr. 911 (1615); Elves' Trial, 2 How. St. Tr. 935 (1615).

92. Duke of Norfolk's Trial, 1 How. St. Tr. 958 (1571); Mary Queen of Scots' Trial, 1 How. St. Tr. 1162 (1586); Udall's Trial, 1 How. St. Tr. 1271 (1586).

93. 5 J. Wigmore, *supra* note 90 at 22 n.45.

94. *Id.* at 26-27.

95. 5 J. Wigmore *id.*, § 1374 at 59. Wigmore also noted that cross-examination had never been required for admission of a deposition taken before a coroner until it became regulated by statute in the 1800s. *See also id.* at 59 n.4 citing Stat. 11 & 12 Vict. c. 42 (1848).

96. *Id.* § 1375 at 61-63.

97. *Id.* § 1376 at 63 (emphasis in original).

98. *Id.* § 1376 at 64.

99. *Id.* § 1402 at 203.

100. *Id.* §§ 1403-10 at 204-27.

101. *Id.* § 1401 at 202.

102. *Id.* § 1398 at 189 (emphasis in original). *See also id.* at n.5:

> The following rulings show the application of the principle: State v. Potter, 6 Idaho 584, 57 Pac. 431 (1899) (depositions taken on preliminary examination by the state not to be used at all at the trial, because not expressly authorized by statute; the opinion ignores the common-law practice, § 1375 *supra*; this is in truth not a deposition at all, but testimony at a former trial); Kaelin v. Commonwealth, 84 Ky. 354, 11 S.W. 594 (1886) (deposition of a person abroad, taken by the accused, not authorized by statute; excluded); Westbrook v. State 14 Okla. Crim. 423, 172 Pac. 464 (1918) (deposition of nonresident witness taken for the defendant rests solely on statutory authority); Blanchard v. State, 21 Okla. Crim. 263, 207 Pac. 96 (1922) (Westbrook v. State approved).
>
> In People v. Turner, 265 Ill. 594, 597, 107 N.E. 162, 163 (1914), the court refused to order a continuance, on application of the defendant, as an alternative to admitting a deposition of a nonresident taken by the defendant; "the Court ought not indirectly to change the law by compelling prosecutors to consent to the introduction of evidence for the defendant not legally admissible."

103. *Id.* at 185-86. *See also id.* at n.4 for particular cases.
104. 26 Va. (5 Rand.) 701 (1827).
105. Peake, *Evidence* 60 (1801).
106. 13 How. St. Tr. 537, (1696).
107. Wigmore claimed that the writer of the treatise misunderstood the opinion in Fenwick's Trial. 5 J. Wigmore, *Evidence* § 1398 at 186 (Chadbourn Rev. 1974). However, Wigmore also noted that the trial of Fenwick was conducted before Parliament, who heard prolonged debate concerning the admissibility of the hearsay deposition. The prosecution had only offered the deposition as corroborating evidence, and it was clear that many of those voting in favor of the receipt of the deposition did so only on the theory that Parliament was not required to follow the inferior court's rules of evidence. *Id.* § 1364 at 26, n.54. *See also* Mattox v. United States, 156 U.S. 237, 240 (1895), in which the Supreme Court agreed that Peake misinterpreted Fenwick's Trial, claiming that the rule in England "clearly" allows the use of the testimony of a deceased witness in a criminal prosecution.
108. 5 J. Wigmore, *Evidence* § 1398 at 186 (Chadbourn Rev. 1974).
109. 156 U.S. 237 (1895).
110. *Id.* at 241-42.
111. *Id.* at 242-43.
112. 194 U.S. 258 (1904).
113. *Id.* at 260.
114. *Id.* at 262.
115. *Id.* at 262-63.
116. *Id.* at 263-64.
117. 380 U.S. 400 (1965).
118. 399 U.S. 149 (1970).
119. 2 J. Wigmore, *Evidence* § 1411 at 1770 (1904).
120. *Id.* at 1770 n.1.
121. U.S. Stat. ch. 20 § 30 (1789).
122. *See* 2 J. Wigmore, *Evidence* § 1381 at 1720 (1904).
123. *Id.* at 1720 n.1.
124. *Id.*
125. 2 J. Wigmore, *Evidence id.* at 1721 n.3 citing United States v. Cameron, 15 Fed. 797 (1883); Warren v. Younger, 18 Fed. 859 (1884). *Contra* Randall v. Venable, 17 Fed. 162 (1884).
126. Ex parte Fisk, 113 U.S. 725 (1884).
127. U.S. Stat. ch. 14 (1892), *cited in* Wigmore, *supra* note 122 at 1721 n. 3.
128. 2 L. Orfield, *Criminal Procedure Under the Federal Rules* § 15:12 at 467 (1966).
129. 15 F. 794 (D. Mo. 1883).
130. 2 L. Orfield, *supra* note 128 at 468-69.
131. Clymer v. United States, 38 F.2d 581 (10th Cir. 1930); Luxenburg v. United States, 45 F.2d 497 (4th Cir. 1930).
132. 28 U.S.C. § 644 was repealed in favor Fed. R. Civ. P. 26.
133. United States v. Hofmann, 24 F. Supp. 847 (D.N.Y. 1938).
134. *Id.*; Wong Yim v. United States, 118 F.2d 667 (9th Cir. 1941); United States v. Dockery, 50 F. Supp. 410 (D.N.Y. 1943). *See also* 2 L. Orfield, *supra* note 128, § 15:13 at 469-72.

135. Fed. R. Civ. P. 26(a), 30, 32.

136. L. Orfield, *The Federal Rules of Criminal Procedure*, 33 Calif. L. Rev. 543, 559 (1945).

137. L. Orfield, *The Preliminary Draft of the Federal Rules of Criminal Procedure*, 22 Tex. L. Rev. 37, 59-60 (1944).

138. Advisory Committee Note on 1974 Amendment to Rule 15, 62 F.R.D. 271, 301 (1974).

139. *Id.*; L. Orfield, *Depositions in Federal Criinal Procedure*, 9 S.C. L. Rev. 376, 380-81 (1957); G. Dession, *The New Federal Rules of Criminal Procedure II*, 56 Yale L. J. 197, 217 (1947).

140. Second Preliminary Draft to the Federal Rules of Criminal Procedure (1944), Note to Rule 17 at 92. The 17 state statutes as of 1944 are set forth in Orfield, *supra* note 137 at 60 n.117.

141. L. Orfield, *Depositions in Federal Criminal Procedure*, 9 S.C. L. Rev. 376, 383 (1957).

142. Advisory Committee Note on 1974 Amendment to Rule 15, *supra* note 138.

143. G. Dession, *supra* note 139 at 217-18.

144. *See* text accompanying notes 109-16 *supra*.

145. 156 U.S. 237 (1895).

146. 194 U.S. 258 (1904).

147. 8 *Moore's Federal Practice* ¶ 15.02[3] at 15-25 (Albany: Matthew Bender, 1975).

148. See text accompanying note 142 *supra*.

149. Advisory Committee Note on 1974 Amendment to Rule 15, *supra* note 138.

150. *Id.* at 301-2.

151. *See e.g.*, L. Orfield, *supra* note 141 at 397; C. McCormick, *Evidence* at 485 (1954); 5 J. Wigmore, *Evidence* § 1398 at 186 (Chadbourn Rev. 1974).

152. See L. Orfield, *supra* note 141 at 411-412.

153. Advisory Committee Note on 1974 Amendment to Rule 15, *supra* note 138 at 302. *See also* 39 F.R.D. 69, 168-211 (1966).

154. C. Wright, *Federal Practice and Procedure: Criminal* § 241 at 8-9 (2d ed. St. Paul: West, 1982).

155. Pub. L. No. 91-452, 84 Stat. 922 (1970).

156. *Organized Crime Control Act of 1970*: Hearings on S.30 Before Subcomm. No. 5 of the House Comm. on the Judiciary, 91st Cong., 2d Sess. at 312 (1970).

157. 18 U.S.C. § 3503(a) (1976).

158. *Id.*

159. Advisory Committee Note on 1974 Amendment to Rule 15, *supra* note 138 at 302.

160. *Organized Crime Control Act of 1970, supra* note 156 at 165 (statement of John N. Mitchell, Attorney General of the United States).

161. 18 U.S.C. § 3503(f) (1976).

162. *Id.* § 3503(b)-(c).

163. *Id.* § 3503(d).

164. *Id.* § 3503(b)

165. *Organized Crime Control Act of 1970, supra* note 156 at 431 (statement of Aaron M. Kohn, Managing Director, Metropolitan Crime Commission of New Orleans).

166. *Id.* at 685-86 (letter to Emanuel Celler, Chairman Comm. on Judiciary, U.S. House of Representatives, from Charles H. Rogovin).

167. Fed. R. Crim. P. 15(a) (1975).

168. *Id.*

169. Advisory Committee Note on 1974 Amendment to Rule 15, 62 F.R.D. 271, 303 (1974).

170. Cong. Rec. S:12875 (July 17, 1975).

171. G. Dession, *supra* note 139 at 217.

172. 11A Cyc. Fed. Proc. § 44.08 at 237 (3d ed. 1980). *See also*, L. Orfield, *supra* note 136 at 558 (1945).

173. *Materiality* as so employed refers to the concept of high incremental probative value as to an important fact of consequence in the litigation, most often an ultimate fact.

174. United States v. Singleton, 460 F.2d 1148 (2nd Cir. 1972).

175. 8 *Moore's Federal Practice* ¶ 15.2[2] at 15-33 (1975).

176. United States v. Egorov, 34 F.R.D. 130 (E.D.N.Y. 1963).

177. United States v. Broke, 246 F.2d 328 (2nd Cir. 1957); United States v. Whiting, 308 F.2d 537 (2nd Cir. 1962).

178. United States v. Glessing, 11 F.R.D. 501 (D. Minn. 1951) (no deposition permitted of members of draft Appeal Board who denied defendant's exemption).

179. 685 F.2d 793, 809 (3rd Cir. 1982).

180. 8 *Moore's Federal Practice* ¶ 15.02[1] at 15-15 (1975).

181. Advisory Committee Note to 1974 Amendment to Rule 15, *supra* note 169.

> The phrase "whenever due to special circumstances of the case it is in the interest of justice," is intended to make clear that the decision by the court as to whether to order the taking of a deposition shall be made in the context of the circumstances of the particular case.

182. *Id.*

183. *Id.* ("Subdivision (a) also makes explicit that only the 'testimony of a prospective witness of a party' can be taken. This means the party's own witness and does not authorize a discovery deposition of an adverse witness."). *See also* Campbell v. Eastland, 307 F.2d 478 (5th Cir. 1962); United States v. Steffes, 35 F.R.D. 24 (D. Mont. 1964).

184. *Id.* ("The principal objective is the preservation of evidence for use at trial. It is not to provide a method of pretrial discovery nor primarily for the purpose of obtaining a basis for later cross-examination of an adverse witness. Discovery is a matter dealt with in Rule 16."). *See also* United States v. Rich, 580 F.2d 929 (9th Cir. 1978); United States v. Gruberg, 493 F. Supp. 234, 253 (S.D.N.Y. 1979); In re Wolfson, 453 F. Supp. 1087 (S.D.N.Y. 1978).

185. United States v. Egorov, *supra* note 176.

186. 8 *Moore's Federal Practice* ¶ 15.03[02] at 15-33-15-34 (1975).

187. Former Fed. R. Crim. P. 15(e) is set forth in full in Chapter 2, Section D4 *supra*.

188. The Confrontation Clause of the Sixth Amendment also requires the government to make a good-faith effort employing "reasonable means" to obtain the presence of a witness at trial beyond the mere showing of an inability to compel

appearance by subpoena before prior testimony may be admitted. For a discussion of the content of such "other reasonable means," *see* Chapter 4, Section B1 *infra.*

189. 590 F.2d 361 (1st Cir. 1978).

190. *Id.* at 366.

191. *Id.* at 365.

192. *Id.* at 366.

193. *Id.* at 368. *Accord*, United States v. Ruthbart, 653 F.2d 462 (10th Cir. 1981).

194. *See* note 152 *supra.*

195. Uniform R. Crim. P. 431(a), 10 U.L.A. 1, 130-39 (1974).

196. Uniform R. Crim. P. 431(a)(3).

197. Uniform R. Crim. P. 431(f)(2).

198. Uniform R. Crim. P. 431(f)(3).

199. Uniform R. Crim. P. 431(h) set forth above. As is self-evident, the Uniform Rules of Evidence are modeled after the Federal Rules of Evidence.

200. *Federal Rules of Criminal Procedure Amendment Act of 1975*: Hearings Before the Senate Comm. on the Judiciary, 94th Cong., 1st Sess. 166 (1975) (statement of John C. Keeney, Acting Assistant Attorney General, Criminal Division).

201. *See* Chapter 2, Section B8 *supra.*

202. *Federal Rules of Criminal Procedure Amendment Act of 1975, supra* note 200 at 134 representing comment submitted originally appearing in Note, *Proposed Amendments to the Federal Rules of Criminal Procedure*, 14 Washburn L. J. 76, 99 (1975).

203. *Id.* at 165 (statement of John C. Kenney, Acting Assistant Attorney General, Criminal Division).

204. *Id.*

205. *Oversight of the Witness Protection Program:* Hearings Before the Subcomm. on Administrative Practice and Procedure of the Senate Comm. on the Judiciary, 95th Cong., 2d Sess. 19 (1978) (statement of Rudolph Guliani, Attorney, New York, N.Y.).

206. *Senate Comm. on the Judiciary, Organized Crime Control Act of 1969*, S. Rep. No. 617, 91st Cong., 1st Sess. 59 (1969).

207. *Oversight of the Witnesses Protection Program, supra* note 205 at 277 (report of the Justice Department's Witness Security Program Review Committee).

208. *Organized Crime Control Act of 1969*: Senate Comm. on the Judiciary, S. Rep. No. 617, 91st Cong., 1st Sess. 41 (1969).

209. *Id.*

210. *Invasion of Privacy*: Hearings Before the Subcomm. on Administrative Practice and Procedure of the Senate Comm. on the Judiciary, 89th Cong., 1st Sess. 1158 (1965) (statement of Nicholas de B. Katzenbach, Attorney General).

211. *Organized Crime Control Act of 1970*, Pub. L. No. 91-452 §§ 501-04, 84 Stat. 922, 933-34 (1970).

As we all know from the movies, federal and local law enforcement personnel have on occasion placed witnesses in "protective custody," hiding them from the "bad guys" until the trial. The Witness Protection Program was, however, the first time the Congress formally authorized and gave encouragement to such activities. It is believed that only Wisconsin among the states has similarly formalized its protective custody program.

212. *Oversight of the Witness Protection Program, supra* note 205 at 59 (statement of William Hall, Director, U.S. Marshals Service).

213. Justice Department Order OBD 2110.2 (Jan. 10, 1975) reprinted in *Oversight of the Witness Protection Program, supra* note 205 at 134-39 (appendix).

214. Sylvester, *New Danger to Witnesses?* 4 Nat'l L. J. No. 36 at 10 (1982).

215. *Id.*

216. *Id.*

217. *Id.*

218. *Id.* at 11.

219. *Oversight of the Witness Protection Program, supra* note 205.

220. *Id.* at 88 (statement of Senator Abourezk, Chairman, Subcomm. on Administrative Practice and Procedure of the Senate Comm. on the Judiciary).

221. Anti-crime legislation enacted October 12, 1984, Pub. L. No. 98-473 provided as follows with respect to the witness protection program:

- Authorized relocation and protection of federal or specified state witnesses and potential witnesses when the attorney general determines that a crime of violence is likely to be committed against those individuals.
- Authorized relocation and protection for the immediate family of the witness, or another person closely associated with the witness, if those individuals may also be endangered.
- Required the attorney general to issue guidelines covering the types of cases for which witnesses can be protected.
- Gave U.S. officials and employees immunity from civil liability for their decisions to protect or not to protect a witness.
- Gave the attorney general discretion to determine how long to protect a witness, and authorized the attorney general to provide the witness with identity documents, housing, transportation to a new home, a payment to meet basic living expenses, and help in obtaining a job.
- Required deductions from living-expense payments to a protected witness to cover court-ordered family support payments.
- Gave the attorney general discretion to disclose or withhold information on the identity or location of a protected witness. Required disclosure of such information to state and local law enforcement officials when the person in question is sought for a crime of violence or an offense punishable by more than one year in prison.
- Provided for a $5,000 fine, five-year prison term or both for anyone convicted of illegally disclosing information about the identity and location of a protected witness.
- Required the attorney general, "to the extent practicable," to obtain information about the suitability of a person for protection and relocation. Such information would include a criminal history, if any, and a psychological evaluation of the person.
- Required the attorney general to determine whether the need for a person's testimony outweighs the risk of endangering people and property in the community where a witness is relocated, and barred relocation if the risk to the public outweighs the need for the person's testimony.
- Required the attorney general to issue a written "memorandum of understanding" to the protected witness specifying the person's responsibilities under

the program. These require no criminal conduct, payment of all legal obligations and civil judgments, agreement to testify and provide information to law enforcement officials, and agreement to take the necessary steps to avoid detection.

- Provided for emergency protection in specified circumstances without the written memorandum.
- Allowed the attorney general to terminate protection of a witness for a substantial breach of the memorandum of understanding.
- Specified procedures for notifying a protected witness of a civil proceeding against him and set out elaborate procedures for enforcing the rights of any litigant who has a judgment against a protected witness. Authorized disclosure to the plaintiff of the identity and location of a protected person who fails to comply with a civil judgment against him. If the attorney general does not make such disclosure upon request, the plaintiff could seek a federal court hearing on the issue.
- Barred the attorney general from relocating any child in connection with protecting a witness if it appears that a person other than the witness has legal custody of that child.
- Provided detailed procedures for safeguarding custody and visitation arrangements involving a protected witness who has legal custody of a child, and required the parent being relocated to seek and abide by modifications in the existing court-ordered custody arrangements if compliance with a visitation order is not possible.
- Specified that the custody and visitation rights of the non-relocated parent may not be infringed if a child is relocated as part of the program.
- Required the Justice Department to pay transportation and security costs necessary to ensure up to 12 visits per year, or up to 30 days, between parents and children.
- Provided for arbitration if no agreement on modifying a custody arrangement is reached within 60 days of a legal action to alter the arrangement.
- Authorized the attorney general to pay restitution or, in the case of death, compensation to any victim injured or killed by a person protected under the federal program.
- Authorized $1 million annually for this compensation program.
- Limited compensation in cases involving death to a maximum of $50,000, and prohibited payments to victims receiving restitution or compensation through other programs or through insurance.

42 Congressional Quarterly 2756-2757 (Oct. 20, 1984).

Chapter 3

Deterrent and Remedial Measures

A. THE CRIME OF INTIMIDATION

During the late 1970's the American Bar Association Criminal Justice Section's Victims Committee focused on the drafting of a model statute making actual or attempted witness intimidation a criminal offense. The model statute,[1] "Intimidation of Witnesses and Victims," was approved by the House of Delegants of the American Bar Association in August 1980.[2] To date it has served as the prototype for state statutes in California, Louisiana, Rhode Island, Pennsylvania, and Wisconsin as well as being highly influential in the enactment by Congress of the Victim and Witness Protection Act of 1982. In light of the importance of the model statute, it is set forth in full with accompanying commentary prepared by the Victims Committee with the exception of Sections 5 and 6, which are presented similarly in Section B below.

Model Statute:
Intimidation of Witnesses and Victims

§ *1. Definitions*

The following words have significance attached to them hereunder through this chapter.

(a) "Malice" means an intent to vex, annoy, harm, or injure in any way another person, or to thwart or interfere in any manner with the orderly administration of justice.

(b) "Witness" means any natural person, (1) having knowledge of the existence or nonexistence of facts relating to any crime or (2) whose declaration under oath is received or has been received as evidence for any purpose; or (3) who has reported any crime to any peace officer, prosecutor, probation or parole officer, correctional officer or judicial officer or (4) who has been served with a subpoena issued under the authority of any court in the state, or of any other state or of the United States, or (5) who would be believed by any reasonable person to be an individual described in Subsections (1), (2), (3), or (4) hereof.

(c) "Victim" means any natural person against whom any crime as defined under the laws of this state or any other state or of the United States is being or has been perpetrated or attempted to be perpetrated.

Commentary

The Committee felt a need to draw a distinction between persuasion, often rather rigorous, which may be exercised by, for example a victim or witness' family members whose motivation for attempting to persuade the person not to testify is legally blameless. Consequently, the malice intended in and defined by the statute should be intentional and knowingly exercised. The committee grappled considerably with this issue. Some members wished to punish all dissuading but for certain narrowly drawn exemptions, but the majority felt that the statute would potentially punish, for instance, a person casually remarking to a potential witness that he or she should not bother getting involved in the process.

The definition of "witness" had to be handled differently from other statutory definitions of the word, as it was intended clearly to cover a person who has become aware of a crime but who has not yet been subpoenaed. This definitional problem is a major reason for non-enforcement of existing statutes. It is the intent of the committee that the definition of witness specifically include both defense and government witnesses.

"Victim" required definition since it is a term rarely found in existing statutes. "Victim" intentionally does not terminate at any particular time, as the committee felt this statute should be broad enough to cover retaliation or attempted retaliation. The Committee was aware of no current victim protection statutes in the United States, although some states could conceivably punish victim intimidation as "obstruction of justice" or by contempt of court proceedings.

The committee recognized that a defense attorney in a criminal case has the affirmative duty to attempt to contact and question witnesses, and did not intend to deter any attorney from fulfilling his ethical, moral or legal obligations to his or her client.

§ 2. *Misdemeanor—Intimidation of Witnesses and Victims*

Except as provided in Section 3, every person who knowingly and maliciously prevents or dissuades or attempts to so prevent or dissuade any witness or victim from attending or giving testimony at any trial, proceeding or inquiry authorized by law or who attempts to prevent or dissuade another person who has been the victim of a crime or who is a witness to a crime or a person acting on behalf of the victim of a crime from (a) making any report of such victimization to any peace officer or state or local or federal law enforcement officer or probation or parole or correctional officer or prosecuting agency or to any judge; (b) causing a complaint, indictment, information, probation or parole violation to be sought and prosecuted and assisting in the prosecution thereof; (c) arresting or causing or seeking the arrest of any person in connection with such victimization, is guilty of a misdemeanor.

Commentary

In this misdemeanor section, the Committee wished to broaden substantially the coverage of many state laws. The Committee felt that society should have some criminal sanction against a person verbally dissuading another from testifying, if done for an improper, i.e., malicious purpose. Note that the broadened definition of witness removes the necessity for language such as "person who becomes a witness" found in many modern statutes.

This section makes it a crime to threaten a third person who wishes to go to the police on behalf of an injured or deceased victim. Under present law with its emphasis on possession of a subpoena, witness protection statutes provide minimal assistance for victims, particularly immediately after the crime is committed, which is often the most critical time framework. The addition of language proscribing the act of threatening someone not to report their victimization is an important advance, and is not clearly covered by existing statutes.

Again it should be emphasized that it is not the intent of this statute to hinder the defense attorney in his ethical, moral or legal obligations to his client relating to the interview of witnesses and victims. Also it should be noted that the coverage of this action has been extended to cover probation and parole violations and the report of any such violation to the appropriate authority.

It was the Committee's intent that this statute cover harassment or intimidation of defense witnesses as well as prosecution witnesses. The Committee heard persuasive testimony that harassment of defense lawyers and witnesses is a serious problem in some areas of the country.

§ 3. Felonious Intimidation of Witnesses and Victims

Every person doing any of the acts described in the misdemeanor section on intimidation of witnesses and victims in Section 2 knowingly and maliciously under any one or more of the following circumstances, is guilty of a felony.

(a) Where such act is accompanied by an express or implied threat of force or violence, upon a witness or victim or any third person or the property of any victim, witness, or any third person,

(b) Where such act is in furtherance of a conspiracy,

(c) Where such act is committed by any person who has been convicted of any violation of this chapter, any predecessor law hereto or any Federal statute or statute of any other state which, if the act prosecuted was committed in this state, would be a violation of this chapter, or

(d) Where such act is committed by any person for pecuniary gain or for any other consideration acting upon the request of any other person. All parties to such a transaction are guilty of a felony.

Commentary

While Section 3 describes a serious felony, its implications are probably more similar to existing law than other sections of the draft statute. What may be slightly novel about this section is its inclusion of a threat directed at any third person (i.e., a spouse) in (a). In the "intimidation for hire" situation in (d), all parties to the transaction are punishable as perpetrators. This may be useful in dealing with organized crime-type activites. The Committee considered making it a felony to attempt to bribe or bribing a victim or a witness. However, it was decided that this type of activity is covered by other statutes. Also, the Committee attempted to use broad enough language in this section to protect prisoners should they be the victim of or witness to a crime.

As is in the misdemeanor section, this section is intended to cover intimidation of defense witnesses as well as government witnesses, and also applies to situations where the defense lawyer is the object of intimidation or harassment.

§ *4. Attempts*

Every person attempting the commission of any act described in the foregoing sections is guilty of the offense attempted without regard to success or failure of such attempt. The fact that no person was injured physically, or in fact intimidate, shall be no defense against any prosectuion under this chapter.

Commentary

Intimidation is one crime in which only unsuccessful attempts are reported or prosecuted. It is critical that in an intimidation statute no vagueness exists. This is contradistinguished from the general law of attempts as defined in many states' sentencing laws, i.e., one-half the sentence of the complete crime. The Committee felt that an attempt at intimidation is as serious as a successful act from the standpoint of a sanction to be imposed. The ABA had previously supported punishing attempt at the same level as a completed offense (1975 Policy on Proposed Federal Criminal Code). Most prosecutions would probably come under this section of the statute. Finally, it is again emphasized that the statute is in no way intended to restrict a defense attorney or district attorney in meeting his or her ethical, moral or legal duties.

* * *

§ *7. Pre-Trial Release*

Any pre-trial release of any defendant, whether on bail or under any other form of recognizance, shall be deemed, as a matter of law, to include a condition that the defendant neither do, nor cause to be done, nor knowingly permit to be done on his behalf, any act proscribed by this chapter hereof and any willful violation of said condition is subject to sanction as prescribed in Section 6(c) whether or not the defendant was the subject of an order under Section 5 (i.e., the section relating to Court Orders).

(a) From and after the effective date of this chapter, any receipt for any bail or or bond given by the clerk of any court, by any court, by any surety or bondsman and/or any written promise to appear on one's own recognizance shall contain in a conspicuous location, notice of this Section 7.

Commentary

This section broadens the potential for revoking pre-trial release of defendants to those situations in which there was no pre-existing order. While in certain states the sole purpose of pre-trial bail is to ensure the defendant's appearance at trial, most take a broader and, in the Committee's view, wiser position. A newly adopted ABA Standard Relating to Pre-trial Release 10-5.2 (iii) and (v) expressly authorized such conditions upon defendants, reflecting a growing recognition that such conditions may be needed in certain areas of the country.

Faced with the growing evidence compiled in numerous studies and hearings of the true extent of the existence of witness intimidation[3] as well as the model statute recommended by the American Bar Association, Congress responded with the enactment of the Victim and Witness Protection Act of 1982.[4] Section 4(a) adds §§ 1512, 1513, and 1515 to Title 18 of the United States Code making intimidation of a witness a criminal offense.

§ *1512. Tampering with a witness, victim, or an informant*

(a) Whoever knowingly uses intimidation or physical force, or threatens another person, or attempts to do so, or engages in misleading conduct toward another person, with intent to—

(1) influence the testimony of any person in an official proceeding;

(2) cause or induce any person to—

(A) withhold testimony, or withhold a record, document, or other object, from an official proceeding;

(B) alter, destroy, mutilate, or conceal an object with intent to impair the object's integrity or availability for use in an official proceeding;

(C) evade legal process summoning that person to appear as a witness, or to produce a record, document, or other object, in an official proceeding; or

(D) be absent from an official proceeding to which such person has been summoned by legal process; or

(3) hinder, delay, or prevent the communication to a law enforcement officer or judge of the United States of information relating to the commission or possible commission of a Federal offense or a violation of conditions of probation, parole, or release pending judicial proceedings;

shall be fined not more than $250,000 or imprisoned not more than ten years, or both.

(b) Whoever intentionally harasses another person and thereby hinders, delays, prevents, or dissuades any person from—

(1) attending or testifying in an official proceeding;

(2) reporting to a law enforcement officer or judge of the United States the commission or possible commission of a Federal offense or a violation of conditions of probation, parole, or release pending judicial proceedings;

(3) arresting or seeking the arrest of another person in connection with a Federal offense; or

(4) causing a criminal prosecution, or a parole or probation revocation proceeding, to be sought or instituted, or assisting in such prosecution or proceeding;

or attempts to do so, shall be fined not more than $25,000 or imprisoned not more than one year, or both.

(c) In a prosecution for an offense under this section, it is an affirmative defense, as to which the defendant has the burden of proof by a preponderance of the evidence, that the conduct consisted solely of lawful conduct and that the defendant's sole intention was to encourage, induce, or cause the other person to testify truthfully.

(d) For the purpose of this section—

(1) an official proceeding need not be pending or about to be instituted at the time of the offense; and

(2) the testimony, or the record, document, or other object need not be admissible in evidence or free of a claim of privilege.

(e) In a prosecution for an offense under this section, no state of mind need be proved with respect to the circumstances—

(1) that the official proceeding before a judge, court, magistrate, grand jury, or government agency is before a judge or court of the United States, a United States magistrate, a bankruptcy judge, a Federal grand jury, or a Federal Government agency; or

(2) that the judge is a judge of the United States or that the law enforcement officer is an officer or employee of the Federal Government or a person authorized to act for or on behalf of the Federal Government or serving the Federal Government as an adviser or consultant.

(f) There is extraterritorial Federal jurisdiction over an offense under this section.

§ *1513. Retaliating against a witness, victim or an informant*

(a) Whoever knowingly engages in any conduct and thereby causes bodily injury to another person or damages the tangible property of another person, or threatens to do so, with intent to retaliate against any person for—

(1) the attendance of a witness or party at an official proceeding, or any testimony given or any record, document, or other object produced by a witness in an official proceeding; or

(2) any information relating to the commission or possible commission of a Federal offense or a violation of conditions of probation, parole, or release pending judicial proceedings given by a person to a law enforcement officer;

or attempts to do so, shall be fined not more than $250,000 or imprisoned not more than ten years, or both.

(b) There is extraterritorial Federal jurisdiction over an offense under this section.

§ *1515. Definitions for certain provisions*

As used in sections 1512 and 1513 of this title and in this section—

(1) the term "official proceeding" means—

(A) a proceeding before a judge or court of the United States, a United States magistrate, a bankruptcy judge, or a Federal grand jury;

(B) a proceeding before the Congress; or

(C) a proceeding before a Federal Government agency which is authorized by law;

(2) the term "physical force" means physical action against another, and includes confinement;

(3) the term "misleading conduct" means—

(A) knowingly making a false statement;

(B) intentionally omitting information from a statement and thereby causing a portion of such statement to be misleading, or intentionally concealing a material fact, and thereby creating a false impression by such statement;

(C) with intent to mislead, knowingly submitting or inviting reliance on a writing or recording that is false, forged, altered, or otherwise lacking in authenticity;

(D) with intent to mislead, knowingly submitting or inviting reliance on a sample, specimen, map, photograph, boundary mark, or other object that is misleading in a material respect; or

(E) knowingly using a trick, scheme, or device with intent to mislead;

(4) the term "law enforcement officer" means an officer or employee of the Federal Government, or a person authorized to act for or on behalf of the Federal Government or serving the Federal Government as an adviser or consultant—

(A) authorized, under law to engage in or supervise the prevention, detection, investigation, or prosecution of an offense; or

(B) serving as a probation of pretrial services officer under this title; and

(5) the term "bodily injury" means—

(A) a cut, abrasion, bruise, burn, or disfigurement;

(B) physical pain;

(C) illness

(D) impairment of the function of a bodily member, organ, or mental faculty; or

(E) any other injury to the body, no matter how temporary.

Section 1512 was drafted to correct several deficiencies in the law as to the protection of victims and witnesses. It applies to activities taken against any person, which includes victims, witnesses, and informants, that occur any time before the person testifies. Prior law did cover many acts of intimidation, such as assault and battery, but it required a relatively high threshold of seriousness to be classified as a crime.[5] For example, prior law did not cover verbal harassment, a very common form of intimidation.[6] It was also not a crime under prior law to intimidate a person who wanted to report a parole or probation violation or to intimidate third parties, such as friends or relatives of the witness.[7] Finally, it was doubtful under the prior law whether a person who provided information about a crime, but who was not expected to testify because the testimony was inadmissible, constituted a "witness," the only category of persons protected. Although the term "witness" was not defined by prior statutes,[8] it was defined by the courts as one who is expected to testify in a court proceeding.[9] Therefore, before

Section 1512 was enacted, a person who provided authorities with information of a crime, but whose testimony was not be admissible in court, if it was hearsay or privileged, for instance, was most likely not protected.

Subsection (a) of Section 1512 prohibits a person from knowingly using or attempting to intentionally use intimidation, physical force, threats, or misleading conduct to achieve three enumerated prohibited results. These prohibited results are, first, influencing the testimony of any person in an official proceeding; second, causing or inducing any person to, in relation to an official proceeding, (a) withhold testimony, records, documents, or other objects; (b) alter, destroy, mutilate, or conceal an object with intent to reduce its integrity or availability for use; (c) evade a legal summons; or (d) be absent; and third, hindering, delaying, or preventing the communication of information relating to the commission or possible commission of a federal offense or a violation of probation, parole, or release. The penalties for a violation of this subsection are fines not exceeding $250,000 or imprisonment up to ten years or both.

Subsection (b) of Section 1512 makes it an offense for a person intentionally to harass or intentionally attempt to harass another person and thereby hinder, delay, prevent, or dissuade that person from (1) attending or testifying in an official proceeding; (2) reporting the commission or probable commission of a crime or a parole, probation, or release violation; (3) arresting or seeking the arrest of another; or (4) seeking, instituting, or assisting a criminal prosecution or a probation or probation revocation proceeding. The violation of this subsection permits penalties of up to one year imprisonment, $25,000 maximum fine, or both.

Subsection (c) of Section 1512 provides that it is an affirmative defense to a charge under Section 1512 that the defendant's conduct was lawful and that his or her intention was to encourage, induce, or cause the other person to testify truthfully. This defense is meant to excuse a judge or prosecutor who threatens a witness or potential witness with a perjury or false swearing prosecution if he or she testifies falsely.

Subsection (d) of Section 1512 plugged some of the loopholes of the prior law by broadening and clarifying the coverage of the section. This subsection provides that for application of this section no official proceeding must be pending or about to be instituted and that the relevant testimony, record, document, or other object need not be admissible. This provision solves the problem previously mentioned of the witness who would not have been protected by previous laws because his or her testimony would not have been admissible. Subsection (e) also broadens the statute's coverage by providing that no state of mind must be proved that any relevant official proceeding is federal or that the relevant judges or enforcement officers are federal.

Section 1513 added to Title 18 of the United States Code by the Victims and Witness Protection Act of 1982 applies to offenses against any person, whether a victim, witness, or informant, that occur after the person has cooperated with law enforcement officials. It was intended to expand the protection of victims, witnesses, and informants by eliminating certain gaps in the prior law relating to retaliation attempts. The protection provided by Section 1513 extends to retaliation against friends, relatives, or associates of victims, witnesses, or informants.[10] Section 1513 prohibits anyone from knowingly engaging in or threatening to perform any conduct that causes bodily injury to another person or damage to another's property with an intent to retaliate against that person for either of two reasons. The first reason is the attendance of a witness at an official proceeding or any testimony, record, document, or other object provided by a witness for an official proceeding. The second reason is the providing of any information relating to the comission or possible commission of a crime or to a parole, probation, or release violation to a law enforcement official. The penalties accompanying this section are up to ten years imprisonment, a maximum $250,000 fine, or both.

The import of Section 1515 is to provide several definitions for Sections 1512 and 1513. An *official proceeding* is defined as a proceeding before a judge or court of the United States, a bankruptcy court, a federal grand jury, or a congressional or federal agency proceeding. *Physical force* means any physical action against another including confinement. *Misleading conduct* encompasses knowingly making a false statement, making an intentionally misleading omission in a statement or an intentional concealment of a material fact resulting in a false impression; and knowingly submitting or inviting reliance on, with intent to mislead, a false, forged, or altered writing or recording or a materially misleading sample, specimen, map, photograph, boundary map, or other object. A *law enforcement officer* is an officer or employee of the federal government, or a person authorized to act for the federal government, who is legally authorized to engage in or supervise the prevention, detection, investigation, or prosecution of an offense or who is a probation or pretrial services officer. *Bodily injury* includes a cut, an abrasion, a bruise, a burn, disfigurement, physical pain, an illness, or an impairment of the function of a bodily member, organ, or mental faculty; or any other injury to the body no matter how temporary.

It is too soon to tell whether making the intimidation of witnesses a separate criminal offense will have a meaningful impact on the problem.[11] Practical considerations involving the allocation of resources make the prospects extremely doubtful. Making intimidation a separate crime is clearly an expression of deep concern over the plight of victims and witnesses. It is certainly questionable, however, whether either the American Bar Association or Congress ever believed that expanding the breadth of conduct involving the intimidation of victims and witnesses classified as criminal beyond the serious conduct already proscribed would in practice ever do much more than that.

B. RESTRAINING ORDER

1. Criminal

The model statute of the American Bar Association provides for the issuance of a court order by any court having jurisdiction over a criminal matter upon a showing of good cause that intimidation has occurred or is likely to occur. Section 5 specifies the orders that may be issued, and Section 6 provides for various punishments that may be handed down for a violation of an order.

§ 5. *Court Orders*

Any court with jurisdiction over any criminal matter may in its discretion upon good cause (which may include but is not limited to credible hearsay or the declaration of the prosecutor or defense attorney) that intimidation or dissuasion of any person who is a victim or who is a witness has occurred or is reasonably likely to occur, issue orders including, but not limited to the following:

(a) An order that a defendant not violate any provision of this chapter.

(b) An order that a person before the court other than a defendant, including, but not limited to, a subpoenaed witness or other person entering the courtroom of said court, not violate any provisions of this chapter.

(c) An order that any person described in this subsection maintain a prescribed geographic distance from any specified witness or victim.

(d) An order that any person described in this subsection have no communication whatsoever with any specified witness or any victim, except through an attorney under such reasonable restrictions as the court may impose.

(e) An order calling for a hearing to determine if an order as described in (a) through (d) should be issued.

(f) An order that a particular law enforcement agency within the jurisdiction of the court provide protection for a victim and/or witness.

Commentary

Section 5 would give judges greater ability than at present (except in a few states, such as Wisconsin) to deal with intimidation. Certain parts of the section, notably (a) which empowers a judge to order a defendant not to violate any other provisions of the law, may be superfluous, but desirable for emphasis, and it may be salutory to provide a "shopping list" of all the things the judge may properly order in one section. The Committee also discussed the possibility of creating a special category of orders relating to domestic relations and child protection but felt such an order was beyond the purview of this statute.

The Committee sought in (b) to recognize that many persons in the courtroom other than the accused may pose possible intimidation problems as when substantial numbers of family members or friends appear in the courtroom although the defendant is in custody. There seems to be no efficacious way of directing orders at persons beyond the court's immediate presence, but recourse to the substantive portions of the statute would be available when a court proceeding reveals intimidation outside the courtroom. Both subpoenaed witnesses and others present in the court were included in (b) since it is common for witnesses to appear voluntarily, rather than pursuant to subpoena. Moreover, much of the intimidation-in-the-courtroom problem seems to flow from "spectators." Candidly, the Committee recognized the limited efficacy of this section, but questioned whether a broader jurisdictional basis could be found.

In addition, the Committee discussed the burden placed on law enforcement agencies and suggested that a protective order be issued only in extreme cases in the judges' discretion. The power of a trial judge to order a particular law enforcement agency over whom he has at least territorial jurisdiction to take protective measures (pursuant to Section 5[f]) varies dramatically from area to area and even within areas. The power of the court in relation to particular peace officers is obviously greatest where it is dealing with a marshall's office or other institution directly responsible to the court itself, and likely to be the weakest where the judge is a state or county official seeking to direct an order to a city police department not a party to the litigation. Even in this latter situation, there is considerable precedent for orders directed at police agencies in many areas (i.e., arrest or search warrants, discovery orders and those regarding conditions of incarceration). If discretion as to the frequency and breadth of such orders is maintained by the courts, many law enforcement agencies may comply without protest, particularly if the community at large is sensitized to the intimidation problem.

In cases where the defendant chooses to represent himself, the court shall issue such orders as will balance the competing interests of the defendant's with the rights of a victim or witness to be free and secure from unwarranted threats or harassment.

§ 6. *Violations of Orders*

Any person violating any order made pursuant to Section 5 may be punished in any of the following ways:

(a) For any substantive offense described in this chapter; where such provision of an order is a violation of any provisions of Section 2 through 4

(b) As a contempt of the court making such order;

  (1) No finding of contempt shall be a bar to prosecution for a substantive offense under this chapter, but

    (a) any person so held in contempt shall be entitled to credit for any punishment imposed therein against any sentence imposed upon conviction of said substantive offense and

    (b) any conviction or acquittal for an substantive offense under Section 2 through 5 shall be a bar to a subsequent punishment for contempt arising out of the same act.

(c) By revocation of any form of pre-trial release and/or the forfeiture of bail and the issuance of a bench warrant for the defendant's arrest or remanding him into custody, said revocation may, after a hearing and upon a showing by clear and convincing evidence, in the sound discretion of the court, be made whether the violation order complained of has been committed by the defendant, personally, or in any way caused or encouraged to have been committed by said defendant.

Commentary

Section 6 provides punishment for violations of orders under Section 5 through contempt power as well as the substantive offense. The summary nature of contempt may, for the immediate less serious situation, be a valuable tool for a trial judge desirous of controlling threatened behavior in the courtroom. Section (c) makes the defendant, in limited cases, rsponsible for actions of those "caused or encouraged" to have acted for him. (See also the commentary to Section 7, infra.) The standard for revocation in (c) is that recommended in the ABA Standards Relating to Pre-trial Release, 10-5.9 (pre-trial detention).

2. Civil

A civil action to restrain harassment of a victim or witness is provided by the Victim and Witness Protection Act of 1982 in the form of Section 1514 to Title 18 of the United States Code.[12] A civil court order was viewed as a valuable supplement to the criminal sanctions of the prior law[13] and the new Sections 1512 and 1513, neither of which explicitly provide for such an order. This section addresses the situation in which the prosecution is in possession of evidence of an actual attempt at witness intimidation or that such an attempt is likely to be forthcoming. Section 1514 applies not only to the acts of the defendant but to acts of the defendant's friends, relatives, and associates that the defendant causes to be done on his or her behalf.

§ ***1514. Civil action to restrain harassment of a victim or witness.***

(a) (1) A temporary restraining order prohibiting harassment of a victim or witness in a Federal criminal case if the court finds, from specific facts shown by affidavit or by verified complaint that these are reasonable grounds to believe that harassment of an identified victim or witness in a Federal criminal case exists or that such order is necessary to prevent and restrain an offense under section 1512 of this title, other than an offense consisting of misleading conduct, or under section 1513 of this title.

(2) (A) A temporary restraining order may be issued under this section without written or oral notice to the adverse party or such party's attorney in a civil action under this section if the court finds, upon written certification of facts by the attorney for the Government, that such notice should not be required and that there is a reasonable probability that the Government will prevail on the merits.

(B) A temporary restraining order issued without notice under this section shall be endorsed with the date and hour of issuance and be filed forthwith in the office of the clerk of the court issuing the order.

(C) A temporary restraining order issued under this section shall expire at such time, not to exceed 10 days from issuance, as the court directs and the court, for good cause shown before expiration of such order, may extend the expiration date of the order for up to 10 days or for such longer period agreed to by the adverse party.

(D) When a temporary restraining order is issued without notice, the motion for a protective order shall be set down for hearing at the earliest possible time and takes precedence over all matters except older matters of the same character, and when such motion comes on for hearing, if the attorney for the Government does not proceed with the application for a protective order, the court shall dissolve the temporary restraining order.

(E) If on two days notice to the attorney for the Government or on such shorter notice as the court may prescribe, the adverse party appears and moves to dissolve or modify the temporary restraining order, the court shall proceed to hear and determine such motion as expeditiously as the ends of justice require.

(F) A temporary restraining order shall set forth the reasons for the issuance of such order, be specific in terms and describe in reasonable detail (and not by reference to the complaint or other document) the act or acts being restrained.

(b) (1) A United States district court, upon motion of the attorney for the Government, shall issue a protective order prohibiting harassment of a victim or witness in a Federal criminal case if the court, after a hearing, finds by a preponderance of the evidence that harassment of an identified victim or witness in a Federal criminal case exists or that such order is necessary to prevent and restrain an offense under section 1512 of this title, other than an offense consisting of misleading conduct, or under section 1513 of this title.

(2) At the hearing referred to in paragraph (1) of this subsection, any adverse party named in the complaint shall have the right to present evidence and cross-examine witnesses.

(3) A protective order shall set forth the reasons for the issuance of such order, be specific in terms, describe in reasonable detail (and not by reference to the complaint or other document) the act or acts being restrained.

(4) The court shall set the duration of effect of the protective order for such period as the court determines necessary to prevent harassment of the victim or witness but in no case for a period in excess of three years from the date of such order's issuance. The attorney for the Government may, at any time within ninety days before the expiration of such order, apply for a new protective order under this section.

(c) As used in this section—

(1) The term "harassment" means a course of conduct directed at a specific person but—

(A) causes substantial emotional distress in such person; and

(B) serves no legitimate purpose; and

(2) the term "course of conduct" means a series of acts over a period of time, however short, indicating a continuity of purpose.

Under Subsection (a) of Section 1514 a court shall issue a temporary restraining order prohibiting harassment of a victim or witness in a federal criminal case if the court finds that there are reasonable grounds to believe that harassment of an identified victim or witness has already occurred.

Such an order may also be issued when established to be necessary to prevent the commission of an offense under Section 1512, other than misleading conduct, or Section 1513. Reasonable grounds to believe that harassment has occurred or will occur if not restrained must be established by specific facts shown by an affidavit or a verified complaint before a temporary restraining order is issued by the court. The duration of the restraining order is up to ten days.

Subsection (b) of Section 1514 allows a court to issue a protective order prohibiting harassment of a federal crime victim or witness after a hearing. The protective order is a stronger version of the temporary restraining order in Subsection (a). For the protective order to issue it must be shown at the hearing by a preponderance of the evidence that harassment of an identified federal crime victim or witness exists or that such an order is necessary to prevent an offense under Section 1512, other than misleading conduct, or Section 1513. The duration of this order may be as long as the court determines is necessary, but it cannot last longer than three years.

Subsection (c) of Section 1514 defines *harassment* as a course of conduct directed at a specific person that causes substantial emotional distress and serves no legitimate purpose.

C. MONETARY RECOVERY

1. Civil Tort Liability

Under some, but by no means all, circumstances, the acts of a defendant in attempting to intimidate a witness not to testify at trial in accordance with his or her prior statement will give rise to civil liability. If the defendant intentionally strikes the witness, a battery has been committed. If the defendant's actions intentionally arouse in the witness a reasonable apprehension of an imminent battery, an assault has been committed. However, the threat of contact to be an assault must be perceived as imminent, which requires an apparent present ability and opportunity of the actor to commit a battery. Thus the statement "If you testify, I will get you" is not an assault. Nor is the statement "You're dead" an assault when made by a defendant in custody. The intentional tort of assault also requires an overt act; that is, words, however strong, do not constitute an assault. Words may on the other hand give character to an otherwise innocuous act sufficient to create an assault.

Intimidation by the defendant is most states can also give rise to civil liability for ensuing damages for the intentional tort of intentional infliction of emotional distress. A defendant who by extreme and outrageous conduct intentionally or recklessly causes severe emotional distress to another is subject to liability for such emotional distress and, if bodily harm to the other results from it, for such bodily harm. To be considered extreme and outrageous the conduct must be more than merely threatening; it must be so shocking as to be beyond all reasonable bounds of decency. Moreover, the emotional distress suffered must be more than minor psychic harm; it must be severe. A few jurisdictions go as far as to prohibit recovery altogether if the emotional distress suffered has not manifested itself in bodily harm. Finally, the defendant is not liable to the extent that the person's emotional response to his or her conduct falls outside the range of reactions of an ordinary person.[14]

As is readily apparent, resort to a civil action for damages for intentional torts flowing from the defendant's intimidation or attempt to intimidate is unlikely to be available in many instances. Most intimidation is verbal conduct (not a battery) not accompanied by an overt act threatening an immediate battery (not an assault). Nor is most verbal intimidation of such a nature as to meet all of the requirements imposed at common law in connection with the tort of intentional infliction of emotional distress. Even with conduct sufficiently extreme and outrageous to qualify, a witness who is not intimidated is extremely unlikely to meet the requirement of severe emotional reaction. A witness who is intimidated is extremely unlikely to turn around and subsequently bring a civil action.

As to those instances in which an action for damages arising from an intentional tort could be successfully prosecuted, various practical problems curtail the likelihood of such suits being brought and thus the deterrent effect of civil liability upon witness intimidation. Lawsuits are costly in terms of both time and money. Moreover, actual damages arising from assault, battery, or intentional infliction of emotional distress will often be slight. Finally, even if a large award of compensatory or punitive damages were warranted, it is highly unlikely that many defendants wil be financially able to pay.[15] Those defendants who are potentially able to pay will most often be associated with organized crime. Few intimidated witnesses would voluntarily chose to extend their period of involvement with such defendants, and with it the risk of action being taken by the defendant rather than mere threats, in the hope of even a large damage award. Money is of no use if you are not around to spend it.

2. Criminal Restitution

As part of the Victim and Witness Protection Act of 1982, Congress provided in Title 18 for the court when sentencing a defendant convicted of any offense under Title 18 of the United States Code, including but not limited to Sections 1512 and 1513 of the same title making witness intimidation a separate crime,[16] to order the defendant as part of the criminal sentence to make restitution to any victim of the offense.

§ *3579. Order of restitution*

(a) (1) The court, when sentencing a defendant convicted of an offense under title or under subsection (h), (i), (j), or (n) of section 902 of the Federal Aviation Act of 1958 (49 U.S.C. 1472) may order, in addition to or in lieu of any other penalty authorized by law, that the defendant make restitution to any victim of the offense.

(2) If the court does not order restitution, or orders only partial restitution, under this section, the court shall state on the record the reasons therefor.

(b) The order may require that such defendant—

(1) in the case of an offense resulting in damages to or loss or destruction of property of a victim of the offense—

(A) return the property to the owner of the property or someone designated by the owner; or

(B) if return of the property under subparagraph (A) is impossible, impractical, or inadequate, pay an amount equal to the greater of—

(i) the value of the property on the date of the damage, loss, or destruction, or

(ii) the value of the property on the date of sentencing,

less the value (as of the date the property is returned) of any part of the property that is returned;

(2) in the case of an offense resulting in bodily injury to a victim—

(A) pay an amount equal to the cost of necessary medical and related professional services and devices relating to physical, psychiatric, and psychological care, including non-medical care and treatment rendered in accordance with a method of healing recognized by the law of the place of treatment;

(B) pay an amount equal to the cost of necessary physical and occupational therapy and rehabilitation; and

(C) reimburse the victim for income lost by such victim as a result of such offense;

(3) in the case of an offense resulting in bodily injury also results in the death of a victim, pay an amount equal to the cost of necessary funeral and related services; and

(4) in any case, if the victim (or if the victim is deceased, the victim's estate) consents, make restitution in services in lieu of money, or make restitution to a person or organization designated by the victim or the estate.

(c) If the Court decides to order restitution under this section, the court shall, if the victim is deceased, order that the restitution be made to the victim's estate.

(d) The court shall impose an order of restitution to the extent that such order is as fair as possible to the victim and the imposition of such order will not unduly complicate or prolong the sentencing process.

(e) (1) The court shall not impose restitution with respect to a loss for which the victim has received or is to receive compensation, except that the court may, in the interest of justice, order restitution to any person who has compensated the victim for such loss to the extent that such person paid the compensation. An order of restitution shall require that all restitution to victims under such order be made before any restitution to any other person under such order is made.

(2) Any amount paid to a victim under an order of restitution shall be set off against any amount later recovered as compensatory damages by such victims in—

(A) any Federal civil proceeding; and

(B) any State civil proceeding, to the extent provided by the law of that State.

(f) (1) The court may require that such defendant make restitution under this section within a specified period or in specified installments.

(2) The end of such period or the last such installment shall not be later than—

(A) the end of the period of probation, if probation is ordered;

(B) five years after the term of imprisonment imposed, if the court does not order probation; and

(C) five years after the date of sentencing in any other case.

(3) If not otherwise provided by the court under this subsection, restitution shall be made immediately.

(g) If such defendant is placed on probation or paroled under this title, any restitution ordered, under this section shall be a condition of such probation or parole. The court may revoke probation and the Parole Commission may revoke parole if the defendant fails to comply with such order. In determining whether to revoke probation or parole, the court or Parole Commission shall consider the defendant's employment status, earning ability, financial resources, the willfulness of the defendant's failure to pay, and any other special circumstances that may have a bearing on the defendant's ability to pay.

(h) An order of restitution may be enforced by the United States or a victim named in the order to receive the restitution in the same manner as a judgment in a civil action.

§3580. Procedure for issuing order of restitution

(a) The court, in determining whether to order restitution under section 3579 of this title and the amount of such restitution, shall consider the amount of the loss sustained by any victim as a result of the offense, the financial resources of the defendant, the financial needs and earning ability of the defendant and the defendant's dependents, and such other factors as the court deems appropriate.

(b) The court may order the probation service of the court to obtain information pertaining to the factors set forth in subsection (a) of this section. The probation service of the court shall include the information collected in the report of presentence investigation or in a separate report, as the court directs.

(c) The court shall disclose to both the defendant and the attorney for the Government all portions of the presentence or other report pertaining to the matters described in subsection (a) of this section.

(d) Any dispute as to the proper amount or type of restitution shall be resolved by the court by the preponderance of the evidence. The burden of demonstrating the amount of the loss sustained by a victim as a result of the offense shall be on the attorney for the Government. The burden of demonstrating the financial resources of the defendant and the financial needs of the defendant and such defendant's dependents shall be on the defendant. The burden of demonstrating such other matters as the court deems appropriate shall be upon the party designated by the court as justice requires.

(e) A conviction of a defendant for an offense involving the act giving rise to restitution under this section shall estop the defendant from denying the essential allegations of that offense in any subsequent Federal civil proceeding or State civil proceeding, to the extent consistent with State law, brought by the victim.

The Model Statute: Intimidation of Witnesses and Victims of the American Bar Association Criminal Justice Section,[17] on which the Victim and Witness Protection Act of 1982 is based, does not contain a similar provision for criminal restitution. Although the absence of such a provision is not explained, undoubtedly the explanation for the omission is the fact that 19 states already had legislation explicitly permitting an order of restitution.[18] In addition, many have thought that the authority to order a criminal defendant to pay restitution is an inherent part of the sentencing power of the court.

In the states without victim compensation programs,[19] restitution may be the only practicable means by which a victim can obtain any financial assistance. In nearly every state it is the only means of recovering for property loss or damage without going to court and obtaining a civil judgment, since victim compensation laws rarely cover property loss. Most state laws authorizing restitution permit the court to impose restitution or not in its discretion. Several require the court to consider restitution as a condition of probation. Only some, like Section 3579(a)(2), establish a presumption of restitution permitting the court in the interests of justice not to order restitution provided the court states its reasons for not so ordering. A few state laws go as far as to make restitution mandatory in specified cases.[20] Historically, the power of the court to order restitution as part of the defendant's sentence has rarely been used. Recently, however, pressure from victims' rights groups coupled with a greater general awareness of and concern for the plight of the crime victim has led to a marked increase in the use of court-ordered restitution.

The Final Report of the President's Task Force on Victims of Crime[21] concludes that the predominant discretionary approach to restitution does not go far enough. The report recommends that legislation be enacted by the states, like Section 3579(a)(2), requiring restitution by the criminal defendant in all cases unless the court provides specific reasons for failing to require it. Nowhere in the report are any suggestions made about a circumstance that might warrant the court in not ordering restitution. The implications of this omission cannot be overlooked.

A significant problem with the increased use of restitution is the additional expense to court systems, particularly the cost of administrative follow-up to insure that restitution orders are not ignored by offenders. A few states including Wisconsin and Maryland impose a surcharge on convicted offenders to support court administration of the restitution program.[22]

3. Victim Compensation Programs

At least 39 states have enacted legislation providing for compensation of victims of violent crimes under specified circumstances.[23] Payments are made from state-administered funds upon application by eligible claimants. Payment does not depend upon the arrest and conviction of the offender, and there is no need for the claimant to secure a civil judgment.

Coverage generally extends to both victims and dependents of victims, and the laws generally define both terms broadly. Most of the statutes condition eligibility on the victim's having reported the crime to the police. Some also require that the victim have cooperated in the investigation and prosecution of the case. Commonly, the laws require the claimant to show financial hardship.

Most of the victim compensation programs are financed from general revenue funds, although some are financed in whole or in part from offender assessments. Some states have created new agencies to administer the programs, and others have incorporated the programs in existing administrative structures or designated existing agencies, such as the courts, to administer the programs.

Compensation generally is permitted for unreimbursed medical expenses, funeral expenses, loss of earnings, and support of dependents of deceased victims. Property loss generally is not reimbursed. A few states permit compensation for additional expenses such as psychiatric services, occupational training, and required household services. Most of the laws set a ceiling on the amount of recovery by an individual claimant, in a few states up to $50,000, but more commonly the maximums range from $10,000 to $15,000. The amount of the award with respect to those elements of damage for which compensation is permitted that have been established by the evidence is generally based upon many factors resulting in practice in only a fraction of the crime victim's loss being reimbursed.[24]

The major problem with victim compensation programs is the lack of adequate funding making less than full reimbursement the rule rather than the exception. In addition many states have imposed minimum loss requirements to save costs, thus often leaving the full burden of crime on those of society who can afford it least. The then current funding situation of the victims compensation programs lead the President's Task Force on Victims of Crime to recommend in 1982 that Congress enact legislation to provide federal funding to assist state crime victims compensation programs. In response, in October of 1984 Congress created a Crime Victims Fund.[25]

NOTES

1. American Bar Association, Criminal Justice Section, *Reducing Victim/Witness Intimidation: A Package*, 6-13 (Washington, D.C., 1981).

2. *See also* American Bar Association, Criminal Justice Section, *Bar Leadership on Victim/Witness Assistance* (Washington, D.C., 1980); American Bar Association, Criminal Justice Section, *Victim/Witness Legislation: Considerations for Policy-makers* (Washington, D.C., 1981); American Bar Association, Criminal Justice Section, *Guidelines for Fair Treatment of Crime Victims and Witnesses* (Washington, D.C., 1983).

3. *See generally*, Chapter 1, Section A and Chapter 2, Section A *supra*.

4. *Victim and Witness Protection Act of 1982*, Pub. L. No. 97-291 §§ 2-9, 96 Stat. 1248-58 (1982).

5. For the offense of influencing a witness, either corruption, threats, or force is required as an element of the crime. For the crime of obstructing criminal investigations, either bribery, misrepresentation, intimidation, force, or threats is required as an element of the offense. 18 U.S.C. §§ 1503, 1510 (1976).

6. *The Omnibus Protection Act of 1982*, Senate Judiciary Committee, S. Rep. No. 532, 97th Cong., 2d Sess. 15 (1982).

7. *Id.* at 14.

8. Several offenses related to *witness*, but the term is not defined by any statute. *See, e.g.*, 18 U.S.C. §§ 1503, 1505 (1976).

9. *See, e.g.*, United States v. Griffin, 463 F.2d 177 (8th Cir. 1972); Hunt v. United States, 400 F.2d 306 (5th Cir. 1968).

10. *See* 18 U.S.C. §§ 1503, 1505 (1976).

11. There have only been two reported cases involving charges under the Victim and Witness Protection Act of 1982. United States v. Johnson, 713 F.2d 654 (11th Cir. 1983) (defendants were convicted under 18 U.S.C. § 1513 when they abducted a close friend of a coconspirator of one of the defendants who was to testify against a defendant. Defendants threatened to kill the friend unless she revealed where the coconspirator/witness had been relocated by the government's witness protection program); United States v. Wilson, 565 F. Supp. 1416 (S.D.N.Y. 1983) (defendant challenges an indictment under which he was convicted for violation of 18 U.S.C. §§ 1512, 1513 for attempting and plotting to murder, and for hiring another to murder, several witnesses and prospective witnesses in his pending trial).

12. The American Bar Association's Model Statute: *Intimidation of Witnesses and Victims*, in Section 5, "Court Orders," provides for similar relief in the context of a pending criminal prosecution. The text of Section 5, with accompanying commentary, appears in Chapter 3 section B1 *supra*.

13. 18 U.S.C. § 1503 (1976).

14. *See generally*, Comment, *Threats Inducing Emotional Reactions*, 39 N.C. L. Rev. 74 (1960); Restatement (Second) of the Law of Torts, §§ 18-20, 21-34, 46-48 (1965); W. Prosser, *Law of Torts* §§ 7-12 (4th ed. St. Paul: West, 1971); E. Kionka, *Torts in a Nutshell: Injuries to Persons and Property* (St. Paul: West, 1977), pp. 147-65.

15. American Bar Association, Criminal Justice Section, *Victim/Witness Legislation: Considerations for Policymakers* 21 (Washington, D.C., 1981) ("Although victims have always had the option of bringing a civil suit against the

offender to collect damages, they rarely do. Often the offender is 'judgment proof,' making any judgment against him worthless.'').

For a discussion of state statutes providing for victim access to income guaranteed by the offender as a result of publicity about the crime, *see id.* at 21-22.

16. For a discusison of Sections 1512 and 1513, *see* Chapter 3 Section A *supra.*

17. *See* Chapter 2, Section A1 *supra.*

18. American Bar Association, Criminal Justice Section, *Victim/Witness Legislation: Considerations For Policymakers* 19 (Washington, D.C., 1981).

With respect to the constitutionality of ordering restitution see *The Unconstitutionality of the Victim and Witness Protection Act Under the Seventh Amendment,* 84 Colum. L. Rev. 1590 (1984).

19. *See* Chapter 3, Section C3 *infra.*

20. Bureau of Justice Statistics, U.S. Department of Justice, *Victim and Witness Assistance* 2 (May 1983); American Bar Association, Criminal Justice Section, *Victim/Witness Legislation: Considerations for Policymakers* 17-20 (Washington, D.C., 1981).

21. The *Statement of Recommended Judicial Practice* of the National Judicial College is in accord.

22. Bureau of Justice Statistics, *supra* note 20 at 2-3.

For a statement of additional concern with court ordered restitution, see Chapter 8, note 6 *infra.*

23. For a history of the development of victim compensation programs, see P. Rothstein, *State Compensation for Criminally Inflicted Injuries,* 44 Tex. L. Rev. 38 (1965); Note, *Compensation for Victims of Crime,* 19 Vand. L. Rev. 220 (1965); R. Yarborough, *S. 2155 of the Eighty-Ninth Congress—The Criminal Injuries Compensation Act,* 50 Minn. L. Rev. 255 (1965); R. Childres, *Compensation for Criminally Inflicted Personal Injury,* 39 N.Y.U. L. Rev. 444 (1964).

For a typical statute, *see* the *Uniform Crime Victims Reparations Act,* 11 U.L.A. 33 (1974).

24. *See generally,* Abt Associates Inc., *Compensating Victims of Crime: An Analysis of American Programs,* United States Department of Justice (Washington, D.C., 1982); American Bar Association, Criminal Justice Section, *Victim/Witness Legislation: Considerations for Policy Makers* 2-16 (Washington, D.C., 1981).

For a directory of ''Offices of State Crime Victim Compensation'' programs, *see* Appendix 2 to American Bar Association, Criminal Justice Section, *Bar Leadership on Victim/Witness Assistance* (Washington, D.C., 1980).

25. Anti-crime legislation enacted October 12, 1984, Pub. L. No. 98-473 provided as follows:

- Created a Crime Victims Fund in the Treasury Department financed through fines collected from persons convicted of federal offenses, with specified exceptions, plus forfeited bonds and collateral.
- Set a $100 million maximum for the fund and required any excess money to go to the Treasury.
- Barred deposits in the fund after Sept. 30, 1988.
- Specified that half the amount in the fund each year shall be available for grants to existing state victim-compensation programs to meet claims, and half to states to provide victim assistance programs such as rape counseling.

• Allowed the attorney general to deduct up to 5 percent of the total in the fund for services to victims of federal crimes. This money would come out of the share allotted to states for victim services.

• Authorized the attorney general, in making annual grants to state victim-compensation programs, to provide funds equal to 35 percent of the amounts awarded to crime victims by the state program during the previous fiscal year, other than awards for property damage.

• Defined an "eligible" program as one that is operated by a state and offers compensation to victims or their survivors for medical expenses, loss of wages and funeral expenses.

• Authorized the attorney general to make grants to states, subject to available funds, for crime victim-assistance programs run by public agencies or non-profit organizations.

• Provided that each state should receive $100,000 under the grant and that any remaining money should be distributed among the states on the basis of population. If there is less than $100,000 per state available, then the money would be distributed to the states equally.

• Authorized a federal court, upon request by a U.S. attorney, to ensure that someone convicted of a crime causing physical harm to an individual does not profit from that crime. A court could order forfeiture of all or part of the proceeds the defendant or his designee received from a contract relating to depiction of the crime in a movie, book, newspaper, magazine, drama, radio or television production.

• Authorized a judge to order the person who contracted with the defendant to pay the specified amount to the attorney general.

• Provided that proceeds paid to the attorney general through forfeiture be held in the Crime Victims Fund for five years, but allowed payment for specified purposes, including a fine or monetary award to the victim. At the end of the five-year period, a court may require all or part of forfeited proceeds to be released for use by the Crime Victims Fund.

42 Congressional Quarterly 2757 (Oct. 20, 1984).

Chapter **4**

Substantive Admissibility of Prior Statements

A. THE PROBLEM

Under the definition of *hearsay* employed at common law as well as that contained in the Federal Rules of Evidence, when a statement offered to prove the truth of the matter asserted is made "other than . . . by the declarant while testifying at the trial or hearing," the statement is hearsay. The out-of-court statement is hearsay regardless of whether the out-of-court declarant later testifies at the trial or hearing at which the out-of-court statement is offered. Thus the definition of hearsay applies to all statements not made under oath at the trial or hearing and thus not subject to contemporaneous cross-examination before the trier of fact.

To recapitulate briefly, exclusion of out-of-court statements as hearsay presents a significant problem for state and federal governments in the prosecution of criminal defendants. Prosecutors often find that by the time of trial victims or occurrence witnesses have changed their stories. Witnesses who change their stories before or at trial are generally referred to as "turncoat" or "flipped" witnesses. On other occasions witnesses lose, or at least appear to lose, their memories. In more extreme cases, witnesses become unavailable altogether either becaue they fail to respond to a subpoena, cannot be located, have fled the jurisdiction, or have met an untimely death. In many, if not most, of the foregoing situations, the witness's testimony will be lost to the trier of fact because the witness was intimidated. *Intimidation* consists of knowingly and maliciously preventing or dissuading an occurrence witness, that is, a person with personal knowledge of relevant facts, from attending or giving testimony at a hearing or trial. In addition, intimidation refers to preventing or dissuading an occurrence witness, whether or not a victim, from reporting a crime or assisting in its investigation.[1] If occurrence witnesses' prior statements are not admissible as substantive evidence by virtue of operaton of the rule against hearsay, an incentive is provided for criminal defendants to intimidate occurrence witnesses in the pursuit of their own liberty.

Neither the common law nor the Federal Rules of Evidence preclude the admission at trial for all purposes of all prior witness statements. On occasion such a statement will satisfy the requirements of a traditional hearsay exception recognized both at common law and under the Federal Rules of Evidence. In addition, the Federal Rules of Evidence now permit the introduction as substantive evidence of certain prior inconsistent statements,[2] consistent statements,[3] prior identification statements,[4] and "other hearsay" statements judged to possess sufficient guarantees of trustworthiness.[5] Moreover, at common law and under the Federal Rules of Evidence prior out-of-court inconsistent statements may be admitted for purposes of impeachment. However, neither the common law nor the Federal Rules of Evidence adequately deal with the difficulties associated with the turncoat, forgetful, or unavailable witness for the prosecution.

To illustrate the difficulties arising in determining admissibility of prior statements of an intimidated turncoat, forgetful, or unavailable witnesses, reference in subsequent discussion will be made to the following hypothetical case:

On July 14, 1984, police in Old Towne received a telephone call that shots were heard in the seven hundred block of Maple Avenue. The police arrived at 709 Maple Avenue at 11:00 p.m. to find three men in the second floor apartment. One man, Jim James, was hanging from the window by his fingertips. Another man, Bob Williams, was lying on the floor with a bullet wound in his leg. A third man, later identified as Harold Harris, was dead in the middle of the room. The officers found cocaine and the equipment necessary to obtain its purity on a table.

On the street below, an officer questioned two witnesses who said they saw a man flee from the building at 10:45 p.m. Mary Mahoney gave a description to the officer but declined to go to the police station to make a written statement because her children would be unattended. John Goodfellow, the other witness, went to the station and gave a tape recorded statement describing the man he saw.

At the police station, Jim James, faced with a narcotics felony charge of possession with intent to sell cocaine, as part of a plea bargain reducing the charge to misdemeanor possession and a recommendation of probation, told a detective that a Sam Smith was going to sell narcotics to Bob Williams and Harold Harris that evening. He, Jim James, was waiting in the apartment because he and Harold had social plans for the evening. During the narcotics sale, Sam Smith pulled a pistol and began firing. At that time, he, Jim James, ran for the window where the police found him. A stenographer took down Jim James' statement and Jim James signed it.

Bob Williams, under similar circumstances, told the grand jury the same story Jim James had given to the police.

Sam Smith was arrested at his home on July 16, 1984. His physical appearance fit the descriptions given by Mary Mahoney and John Goodfellow. Sam Smith is subsequently identified by John Goodfellow at a lineup.

The prosecution appeared to have a solid case. Just before trial, however, upon recontact, Mary Mahoney changed her description. Bob Williams was found floating face up in the river with a bullet in his head. At trial, John Goodfellow testifies he does not now recall seeing anyone on the evening of July 14 outside 709 Maple Avenue but he does admit it is his voice on the tape recording. John Goodfellow acknowledges his presence at a lineup but testifies that at the lineup he was unable to identify anyone as being present at the scene of the crime. Jim James refuses to answer any questions even though he has been given testimonial immunity with respect to the murder and any related drug charges and ordered to answer. The prosecutor finally calls Mary Mahoney hoping that under oath she will give an accurate account of what she perceived but she testifies giving a different description of the person leaving the building.[6]

The out-of-court statements of the four witnesses to the incident if offered to prove the truth of the matter asserted are hearsay.[7] Accordingly, each of the four out-of-court statements is admissible as substantive evidence under the Federal Rules of Evidence only if it qualifies as a prior inconsistent statement of an in-court witness under Rule 801(d)(1)(A), qualifies as a prior identification statement of an in-court witness under Rule 801(d)(1)(C), or satisfies a hearsay exception contained in Rule 803 or Rule 804. At common law each statement is admissible as substantive evidence only if it satisifes the requirements of a traditional hearsay exception. Under the Federal Rules of Evidence and at common law a prior statement of a witness inconsistent with the witness's in-court testimony is admissible to impeach credibility.

B. FORMER TESTIMONY

Prior statements of a victim or witness are admissible under the former testimony exception to the hearsay rule if the declarant is unavailable as a witness at trial and the prior statement was given as testimony at another hearing of the same or a different proceeding, or at a deposition, if the party against whom the testimony is offered had an opportunity and similar motive to develop the witness's testimony by direct, cross-, or redirect examination. Thus prior statements of a witness whose testimony at trial is unavailable as a result of intimidation by the defendant given at a preliminary hearing, or a hearing on a motion to suppress a confession, an identification, or illegally seized evidence are admissible as substantive evidence. Since the accused is not present at a grand jury proceeding when a witness testifies, testimony given by the witness before the grand jury fails to meet the requirements of the former testimony hearsay exception, that is, the accused did not have an opportunity to develop the witness's testimony when given by direct, cross-, or redirect examination.

1. Unavailability Requirement

At common law the requirement of unavailability evolved separately in connection with particular hearsay exceptions rather than along general lines. However, as the Advisory Committee's Note to Rule 804(a) of the Federal Rules of Evidence points out, "no reason is apparent for making distinctions as to what satisfies unavailability for the different exceptions." Accordingly, Rule 804(a) alters this pattern by treating unavailability as a single concept applicable to each exception requiring unavailability as a prerequisite[8] including the hearsay exception for former testimony, Rule 804(b)(1). Rule 804(a) provides as follows:

Hearsay Exceptions; Declarant Unavailable

(a) Definition of unavailability. "Unavailability as a witness" includes situations in which the declarant—

(1) is exempted by ruling of the court on the ground of privilege from testifying concerning the subject matter of his statement; or

(2) persists in refusing to testify concerning the subject matter of his statement despite an order of the court to do so; or

(3) testifies to a lack of memory of the subject matter of his statement; or

(4) is unable to be present or to testify at the hearing because of death or then existing physical or mental illness or infirmity; or

(5) is absent from the hearing and the proponent of his statement has been unable to procure his attendance (or in the case of a hearsay exception under subdivision (b)(2), (3) or (4), his attendance or testimony) by process or other reasonable means.

A declarant is not unavailable as a witness if his exemption, refusal, claim of lack of memory, inability, or absence is due to the procurement or wrongdoing of the proponent of his statement for the purpose of preventing the witness from attending or testifying.

The definition of *unavailability* contained in Rule 804(a) provides five alternatives, each alone sufficient to meet the requirement. The thrust of the alternative definitions of unavailability concerns the unavailability of the testimony of the witness, which includes, but is not limited to, situations in which the witness is not physically present in court. Physical presence on the witness stand does not make a witness available within the meaning of the rule if the witness exercises a privilege, simply refuses to answer, or tstifies to a lack of memory about the subject matter of his or her prior statement.[9]

Rule 804(a)(1) provides that a witness exempt from testifying concerning the subject matter of his or her statement on the grounds of privilege is unavailable. An actual claim of privilege must be made by a witness, other than a criminal defendant,[10] and allowed by the court before the witness will be considered unavailable on the basis of a privilege.[11] Rule 804(a)(2) provides that one who persists in refusing to testify concerning the subject matter of his or her statement, despite an order of the court to do so, is unavailable.[12] Silence resulting from misplaced reliance upon a privilege without making a claim, or in spite of a court denial of an asserted claim of privilege, constitutes unavailability under this subsection.[13]

Rule 804(b)(3) provides that a witness who testifies to a lack of memory of the subject matter of his or her statement is unavailable. A witness may either truly lack recollection or, for a variety of reasons, including fear arising from intimidation by the accused and concern of a possible perjury prosecution, feign lack of recollection. In either event, the witness is unavailable to the extent that he or she asserts lack of recollection of the subject matter of the prior statement even if the witness recalls other events.[14] Rule 804(a)(4) provides that a witness unable to be present, or to testify at the hearing, because of death or then existing physical or mental illness or infirmity is unavailable. Death is the most obvious basis. Mental illness or physical disability of a serious nature are equally compelling. If the reason for the government witness's unavailability is only temporary, and the witness's testimony important, considerations underlying the Confrontation Clause may require resort to a continuance.[15]

Rule 804(a)(5) provides that in both civil and criminal cases, a declarant is unavailable if his or her presence cannot be secured by process or other reasonable means. In federal civil cases, a subpoena may be served at any place within the district or within 100 miles of the place of the trial.[16] In federal criminal cases, a subpoena may be served at any place within the United States.[17] In all criminal cases, the Confrontation Clause[18] itself requires that before former testimony, Rule 804(b)(1), may be introduced against the accused as a substitute for in-court testimony, the government must make a good faith effort to obtain the presence of the witness at trial. Witnesses who are in state or federal prison can be required to appear in state or federal court pursuant to a subpoena to the individual and a writ of habeas corpus *ad testificandum* issued to the appropriate prison authority. Whether the government has shown good faith in attempting first to locate the witness and second in procuring the witness's attendance by process or voluntarily by reasonable means must be determined on a case-by-case basis after careful review of the particular facts and circumstances.[19]

Determination of unavailability is a matter for the court.[20] The party offering the statement has the burden of showing unavailability. A witness is not "unavailable" under any of the subdivisions of Rule 804(a) if the circumstances that would otherwise constitute unavailability are due to the procurement or other wrongdoing of the proponent of the statement.[21]

2. Specified Criteria

At common law and under the Federal Rules of Evidence, testimony given by a witness at another hearing of the same or a different proceeding, or in a deposition taken in compliance with law in the course of the same or another proceeding, is admissible as a hearsay exception if (1) the witness is unavailable, and (2) the party against whom the testimony is being offered, or in a civil action or proceeding a person in privity or under the Federal Rules of Evidence a predecessor in interest, had an opportunity and similar motive to develop the testimony by direct, cross-, or redirect examination. Rule 804(b)(1) provides as follows:

Hearsay Exceptions; Declarant Unavailable

* * *

(b) Hearsay exceptions. The following are not excluded by the hearsay rule if the declarant is unavailable as a witness:

(1) Former testimony. Testimony given as a witness at another hearing of the same or a different proceeding, or in a deposition taken in compliance with law in the course of the same or another proceeding, if the party against whom the testimony is now offered, or, in a civil action or proceeding, a predecessor in interest, had an opportunity and similar motive to develop the testimony by direct, cross, or redirect examination.

The exception for former testimony involves the admission of testimony taken under oath and subject to cross-examination. However, the demeanor of the witness has not been, and will not be, observed by the trier of fact. Imposing the requirement of unavailability represents a strong preference for the personal appearance of the witness as an aid in evaluating his or her testimony. The additional requirement that the same party, or a person in a civil action in privity at common law or the apparently slightly broader category of a predecessor in interest under Rule 804(b)(1),[22] possessed a similar motive and adequate opportunity to develop the prior testimony is designed to insure that the prior opportunity was functionally equivalent to the circumstances that would surround the party's development of the witness's testimony if the witness was in fact available to testify at trial. An adequate opportunity to develop the witness's testimony at the earlier hearing may be the opportunity to conduct direct and redirect or cross-examination. Both opportunities are treated as equivalent for this purpose.

(a) Same Party or, in Civil Action, Predecessor in Interest

Early cases interpreting the common law requirement of identity of parties imposed the concept of mutuality. This concept meant that both the party offering and the party against whom the former testimony was offered had to have been parties to the former suit. Under the guidance of Wigmore,[23] the requirement of mutuality was abandoned at common law in favor of admissibility of former testimony against a party to the prior hearing in criminal cases and against a party to the former suit, or someone in privity, in civil actions.

Rule 804(b)(1), as proposed by the Advisory Committee, would have completely eliminated any requirement regarding the identity of parties in favor of permitting introduction of evidence against a party whenever a party in the former action, possessing a motive and interest similar to that of the party against whom the evidence is now offered, had an opportunity to develop the prior testimony of the witness by direct and redirect or cross-examination.[24] Congress rejected this proposal, reasoning that it is "generally unfair to impose upon the party against whom the hearsay evidence is being offered responsibility for the manner in which the witness was previously handled to another party."[25] Congress thought that it was generally unacceptable to impose the examination of another, and with it the quality of the attorney selected, tactical decisions, access to information, and state of preparation, upon a nonparty to the prior litigation.[26] The sole exception to this principle was thought to be when the party's predecessor in interest in a civil case had an opportunity and similar motive to examine the witness.

(b) Similar Motive to Develop Testimony

As to the party, person in privity, or predecessor in interest in civil actions, and the party to the prior hearing in a criminal case who had an opportunity to develop the witness's testimony by direct and redirect or cross-examination, the former testimony will be admitted against the party only if such litigant had a similar motive to develop the testimony at the prior hearing. At common law the requirement of similar motive is couched in terms of substantial identity of issues. Rule 804(b)(1) employs the term *similar motive*, recognizing that identity of issues is significant only in that it bears on the litigant's motive in developing fully the witness's testimony.[27] Conversely, a similar motive will usually have existed at the prior hearing when the issue at the prior hearing and at the current hearing are substantially identical.[28] One instance in which the motive to develop the testimony may not be similar even though the issue is substantially identical is when the initial case against the same party involves only the possibility of a small judgment or fine. All issues at the earlier hearing need not be the same. Only the particular issues about which the testimony was first offered need be substantially identical to the issue upon which the testimony is offered in the current action.[29] Similarly, neither the form of the proceeding, the theory of the case, nor the nature of the relief sought need be the same.[30]

(c) The Adequate Opportunity Dilemma

The adequacy of an opportunity to cross-examine a witness at a prior hearing is best illustrated by reference to the preliminary hearing. Under Rule 804(b)(1) the government may offer testimony given by the witness at the preliminary hearing against the same criminal defendant if the witness becomes unavailable. If the defendant was afforded a full and fair opportunity to conduct a meaningful cross-examination of the witness, the preliminary hearing testimony is admissible. The question is whether, given the circumstances surrounding the preliminary hearing, the particular defendant was afforded such opportunity.

Analysis is complicated by the nature of the preliminary hearing itself, tactical questions faced by counsel for the accused, and whether meaningful discovery is available before the preliminary hearing. A preliminary hearing is ordinarily a much less searching exploration of the merits of a case than a trial, simply because its function involves the more limited one of determining whether probable cause exists to hold the accused for trial. Defense counsel, faced with the testimony of a witness, realizes that to the extent his or her interrogation attempts to discredit the witness, by, for example, attacking powers of observation, or by showing bias, the effort is extremely unlikely to affect the result. Moreover, in practice discovery to which the defendant is ultimately entitled will frequently be incomplete, or even nonexistent, at the time of the preliminary hearing, making effective destructive cross-examination more difficult. As a result defense counsel often tries to use cross-examination at a preliminary hearing primarily to effect discovery rather than impeach credibility.

Extensive cross-examination of prosecution witnesses at the preliminary hearing may be of value to the defense even when there is little likelihood of successfully challenging the prosecution's showing of probable cause and little to be gained by way of discovery. This is because "the skilled interrogation of witnesses [at the preliminary hearing] by an experienced lawyer can fashion a vital impeachment tool for use in cross-examination of the State's witnesses at trial."[31] In many instances witnesses are more likely to make damaging admissions or contradictory statements at the preliminary hearing, because they are less thoroughly briefed for that proceeding than they are for trial. Also, with respect to some witnesses, the more they say before trial, the more likely that there will be some inconsistency between their trial testimony and their previous statements. Arguably, such inconsistencies will have a more damaging impact upon the witness's credibility when the inconsistency is with preliminary hearing testimony, as opposed to prior statements given to the police, since the preliminary hearing testimony was given under oath at a judicial setting.

Cross-examination designed to lay the foundation for future impeachment, however, also carries with it certain dangers for the defense. If the cross-examination focuses too much on potential weaknesses in the witness's testimony, it may educate the witness about these weaknesses. The witness may "rehabilitate himself for the trial and state that at the hearing he was confused, but that everything is now clear in his mind."[32] If the witness is one who otherwise might "soften" his or her view of the facts as time passes and the witness's emotional involvement lessens, extensive cross-examination at the preliminary hearing may only harden the witness's position and make him or her less able to retreat to a more friendly position. In addition, if the witness becomes unavailable at trial, the defense counsel may find that he or she has perpetuated testimony more damaging than that which would have existed without the cross-examination. Finally, counsel may be working at cross-purposes in seeking to discover and impeach simultaneously. If the defense counsel vigorously cross-examines the witness in an effort to get a contradiction or concession on record, the witness will normally dig in and give a minimum of information in an effort to save his or her testimonial position. More than likely the witness will also be uncooperative if counsel thereafter attempts to interview the witness before trial. Conversely, if counsel engages the witness in routine examination, amiable and ranging, counsel may be able to pick up many clues for investigating and planning his or her defense.[33]

In spite of the foregoing, determining the adequacy of an opportunity to conduct meaningful cross-examination primarily focuses not on the practical realities facing defense counsel but upon the scope and nature of the opportunity for cross-examination permitted by the court.[34] Accordingly, a decision by counsel not to cross-examine a witness at the preliminary hearing, or to do so only to a limited extent, no matter how much practical sense the decision makes, does not appear to affect the adequacy of opportunity. The presence of different counsel in the two proceedings clearly does not affect the determination of the adequacy of an opportunity to develop the testimony of the witness.[35]

C. PRIOR INCONSISTENT STATEMENTS

1. Federal Rule of Evidence 801(d)(1)(A)

(a) The Orthodox Rule

The wisdom of admitting a prior inconsistent statement of an in-court witness available for cross-examination as substantive evidence has been thoroughly debated in the literature.[36] Although it is unnecessary to rehash this dialogue in detail, a short summary of the rival contentions is useful to place the relevant issues in perspective.

The hearsay rule as developed by the common law excluded use of a witness's prior out-of-court statement to prove the truth of the matter stated. The prohibition included both prior consistent and inconsistent statements of the in-court witness. Denial of substantive effect to a witness's prior inconsistent statements, referred to hereinafter as the "orthodox rule," was based on a threefold rationale of lack of trustworthiness: (1) the statement was not made under oath, (2) the trier of fact did not observe the declarant's demeanor at the time the statement was made, and (3) the declarant was not subject to contemporaneous cross-examination before the trier of fact by the party against whom the statement is being offered.[37] Although it is certainly correct that a prior statement—unless made at an earlier trial, hearing, or deposition—will rarely have been made under oath, critics of the orthodox rule have downplayed the value of the oath and of the penalties for perjury as safeguards of trustworthiness; of all recognized exceptions to the hearsay rule, only the former testimony exception requires that the statement have been made under oath.[38] Critics of the orthodox rule have also rejected the justification behind the traditional requirement that the trier of fact observe the witness's demeanor when he or she makes the statement. As Judge Learned Hand stated in dismissing the requirement:

> If, from all that the jury see of the witness, they conclude that what he says now is not the truth, but what he said before, they are nonetheless deciding from what they see and hear of that person and in court.[39]

The core of the theoretical dispute over substantive admissibility of a witness's prior inconsistent statements concerns the final challenge to the trustworthiness of such statements—lack of contemporaneous cross-examination. The critical question may be stated as follows: What is the value of cross-examination that is not conducted contemporaneously with the making of the statement whose truth is in question before the same trier of fact that must determine whether the statement is truthful?

The argument that noncontemporaneous cross-examination cannot serve the function performed by cross-examination conducted at the time of the witness's statement is illustrated by the following example. W, testifying on direct examination for the prosecution, states at trial that the defendant threw the first punch leading to a barroom fight. On cross-examination, defense counsel forces W to admit that he feels sorry for the badly injured complainant and that in fact the complainant was the first aggressor. Now assume that W had recanted before trial. If W's prior statement that the defendant threw the first punch was to be introduced at trial, the scenario would be as follows: The defendant calls W, who testifies that the complainant threw the first punch. On cross-examination by the prosecution W admits making the statement and explains upon redirect examination by defense counsel that he made the prior statement accusing the defendant of throwing the first punch only because he felt sorry for the badly injured complainant.

In both of the above situations, the jury faces a choice between two statements and has before it the witness's explanation for their inconsistency. The crucial difference, according to the proponents of the orthodox rule, is that in the first case the jury has seen the witness break down as a result of adversarial confrontation. Cross-examination by defense counsel has fulfilled its purpose. The jury first saw and heard the witness testify to one fact and then saw and heard him recant, thus entirely destroying the value of his initial testimony. In the second situation, although the jury hears W's explanation of his prior statement, the explanation is generally made during examination by the party who is depending on W's present testimony, that is, on redirect examination. Proponents of the orthodox rule argue against the usefulness of such subsequent examination designed to rebuild a witness's credibility:

> Cross-examination presupposes a witness who affirms a thing being examined by a lawyer who would have him deny it, or a witness who denies a thing being examined by a lawyer who would have him affirm it. Cross-examination is in its essence an adversary proceeding. The extent to which the cross-examiner is able to shake the witness or induce him to equivocate is the very measure of the cross-examiner's success.[40]

Under this view the jury in the first case finds that the defendant's adversial, destructive cross-examination aids it in determining the truth of the testimony, but in the second case the jury sees only defense counsel attempting to rehabilitate an impeached witness—a less persuasive, less dramatic, and far less clear-cut event.[41]

Opponents of the orthodox rule have contended that this difference is meaningless and that examination of the witness need not be contemporaneous with the making of the statement to be effective:

> The line of questioning in each instance is virtually identical, except that in the contemporaneous version the witness recants his prior version at the conclusion of the cross-examination while in the subsequent cross-examination he has already done so. The only difference lies in the eye of a first-triumphal flourish.[42]

Moreover, it is argued that the orthodox rule assumes that the cross-examiner at trial will be successful in "breaking down" the witness à la Perry Mason, which obviously is a rare event. Subsequent cross-examination, that is, redirect, relating to a prior inconsistent statement, according to this argument, will more often have a significant impact upon the jury. As stated by the United States Supreme Court in California v. Green:

> The defendant's task in [subsequent] cross-examination is, of course, no longer identical to the task that he would have faced if the witness had not changed his story and hence had to be examined as a "hostile" witness giving evidence for the

prosecution. This difference, however, far from lessening, may actually enhance the defendant's ability to attack the prior statement. For the witness, favorable to the defendant, should be more than willing to give the usual suggested explanation for the inaccuracy of his prior statement, such as faulty perception or undue haste in recounting the event. Under such circumstances, the defendant is not likely to be hampered in effectively attacking the prior statement, solely because his attack comes later in time.[43]

Critics of the orthodox rule have not rested with a defense of the merits of subsequent cross-examination. They have also attacked the basic rationale of the orthodox rule, asserting that the primary reason for disallowing substantive use of a witness's prior inconsistent statement as hearsay—that is, that the declarant was not then subject to cross-examination—simply ignores the realities of the situation. By hypothesis, the witness is present before the trier of fact, is under oath, and is subject to cross-examination. The witness can deny making the prior statement or explain the circumstances surrounding the utterance, and his or her demeanor may be observed throughout. Such critics would support admission as substantive evidence of Mary Mahoney's prior oral inconsistent description of the perpetrator as testified to by the police officer.

For essentially the foregoing reasons, Wigmore concluded that courts should grant substantive value to prior inconsistent statements of in-court witnesses.[44] C. McCormick, supporting Wigmore's position, argued that prior statements are even more trustworthy than later in-court statements, because they are made closer in time to the event.[45] This argument, which draws on the obvious principle tht memory fades with time, suggests as well that there is less likelihood that the earlier statement is the result of corruption, false suggestions, intimidation, or appeals to sympathy or prejudice. McCormick also contended that substantive admissibility was needed to protect parties from the turncoat witness, who by changing his or her story deprives the party calling the witness of essential evidence.[46]

As the final string to their bow, critics of the orthodox rule have argued that when the rule is followed, prior inconsistent statements are still allowed into evidence, accompanied by an instruction to the jury to consider the prior inconsistent statement as bearing solely upon the credibility of the witness's in-court testimony and specifically providing that the statement cannot be treated as evidence of the facts asserted therein.[47] E. Morgan called this practice a "pious fraud."[48] He and others have argued that a jury faces an impossible task when asked to accept a statement as bearing on a witness's credibility while ignoring its substantive content.[49]

In summary, the opponents of the orthodox rule argue that as long as the witness is in court and subject to cross-examination, the hearsay problems are eliminated and prior inconsistent statements of the witness should be substantively admissible. They contend further that substantive admissibility is desirable because the proximity of prior statements to the event in question makes them more trustworthy than in-court testimony and because substantive admissibility protects parties from turncoat witnesses. Finally, they argue that the juries are unable and in any event unwilling to distinguish between statements admitted substantively and those admitted solely as evidence of the witness's credibility.

Supporters of the orthodox rule have also devised arguments to buttress their position. One enduring argument is that a witness's prior inconsistent statement should be denied substantive effect because it is technically hearsay in that the witness was not under oath and was not subject to cross-examination before the trier of fact when the statement was made. They also contend that prior inconsistent statements are often biased as a result of coercion, deception, or subtle influence on the part of the person eliciting the statement, who is often an investigator or police officer.[50] Carrying this argument one step further, the rule's supporters assert that prior inconsistent statements may be completely fabricated,[51] a danger that they assert can be eliminated adequately only by the requirement that testimony not be accepted substantively unless it is given in court, under oath, and subject to cross-examination. Implicitly rejected by this argument is the view that examination of either the declarant when he or she testifies in court or the witness presenting extrinsic proof of the prior inconsistent statement will successfully expose a fabrication or bring to light any illegitimate influence that acted to color the declarant's prior statement. Proponents of the orthodox rule also argue that no need for a change exists since present hearsay exceptions permit substantive admission of prior inconsistent statements that are in fact sufficiently trustworthy. Finally, they point out that prior inconsistent statements may be used to impeach—and thus to neutralize—an opponent's witness. If a party's own witness unfavorably changes his or her story before trial, the party may simply refrain from calling the witness. At common law, if the party calling the witness is surprised and affirmatively damaged by the witness's testimony, the party may impeach the witness with his or her prior inconsistent statement.[52] Confrontation with the inconsistent statement, coupled with fear of perjury prosecution, are asserted to be be sufficient to encourage the witness to adopt the prior statement if the witness actually believes it to be true.

(b) Advisory Committee's Proposal and Congressional Reaction

In the face of the controversy over the substantive admissibility of prior inconsistent statements, Congress enacted Rule 801(d)(1)(A), which reads as follows:

(d) Statements which are not hearsay. A statement is not hearsay if—

(1) Prior statement by witness. The declarant testifies at the trial or hearing and

is subject to cross-examination concerning the statement, and the statement is (A) inconsistent with his testimony, and was given under oath subject to the penalty of perjury at a trial, hearing, or other proceeding, or in a deposition.

Rule 801(d)(1)(A) emerged from Congress only after a seesaw battle that evidenced deep concern over the trustworthiness of prior inconsistent statements. As drafted by the Advisory Committee and submitted by the Supreme Court, rule 801(d)(1)(A) provided for substantive admissibility of all prior inconsistent statements:

(d) Statements which are not hearsay. A statement is not hearsay if:

(1) Prior statements by witness. The declarant testifies at the trial or hearing and is subject to cross-examination concerning the statement, and the statement is (A) inconsistent with his testimony.[53]

The Advisory Committee, following the path of the California Law Revision Commission,[54] concluded that the arguments in favor of treating prior inconsistent statements as hearsay did not withstand analysis. Specifically, the Advisory Committee stated in its Note that the absence of an oath, cross-examination, and observation of demeanor at the time that the prior statement was made could each be adequately supplied by later examination at trial.[55]

The version of rule 801(d)(1)(A) enacted into law, however, shows that the Advisory Committee failed to persuade Congress that substantive admissibility for all prior inconsistent statements was desirable. Rather, as the legislative history of Rule 801(d)(1)(A) suggests, Congress ultimately came to accept arguments asserting the untrustworthiness of most prior inconsistent statements, particularly those arguments that pointed to the risk of total fabrication.[56] Congressional consideration of proposed rule 801(d)(1)(A) commenced in the House Committee on the Judiciary. Initially, a subcommittee report recommended adoption of a compromise rule patterned after decisions of the United States Court of Appeals for the Second Circuit. The Second Circuit had approved substantive admissibility of prior inconsistent statements given under oath at a former trial or in grand jury testimony in the same proceeding.[57] The House subcommittee incorporated the Second Circuit's position into the proposed rule as follows:

(A) Inconsistent with his testimony and was given under oath and subject to the penalty of perjury at a trial or hearing or in deposition or before a grand jury.[58]

The full House Judiciary Committee next added a requirement that, to be admissible substantively, the prior statements must have been subject to contemporaneous cross-examination. This committee also struck the reference to grand jury proceedings. The committee's final version of rule 801(d)(1)(A), which eventually was passed by the House, stated:

(A) Inconsistent with his testimony and was given under oath subject to cross-examination, and subject to the penalty of perjury at a trial or hearing or in a deposition.[59]

The House Judiciary Committee's report indicated the nature of the concerns that prompted both the committee and the full House to place limitations on proposed rule 801(d)(1)(A). Under the House's approach, "[u]nlike in most other situations involving unsworn or oral statements, there can be no dispute as to whether the prior statement was made; and . . . the context of a formal proceeding, an oath, and the opportunity for cross-examination provide firm additional assurance of the reliability of the prior statement."[60] Although rule 801(d)(1)(A) was to apply in both civil and criminal proceedings, various statements in the legislative record suggest that in attacking the reliability of a witness's prior inconsistent statements, the House was focusing on the rule's potential impact upon the criminal defendant.[61] The House was concerned that a defendant could be convicted solely on the basis of a witness's alleged out-of-court statement, even though the statement was disputed by the witness's own testimony, and no certain evidence existed establishing that the witness had accurately recounted the information in the statement and, more fundamentally, that the statement had ever been made. The House was unwilling to accept the risk that proposed rule 801(d)(1)(A), making all prior inconsistent statements admissible substantively against a criminal defendant, would result in the criminal defendant being convicted in substantial reliance on evidence as to a prior statement of the witness that was in fact never made.

This risk of fabrication can be appreciated by considering the following illustration. Assume that the prosecution calls a witness to the stand to testify concerning certain events that took place in a bar the night of a bank robbery. A policeman has advised the prosecution that when he went into the bar, a patron told the policeman that he was a friend of the defendant and that the defendant had been in the bar earlier that evening. The policeman is prepared to testify that the patron friend of the defendant told him that the accused arrived at the bar very sweaty and out of breath carrying a brown paper bag and furthermore that the defendant admitted to the patron friend that he had just robbed a bank. The patron friend of the defendant at trial admits talking to the police officer but adamantly maintains that what he told the police officer was that when he saw the defendant in the bar that evening, the defendant did not say anything to him, that the defendant was in normal health, and that the defendant was not carrying anything.

Consider the position of the accused's attorney who is attempting to cross-examine the police officer about whether an oral inconsistent statement was made by the witness. Since the police officer in fact spoke to the witness, cross-examination about time, location, and so on will be unavailing. The situation involving the police officer and the patron friend resolves itself ultimately into a "Yes we did" versus "No I didn't" situation; that is, the police officer will swear that a statement was made, and the alleged declarant of the statement will swear it was not made.

The House believed that given such a situation the jury would too often uncritically merely accept the testimony of the police officer about the existence of the highly incriminating oral inconsistent statement. The House further believed that given the oral nature of the alleged prior inconsistent statement, there was an unacceptable probability that the police officer fabricated his testimony and thus that the defendant would be unjustly convicted. The House accordingly amended rule 801(d)(1)(A) to limit substantive admissibility of prior inconsistent statements to those made at a formal proceeding where almost absolute certainty that the prior statement was made can be assured.

After the House adopted its version of rule 801(d)(1)(A),[62] consideration of the matter moved to the Senate Committee on the Judiciary. The Report of the Senate Committee on the Judiciary recognized that House opposition to proposed rule 801(d)(1)(A) permitting all prior inconsistent statements to be admitted as substantive evidence arose in great measure from a concern that a criminal defendant could be convicted in substantial reliance or even solely upon untrustworthy evidence admitted under the rule,[63] such as, for example, our alleged oral statement of the patron friend directly implicating an accused testified to by a police officer denied by the alleged declarant in open court to have been made. The Senate committee, however, recommended reinstatement of the rule proposed by the Advisory Committee and the Supreme Court. In its report the Senate committee expressed the view that the requirements of oath and opportunity for cross-examination were "unnecessary," since those elements were present when the witness testified at trial.[64] In support of unrestricted admission of prior inconsistent statements, the Senate Committee also pointed out that rule 801(d)(1)(A) addresses admissibility, not the sufficiency of the evidence to send a case to the jury.[65] The Senate committee added that factual circumstances could well arise in which, if a prior inconsistent statement were the sole evidence, "dismissal would be appropriate."

The Senate Committee's position, even if correct,[66] does not reach the heart of the problem, since only a very small percentage of the cases that merit concern will involve the sole evidence issue. If admitted substantively, evidence of prior inconsistent statements may have its greatest impact operating on the margin, that is, at the point the jury actually determines whether guilt has been proved beyond a reasonable doubt. As the jury makes its critical determination of guilt or innocence, a prior inconsistent statement of questionable trustworthiness will often constitute the straw —more likely the boulder—that breaks the defendant's back by tipping the scales in favor of his or her guilt. This paramount danger clearly supports the concern for certainty of making exhibited by the House.

After the full Senate eventually accepted the recommendation of its committee, the conflicting House and Senate proposals were referred to the Conference Committee. The version of rule 801(d)(1)(A) that emerged from the Conference Committee, which was the version finally enacted by Congress, is as interesting for its packaging as for its resolution of the disputed issues. The conference report[67] stated that the Senate version of rule 801(d)(1)(A), which contained the approach originally proposed by the Advisory Committee, was adopted with an amendment providing that prior inconsistent statements are admissible as substantive evidence only if they were made at a trial, hearing, deposition, or other proceeding under oath and subject to the penalty of perjury. The report stated that the "other proceeding" provision would allow testimony given before a grand jury.

Despite the suggestion by the Conference Committee that it had largely adopted the Senate's version of rule 801(d)(1)(A), the rule proposed by the Conference Committee and accepted by Congress clearly incorporates the substance of the House version of the rule. Enacted Rule 801(d)(1)(A) limits substantive admissibility to those prior inconsistent statements for which there is (1) almost absolute certainty that the statement was made and (2) certain additional assurance of trustworthiness because of the requirement that the prior statement must have been given in a formal proceeding. Thus even though Congress did delete the House's requirement of an opportunity for contemporaneous cross-examination, it is clear that Congress ultimately accepted the House's basic position that only the most trustworthy prior inconsistent statements should be admissible in a criminal action. By the same token, it rejected the contention advanced by supporters of the Advisory Committee and Senate position that protection of the criminal defendant from unwarranted conviction based solely upon a prior inconsistent statement is properly the function of rules designed to evaluate the sufficiency of evidence rather than of rules governing its substantive admissibility.[68]

(c) An Assessment

Although certainty of making of the prior statement is clearly a legitimate consideration in determining admissibility, the safeguards provided in Rule 801(d)(1)(A) to insure that the statement was made are overly strict. For example, the rule excludes substantive admission of prior inconsistent statements contained in an affidavit prepared by the witness's attorney, executed under oath, and submitted to court in the same or another proceeding. Rule 801(d)(1)(A) also excludes a signed or handwritten statement that the witness either acknowledges or other evidence establishes to be his or her signature or handwriting. The rule similarly excludes an oral statement, not under oath, that the witness during testimony admits having made.[69] Yet each of the foregoing circumstances possesses adequate assurance of certainty of making to satisfy the legitimate concern of Congress that convictions not be based upon fabricated out-of-court statements of witnesses.

Unfortunately, this overly restrictive interpretation adopted in Rule 801(d)(1)(A) often renders the rule unhelpful in problems involving an intimidated witness. One might argue that prosecutors who want to rely on the rule should make attempts to place all witnesses before the grand jury and elicit from them the statements the prosecutors want to preserve. Although this is an alternative available to federal prosecutors, if a grand jury proceeding is not immediate the potential criminal defendant may intimidate the witness before the proceeding occurs. Placing an already intimidated witness before a grand jury will not accomplish the preservation of the witness's statements previously made to investigators. In state prosecutions, where reliance is more likely to be placed on a preliminary hearing determination of probable cause rather than a grand jury indictment, the problem may be even more acute. Before such hearings the defendant is given time to find counsel, and counsel is given time to prepare. As the length of the time between the crime and the preliminary hearing increases, the opportunity for intimidation also increases.

As suggested in Chapter 7, what needs to be done is to expand the breadth of coverage of Rule 801(d)(1)(A) to include statements made before the conduct of a formal hearing to the full extent warranted by considerations of trustworthiness and certainty of making.

2. The Requirement of Inconsistency

Although at common law prior inconsistent statements are not admissible as substantive evidence, they are admissible for the limited purpose of impeachment. Pursuant to this rule of limited admissibility, courts developed standards for determining whether a prior statement was inconsistent with testimony at trial. In construing the provisions of Rule 801(d)(1)(A) making certain prior inconsistent statements admissible as substantive evidence, federal courts have looked to the body of common law concerning prior statements for impeachment to determine whether a particular statement is inconsistent with testimony at trial.[70] Some common law jurisdictions follow a strict test of inconsistency by resolving doubts about the meaning of the statements in favor of the witness and then admitting the prior statement for impeachment purposes only if it could not be reconciled with the testimony of the witness at trial.[71] Most courts, however, follow a more liberal test. McCormick suggested the following as both the proper and the predominant standard: "[C]ould the jury reasonably find that a witness who believed the truth of the facts testified to would have been unlikely to make a prior statement of this type?"[72] Wigmore also favored a liberal test: "Do the two expressions appear to have been produced by inconsistent beliefs?"[73] Federal courts before enactment of the Federal

Rules of Evidence had themselves adopted the approach suggested by McCormick and Wigmore. For example, in United States v. Barrett, with respect to the admission of a prior statement only for impeachment, the court articulated the following standard:

> To be received as a prior inconsistent statement, the contradiction need not be "in plain terms." It is enough if the proffered testimony, taken as a whole, either by what it says or by what it omits to say, affords some indication that the fact was different from the testimony of the witness whom it is sought to contradict.[74]

The prior statement that is inconsistent with the in-court testimony of the witness may consist of a previously expressed opinion whether or not the particular subject matter as presented in the form of the statement would be proper if offered at trial.[75] The inconsistency may itself consist of the omission from a prior statement of a matter that would reasonably be expected to have been mentioned if true[76] or the failure to speak at all of a matter asserted at trial under circumstances in which it would have been natural to do so.[77] Similarly, under circumstances that would normally call for a denial if untrue, the failure to respond to the statement of another may be treated as an adoption by silent acquiescence. Finally, an inconsistency may consist of a photograph, sketch, or identi-kit picture previously adopted by the witness as an accurate portrayal of an individual differently described or identified by that witness in court.[78]

3. The Forgetful Witness

When a witness testifies at trial to a lack of recollection about a particular subject, two issues arise with respect to whether a prior statement of the witness relating to that subject may be admitted under Rule 801(d)(1)(A), provided that the prior statement was given under oath, subject to the penalty of perjury at a trial, hearing, or other proceeding or in a deposition: first, whether current lack of recollection and the prior statement are inconsistent; second, whether a witness who testifies to a lack of current recollection about the subject matter of a prior statement is at trial "subject to cross-examination concerning the statement" as required by Rule 801(d)(1)(A). Analysis of both issues is effected by whether the witness, such as John Goodfellow in our hypothetical case, really cannot remember or on the other hand is feigning his lack of ability to recall.

(a) True Lack of Recollection

When the witness truly lacks recollection, determination of both issues is relatively clear. Even the liberal test for inconsistency advanced by McCormick and Wigmore and adopted by Rule 801(d)(1)(A) does not seem to reach the situation in which the witness testifies truthfully to a total lack of recollection of the facts related in the prior statement. True loss of memory and a prior statement are simply not incompatible; they do not evidence inconsistent belief, only a lack of current recollection.[79] Moreover and probably more importantly, if the witness truly lacks recollection, the rationale underlying the requirement of inconsistency is defeated. The Advisory Committee justified the substantive admissibility of prior inconsistent statements on the ground that "the requirement that the statement be inconsistent with the testimony given assures a thorough exploration of both versions while the witness is on the stand."[80] If the witness truly lacks recollection of the underlying event, however, there are not two versions to be explored. Any examination of the witness is a formality at best. The witness does not recall the event and therefore cannot testify concerning the truth or falsity of the prior statement.[81] Thus not only is a prior statement about a particular event not inconsistent with trial testimony confessing a true lack of recollection, the witness is also not subject to the meaningful cross-examination by the defendant concerning the subject matter of the statement that Rule 801(d)(1)(A) contemplates.[82] Accordingly, if at Sam Smith's trial John Goodfellow is truly unable to recall the man fleeing the building, even assuming his prior statement had been made before a grand jury, Sam Smith's prior statement would not be admissible as substantive evidence under Rule 801(d)(1)(A).[83]

(b) Feigned Lack of Recollection

A witness may be moved to assert lack of recollection at trial to avoid giving damaging testimony even though he or she does recall the event if, for example, the witness is intimidated by the defendant or the defendant's associates, if the witness is a friend of the defendant, or if the witness simply wants to avoid peer or community castigation as a "squealer." Wigmore expressed well the concern of courts with his observation that "the unwilling witness often takes refuge in a failure to remember, and the astute liar is sometimes impregnable unless his flank can be exposed to an attack of this sort."[84] Whether a prior statement of a witness who is sufficiently shown to have feigned a lack of recollection should be admissible as substantive evidence under Rule 801(d)(1)(A) or otherwise is a difficult issue to resolve. No one wants to reward witness intimidation. Such reward would befall the criminal defendant if the prior statement of a witness feigning lack of recollection is denied substantive admissibility. On the other hand, a criminal defendant should not be convicted for one crime on the strength of untrustworthy evidence admitted solely because the defendant has committed another crime, that is, intimidated a witness.

Several courts have undertaken to evaluate claims of lack of recollection by a party's own witness and, upon concluding that the witness was feigning lack of recollection, have developed rationales in support of substantive admissibility of the witness's prior satement.[85] Two courts, the Second Circuit in United States v. Insana[86] and the California Supreme Court in People v. Green,[87] have thoroughly addressed this question. Both courts found the prior statement admissible, but, interestingly, the courts adopted incompatible rationales for admissibility.

In *Insana* the defendant was tried and convicted of mail fraud. The government had subpoenaed Warren Schurman, a codefendant who had pled guilty, as a witness against the defendant, Peter Insana, at trial. In testimony before the grand jury and in a statement given to the United States Attorney's Office, Schurman had related in full the details of the mail-fraud scheme, including Insana's participation. At trial Schurman first "reluctantly" identified Insana and admitted having certain conversations with him. He then became unresponsive stating, "I don't want to hurt nobody" and claimed a lack of recollection of certain facts. The trial court declared Schurman a hostile witness and permitted the government to read to Schurman in the presence of the jury questions and answers from the transcript of his grand jury testimony.[88] When the government asked whether he gave those answers at the grand jury proceeding, Schurman responded vaguely: "I don't remember. . . If he has it on the record I guess I must have." Among the errors presented on appeal was the hearsay objection to the admission of Schurman's grand jury testimony as substantive evidence. In confirming the conviction, the Second Circuit reasoned as follows:

> The question presented . . . is whether former sworn testimony with respect to the facts can be considered inconsistent with a present disavowal of memory of those facts. . . . [U]nder the particular circumstances of this case we answer the question in the affirmative. . . .
>
> The conclusion that prior testimony inconsistent with a present lack of memory may be admissible as a contradiction is not a novel one. . . . The general theory of admitting a prior inconsistent statement is the cancellation of an adverse answer by which a party is surprised; however, where a witness gives no testimony injurious to the party calling him because of lack of memory, there is no reason or basis for impeachment under the rule. . . . But . . . this analysis "is not quite the whole story."
>
> Where, as here, a recalcitrant witness who has testified to one or more relevant facts indicates by his conduct that the reason for his failure to continue to so testify is not a lack of memory but a desire "not to hurt anyone," then the court has discretionary latitude in the search for truth, to admit a prior sworn statement which the witness does not in fact deny he made. . . . By conceding that his lack of memory was due to his desire not to hurt anyone, [Schurman] *impliedly admitted* the truth of the extrajudicial statements harmful to the defendant. Thus we believe that these statements are admissible not only to impeach his claim of lack of memory but also as an implied affirmaiton of the truth.[89]

Notice the reasoning behind the court's holding that Schurman's prior statements were substantively admissible: Schurman, by admitting that the motivation for his failure to testify was a desire "not to hurt anyone," impliedly admitted the truth of the prior statements. In providing this rationale for admissibility, the court without citation placed a new gloss on the common-law doctrine of adopted testimony. Under that doctrine a prior inconsistent statement offered to impeach a witness is given substantive effect if the witness actually admits in open court that the facts contained in the prior statement are true.[90] In *Insana* the Second Circuit, on the basis of a concept of implied affirmation of truth, expanded the common-law doctrine to render admissible as substantive evidence the prior statements of a witness who feigns loss of memory at trial.[91]

The court complicated its opinion by referring to the inconsistency between Schurman's prior testimony and his professed lack of recollection at trial. It is unclear whether the court regarded this inconsistency as an independent ground of substantive admissibility or merely as a justification for the admission of the prior statement to impeach Schurman's professed lack of recollection. In United States v. DeSisto, which was cited in *Insana*, the Second Circuit several years before the adoption of the Federal Rules of Evidence modified the common law by accepting as substantive evidence prior inconsistent statements made by a witness before a grnad jury and at a former trial.[92] *DeSisto*, however, provides no support for the proposition that a prior statement of fact is inconsistent with an assertion at trial of lack of recollection of the underlying event. Moreover, for the *Insana* court to have held Schurman's prior statements admissible as substantive evidence because of their inconsistency with his asserted lack of recollection at trial would have undermined the rationale the court subsequently gave for the substantive admissibility of the statements—that a witness who feigns lack of recollection impliedly admits the truth of the prior statements.

In discussing the effect of prior inconsistent statements, the court in *Insana* on occasion employed language indicating that it was considering whether the inconsistent statements could be admitted solely to impeach Schurman's professed lack of recollection. As the court concedes, however, under the common law as applied by federal courts at the time, a prior inconsistent statement not also admissible as substantive evidence could not be used to impeach a party's own witness unless the witness's testimony affirmatively damaged the party.[93] Since Schurman's purported lack of recollection was not affirmatively damaging, his prior statements could not be employed solely for the purpose of impeachment, even if they were considered inconsistent with his professed lack of recollection. The court's concluding remark that the statements were "admissible not only to impeach [Schurman's] claim of lack of memory but also as an implied affirmation of the truth"[94] can thus only mean that because the statements were substantively admissible pursuant to the adopted testimony doctrine, they could also be considered as impeaching the witness's claim of lack of recollection. Since the court had concluded that Schurman feigned lack of recollection, the jury could consider the statements for their truth as adopted testimony. The prior statements thus being admissible as substantive evidence, the jury could in turn consider the statements in determining whether Schurman was in fact feigning lack of recollection and in the process impliedly admitting the truth of his prior statements.[95]

In People v. Green[96] the California Supreme Court adopted a different approach to the problem of feigned lack of recollection. John Green was convicted of supplying marijuana to a minor, Melvin Porter. In his testimony before the grand jury and in an oral statement to a police officer, Porter asserted that defendant Green had sold him the marijuana. At trial, Porter, while admitting remembering events leading up to and following the crucial moment when he obtained possession of the marijuana, testified to a lack of recollection concerning the sale itself. The trial court admitted the statements Porter made to the officer and before the grand jury under Section 1235 of the California Evidence code, which provided that prior inconsistent statements were admissible as substantive evidence if the witness had an opportunity at trial to explain or deny the statements. Without reaching the issue whether the statements were properly admitted under the statute, the California Supreme Court reversed on the ground that defendant's Sixth Amendment right of confrontation had been violated. After the United States Supreme Court vacated that judgment and remanded on the confrontation issue,[97] the state supreme court was required to decide whether Porter's prior statements were inconsistent with his testimony at trial and therefore admissible as substantive evidence under Section 1235. The court acknowledged the general principle that when the state is examining its own witness, "testimony of [the] witness that he does not remember an event is not 'inconsistent' with a prior statement by him describing that event."[98] Finding that Porter was feigning loss of memory, however, the court stated that:

> [J]ustice will not be promoted by a ritualistic invocation of this rule of evidence. Inconsistency in effect, rather than contradiction in express terms, is the test for admitting a witness' prior statement. . . . [W]e conclude that Porter's deliberate evasion . . . in his trial testimony must be deemed to constitute an *implied denial* that defendant did in fact furnish him with the marijuana as charged. His testimony was thus materially inconsistent with . . . his extra judicial declaration to Officer Wade, in . . . which he specifically named defendant as his supplier.[99]

Having found Porter's prior statements to be inconsistent with his feigned lack of recollection at trial, the court held that the statements were properly admitted under Section 1235 as substantive evidence.

Even if a court determines that a prior statement about an event is inconsistent with what is sufficiently established to be feigned lack of recollection of the event at trial, to admit the prior statement under Rule 801(d)(1)(A) the court must also find that the witness is "subject [at trial] to cross-examination concerning the statement." When the witness testifies in court to a lack of recollection of the underlying event, however, the opportunity for effective subsequent cross-examination is not present. There are not two versions of the event to explore and the jury does not have the opportunity to observe the witness trying to explain away the inconsistency raised. Thus even if a court adopts the rationale of People v. Green to find a prior statement inconsistent with feigned lack of recollection at trial, the statement should still not be substantively admissible under Rule 801(d)(1)(A), because there is no opportunity for effective subsequent cross-examination of the witness by the defendant about the subject matter of the statement. The California Supreme Court did not feel compelled to grapple with this problem in *Green*, apparently, because Section 1235 of the California Evidence Code, unlike Rule 801(d)(1)(A), does not on its face require that the witness be subject to cross-examination.

Feigned lack of recollection most frequently if not always constitutes a tacit admission rather than a denial of the prior statement; thus the rationale of *Insana* more accurately comports with reality than does the rationale of *Green*. In *Green*, for example, Porter revealed the real motive behind his evasive testimony with the following statement: "Like I already said, I mean I've got a conscience, and I don't want to."[100] Similarly, in *Insana* Schurman confessed at one point that he did not "want to hurt nobody."[101] Ordinarily, when a witness wants to avoid giving damaging testimony because the witness has been intimidated by the defendant, is a friend of the defendant, or simply wants to avoid the consequences of being labeled a "squealer," he or she will either deny having any relevant knowledge or testify contrary to what the witness knows the facts are. When faced with a prior statement given under oath, however, feigned lack of recollection of the underlying event is the strategy best suited to avoid a future perjury prosecution. Given the facts of cases like *Green* and *Insana*, the government will undoubtedly argue to the jury that the witness's conduct should be considered an admission of the truth of the prior statement. If the jury agrees that the witness is falsifying loss of memory, it too will more likely consider the witness's testimony to be an admission rather than a denial of the statement. A court that agrees with this analysis could not admit the statement as a prior inconsistent statement under Rule 801(d)(1)(A), but it could under *Insana* determine that there is sufficient evidence that the witness is feigning lack of recollection to allow the jury to give the prior statement substantive effect as adopted testimony.[102]

Although the foregoing highlights that feigned lack of recollection clearly more often than not is consistent with prior testimony and therefore that the requirement of "subject to cross-examination concerning the statement" set forth in Rule 801(d)(1)(A) does not come into play, courts appear hesitant to adopt the *Insana* approach. Perhaps judges are reluctant to engage in a determination of the state of mind of the in-court declarant, a function normally assigned to the jury.[103] Moreover, and of critical importance, it is unusual for there to be sufficient evidence upon which the court could in good conscience decide that the prosecution has established that the witness is feigning lack of recollection when the witness does not so indicate. Most witnesses simply state "I don't remember." Few will say "I don't remember. I'm afraid, and I don't want to hurt anyone." Thus the *Insana* doctrine of adopted testimony by the establishment of feigned lack of recollection will not often become available.

In summary, a court that wants to prevent a criminal defendant from circumventing the effectiveness and integrity of the fact-finding process by simply intimidating a prosecution witness to feign a lack of recollection thus has available the approaches of *Insana* and *Green*, neither of which is entirely satisfactory. Both alternatives allow the admission of the relevant portions of prior statements of the witness as substantive evidence. Both require, however, that the judge evaluate the credibility of the witness to determine that the witness is feigning lack of recollection, a function normally reserved for the jury. To date courts for good reason appear very reluctant to apply the expanded implied adoption rationale of *Insana* to any but the most obvious instances of feigned lack of recollection at trial. On the other hand, the approach of the California Supreme Court in *Green* treating the prior statements as inconsistent contradicts the reality of the situation, since in most if not all cases of feigned lack of recollection the witness impliedly admits rather than denies his or her prior statements. In any event, such prior "inconsistent" statements of the witness will be admissible under Rule 801(d)(1)(A) only if the court somehow concludes that the witness is subject to meaningful cross-examination at trial. Any finding that a witness who claims lack of recollection of the subject matter of his or her alleged prior inconsistent statement is "subject to cross-examination concerning the statement" would be contrary to the intent of the Federal Rules of Evidence and a travesty of justice. As clearly stated in Rule 804(a)(3), a declarant who "testifies to a lack of memory of the subject matter of his statement" is "unavailable as a witness." A declarant who is "unavailable as a witness" is obviously not "subject to cross-examination concerning the statement" as required by Rule 801(d)(1)(A).[104]

D. FEDERAL RULE OF EVIDENCE 803(24)

At common law a hearsay statement not meeting a traditional hearsay exception is inadmissible. No general provision exists for the admissibility of a trustworthy and necessary hearsay statement falling outside of all specifically recognized pigeonhole-class type exceptions. The Federal Rules of Evidence depart from the common law by providing two "other [hearsay] exceptions." Rules 803(24) and 804(b)(5) permit introduction of hearsay statements possessing circumstantial guarantees of trustworthiness that are equivalent to those present with respect to the specifically enumerated class type exceptions. Rule 804(b)(5) is identical to Rule 803(24) with the sole exception that Rule 804(b)(5) requires that the declarant be unavailable at trial. Rule 803(24) does not exclude the following hearsay statements:

The following are not excluded by the hearsay rule, even though the declarant is available as a witness:

* * *

(24) Other Exceptions. A statement not specifically covered by any of the foregoing exceptions but having equivalent circumstantial guarantees of trustworthiness, if the court determines that (A) the statement is offered as evidence of a material fact; (B) the statement is more probative on the point for which it is offered than any other evidence which the proponents can procure through reasonable efforts, and (C) the general purposes of these rules and the interests of justice will best be served by admission of the statement into evidence. However, a statement may not be admitted under this exception unless the proponent of it makes known to the adverse party sufficiently in advance of the trial or hearing to provide the adverse party with a fair opportunity to prepare to meet it, his intention to offer the statement and the particulars of it, including the name and address of the declarant.

Exceptions contained within Rule 803 include those hearsay statements that have been considered sufficiently trustworthy to be admissible without requiring imposition of the time and expense associated with the production of an available declarant or in spite of the fact that the declarant of the statement actually testifies at trial. Thus a party proposing to introduce a prior statement pursuant to Rule 803(24) need not actually call an available declarant. Moreover, statements meeting the requirements of a Rule 803 hearsay exception, including Rule 803(24), are also admissible if the declarant is unavailable. Nevertheless, since Rule 804(b)(5) is identical to Rule 803(24) with the exception of the fact that the declarant *must* be unavailable, statements of an unavailable declarant are traditionally considered under the "other [hearsay] exception" of Rule 804(b)(5) and not under Rule 803(24).

Rule 803(24) contains five express requirements, all of which must be determined by the court to have been satisfied before the statement may be admitted. The requirement that the statement be offered as evidence of a material fact probably means that not only must the fact the statement is offered to prove be relevant but that the fact be of substantial importance in determining the outcome of the litigation.[105] Introduction of the hearsay statement must be necessary by being more probative on the point for which it is offered than any other evidence that the proponent may reasonably procure. Whether a particular effort to procure alternative proof of a matter may reasonably be demanded must depend upon the fact at issue considered in the context of the litigation.[106] The requirement that the general purposes of the rules of evidence and the interests of justice be best served by admission of the statement into evidence is of little practical importance in determining admissibility. In addition, a hearsay statement may not be admitted under the "other [hearsay] exception" of Rule 803(24) unless the proponent of it makes known to the adverse party, sufficiently in advance of the trial or hearing to provide the adverse party with a fair opportunity to prepare to meet it, the proponent's intention to offer the statement and the particulars of it, including the name and address of the declarant. Finally, the requirement of "equivalent circumstantial guarantees of trustworthiness" requires that the court undertake a search for trustworthiness—trustworthiness equivalent to that possessed by statements falling within the enumerated hearsay exceptions of Rule 803.

Mississippi v. Durham,[107] a case decided before adoption of the Federal Rules of Evidence, illustrates the need to give effect to Rule 803(24). In *Durham* the daughter of a Mr. Wood brought an action against the county sheriff to recover for the death of her father. Sheriff Durham had arrested Wood for driving in a "well-intoxicated" condition. After the arrest the sheriff took Wood to jail. Testimony at trial conflicted concerning whether subsequently Wood became ill or Durham beat him. Critical to the determination was a tape recording of a conversation between a deputy sheriff and Eddie Brooks, a trusty at the jail when Durham arrested Wood. In the recording Brooks stated to the deputy sheriff that he had seen Wood physically abused at the jail. Knowing that Brooks would deny the facts stated in the taped conversation, Wood's daughter called him to the stand. The trial court overruled Durham's objection that the daughter was impeaching her own witness and permitted introduction of the tapes solely for impeachment. The Fifth Circuit, in reversing a jury verdict for the plaintiff, reiterated its position that a party could not call a witness whose testimony the party knew would be adverse in order to use the guise of impeachment to get the substance of the witness's prior statement before the jury.[108]

If *Durham* had risen under the Federal Rules of Evidence, the tape recording would undoubtedly have been declared admissible as substantive evidence under Rule 803(24). No real question existed with respect to the making of the statement or the accuracy of reporting. Because Brooks had nothing to gain by making such a statement to a deputy sheriff, the circumstances of its making provided clear evidence of trustworthiness. The statement indicated Brooks's personal knowledge of the events—he saw Wood physically abused. Probative value, necessity for introduction, assurance of truthworthiness based upon certainty of making and the totality of surrounding circumstances, including the corroborating facts and an assessment of credibility, and the interests of justice all compel introduction of such a statement as substantive evidence.

An important application of Rule 803(24) can be found in United States v. Iaconetti.[109] In *Iaconetti* Judge Weinstein at trial applied Rule 803(24) as an alternative basis for the admission of a witness's prior consistent statements.[110] The defendant was convicted of solicitation, acceptance of a bribe, and extortion. The government had recorded conversations in which the defendant had solicited a bribe from Michael Lioi; the defendant attempted at trial to explain away the conversations as a practical joke.[111] To rebut this explanation, the prosecution offered two witnesses to recount statements Lioi had made to them following his conversations with defendant. Because Lioi also testified at the trial, Judge Weinstein applied Rule 803(24) rather than Rule 804(b)(5) as the alternative basis for his holding that the testimony of the two rebuttal witnesses was properly admitted.

Noting that application of Rule 803(24) requires careful exercise of discretion, Judge Weinstein found that all requirements of that rule were met on the facts of *Iaconetti.* That the declarant, Lioi, was available for cross-examination, that he made the statements to the two witnesses minutes after being offered the bribe, and that the witnesses were a business partner and attorney of Lioi all minimized the risk of faulty memory and insincerity. Equivalent circumstantial guarantees of trustworthiness were thus present. Judge Weinstein deemphasized the requirement that the hearsay statements be evidence of a material fact as being literally only a restatement of the relevance requirement. Concluding that the materiality requirement must have been meant to exclude trivial statements, Judge Weinstein found that the materiality requirement was met in *Iaconetti* because the witnesses's testimony was of great importance in rebutting defendant's explanation of the conversations with Lioi. Because of the direct conflict at trial between the defendant's and Lioi's explanations of those conversations, evidence of the immediate reaction of Lioi to the conversations was the most probative evidence reasonably available to resolve the conflict. The general purpose of the rules and the interests of justice were served by admission of the statements because the jury needed the evidence to resolve the conflict of credibility. Finally, Judge Weinstein found that notice given after the trial began and just five days before the witnesses were called was sufficient, because the need for the testimony was not apparent until that time.[112]

In United States v. Leslie[113] the Fifth Circuit relied on Judge Weinstein's interpretation of Rule 803(24) to hold admissible several witnesses's prior inconsistent statements. Defendant was convicted of the interstate transportation and sale of a stolen vehicle. At trial, upon the government's request, the court called three alleged accomplices who testified that the defendant did not know the car was stolen. The prosecution impeached this testimony with inconsistent written statements that the witnesses had given the FBI following their arrests. Although the witnesses admitted making the prior statements, they denied the truth of some of the statements and testified that they could not recall whether parts of others were true. Two of the three further testified to being under the influence of drugs when they gave the statements, and all three said they expected favorable treatment for their cooperation with the FBI. The government introduced evidence to show that the statements were freely given, without promise of reward and uninfluenced by drugs.

The court reviewed *Iaconetti* carefully before concluding that the jury could properly consider the witnesses's prior inconsistent statements as substantive evidence pursuant to Rule 803(24).[114] The requirement of "equivalent circumstantial guarantees of trustworthiness" was met because of the strong indicia of trustworthiness for each of the statements. The court deemed "most significant" that the witnesses admitted making the statements.[115] In addition, the statements were substantially identical despite having been given only a few hours after arrest and before the witnesses had had an opportunity to agree on a single story. Moreover, the witnesses were available at trial for cross-examination about the statements. The court, perhaps too lightly, discounted the witness's mere "hope" of better police treatment in exchange for favorable statements. Finally, the court found the evidence that the witnesses were under the influence of drugs unconvincing in light of the testimony of agents and others who dealt with the witnesses when they made the statements.

The Fifth Circuit in *Leslie* easily found that the other four requirements of Rule 803(24) were also met. The statements were evidence of important facts concerning the ride. The statements were more probative on this issue than any other evidence the prosecutor could reasonably produce, because only the four persons who committed the theft knew what had been planned. The direct conflict within each witness's story justified the conclusion that introduction of the statements best served the interests of justice. The court excused noncompliance with the notice requirement on the ground that defendant had not been harmed.[116]

The leading opinions in *Iaconetti* and *Leslie* demonstrate[117] that in determining whether the "equivalent circumstantial guarantees of trustworthiness" required by Rule 803(24) for admissibility of hearsay statements are present, four criteria will be applied: (1) certainty that the statement was made;[118] (2) assurance of personal knowledge of the declarant of the underlying event;[119] (3) practical availability of the declarant at trial for meaningful cross-examination concerning the underlying event;[120] and finally, (4) an ad hoc ascertainment of trustworthiness based upon the totality of the surrounding circumstances including corroborating facts and an assessment of credibility of the declarant, considered in light of the class type exceptions to the hearsay rule supposed to demonstrate such characteristics. Relevant factors bearing upon such an ad hoc ascertainment of trustworthiness include the declarant's partiality, that is, interest, bias, corruption, or coercion; the presence or absence of time to fabricate; and suggestiveness brought on by the use of leading questions.

As so interpreted, Rule 803(24) permits the introduction of some statements not given in a formal proceeding, a requirement for admissibility under Rule 801(d)(1)(A). As so interpreted, Rule 803(24), however, still requires that the declarant be available at trial and subject to meaningful cross-examination. Thus Rule 803(24) does not extend to the statements given by either John Goodfellow, Jim James, or Bob Williams in our hypothetical case; none of these individuals is available to testify at trial subject to meaningful cross-examination. As applied to Mary Mahoney's statement, Rule 803(24) would probably not permit introduction. Although Mary Mahoney is available at trial, there may be a substantial question about the certainty of making of her statement. Her statement was not tape recorded as was John Goodfellow's. Rather, Mary Mahoney allegedly gave only an oral statement to a police officer. At trial Mary Mahoney may deny making the statement claimed by the police officer. There is also an absence of corroborating facts establishing that Mary Mahoney's oral statement, if made, identifying the person leaving the building as Sam Smith was accurate. The opportunity Mary Mahoney had to observe the person fleeing the building is questionable. Such factors coupled with the different description given by Mary Mahoney at trial make it unlikely that a court would find the prosecution has established that the alleged oral statement possesses the equivalent circumstantial guarantees of trustworthiness required by Rule 803(24). Finally, Mary Mahoney's statement of identification may not be sufficiently probative in light of other available evidence. If the statement of either Jim James or Bob Williams is admitted, Mary Mahoney's statement may not add enough to the prosecution's case to warrant application of Rule 803(24). Conversely, if neither of these witnesses statements is admissible, a person leaving the building at a relevant time may not, taken alone, be sufficiently "material" to warrant application of Rule 803(24).

E. FEDERAL RULE OF EVIDENCE 804(b)(5)

Rule 804 sets forth exceptions to the hearsay rule applicable only when the declarant is unavailable. *Unavailability* as defined in Rule 804(a) relates to the unavailability of the testimony of the witness at trial.[121]

Definition of Unavailability. "Unavailability as a witness" includes situations in which the declarant—

(1) is exempted by ruling of the court on the ground of privilege from testifying concerning the subject matter of his statement; or

(2) persists in refusing to testify concerning the subject matter of his statement despite an order of the court to do so; or

(3) testifies to a lack of memory of the subject matter of his statement; or

(4) is unable to be present or to testify at the hearing because of death or then existing physical or mental illness or infirmity; or

(5) is absent from the hearing and the proponent of his statement has been unable to procure his attendance (or in the case of a hearsay exception under subdivision (b)(2), (3) or (4), his attendance or testimony) by process or other reasonable means.

A declarant is not unavailable as a witness if his exemption, refusal, claim of lack of memory, inability, or absence is due to the procurement or wrongdoing of the proponent of his statement for the purpose of preventing the witness from attending or testifying.

Rule 804(b)(5) creates an exception for the hearsay statement of an unavailable witness that does not fall within one of the specific exceptions contained in Rule 804(b) if the hearsay statement meets the following requirements: (1) it has "equivalent circumstantial guarantees of trustworthiness"; (2) it is "evidence of a material fact"; (3) it is "more probative on the point for which it is offered" than any other reasonably available evidence; (4) admission of the statement would promote the interests of justice and the purpose of the federal evidence rules; and (5) the proponent notifies the opposing party of his or her intention to offer the statement sufficiently in advance of the trial to allow the opponent to meet the statement. As previously mentioned, the requirements of Rule 804(b)(5) are identical to those specified in Rule 803(24) except that the declarant under Rule 804(b)(5) must be unavailable. The unavailability of the declarant strongly suggests that a court require greater circumstantial indications of trustworthiness under Rule 804(b)(5) than under Rule 803(24), because cross-examination to test the trustworthiness of the statement is not possible. The cases evidence a trend toward this position.

In United States v. Carlson,[122] the Eighth Circuit held admissible under Rule 804(b)(5) prior statements of a witness who was practically unavailable at trial, having asserted his Fifth Amendment rights. Defendants were convicted of distributing and conspiring to distribute cocaine. James Tindall testified before the grand jury that he had purchased cocaine from one defendant and sold it to the other, but he refused to testify at trial. The Eighth Circuit held that under these circumstances the district court's admission of the grand jury testimony pursuant to Rule 804(b)(5) was proper. According to the appellate court, the requirements specified in Rule 804(b)(5) mandate that the court undertake a two-part inquiry into the trustworthiness of the statement and the necessity for its admission at trial. As to the first inquiry, the court found strong indicia of trustworthiness in Tindall's grand jury testimony. Tindall had firsthand knowledge of the cocaine transactions about which he testified because he had participated in them. Additionally, at trial Tindall reaffirmed that he had told the truth during his grand jury testimony. As to the second inquiry, the court found the necessity for admitting the testimony substantial, becaue there were no other witnesses to the cocaine transaction between Tindall and defendant Donald Carlson.

As in *Iaconetti* and *Leslie*, little difficulty was encountered in *Carlson* in finding that the other requirements of the hearsay exception were met. Tindall's grand jury testimony was evidence of the material fact that defendant acted with intent and knowledge in distributing and conspiring to distribute cocaine. The trustworthiness of the grand jury testimony combined with its necessity compelled the conclusion that admission of the testimony into evidence at trial served the interests of justice. Finally, the court cited *Iaconetti* for the proposition that notice given during trial is permissible in the proper circumstances. The circumstances were proper in *Carlson* because the government notified the defendant when it became apparent that Tindall woulds not testify. Moreover, the defendant was not prejudiced by the delayed notice having been advised two days before the admission of the testimony in evidence.

Notably absent in *Carlson* was corroborating evidence of the underlying circumstances, the cocaine transaction. The court in *Carlson* was willing to accept Tindall's reaffirmation at trial that he had told the truth before the grand jury as sufficient corroborative indicia of trustworthiness. Absent such affirmation, as is the case with the unavailable declarants in our hypothetical case, other courts have focused on the existence of corroborating testimony of other witnesses concerning the underlying events.[123] Even if some such corroboration exists, courts have often refused to declare a prior statement to be sufficiently trustworthy if either the circumstances of its making involve governmental pressure likely to have made the declarant partial by reason of self-interest or suggestiveness in the taking of the prior statement through the use of leading questions is shown.[124]

United States v. Boulahanis[125] stresses the importance of evidence providing sufficient corroborating indicia of trustworthiness as to a hearsay statement offered under Rule 804(b)(5). In *Boulahanis* appellants were convicted of extortion. Appellants and one Frank Renella appeared at a Greek social club in Chicago where they proceeded to beat up the owner, Nick Velentzas. Velentzas went to the FBI the next day and was outfitted with a tape recorder. That night Velentzas was able to tape record a conversation in which the appellants and Renella told Velentzas to pay $300 for the last month and an additional $500 for each month thereafter. Only then would they leave Velentzas alone and also prevent others from bothering him. Several days later Renella turned himself into the FBI and made statements incriminating himself and the appellants. In addition to this evidence, one James Chiampas, a bystander at the club, testified at the grand jury that he saw the appellants and Renella beat up Velentzas.

By the time of trial, Velentzas had been murdered by persons unknown, and Renella had fled, possibly fearing for his life. Chiampas was subpoened for trial even though he had told the goverment he would not testify because he was afraid of being killed. At the trial Chiampas refused to testify although ordered twice by the court to do so. The trial court admitted Chiampas's grand jury testimony but refused to admit Renella's statements. The tape recording of the conversation at the social club made by Velentzas was also admitted in evidence.[126]

The defendants appealed, asserting that admission of the grand jury testimony of Chiampas was in error.[127] The Seventh Circuit upheld the admission of the grand jury testimony pursuant to Rule 804(b)(5) after first finding the testimony sufficiently trustworthy and "more probative on the point for which it is offered than any other evidence which the proponent can reasonably procure."[128] As to the finding of trustworthiness, the court stressed that Chiampas voluntarily testified at the grand jury, he lacked a motive to falsify, and that his testimony was corroborated by other evidence.

Chiampas had testified before the grand jury under oath of course, and hence subject to being prosecuted if he perjured himself, but also, far as appears, without having been pressured to testify. It is conceded that he was a disinterested witness—a mere bystander, with no axe to grind. And his testimony was corroborated at every point by the tape of the conversation, and on most points by testimony of eyewitnesses as well as including Scalise [one of the appellants].[129]

The court recognized that the corroboration available undermined the condition that the evidence be more probative than other evidence; that is, "the taped conversation provided all the evidence the government needed to show extortion by the appellants."[130] The court, however, stated that the rule did not require that evidence be essential as long as the evidence was the "most probative evidence reasonably available on a material issue in the case."[131] The court found the evidence to be such, for it was important for the government to show that the appellants had beaten up Velentzas the night before the tape-recorded conversation. Chiampas testimony was thus "material" to prove that the taped conversation was extortionate and not a business transaction. Finally, at the time offered, the government did not know that one of the appellants would testify to the fight.

United States v. Bailey[132] represents a well-written analysis rejecting as insufficient the corroborative evidence offered to indicate trustworthiness. In *Bailey* the defendant appealed his conviction for armed bank robbery alleging reversible error because the trial court admitted a written statement of a witness who refused to testify at trial. Two men had robbed a bank. Witnesses at the robbery were unable to identify Milton Bailey at trial as one of the men, although two witnesses had identified him earlier from a photographic display. The other man, Johnny Stewart, was identified from palm prints left at the scene of the crime. Stewart negotiated a plea that required him to furnish a statement concerning the robbery. Stewart gave two oral statements, one of which was transcribed and signed by Stewart acknowledging its veracity. At trial Stewart refused to testify even after being ordered to do so. The government then asked the court to permit introduction of the written statement pursuant to Rule 804(b)(3)[133] or Rule 804(b)(5). The trial court permitted introduction of the written statement pursuant to Rule 804(b)(5).

On appeal the defendant claimed that the requirements of Rule 804(b)(5) were not satisfied because notice of intent to offer the written statement was not given until after the trial commenced and because the statement did not possess guarantees of trustworthiness equivalent to other hearsay exceptions under Rule 804(b). The Third Circuit agreed with the Eighth Circuit's opinion in *Carlson* that notice at trial was sufficient provided "the proponent of the evidence is without fault in failing to notify his adversary prior to trial and the trial judge has offered sufficient time, by means of granting a continuance, for the party against whom the evidence is to be offered to prepare to meet and contest its admission."[134] In *Bailey* the government could not foresee Stewart's refusal to testify; the trial court had also offered defense counsel time to conduct interviews and review evidentiary questions.

The Third Circuit, however, did agree with the defendant that the written statement did not possess sufficient circumstantial guarantees of trustworthiness. The trial court had admitted the statement because of one corroborated fact. Other evidence showed that the bank robbers fled in Bailey's girlfriend's car. The statement of Stewart mentioned that Stewart and Bailey traveled to a city in that car. The appellate court did not find this single fact to be sufficient.[135] Moreover, the court held that trustworthiness of a statement should not be based solely on the existence of corroborating facts but also by evaluating "the circumstances in which the declarant made the statement and the incentive he had to speak truthfully or falsely."[136] The court found that the statement was not sufficiently established to be trustworthy in light of the fact that the statement was made as part of a negotiation for a reduction in charges during a face-to-face meeting with two FBI agents.

An unusual application of Rule 804(b)(5) highlighting the importance of the opportunity to acquire personal knowledge and the absence of time within which the declarant could fabricate his or her prior statement occurred in United States v. Medico.[137] *Medico* involved the introduction under Rule 804(b)(5) of an unknown bystander's report of the license plate of a fleeing car used by escaping bank robbers. An unknown bystander had given the number to a customer of the bank on the street. That customer immediately relayed the information through the bank door to Carmody, a bank employee. Carmody wrote the number down on his checkbook. The court stated:

> The two unavailable witnesses were at the scene of the crime. One was in position to perceive and describe the car and license plate number the robbers used to effect their escape; and while the other did not claim to have himself observed the car or the license plate, he relayed to Carmody that information just told to him by the first bystander who personally had seen the robbers drive away in the getaway car. The time frame in which the information was passed from the eyewitness to the bank customer and then from the customer to Carmody was very brief and followed the actual getaway so closely, that the likelihood of inaccuracies is small and the possibility that truth was undercut by speculation or fabrication reduced. The probability that the information was accurate is enhanced by the fact that Carmody transcribed it onto his checkbook as it was being told him.[138]

Thus in *Medico* the Second Circuit concluded that a statement by a noninvolved bystander likely to possess personal knowledge made within such a short time frame after the incident sufficiently reduced the risk of faulty memory and the chance of fabrication to warrant a finding that the statement possessed sufficient indicia of trustworthiness.

Inferences arising from governmental pressure and suggestiveness in the taking of the witness's prior statement may also play a prominent role in the court's decision about whether the particular statement possesses adequate assurance of trustworthiness. For example, in United States v. Gonzalez,[139] the unavailable declarant was arrested while attempting to import marijuana across the border by truck. At the time of his arrest, Rugelio Guerrero stated he had been hired by a Mexican, but he would not identify the man. After his own conviction for possession of marijuana, he was called before the grand jury. Faced with prolonged confinement for contempt if he refused to testify, Guerrero answered leading questions of the prosecutor that suggested that the person who hired him was the defendant, Ramiro Gonzalez. At Gonzalez's trial, however, Guerrero refused to testify, although he had already been convicted, given immunity, and ordered to do so. The trial court admitted the grand jury testimony pursuant to Rule 804(b)(5). The Fifth Circuit reversed[140] on the ground that the statement failed to possess "equivalent guarantees of trustworthiness," because the government pressured the witness with threats of unlimited number of contempt proceedings at the grand jury and then used leading questions suggesting the proper responses.[141]

In our hypothetical case, with respect to the three witnesses whose testimony proved unavailable at trial, only John Goodfellow is an uninterested bystander whose statement describing the events of July 14, 1984 was preserved in a manner providing sufficient assurance of certainty of making. His statement describing a person fitting Sam Smith's description leaving the building is corroborated by Mary Mahoney's earlier oral statement and by Jim James's and Bob Williams's subsequent adequately preserved statements. Unless either the statement of Jim James or Bob Williams is admitted, however, John Goodfellow's statement would not be particularly probative. Merely identifying a man fitting Sam Smith's description as leaving the building is not highly probative as to his having committed the crime in a second floor apartment. Whether merely placing a person fitting Sam Smith's description at the scene would be considered sufficiently "material" within the meaning of Rule 804(b)(5) to warrant admission under the "other exception" is unclear. On the other hand, if either Jim James's or Bob Williams's statement is admissible, John Goodfellow's statement may not be more probative on any material issue than other available evidence. Given the nature of both Jim James and Bob Williams's statements specificially incriminating Sam Smith, John Goodfellow's statement adds little if anything to the prosecution's case.

Jim James's and Bob Williams's statements corroborate each other and are corroborated in part by the statements of John Goodfellow and Mary Mahoney. However, neither Jim James nor Bob Williams are disinterested occurrence witnesses. Each one was at risk with respect to possible criminal charges arising from the busted drug deal. Moreover, each one would have an incentive to incriminate another for the murder to remove suspicion from himself. Each one would thus have an incentive to finger someone for the murder in exchange for a plea bargain or total immunity on the drug charges even if he did not know who did the shooting. The position of Jim James and Bob Williams also made them vulnerable to pressure form the government to cooperate in the more important murder investigation or face vigorous prosecution on the drug charges. The statements by both Jim James and Bob Williams occurred well after the event, thus presenting each sufficient time for fabrication. The two also had time and opportunity to confer on a story before the police arrived. The grand jury testimony given by Bob Wiliams may have been designed specifically to corroborate Jim James's story. In addition, the statement of Jim James was during a face-to-face interrogation by the police while the statement of Bob Williams was made before the grand jury. The police in interrogating witnesses and the prosecuting attorney before the grand jury often proceed by the use of leading questions. Both statements thus raise concern over suggestiveness introduced by government use of leading questions eliciting responses from a witness obviously possessing a motive to cooperate with the questioner for his own ends. Moreover, as a practical matter, neither the police nor the prosecuting attorney possesses substantial reason to question the witness to insure adequacy of opportunity to perceive. Given the foregoing, a court is unlikely to find that the prosecution has made a sufficient showing of "equivalent circumstantial guarantees of trustworthiness" with respect to any of the statements of the three unavailable declarants implicating Sam Smith to satisfy Rule 804(b)(5).[142]

F. PRIOR STATEMENT OF IDENTIFICATION

1. The Prerequisites

An out-of-court statement made by a declarant after perceiving an individual identifying the individual as the person who had performed an act, usually committing a crime, falls squarely within the definition of hearsay. Nevertheless, at common law the general unsatisfactory and inconclusive nature of courtroom identifications, compared with those made out of court under less suggestive circumstances, resulted in many courts admitting prior statements of identification of a witness to corroborate the witness's in-court identification. The recent trend at common law has been to treat a statement of prior identification of an out-of-court declarant who also testifies in court as substantive evidence not barred by the hearsay rule on the ground that the declarant is in court, under oath, before the trier of fact, and subject to cross-examination. Rule 801(d)(1)(C) of the Federal Rules of Evidence is in accord with this recent trend:

(d) Statements which are not hearsay. A statement is not hearsay if—

(1) Prior statement by witness. The declarant testifies at the trial or hearing and

is subject to cross-examination concerning the statement, and the statement is—(C) one of identification of a person made after perceiving him.

Under Rule 801(d)(1)(C), when a witness testifies and is subject to cross-examination, the witness's prior statement is defined as "not hearsay" and thus not barred by operation of the hearsay rule, when it is one identifying a person made after perceiving the subject, usually at a lineup, at a one-on-one viewing often called a showup, in a photograph, in a sketch, or at a prior hearing. The concept of "after perceiving him" refers to perceiving the individual or a representation of the person once again after the event in question.[143] Thus Rule 801(d)(1)(C) is not limited to identification following corporal perception but applies as well to photographs and sketches.[144] The rule has no requirement that the witness first be impeached. The theory is that courtroom identification is so unconvincing as practically to impeach itself, thus justifying the corroboration.[145] The purpose of Rule 801(d)(1)(C) is to "permit the introduction of [more meaningful] identifications made by a witness when memory was fresher and there had been less opportunity for influence to be exerted upon him."[146] The circumstances of the prior identification may be considered by the trier of fact in determining the weight to be accorded.

Rule 801(d)(1)(C) only requires that the person who made the identification testify at the trial or hearing and be subject to cross-examination. It seems reasonable to assume that the rule also contemplates that the declarant will testify in court on the subject of identification and not simply be available to be recalled to the stand by the defendant for cross-examination. Rule 801(d)(1)(C) does not limit testimony establishing the statement of identification made after perception solely to that of the identifying witness. Testimony of any person who was present, for example, a police officer, is admissible.[147] However, because overproof may mislead the jury by unduly emphasizing the prior identification, the number of persons who may testify to the prior identification rests in the discretion of the court.

Rule 801(d)(1)(C) does not require on its face, nor has a requirement been imposed, that the identifying witness make a positive in-court identification or that the witness identify the defendant in court at all.[148] Moreover, nothing in the text of the rule prohibits introduction of an out-of-court statement identifying the defendant made by a declarant who in court denies that the defendant is the person involved in the crime. In addition, Rule 801(d)(1)(C) permits introduction of evidence about a statement of prior identification of a witness who fails to recall at trial whom it is he or she previously identified or who at trial denies having made the prior statement of identification. Finally, although it may be argued that a witness who lacks current recollection of the identity of the individual who had performed the act in issue, whether such lack of recollection is real or feigned, is not "subject to cross-examination concerning the statement" as required by Rule 801(d)(1),[149] legislative history nevertheless indicates at least some support for applicability of Rule 801(d)(1)(C) even in this context.[150]

In summary, the text and legislative history of Rule 801(d)(1)(C) place no restrictions upon admissibility provided the alleged out-of-court declarant is in court available to be cross-examined concerning the statement.[151] Thus in our hypothetical case, even though John Goodfellow testifies at trial that he does not recall seeing anyone leave the building and that he did not identify anyone at the lineup, any person present at the lineup, in particular a police officer, may testify that John Goodfellow identified Sam Smith. Moreover, the testimony of the police officer is received as substantive evidence. The position advocated in the legislative history and adopted by the courts stems in great part from a concern that a witness's failure positively to identify the accused in court may be the direct result of intimidation by the accused or the accused's friends against the witness designed to cause the witness to change his or her testimony.[152]

2. Critique

Contrary to the current position taken by the courts, it is suggested that when the witness is unable positively to identify the defendant in court, the rationale supporting Rule 801(d)(1)(C) fails to apply. Rule 801(d)(1)(C)'s treatment of prior statements of identification as "not hearsay" rests upon the need to introduce evidence supportive of the witness's positive in-court identification by virtue of the self-impeaching character of an in-court identification and the availability of the declarant for meaningful cross-examination concerning identification of the accused both before and in court. When the witness fails to make a positive in-court identification, the rationale for "not hearsay" treatment is thus inapplicable.[153] Moreover, Congress expressed deep concern that certainty of making, accuracy of reporting, and circumstantial guarantees of trustworthiness accompany the admission as substantive evidence of out-of-court statements of in-court witnesses, whether offered under Rule 801(d)(1)(A) or Rules 803(24 and 804(b)(5). Such concern applies with equal force to a prior statement of a witness offered under Rule 801(d)(1)(C). It is suggested that the fact that in some instances pressure may have been placed upon the witness to alter his or her in-court testimony is an insufficient justification to permit blanket admissibility under Rule 801(d)(1)(C).

Rule 801(d)(1)(C) should apply only when the witness makes a positive in-court identification, thereby making the out-of-court declaration a prior consistent statement.[154] When the alleged out-of-court statement is not a prior consistent statement, it is suggested that blanket admissibility is neither mandated by the language of Rule 801(d)(1)(C) nor warranted. Certainty of making, accuracy of reporting, and circumstantial guarantees of trustworthiness in the particular case need to be established before the statement of identification after perception should be admitted as substantive evidence against the criminal defendant. Accordingly, when the witness fails for any reason to make a positive in-court identification, the admissibility of an alleged prior statement of the declarant identifying the defendant after perceiving the defendant ought to be governed by other rules. Thus if the witness denies that the accused is the perpetrator of the offense, principles regarding impeachment of a party's own witness under Rule 607,[155] principles relating to introduction as substantive evidence of a prior inconsistent statement as provided by Rule 801(d)(1)(A),[156] and principles associated with the "other [hearsay] exception" of Rule 803(24)[157] should govern admissibility of the alleged prior statement of identification.[158] When the witness claims lack of recollection about the identity of the perpetrator, admissibility of the alleged prior statement of identification should be governed by the "other [hearsay] exception" contained in Rule 804(b)(5).[159]

3. Constitutional Considerations

With respect to prior identification of the criminal defendant, various constitutional safeguards must be satisfied before an out-of-court identification may be introduced at trial at common law to corroborate or under Rule 801(d)(1)(C) as substantive evidence. Initially, if a corporal identification, whether at a lineup or a showup, is conducted at or after the instigation of adversary judicial criminal proceedings, the accused is entitled to the presence of counsel. As provided by the Supreme Court in United States v. Wade[160] and Gilbert v. California,[161] failure to provide counsel renders the pretrial identification inadmissible. In-court identification of the defendant when counsel was not provided as required will be excluded, unless the prosecution establishes by clear and convincing evidence that the in-court identification was based upon the observation of the suspect other than at a lineup or showup. Among the factors to be considered in making this determination are the prior opportunity to observe the alleged criminal act, the existence of any discrepancy between any prelineup description and the defendant's actual description, any identification before a lineup of another person, a picture identification of the defendant before the lineup, failure to identify the defendant on a prior occasion, and the lapse of time between the alleged act and the lineup identification. The right to counsel announced in *Wade* and *Gilbert* attaches only to corporal identifications. There is no requirement of defense counsel when the witness views police or prosecution photographs or sketches.[162]

With respect to lineups, showups, and photographic or sketch identifications, the requirements of due process must also be met before the prior identification may be admitted. The pretrial identification procedure may not be suggestive unless required by the exigencies of the circumstances.[163] Admitting testimony concerning a suggestive identification not required by the exigencies of the circumstances does not violate due process, however, as long as the identification possesses sufficient reliability so that there is not a very substantial likelihood of misidentification. Factors considered in determining reliability include the opportunity of the witness to view the criminal at the time of the crime, the witness's degree of attention, the accurcy of the witness's prior description of the criminal, the level of certainty demonstrated at the confrontation, and the time between the crime and the confrontation. Against these factors weighs the corrupting effect of the suggestive identification itself. If application of the foregoing standard excludes the pretrial identification, an in-court identification will not be permitted if the pretrial procedure was so impermissibly suggestive as to create a very substantial likelihood of irreparable misidentification.[164]

G. PAST RECOLLECTION RECORDED

A prior statement of a witness who claims lack of recollection at trial of the subject matter of the statement may fall within the common law hearsay exception for past recollection recorded, known as recorded recollection under Rule 803(5) of the Federal Rules of Evidence. For example, in United States v. Williams,[165] the Sixth Circuit permitted the introduction as past recollection recorded of a statement prepared by a government agent, recording the oral statement of the declarant, repeating an alleged admission of the defendant. The written statement was signed and sworn to by the declarant. In *Williams* the defendant was charged with cashing government checks bearing forged endorsements. The only issue at trial was whether the defendant intentionally cashed the checks knowing they bore false endorsements. A witness, Gary Ball, testified that he did not then recall whether the defendant had ever told him where he had received the checks that were cashed at Ball's junkyard. In an earlier conversation with a special agent, however, Ball claimed that the defendant had told him that he, the defendant, had obtained the checks before the payees received their mail. The special agent wrote out Ball's statement, which Ball then attested and signed. At trial Ball testified that when he had spoken with the special agent, his conversation with Williams was fresh in his mind and that his signed statement was a true and correct statement at that time. The trial court permitted Ball's signed statement to be admitted as recorded recollection under Rule 803(5). On appeal the Sixth Circuit affirmed.

Rule 803(5) provides as follows:

> The following are not excluded by the hearsay rule, even though the declarant is available as a witness:
>
> * * *
>
> (5) Recorded Recollection. A memorandum or record concerning a matter about which a witness once had knowledge but now has insufficient recollection to enable him to testify fully and accurately, shown to have been made or adopted by the witness when the matter was fresh in his memory and to reflect that knowledge correctly. If admitted, the memorandum or record may be read into evidence but may not itself be received as an exhibit unless offered by an adverse party.

The hearsay exception for recorded recollection provided by Rule 803(5) requires that the witness at trial testify that the statement was accurate when made or, if the witness has entirely forgotten the exact situation in which the recording was made, that the witness is confident from the circumstances that he or she would not have written or adopted such description of the facts unless that description truly described the witness's observations at the time.[166] Moreover, the proponent of the statement must establish that the witness once had personal knowledge of the matter stated.[167]

In instances of the truly forgetful witness, the testimony of the in-court witness may satisfy these requirements.[168] However, in instances of feigned forgetfulness caused by witness intimidation, witnesses whose prior statements were recorded will not testify at trial to the effect that they remember now having personal knowledge then but that they do not recall now what they knew then. The intimidated witness will simply testify to an absence of recollection including an absence of recollection as to the state of the witness's personal knowledge when the recorded statement was made. Thus John Goodfellow can prevent the introduction of the tape recording of his statement under the hearsay exception for recorded recollection by claiming at trial that he does not remember being outside the building and he does not now recall that when he made the recorded statement he had personal knowledge of the matters stated. In short, Rule 803(b)(5) will not permit admission of the prior recorded statement of an occurrence witness when the occurrence witness has been intimidated to hide behind a total veil of forgetfulness.

H. CONFRONTATION CLAUSE ISSUES

The Confrontation Clause of the Sixth Amendment provides that "[i]n all criminal prosecutions, the accused shall enjoy the right . . . to be confronted with the witnesses against him."[169] The Confrontation Clause once presented several interesting questions regarding the admission of prior out-of-court statements as substantive evidence pursuant to what are now Rules 801(d)(1)(A), 803(24), 804(b)(1), and 804(b)(5). The Supreme Court has since resolved many, but not all, of the questions surrounding the rules of evidence and the Confrontation Clause. The basic questions presented fall within two major categories: those involving a declarant who is available for trial in the sense that he or she can admit, deny or explain the prior statement and those involving a declarant who is not so available.

1. Available Declarant

In California v. Green,[170] the Supreme Court addressed the relationship between the right of confrontation and substantive admissibility of prior inconsistent statements. John Green was convicted of supplying marijuana to Melvin Porter, a minor. Both at a preliminary hearing and in an oral unsworn statement to police officer Wade, Porter identified Green as his supplier. At trial, however, Porter was evasive and uncooperative, claiming he could not recall who supplied him the marijuana because he was under the influence of LSD at the time of the transaction. The trial court admitted both prior statements under Section 1235 of the California Evidence Code, which provided that a witness's prior inconsistent statements were admissible as substantive evidence if the witness had an opportunity at trial to admit, deny, or explain the statements. The California appellate courts reversed the defendant's conviction on the ground that his right of confrontation had been violated by the admission of the prior statements as substantive evidence. The United States Supreme Court, upholding the constitutional validity of Section 1235, vacated the judgment of the California Supreme Court.[171]

To analyze whether the admission of the oral unsworn statement made to police officer Wade violated the Confrontation Clause, the Supreme Court identified the three purposes of confrontation: to ensure that the witness gives his or her statement under oath; to provide an opportunity for cross-examination; and to allow the jury to assess the demeanor of the witness making the statement.[172] Conceding that a prior out-of-court statement might be made under circumstances having none of these protections, the Supreme Court nevertheless found that each of the purposes of confrontation could be satisfied when the declarant testified at trial:

> [A]s far as the oath is concerned, the witness must now affirm, deny, or qualify the truth of the prior statement under the penalty of perjury.
>
> Second, the inability to cross-examine the witness at the time he made his prior statement cannot easily be shown to be of crucial significance as long as the defendant is assured of full and effective cross-examination at the time of trial.
>
> * * *
>
> . . . The witness who now relates a different story about the events in question must necessarily assume a position as to the truth value of his prior statement, thus giving the jury a chance to observe and evaluate his demeanor as he either disavows or qualifies his earlier statement.[173]

Therefore prior inconsistent statements satisfying the requirements of Rule 801(d)(1)(A) do not run afoul of the Confrontation Clause. For a prior inconsistent statement to be admitted under the rule, the declarant must be under oath subject to cross-examination and redirect examination before the jury regarding the statement; the jury can evaluate such responses.

In *Green* the Supreme Court specifically declined to decide the question of the admissibility of the prior statement to police officer Wade, because at trial Porter did not affirm, deny, or explain the truth of the prior statement but instead testified to a lack of recollection of the underlying event.[174] This raised the issue whether defendant was "assured of full and effective cross-examination at the time of trial." The Supreme Court explained:

> Whether Porter's apparent lapse of memory so affected Green's right to cross-examine [at trial] as to make a critical difference in the application of the Confrontation Clause in this case is an issue which is not ripe for decision at this juncture. The state court did not focus on this precise question. . . . Nor has either party addressed itself to the question. Its resolution depends much upon the unique facts in this record, and we are reluctant to proceed without the state court's views of what the record actually discloses relevant to this particular issue.[175]

On remand, the California Supreme Court squarely addressed the question reserved in *Green* and held that Porter's prior oral statement to police officer Wade was properly admitted "insofar as the Sixth Amendment is concerned."[176] The California Supreme Court considered in turn each of the three purposes of confrontation identified by the Supreme Court. As to oath, it quoted the Supreme Court's opinion in *Green* for the proposition that because Porter was under oath at trial he was required to " 'affirm, deny, or qualify the truth of the prior statement under the penalty of perjury.' "[177] In fact, Porter had testified at trial to a lack of recollection of the underlying event, and he therefore never addressed the truth of his prior statements while under oath. The California Supreme Court also concluded that defendant had an "adequate opportunity" to cross-examine Porter at trial. Although defense counsel had asked Porter only one question on cross-examination, the court suggested that he could have sought to rehabilitate the then friendly Porter "by providing him with 'the usual suggested explanations for the inaccuracy of his prior statement, such as faulty perception or undue haste in recounting the event.' "[178] Finally, with respect to demeanor, it found sufficient that the trier of fact had the opportunity to observe Porter's demeanor and evaluate his credibility as he testified at trial to lack of recollection.[179]

The California Supreme Court's analysis of the reserved question in *Green* is less than satisfactory. The United States Supreme Court remanded the case for a determination whether Porter's "apparent lapse of memory" so affected defendant's opportunity to cross-examine that he was deprived of his Sixth Amendment right of confrontation. The Supreme Court thought that the question depended "much upon the unique facts in [the] record,"[180] but the California Supreme Court apparently disagreed. It simply concluded without any factual discussion that the defendant had had an "adequate opportunity" to cross-examine. The only assistance the court offered on how defense counsel might have taken advantage of that opportunity was the suggestion that he could have rehabilitated Porter.[181]

It is suggested that the Supreme Court erred in the first place in remanding the question of the constitutional admissibility of the statement made to police officer Wade for a determination of the potential effectiveness of the defendant's ability to cross-examine. Whether Porter's lack of recollection at trial made a "critical difference" to Green's ability to cross-examine did not depend on the "unique facts" in the record. A witness's lack of recollection of the event underlying his or her earlier statement always makes a "critical difference"; the facts of a particular case cannot make cross-examination of that witness potentially effective. Because a witness cannot credibly admit, deny, or explain the inaccuracy of his or her prior statement at trial when the witness claims lack of recollection of the underlying event, the criminal defendant does not have an opportunity to refute effectively by cross-examination the truth of the prior statement.[182] For reasons presented earlier, the forgetful witness who "testifies to a lack of memory as to the subject matter of his statement," Rule 804(a)(3), should be deemed unavailable.[183] Accordingly, the prior statements of such a declarant should not be admitted under Rule 801(d)(1)(A) but should be considered pursuant to Rule 804(b)(5), the "other [hearsay] exception" category for the unavailable witness. As an unavailable witness, the declarant's prior statements would be analyzed differently for Confrontation Clause purposes.

2. Unavailable Declarant

As previously mentioned, in California v. Green the United States Supreme Court was called upon to decide the admissibility of preliminary hearing testimony of an unavailable witness, the court treating Porter's alleged lapse of memory as constituting unavailability for the purpose of addressing the question. Noting that Porter was under oath at the preliminary hearing and that Green had the right to cross-examine Porter at the time, the court held that substantive admissibility of Porter's preliminary hearing testimony did not violate the defendant's right of confrontation:

> We also think that Porter's preliminary hearing testimony was admissible as far as the Constitution is concerned wholly apart from the question of whether respondent had an effective opportunity for confrontation at the subsequent trial. For Porter's statement at the preliminary hearing had already been given under circumstances closely approximating those that surround the typical trial. Porter was under oath; respondent was represented by counsel—the same counsel in fact who later represented him at the trial; respondent had every opportunity to cross-examine Porter as to his statement; and the proceedings were conducted before a judicial tribunal, equipped to provide a judicial record of the hearings.
>
> * * *
>
> . . . In the present case respondent's counsel does not appear to have been significantly limited in any way in the scope or nature of his cross-examination of the witness Porter at the preliminary hearing. If Porter had died or was otherwise unavailable, the Confrontation Clause would not have been violated by admitting his testimony given at the preliminary hearing—the right of cross-examination then afforded provides substantial compliance with the purposes behind the confrontation requirement, as long as the declarant's inability to give live testimony is in no way the fault of the State. * * * As in the case where the witness is physically unproducible, the State here has made every effort to introduce its evidence through the

live testimony of the witness; it produced Porter at trial, swore him as a witness, and tendered him for cross-examination. Whether Porter then testified in a manner consistent or inconsistent with his preliminary hearing testimony, claimed a loss of memory, claimed his privilege against compulsory self-incrimination or simply refused to answer, nothing in the Confrontation Clause prohibited the State from also relying on his prior testimony to prove its case against Green.[184]

As indicated by the foregoing quotation, *Green* requires "an opportunity to effectively cross-examine and merely providing an opportunity to cross-examine at the preliminary hearing is not per se adequate opportunity."[185] Ordinarily, however, unless the defense was limited by "unusual circumstances," the opportunity for cross-examination provided in the typical preliminary hearing will be found to have been sufficient.[186]

Decisions interpreting *Green* have generally agreed that the question is whether the defense had the opportunity to cross-examine effectively, not whether defense counsel actually engaged in an extensive cross-examination.[187] Nevertheless, the matter is not totally without doubt. In Ohio v. Roberts,[188] the United States Supreme Court held that *Green* permitted admission of preliminary hearing testimony of an unavailable prosecution witness who had been called by the defense at the preliminary hearing but had been examined as a hostile witness. Although defense counsel had not formally asked that the witness be declared hostile and that he be allowed to cross-examine her, that is, lead and impeach, his questions had been the functional equivalent of cross-examination. The Supreme Court noted that counsel in his "direct examination" had challenged the witness's perception of events and her veracity and had not been limited "in any way" in this line of questioning. The result was, as in *Green*, a "substantial compliance with the purposes behind the confrontation requirement." However, the Supreme Court added that in light of the facts before it there was no need to determine whether *Green* applied when a defense counsel had not actually engaged in extensive questioning of the witness.[189]

Six months after it decided *Green*, the United States Supreme Court held in Dutton v. Evans,[190] that the defendant's right of confrontation was not violated by the substantive admission under a Georgia coconspirator hearsay exception of an out-of-court declaration of a nonappearing but available witness. Three men, Wade Truett, Venson Williams, and Alex Evans, were charged with the murder of three police officers. Truett was granted immunity in return for his testimony, and Williams and Evans were indicted for the murders and tried separately. At Evans's trial there were 20 prosecution witnesses, but the most damaging testimony came from Truett. He testified that he, Williams, and Evans were stealing a car when the three police officers confronted them; they seized a gun from one officer and used that gun to murder all three. Another witness at Evans's trial, a man named Shaw, testified that he and Williams had been fellow prisoners when Williams was being held prior to arraignment. Shaw said that when

Williams returned to the cell after arraignment, he asked him how he made out in court. According to Shaw, Williams responded, "If it hadn't been for that dirty son-of-a-bitch Alex Evans, we wouldn't be in this now." Although Williams was available to either side, he was not called to testify at Evans's trial. Defense counsel objected to Shaw's testimony on the grounds that it was hearsay and that it violated Evans's right of confrontation.

The trial court admitted the testimony pursuant to a Georgia statutory coconspirator hearsay exception and overruled the confrontation objection. Defense counsel then cross-examined Shaw at length. Evans was convicted, and the Georgia courts upheld that conviction on direct appeal. A federal district court denied Evans's writ of habeas corpus, but the Fifth Circuit reversed, holding that admission of Shaw's testimony under the Georgia coconspirator hearsay exception violated Evans's right of confrontation.[191]

In a five-to-four decision, the Supreme Court reversed.[192] Justice Stewart, writing the plurality opinion,[193] first carefully reasserted that the Confrontation Clause was not a codification of the common law rule of hearsay and its exceptions, nor did the Confrontation Clause render all hearsay inadmissible.[194] He also rejected with little difficulty the defendant's argument that because the Georgia coconspirator hearsay exception did not conform to the federal exception it was constitutionally invalid. Stewart identified the issue as whether the "mission" of the Confrontation Clause was satisfied:

> The decisions of this Court make it clear that the mission of the Confrontation Clause is to advance a practical concern for the accuracy of the truth-determining process in criminal trials by assuring that "the trier of fact [has] a satisfactory basis for evaluating the truth of the prior statement." California v. Green.[195]

In *Green*, the court remanded for a determination whether the declarant's lack of recollection at trial "so affected" the defendant's opportunity to cross-examine that the defendant was deprived of his right of confrontation. In *Evans* the defendant had no opportunity to cross-examine the declarant, who was physically absent from trial, not just practically unavailable. According to Stewart, however, the issue was no longer the existence of an opportunity for full and effective cross-examination but whether the "trier of fact [has] a satisfactory basis for evaluating the truth of the prior statement."[196] Although Stewart's opinion is abstruse, he appears to have looked to the criteria of certainty of making, indicia of trustworthiness, and probative impact in determining whether the jury in *Evans* had such a satisfactory basis.[197]

Stewart first found that the jury had a satisfactory basis for evaluating whether Williams actually made the statement to Shaw. Shaw was present in court and defense counsel effectively cross-examined him on the question of whether he actually heard Williams make the statement.[198] According to

Justice Stewart, the opportunity to cross-examine the reporting witness, while the witness is under oath, in the presence of the ultimate trier of fact is a sufficient guarantee of certainty of making.[199]

Stewart next found that Williams's statement possessed those indicia of trustworthiness "widely viewed as determinative" of when a statement should be placed before a jury without confrontation of the declarant. The statement contained no express assertion of past fact and consequently carried on its face a warning to the jury against giving the statement more than the little probative value it deserved. Williams's personal knowledge of the facts surrounding the murder was well established. There was little likelihood that Williams had faulty recollection of the crime, and the circumstances under which the statement was made negated any motive to misrepresent. Although *Green* had quoted Wigmore to characterize cross-examination as "the greatest legal engine ever invented for the discovery of truth,"[200] Justice Stewart in *Evans* summarily dismissed as "wholly unreal" the possibility that cross-examination of Williams would have aided the jury in determining whether his statement, though made, might have been untrustworthy.[201]

Justice Stewart's plurality opinion in *Evans* is exceptionally unclear about the standard a court should apply to determine the constitutional admissibility of an out-of-court declaration by a nonappearing witness. Stewart's concern was that the trier of fact have a satisfactory basis for evaluating the truth of the prior statement. He looked to the indicia of trustworthiness possessed by the statement, the certainty with which the making of the statement was established, and the importance of the statement in the litigation, but he failed to advise lower courts of the proper weight to be accorded each of these factors. For example, it is not apparent whether Stewart intended an evaluation of incremental probative value to be an independent criterion in the confrontation analysis he announced or whether he was merely stating that any error in admitting Williams's statement was harmless. Moreover, even if incremental probative value is a relevant criterion, Stewart's opinion leaves unclear whether all hearsay statements that are crucial to a case must be excluded or whether necessary hearsay may nevertheless be admitted if indicia of trustworthiness are adequately established.

This question was answered in Ohio v. Roberts.[202] In *Roberts* the defendant was charged with forgery of a check in the name of Bernard Isaacs and with possession of stolen credit cards belonging to Isaacs and his wife. At a preliminary hearing defense counsel called Isaac's daughter Anita to establish that she had permitted the defendant to use her apartment and to attempt to elicit from her an admission that she had given the defendant the checks and the credit cards without informing him that she did not have permission to use them. The daughter denied giving the defendant the items. The government issued five subpoenas to Anita for four different trials. She was not at her residence and did not appear at trial.

After the preliminary hearing, defense counsel resigned to accept an appointment as municipal county judge. New counsel appeared at trial. The defendant testified that Anita had given him her parents' checkbook and credit cards. The state, on rebuttal, offered the preliminary hearing transcript of Anita's testimony relying on the Ohio evidence code, which permits the use of preliminary examination testimony of a witness "who cannot for any reason be produced at trial."[203] At a *voir dire* hearing, the trial court determined that Anita was unavailable because no one was aware of her whereabouts.

The Ohio Court of Appeals reversed the defendant's conviction, holding that the state had made insufficient efforts to seek Anita's whereabouts. The Ohio Supreme Court affirmed the reversal on a different ground, after first declaring that the trial court could reasonably infer from testimony at *voir dire* that due diligence could not have procured the attendance of Anita. The Ohio Supreme Court found the transcript inadmissible because the mere opportunity to cross-examine at a preliminary hearing "did not afford constitutional confrontation for purposes of trial."[204] Since defense counsel at the preliminary trial did not have Anita declared hostile and thus subject to cross-examination, that is, the use of leading questions, the lack of actual cross-examination violated defendant's confrontation rights.[205]

On appeal the United States Supreme Court reversed the Ohio Supreme Court and found the preliminary hearing testimony admissible. The United States Supreme Court reasoned that with respect to former testimony the Confrontation Clause establishes a preference for a face-to-face confrontation. Thus the prosecution must produce the declarant or establish the unavailability of the declarant. Moreover, with respect to every hearsay statement, whether or not crucial to a case, of both an available or unavailable witness, the hearsay statement must possess "indicia of reliability" to be admitted. The Supreme Court continued:

> The Court has applied this "indicia of reliability" requirement principally by concluding that certain hearsay exceptions rest upon such solid foundations that admission of virtually any evidence within them comports with the "substance of the constitutional protection." Mattox v. United States, 156 U.S., at 244. . . . This reflects the truism "hearsay rules and the Confrontation Clause are generally designed to protect similar values," California v. Green, 399 U.S. at 155, . . . and "stem from the same roots," Dutton v. Evans, 400 U.S. 74, 86 . . . (1970). It also responds to the need for certainty in the workday world of conducting criminal trials.
>
> In sum, when a hearsay declarant is not present for cross-examination at trial, the Confrontation Clause normally requires a showing that he is unavailable. Even then, his statement is admissible only if it bears adequate "indicia of reliability." Reliability can be inferred without more in a case where the evidence falls within a firmly rooted hearsay exception. In other cases, the evidence must be excluded, at least absent showing of particularized guarantees of trustworthiness.[222]

The Supreme Court found that the direct examination of Anita afforded such "indicia of reliability" since the defense counsel had explored the underlying events in detail. It found no substance in the contention that confrontation was violated because of the change in attorney.

The Supreme Court delineated several important doctrines in *Roberts.* Although declining to "map out a theory of the Confrontation Clause that would determine the validity of all hearsay exceptions,"[207] the Supreme Court stated without qualification that sufficient trustworthiness can be "inferred without more" with respect to evidence falling squarely within a "firmly rooted hearsay exception." The common law hearsay exception for prior testimony is clearly among the "firmly rooted." Each of the hearsay exceptions specifically denominated in Rules 801(d)(2), 803, and 804 are similarly clearly within the "firmly rooted." The Supreme Court also provided for the admission of statements not falling within a "firmly rooted" hearsay exception if such statement possesses "particularized guarantees of trustworthiness." Notably, the court's language exactly fits the requirements of Rules 803(24) and 804(b)(5). Pursuant to each rule, evidence can be admitted only if it possesses "equivalent circumstantial guarantees of trustworthiness" to the "firmly rooted" hearsay exceptions. Thus evidence properly admitted pursuant to Rule 804(b)(5) also meets the requirements of the Confrontation Clause.

3. Synopsis

Evidence offered under Rule 801(d)(1)(A) is admissible only if the declarant testifies at the trial and is subject to cross-examination regarding the statement. *Green* establishes that if the declarant is available for cross-examination at trial regarding the prior inconsistent statement and its underlying subject matter, there is no Confrontation Clause prohibition. Thus evidence admitted pursuant to Rule 801(d)(1)(A) does not run afoul of the Sixth Amendment right of confrontation. The same is true for evidence admitted pursuant to Rule 803(24), which also in practice requires that the witness be available to admit, deny, or explain the prior statement. Whether a particular witness who at trial claims to lack recollection of the subject matter of his or her prior statement is subject to cross-examination is the question reserved in *Green.* As previously discussed, a no answer is suggested.[208]

When the declarant is unavailable, Rule 804(b)(5) permits admission of a prior statement only if the statement possesses "equivalent circumstantial guarantees of trustworthiness" to that of statements admitted pursuant to the "firmly rooted" hearsay exceptions. *Roberts* declares such evidence sufficiently trustworthy to satisfy the mission of the Confrontation Clause.

Returning to our hypothetical case, to the extent that Mary Mahoney's, John Goodfellow's, Jim James's, or Bob Williams's statements are admissible pursuant to either Rule 801(d)(1)(A), Rule 803(24), or Rule 804(b)(5), their prior statements would not run afoul of the Confrontation Clause. As discussed previously, however, it is unlikely that any of these witnesses's prior statements would be found to qualify for admission pursuant to any of such rules.

I. THE WAIVER DOCTRINE

Several courts have recently employed a different approach to support admission of a prior statement of a witness whose trial testimony was lost to the trier of fact because of witness intimidation by or on behalf of the criminal defendant. The approach employed permits introduction into evidence of the prior statement of the intimidated unavailable witness without regard to whether the prior statement meets either a traditional hearsay exception or the requirements of Rule 804(b)(5). When witness intimidation arising from the acts of the defendant or the defendant's agents is sufficiently established, these courts have declared that the defendant has waived his or her hearsay objection and confrontation rights. This waiver doctrine, however, is based upon certain questionable assumptions. Moreover, it is not an available solution to the witness intimidation question when, as is usually the case, the prosecution possesses insufficient evidence to satisfy the court that intimidation by the defendant or the defendant's agents caused the loss of the witness's testimony at trial.

1. The Doctrine in Operation

In United States v. Carlson,[209] the grand jury testimony of a witness who refused to testify at trial because of threats of reprisal by defendant Donald Carlson was admitted into evidence under Rule 804(b)(5). The Eighth Circuit on appeal, after affirming the Rule 804(b)(5) determination, declined to decide whether the evidence was sufficiently trustworthy to meet the standards *Evans* set for the Confrontation Clause.[210] Instead, the court found that the existence of intimidating acts by the defendant constituted a waiver of his right of confrontation.[211]

In United States v. Thevis,[212] the Fifth Circuit employed the same waiver doctrine in determining whether grand jury testimony was admissible over hearsay and Confrontation Clause objections. In *Thevis* the defendants were convicted at trial of racketeering activity involving an interstate pornography business and for violating the civil rights of Roger Underhill by murdering him to prevent his testimony. Originally, the defendants were indicted solely for their racketeering activities. Before the grand jury, the principal witness against the defendants was an unindicted coconspirator, Roger Underhill. Before trial Underhill was murdered. Witnesses placed Thevis at the place of the murder at the time of the murder. Additionally, Thevis's cellmate claimed that Thevis boasted of the killing. The government obtained an additional indictment charging the defendants with conspiracy to murder Underhill.

The government in advance of trial notified the trial court and the defendants that it intended to introduce Underhill's grand jury testimony pursuant to Rule 804(b)(5). The trial court instructed the government to proceed by initially offering evidence about the conspiracy to murder charge. After the introduction of such evidence, the trial court found the grand jury testimony sufficiently trustworthy to be introduced pursuant to Rule 804(b)(5). The trial court, however, even after *Roberts*, then assumed that the Confrontation Clause required something more than Rule 804(b)(5), ultimately concluding that the admission of the grand jury testimony would violate the defendant's Confrontation Clause rights. In the case at hand, however, the trial court held that the defendants had waived their confrontation rights by their act of murdering the witness, thus making Underhill's grand jury testimony admissible.

On appeal, the Fifth Circuit rejected the trial court's ruling that once evidence is admitted pursuant to Rule 804(b)(5), a court must still find satisfaction or waiver of confrontation rights: a prior statement properly admitted under Rule 804(b)(5) satisfies the Confrontation Clause. The court, however, expressed grave doubt that the grand jury testimony had been properly admitted under Rule 804(b)(5).[213] The court declined to determine if grand jury testimony was ever admissible. Instead, the Fifth Circuit held that intimidation of a witness by the criminal defendant depriving the trier of fact of the witness's testimony constituted a waiver by the criminal defendant of the right of confrontation and any objection to admission of the witness's prior statement under the hearsay rule.[214] The rationale presented was one of deterrence, that is, a defendant should not be permitted to benefit from his or her own act of depriving the trier of fact of relevant testimony of a potential witness.[215]

2. Finding a Waiver

The waiver doctrine as applied broadly to both confrontation and hearsay concerns eliminates any need to determine the presence of equivalent circumstantial quantities of trustworthiness of the out-of-court statement pursuant to Rule 804(b)(5) if a firmly rooted hearsay exception is not applicable. Although the waiver doctrine relieves the court of what may very well be a difficult determination, the doctrine in its place requires that the court determine whether the defendant "caused" the unavailability of the witness. The burden of persuasion placed upon the government, the party seeking to introduce the prior statement of the unavailable declarant, with respect to such a judicial determination will in most cases be impossible to meet.

The Tenth Circuit has discussed in detail the burden of persuasion trial courts within its circuit must employ in finding a waiver. In United States v.

Balano,[216] the defendant was accused of dealing in interstate stolen goods. The indictment arose from the grand jury testimony of Dominick Carullo. At trial Carullo refused to testify. The trial court held an evidentiary hearing outside the presence of the jury in which Carullo stated that he would not explain the reasons why he would not testify but that his grand jury testimony was truthful. An FBI agent testified that after his grand jury appearance, Carullo told him in an interview that threats had been made, and that he would not testify. Notes made at the interview confirmed the agent's testimony. The trial court found a waiver of confrontation and hearsay claims.

On appeal, the Tenth Circuit affirmed the finding of a waiver. The court first considered the use of a reasonable doubt standard, which would require the prosecution to show beyond a reasonable doubt that the defendant caused the unavailability of the witness. If such a standard was adopted, the court stated that Carullo's statement describing the intimidation as recorded by the FBI agent would be insufficient to find a waiver. Often the only evidence of intimidation will be a statement by the intimidated witness to government officials. The court, therefore, rejected the beyond-a-reasonable-doubt standard. In rejecting this standard, however, the court also stated that a prima facie showing of coercion, that is, evidence sufficient to support a finding of more probably true than not true, was insufficient to find a waiver. Instead, the Tenth Circuit concluded the trial court to find a waiver must determine, after holding an evidentiary hearing outside the presence of the jury, that the existence of intimidation by the defendant has been demonstrated to be more probably true than not. In *Balano* the court noted that Carullo's reiteration of the grand jury testimony's truthfulness could lead a trial court to give greater credence to statements regarding intimidation and that the FBI agent's statement and his notes, which included reference to two specific threats, also corroborated the existence of intimidation.

Actually, *Balano* does not set a very high standard for the government's burden of persuasion. The court presumed that because Carullo stated that his grand jury testimony was truthful, his present silence must be due to fear of reprisal by the defendant. Moreover, statements by an investigator about what the declarant stated may be of questionable worth as even the court recognized. Given even this low standard for finding a waiver, however, few cases would meet the standard. A witness will rarely reiterate the truth of his or her grand jury testimony. A successfully intimidated witness may be dead or otherwise physically unavailable or claim not to remember and thus does not know if his or her prior testimony is the truth. Moreover, an intimidated witness will most often be too frightened to speak to law officials about intimidation.

The Fifth Circuit in United States v. Thevis[217] adopted a tougher standard for finding a waiver. The court also rejected the reasonable-doubt standard but was unwilling to use the more-probably-true-than-not standard. The court held that the reasonable-doubt standard related only to the necessity of proving every element of the offense. Admission of grand jury testimony, however, is merely an evidentiary ruling and not a ruling as to a defendant's substantive guilt. The importance of the fact-finding process and confrontation's role in ascertaining the truth, however, prevents use of a mere more-probably-true-than-not standard. Instead, since trustworthiness of evidence is the central purpose of both the hearsay rule and Confrontation Clause, the proper standard should be clear and convincing evidence.[218] In reaching this conclusion, the Fifth Circuit relied on the Supreme Court's ruling that an in-court identification following a tainted out-of-court identification is not admissible unless the prosecution shows by clear and convincing evidence that the in-court identification has an independent basis.[219] In *Thevis* itself, Thevis's admission to a cellmate that he murdered the declarant coupled with eyewitnesses who placed him at the scene provided the clear and convincing evidence.

If evidence is usually lacking to pass the more-probably-true-than-not standard, clearly, very few cases will involve evidence that will meet the clear-and-convincing standard as the government's burden of persuasion. Murdered witnesses cannot reiterate the truthfulness of their grand jury statements. Defendants do not usually boast of their murders as did Thevis. If no evidence connects the defendant to the unavailability of a witness as is most often the case,[220] the waiver doctrine is simply inapplicable, no matter what burden of persuasion is imposed. Mere suspicion aroused by a witness's death or sudden forgetfulness is insufficient to support a determination that "the defendant must have done something."

3. A Better Approach

The waiver doctrine rests on a faulty assumption that somehow intimidating acts are always highly probative on the issue of the accused's consciousness of guilt concerning the particular charge and thus always serve to corroborate significantly the trustworthiness of the grand jury testimony or other prior out-of-court statement being offered. In fact, the waiver doctrine previously described permits the introduction of testimony whether or not it is trustworthy.[221] A defendant has an incentive to intimidate a witness whenever the witness is going to give damaging evidence regardless of the truth of such evidence. Since the declarant's evidence is harmful even if untruthful, the incentive to eliminate the evidence through intimidation, including murder, is substantially if not almost totally identical. Any small reduction in incentive that does arise stems from the assumption that an innocent defendant is more likely to be able to present a strong defense including refutation of the prior out-of-court statement. For instance, in our hypothetical case Jim James and Bob Williams may have had more to do with the murder of Harold Harris than indicated. Accordingly, their statements may have been made to point the finger toward someone else. Alternatively, even if not involved in the murder, Jim James and Bob Williams would have a motive to identify a particular person as having committed the murder in exchange for a plea bargain or immunity on the drug charges. One could easily foresee that under such circumstances Jim James and Bob Williams might have fabricated a story before the police arrived naming Sam Smith to avoid naming the actual perpetrator or because they did not know the identity of the actual perpetrator. Sam Smith had good reason to intimidate them since their testimony would be extremely damaging to him whether he committed the murder or not, especially if he did not have a strong alibi for the time of the murder.

Although Sam Smith's acts of intimidation are themselves criminal, it is suggested that such acts should not constitute a waiver of Sam Smith's right to a fair trial for the murder of Harold Harris, a totally separate consideration. Jim James and Bob William's potential testimony was sufficiently damaging to encourage intimidation. Nevertheless, surrounding circumstances indicate that their motives in making their prior statements may not have been to tell the truth. The waiver doctrine thus permits evidence to be admitted solely on the basis that the defendant, Sam Smith, committed acts of intimidation against witnesses, which acts do not themselves sufficiently, if at all, demonstrate the trustworthiness of the witnesses' prior statements.

A better approach to the question of the effect of the conduct of the defendant in denying the trier of fact of the benefit of the witness's in-court testimony is to follow the mandates of the Confrontation Clause as interpreted by the United States Supreme Court in Ohio v. Roberts:

> The Court has applied this "indicia of reliability" requirement principally by concluding that certain hearsay exceptions rest upon such solid foundations that admission of virtually any evidence within them comports with the "substance of the constitutional protection." Mattox v. United States, 156 U.S., at 244. . . . This reflects the truism "hearsay rules and the Confrontation Clause are generally designed to protect similar values," California v. Green, 399 U.S. at 155, . . . and "stem from the same roots," Dutton v. Evans, 400 U.S. 74, 86 . . . (1970). It also responds to the need for certainty in the workday world of conducting criminal trials.
>
> In sum, when a hearsay declarant is not present for cross-examination at trial, the Confrontation Clause normally requires a showing that he is unavailable. Even then, his statement is admissible only if it bears adequate "indicia of reliability." Reliability can be inferred without more in a case where the evidence falls within a firmly rooted hearsay exception. In other cases, the evidence must be excluded, at least absent showing of particularized guarantees of trustworthiness.[222]

Under *Roberts*, the Confrontation Clause normally requires that the in-court testimony of the declarant be shown to be unavailable before hearsay statements of the declarant may be admitted in evidence against the accused. Assuming it is established that the witness is unavailable for any of the reasons specified in Rule 804(a),[223] *Roberts* provides in addition that the statement may be admitted under the Confrontation Clause "only if it bears adequate 'indicia of reliability.' "[224] Although "reliability can be inferred without more in a case where the evidence falls within a firmly rooted hearsay exception," with respect to grand jury testimony and oral, written, or recorded statements given to the police, such hearsay statements of an unavailable witness may be admitted as sufficiently reliable only if "a showing of particularized guarantees of trustworthiness,"[225] identical to "equivalent circumstantial guarantees of trustworthiness" mandated in Rule 804(b)(5),[226] is made.

A sufficient showing that the defendant has intimidated the witness to the point of the witness refusing to testify or feigning a lack of recollection or that the defendant has prevented even the physical appearance of the witness at trial by murder or other means obviously makes the witness "unavailable," thus satisfying the first prong of the two-prong *Roberts* test. Moreover, witness intimidation, including physical elimination of a witness, normally will give rise to an inference that the accused is conscious of his own guilt. As stated in United States v. Gonsalves such evidence of witness intimidation is admissible:

> Evidence of bad conduct, like the threat at issue here, is inadmissible to prove character in order to show the defendant acted in conformity therewith. Fed. R. Evid. 404(a). Such evidence may, however, be admissible for other purposes, such as to show intent, knowledge, or identity. Fed. R. Evid. 404(b). This court has recently held that "[e]vidence of threats to witnesses can be relevant to show consciousness of guilt." United States v. Monahan, 633 F.2d 984, 985 (1st Cir. 1980) (per curiam). Like evidence of flight from the scene of a crime, bribery of an adverse witness, or the destruction of incriminating evidence, threats made by a defendant respecting a specific hostile witness may imply that the party making the threat has something specific to hide. The desire to "cover something up," in turn, implies a consciousness of guilt of the particular crime charged. See 2 Wigmore on Evidence §§ 273-77 (Chadbourn Revision 1979).[227]

Witness intimidation, including physical elimination of a witness, may also be said to give rise to an inference of consciousness of guilt giving rise not to the ultimate inference that the defendant committed the particular crime charged but to an intermediate inference that the defendant knows that the prior statement to the authorities of the witness who was intimidated is true and correct. Thus intimidation may be said to give rise to an inference flowing from consciousness of guilt that would constitute a corroborating circumstance tending to establish the "particularized guarantees of trustworthiness" described in Roberts, the counterpart to the "equivalent circumstantial guarantees of trustworthiness" mandated by Rule 804(b)(5). In determining whether the out-of-court statement of the witness may be admitted under the "other [hearsay] exception" of Rule 804(b)(5), each of the criteria previously discussed must also be considered.[228]

The inference of trustworthiness arising from the fact that the accused prevented the declarant from repeating the out-of-court statement in court is at most a single fact to be considered by the court together with all other relevant facts in determining whether particularized-equivalent circumstantial guarantees of trustworthiness required for admissibility have been established. Exactly how important a fact intimidation resulting in the loss at trial of the witness's testimony may be in determining the admissibility of the witness's prior out-of-court statement obviously depends upon the totality of surrounding circumstances. Nevertheless, it is suggested that given the basic assumption that an innocent defendant would have the same or almost the same incentive to intimidate a witness who is going to testify against the defendant as would a guilty defendant, the inference arising from the act of intimidation to consciousness of guilt, to particularized-equivalent circumstantial guarantees of trustworthiness, will almost always, if not always, be overvalued by the trial court. As is indicated by *Thevis* and *Balano*, once the trial court concludes that the defendant intimidated the witness causing a loss of his or her testimony at trial,[229] the trial judge will naturally seek to keep the defendant from benefiting from these acts of intimidation and to discourage such conduct in the future by giving the inference arising from intimidation to particularized-equivalent guarantee of trustworthiness more than the low probative value it deserves. Therefore, if the trial court is permitted to consider the inference from intimidation to consciousness of guilt, to particularized-equivalent circumstantial guarantees of trustworthiness, the prior statement of the witness will all too often be admitted under Rule 804(b)(5). To prevent such a natural reaction, the trial court should simply be prohibited from considering the inference arising from intimidation in determining whether particularized-equivalent circumstantial guarantees of trustworthiness exist under the Confrontation Clause and Rule 804(b)(5).[230]

In short, *Roberts* compels the conclusion that a finding that the defendant has by his or her actions made the in-court testimony of the out-of-court declarant unavailable for any of the reasons specified in Rule 804(a) should not constitute a waiver of either the Confrontation Clause or the hearsay rule. The defendant is entitled to confront witnesses who appear against the defendant in court *and* to be convicted solely upon trustworthy evidence. The inference arising from intimidation to particularized-equivalent guarantees of trustworthiness of the intimidated witness's prior statements is weak at best. The trial court should not consider the inference in determining particularized-equivalent circumstantial guarantees of trustworthiness under Rule 804(b)(5) as to the prior statement because of the undue tendency of the court to overvalue such an inference in order (1) to prevent a defendant from having successfully deprived the trier of fact of the witness's evidence and (2) to deter acts of witness intimidation by other defendants in the future. The determination of particularized-equivalent guarantees of trustworthiness mandated by the Confrontation Clause for admissibility of prior statements of an unavailable witness under Rule 804(b)(5) cannot be sacrificed in the pursuit of such goals, as noble as such goals may be. The proper means of deterence is to provide that acts of witness intimidation are considered criminal and proceed to try, convict, and punish the defendant for having committed the crime that resulted in the loss of the witness's testimony. The criminal justice system should not seek to deter witness intimidation at the cost of permitting the defendant to be convicted on the particular offense charged on the basis of untrustworthy hearsay evidence.

On the other hand, evidence of witness intimidation as giving rise to the inference of consciousness of guilt for the further inference that the defendant committed the particular offense charged may itself be admitted provided the probative value of the evidence is not substantially outweighed by the danger of unfair prejudice[231] arising from the bad man inference, that is, if the defendant did something bad, the defendant must also have committed the crime for which he or she is on trial, or if the defendant did something bad, the defendant must have done other bad things for which he or she was not punished, thus making it easier for the jury to convict the defendant of the crime charged than if they were dealing with a "truly innocent person."

J. SUMMARY

Despite the many hearsay exceptions contained in the Federal Rules of Evidence and its new category of "not hearsay," in a criminal trial involving a successfully intimidated witness, the government will often find that prior statements of the witness are inadmissible. Rule 801(d)(1)(A) defining certain prior inconsistent statements as "not hearsay" is not applicable when a witness is successfully intimidated before he or she has testified in any formal proceeding such as happened to Mary Mahoney in our hypothetical case. Even if the witness, such as Bob Williams, does testify in a formal proceeding, the rule is not applicable if the witness is murdered before trial, feigns a lack of recollection at trial, refuses to testify, or if the witness's testimony is otherwise unavailable at trial. Thus none of the prior statements of John Goodfellow, Jim James, Mary Mahoney, or Bob Williams is admissible pursuant to Rule 801(d)(1)(A). None of the declarants could be subject to meaningful cross-examination at trial with respect to the content of their out-of-court statements as required by Rule 801(d)(1)(A).

The "other exceptions" hearsay exceptions of Rule 803(24) and Rule 804(b)(5) are also unhelpful in most cases. Both rules, as interpreted, require that there be substantial, almost indisputable, certainty of making regarding the statement. The "other exceptions" hearsay exceptions of Rules 803(24) and 804(b)(5) therefore will rarely be applied to include an oral statement such as that given to police officers by Mary Mahoney. Additionally, both rules require a showing of equivalent circumstantial guarantees of trustworthiness to categorical hearsay exceptions. Thus even statements given in a formal proceeding or otherwise sufficiently shown to have been made may not be admissible if questions exist about interest or motive, time to fabricate, lack of personal knowledge, governmental influence through threats of prosecution or contempt, or the use of leading questions.

The waiver doctrine relieves the court from any determination regarding the trustworthiness of hearsay or the accused's right of confrontation by simply holding that the defendant waives such objections when he or she personally or through agents intimidated the witness. The doctrine is flawed analytically and subject to abuse. More importantly, it requires that the government establish that the defendant actually did intimidate the witness. As in our hypothetical case, such evidence is most often lacking.

In conclusion, neither the common law nor the Federal Rules of Evidence adequately provide for substantive admission of prior statements of government witnesses who have been successfully intimidated. In our hypothetical case, the result is that the government will lose its prosecution of Sam Smith. Such a result will only serve further to encourage defendants and their agents to intimidate to the point of even killing witnesses to prevent testimony at trial. In addition, and of substantial importance, witnesses remain in danger until the trial. Rule 804(b)(5) determinations will most usually result in favorable rulings to the defendant. Even assuming the waiver doctrine should be applied, sufficient evidence of intimidation to justify a finding of waiver will usually be absent. Thus the defendant's chances of preventing incriminating evidence from being admitted are high if the defendant succeeds at any time before trial in intimidating the witness. This suggests that the criminal justice system expand the opportunities for the early preservation and ultimate admission as substantive evidence of out-of-court statements of all potential witnesses to the extent justified by considerations of certainty of making and trustworthiness and thereby reduce the incentive of the accused to intimidate witnesses. Proposals to this end are set forth in Chapter 7.

NOTES

1. American Bar Association, Criminal Justice Section, *Reducing Victim/Witness Intimidation: A Package* 7-8 (Washington, D.C., 1981).
2. Fed. R. Evid. 801(d)(1)(A).
3. Fed. R. Evid. 801(d)(1)(B).
4. Fed. R. Evid. 801(d)(1)(C).
5. Fed. R. Evid. 803(24) and Fed. R. Evid. 804(b)(5).
6. The hypothetical case is based upon an actual case as related by Robert B. Lawler, Chief of the Appeals Division of the District Attorney's Office for Philadelphia, Pennsylvania.

7. The common law defines *hearsay* as "testimony in court, or written evidence, of a statement made out of court, the statement being offered as an assertion to show the truth of matters asserted therein, and thus resting for its value upon the credibility of the out-of-court asserter." C. McCormick, *Evidence* § 246 at 584 (Cleary ed. 1972). Rule 801(a)-(c) of the Federal Rules of Evidence is in accord:

The following definitions apply under this article:

(a) Statement. A "statement" is (1) an oral or written assertion or (2) nonverbal conduct of a person, if it is intended by him as an assertion.

(b) Declarant. A "declarant" is a person who makes a statement.

(c) Hearsay. "Hearsay" is a statement, other than one made by the declarant while testifying at the trial or hearing, offered in evidence to prove the truth of the matter asserted.

8. An exception to this unified approach exists only with respect to imposition of a requirement regarding procuring testimony of a witness absent from the hearing applicable solely to Rules 804(b)(2), (3), and (4), in which the proponent of the hearsay statement is unable to procure the witness's attendance by process or other reasonable means, Rule 804(a)(5). The exception by its terms is inapplicable to former testimony, Rule 804(b)(1).

9. Mason v. United States, 408 F.2d 903, 906 (10th Cir. 1969) ("We consider, as did the trial court, that the important element is whether the testimony of the witness is sought and is available and not whether the witness's body is available.").

10. United States v. Lieberman, 637 F.2d 95, 103 (2d Cir. 1980) ("There is no question that Gaines was unavailable to testify. He was a defendant, and the government could not call him as a witness. See Fed. R. Evid. 804(a)(1).").

11. United States v. Elmore, 423 F.2d 775, 778 (4th Cir. 1970) ("The requirement that the declarant be unavailable to testify is satisfied by the fact that West successfully asserted his fifth amendment privilege against self-incrimination and declined to answer any questions about the matter."). *See also* Advisory Committee's Note to Rule 804(a)(1) ("A ruling by the judge is required, which clearly implies that an actual claim of privilege must be made.").

12. United States v. Zappola, 646 F.2d 48, 54 (2d Cir. 1981) ("In United States v. Oliver, 626 F.2d 254 (2d Cir. 1980), this circuit held that an order from the court is an essential component in a declaration of unavailability under Rule 804(a)(2). Id. at 261. It is clear that in this case, the district court did not order Marano to testify. Instead, the district court relied on his assertion that he would refuse to testify even if ordered to by the court. The procedure that should have been followed by the court when faced with Marano's refusal to testify was (1) the issuance of an order, outside the presence of the jury, directing him to testify and (2) a warning the continued refusal to testify despite the court's order would be punishable by contempt.").

13. United States v. Mobley, 421 F.2d 345, 350-51 (5th Cir. 1970) ("Oliver's silence in reliance, albeit misplaced, upon Fifth Amendment rights, makes him no less unavailable than death or absence from the country or physical inability to speak.").

14. McDonell v. United States, 472 F.2d 1153, 1155 (8th Cir. 1973) ("Since [the witness] testified to a lack of memory as to a material portion of the subject matter of his prior testimony, he would be 'unavailable' under Rule 804 and his former

testimony on the subject would be admissible. Such a rule of evidence is supported by textwriters and case law. See generally, M. Ladd and R. Carlson, Cases and Materials on Evidence, 1001-1025 (1972); McCormick on Evidence, 611-12 (2d ed. 1972).").

15. 4 *Weinstein's Evidence* ¶ 804(a)]01] at 804-39-40 (New York: Matthew Bender, 1979) ("In a civil case, or in a criminal case where defendant offers the hearsay statement, it is easier to find unavailability even when the disability is only temporary. In such a case, Wigmore's formula may be appropriate: 'The duration of the illness need only be in probability such that with regard to the importance of the testimony the trial cannot be postponed.' [5 Wigmore, Evidence § 1406(a) at 219 (Chadbourn Rev. 1974)]. This is a matter for the trial judge's discretion. In reaching his decision he may consider such factors as the nature of the disability and its expected duration, the length of time the case has been pending and whether delays, if any, are attributable to the proponent of the hearsay, the nature of the case, the significance of the disabled witness' testimony, the availability of other evidence on the same point, and whether the nature of the expected trestimony and the subject of the hearsay statement is such that cross-examination would be expected to be particularly helpful.").

16. Fed. R. Civ. P. 45(e).

17. Federal Rule of Criminal Procedure 17(e) provides:

> (e) Place of Service.
>
> (1) In United States. A subpoena requiring the attendance of a witness at a hearing or trial may be served at any place within the United States.
>
> (2) Abroad. A subpoena directed to a witness in a foreign country shall issue under the circumstances and in the manner and be served as provided in Title 28, U.S.C. § 1783.

28 U.S.C. § 1783 provides that a federal court may issue a subpoena to a United States national or resident present in a foreign country, "if the court finds that particular testimony . . . by him is necessary in the interest of justice, and, in other than a criminal action or proceeding, if the court finds, in addition that it is not possible to obtain his testimony in admissible form without his personal appearance."

18. United States Constitution, Amendment VI ("In all criminal prosecutions, the accused shall enjoy the right . . . to be confronted with the witnesses against him.").

19. *See, e.g.*, Ohio v. Roberts, 448 U.S. 56 (1980); Mancusi v. Stubbs, 408 U.S. 204 (1972); Barber v. Page, 390 U.S. 719 (1968).

20. Fed. R. Evid. 104(a).

21. Motes v. United States, 178 U.S. 458, 474 (1900) (prior testimony properly excluded when the unavailabilty of the witness at trial was due to the "negligence" of the United States in removing him from custody before the trial and permitting him to stay in a hotel room in the custody of another government witness from which he escaped rather than in jail); United States v. Mathis, 550 F.2d 180, 181-82 (4th Cir. 1976):

> Karen Jones was not available to testify in person because she could not be located; inadvertently she had been released from a District of Columbia penal institution pursuant to a court order requiring the release of another prisoner bearing the same name.

Jones' prior testimony was admissible under Rule 804 of the Federal Rules of Evidence if her attendance at the trial could not be procured by process or other reasonable means, Rule 804(a)(5). The record shows that reasonable efforts were made to find her, but to no avail. Motes v. United States, 178 U.S. 458, 20 S.Ct. 993, 44 L.Ed. 1150 (1900) is inapposite. In the instant case, unlike *Motes*, the disappearance of Jones was due to inadvertence, not reckless disregard of an obligation to produce her, and there is no evidence that the prison official who released her knew that she would be needed as a witness.

22. In re Screws Antitrust Litigation, 526 F. Supp. 1316 (D. Mass. 1981); In re IBM Peripheral EDP Devices Antitrust Litigation, 444 F. Sup. 110 (N.D. Cal. 1978); Matter of Johns-Manville Asbestos Cases, 93 F.R.D. 853 (N.D. Ill. 1982), each declared that *predecessor in interest* means something more than "similar motive," something in the nature of a "special relationship," but at the same time not equating "special relationship" solely with the common law concept of privity.

23. 5 J. Wigmore, *Evidence* § 1388 at 111 (Chadbourn Rev. 1974).

24. Advisory Committee's Note to proposed Rule 804(b)(1), 56 F.R.D. 183, 324 (1973):

> As a further assurance of fairness in thrusting upon a party the prior handling of the witness, the common law also insisted upon identity of parties, deviating only to the extent of allowing substitution of successors in a narrowly construed privity. Mutuality as an aspect of identity is now generally discredited, and the requirement of identity of the offering party disappears except as it might affect motive to develop the testimony. * * * The question remains whether strict identity, or privity, should continue as a requirement with respect to the party against whom offered. The rule departs to the extent of allowing substitution of one with the right and opportunity to develop the testimony with similar motive and interest. This position is supported by modern decisions. McCormick § 232, pp. 489-490; 5 Wigmore § 1388.

25. Report of House Committee on the Judiciary, 93rd Cong., 1st Sess., Fed. R. Evid., No. 93-650, p. 15 (1973).

26. *Compare* C. McCormick, *Evidence* § 256 at 620 (Cleary ed. 1972) ("Identity of interest in the sense of motive, rather than technical identity of cause of action or title, is the test. The argument that it is unfair to force upon a party another's cross-examination or decision not to cross-examine a witness loses its validity with the realization that other hearsay exceptions involve no cross-examination whatever, and further that the choice is not between perfect and imperfect conditions for the giving of testimony but between imperfect conditions and no testimony at all.").

27. Advisory Committee's Note to proposed Rule 804(b)(1), 56 F.R.D. 183, 324 (1973) ("The common law did not limit the admissibility of former testimony to that given in an earlier trial of the same case, although it did require identity of issues as a means of insuring that the former handling of the witness was the equivalent of what would now be done if the opportunity were presented. Modern decisions reduce the requirement to 'substantial' identity. McCormick § 233. Since identity of issues is significant only in that it bears on motive and interest in developing fully the testimony of the witness, expressing the matter in the latter terms is preferable.")

28. United States v. Wingate, 520 F.2d 309 (2d Cir. 1975).

29. United States v. Atkins, 618 F.2d 366 (5th Cir. 1980).

30. C. McCormick, *Evidence* § 257 at 621 (Cleary ed. 1972) ("Thus, in criminal cases where the first indictment charges one offense, e.g., robbery, and the second, another distinct offense, such as murder of the person robbed, it is usually considered sufficient that the two indictments arise from the same transaction. Other patterns recur in the cases. One involves introducing at the trial of a criminal case testimony given at the preliminary hearing. In another, testimony given against the accused in an earlier criminal trial is offered against him in a civil case to which he is a party.").

31. Coleman v. Alabama, 399 U.S. 1, 9 (1970).

32. F. Bailey and H. Rothblatt, *Successful Techniques for Criminal Trials* § 25 at 26 (Rochester: Lawyers Cooperative, 1971).

33. A. Amsterdam, B. Segal, and M. Miller, *Trial Manual for the Defense of Criminal Cases* § 139 at 1-129 (3d ed. Philadelphia: ALI-ABA, 1977).

34. Ohio v. Roberts, 448 U.S. 56, 68-70 (1980):

> In [California v. Green, 399 U.S. 149 (1970)], at the preliminary hearing, a youth named Porter identified Green as a drug supplier. When called to the stand at Green's trial, however, Porter professed a lapse of memory. Frustrated in its attempt to adduce live testimony, the prosecution offered Porter's prior statements. The trial judge ruled the evidence admissible, and substantial portions of the preliminary hearing transcript were read to the jury. This Court found no error. . . . [T]he Court rejected Green's Confrontation Clause attack. It reasoned:
>
> > "Porter's statement at the preliminary hearing had already been given under circumstances closely approximating those that surround the typical trial. Porter was under oath; respondent was represented by counsel—the same counsel in fact who later represented him at the trial; respondent had every opportunity to cross-examine Porter as to his statement; and the proceedings were conducted before a judicial tribunal, equipped to provide a judicial record of the hearings." 399 U.S. at 165.
>
> These factors, the Court concluded, provided all that the Sixth Amendment demands: "substantial compliance with the purposes behind the confrontation requirement." *Id.* at 166.
>
> This passage and others in the *Green* opinion suggest that the *opportunity* to cross-examine at the preliminary hearing—even absent actual cross-examination—satisfies the Confrontation Clause. Yet the record showed, and the Court recognized, that defense counsel in fact had cross-examined Porter at the earlier proceeding. *Id.* at 151. Thus, Mr. Justice Brennan, writing in dissent, could conclude only that "[p]erhaps" "the mere opportunity for face-to-face encounter [is] sufficient." *Id.*, at 200, n.8. . . .
>
> We need not decide whether the Supreme Court of Ohio correctly dismissed statements in *Green* suggesting that the mere opportunity to cross-examine rendered the prior testimony admissible. . . . Nor need we decide whether de minimis questioning is sufficient, for defense counsel in this case tested Anita's testimony with the equivalent of significant cross-examination.

35. Ohio v. Roberts 448 U.S. 56, 72 (1980) ("Nor does it matter that, unlike [California v. Green, 399 U.S. 149 (1970)], respondent had a different lawyer at trial

from the one at the preliminary hearing. Although one might strain one's reading of *Green* to assign this factor some significance, respondent advances no reason of substance supporting the distinction. Indeed, if we were to accept this suggestion, *Green* would carry the seeds of its own demise; under a 'same attorney' rule, a defendant could nullify the effects of *Green* by obtaining new counsel after the preliminary hearing was concluded.'').

36. *See, e.g.*, J. Falknor, *The Hearsay Rule and Its Exceptions*, 2 U.C.L.A. L. Rev. 43 (1954); C. McCormick, *The Turncoat Witness: Previous Statements as Substantive Evidence*, 25 Tex. L. Rev. 573 (1947); E. Morgan, *Hearsay Dangers and the Application of the Hearsay Concept*, 62 Harv. L. Rev. 177 (1948); M. Reutlinger, *Prior Inconsistent Statements: Presently Inconsistent Doctrine*, 26 Hastings L. J. 361 (1974); E. Silbert, *Federal Rule of Evidence 801(d)(1)(A)*, 49 Temp. L. Q. 880 (1976).

37. 5 J. Wigmore, *Evidence* § 1362 at 3-10 (Chadbourn Rev. 1974).

38. C. McCormick, *Handbook of the Law of Evidence* § 39 at 74 (St. Paul: West, 1954).

39. Di Carlo v. United States, 6 F.2d 364, 368 (2d Cir. 1925).

40. Ruhala v. Roby, 379 Mich. 102, 124, 150 N.W.2d 146, 156 (1967).

41. The difference becomes more pronounced in cases in which the witness professes a lack of memory about whether he made the prior statement or about its subject matter. The effectiveness of rehabilitative redirect in these cases varies inversely with the extent of the witness's memory loss. Probably at some point the inability of the criminal defense attorney to conduct effective redirect examination of a witness forgetful of the substance of the alleged inconsistent statement would preclude substantive admission of the prior statement as violative of the Sixth Amendment right to confrontation. *See* California v. Green, 399 U.S. 149, 168-69 (1970).

42. A letter to the Chairman of the Senate Judiciary Committee from the Standing Committee on Rules of Practice and Procedure and the Advisory Committee on Rules of Evidence of the Judicial Conference of the United States (May 22, 1974), quoted in 4 *Weinstein's Evidence* at 801-4 (1979).

43. 399 U.S. 149, 160 (1970). *See also* 4 *Weinstein's Evidence* at 801-14-801-15 (1979) (''[N]ot only does the witness . . . recant his earlier story, but he also explains, in not unplausible fashion, the reason why he did so. This is a cross-examination successful beyond the dreams of avarice.''). With respect to the likelihood of successfully ''breaking down'' the witness, *see* Dutton v. Evans, 400 U.S. 74, 89 (1970).

44. 3A J. Wigmore, *Evidence* § 1018 at 996 (Chadbourn Rev. 1970). *See also* J. Maguire, *The Hearsay System: Around and Through the Thicket*, 14 Vand. L. Rev. 741, 767-68 (1961).

45. C. McCormick, *supra* note 38 at 76.

46. C. McCormick, *supra* note 36 at 575.

47. 1 E. Devitt and C. Blackmar, *Federal Jury Practice and Instructions* § 17.16 (3d ed. St. Paul: West, 1977):

> ***Effect of Prior Inconsistent Statements or Conduct—***
> ***By a Witness Not a Party***
>
> Evidence that at some other time a witness, . . . has said or done something, or has failed to say or do something, which is inconsistent with the witness'

testimony at the trial, may be considered by the jury for the sole purpose of judging the credibility of the witness; but may never be considered as evidence or proof of the truth of any such statement.

48. E. Morgan, *supra* note 36 at 193.

49. E. Morgan, *id. See also* United States v. Duff, 332 F.2d 702, 707 (6th Cir. 1964) ("[The] jury could hardly help considering the content of the statement as substantive evidence."); Bruton v. United States, 391 U.S. 123, 126 (1968) ("[B]ecause of the substantial risk that the jury, despite instructions to the contrary, looked to the incriminating extra-judicial statements in determining petitioner's guilt, admission of Evans' confession in this joint trial violated petitioner's right of cross-examination."); Shepard v. United States, 290 U.S. 96, 104 (1933) (Cardozo, J.) (evidence in admissible and gravely prejudicial for one purpose but admissible and not objectionable for another should be excluded from consideration by the jury since the task of ignoring the evidence for the one aspect while considering it for the other is too subtle for the ordinary mind).

50. *See* Hearings on H.R. 5464 Before the Senate Comm. on the Judiciary, 93d Cong., 2d Sess. 302 (1974) (statement of Herbert Semmel):

> The problems of inaccurate repetition, ambiguity and incompleteness of out-of-court statements may be found in both written and oral statements, although the problem is more acute in oral statements. But written statements are also subject to distortion. We are all familiar with the way a skilled investigator, be he a lawyer, police officer, insurance claim agent, or private detective, can listen to a potential witness and then prepare a statement for signature by the witness which reflects the interest of the investigators' client or agency. Adverse details are omitted; subtle changes of emphasis are made. It is regrettable but true that some lawyers will distort the truth to win a case and that some police officers will do the same to "solve" a crime, particularly one which has aroused the public interest or caused public controversy. Or the police officer may be seeking to put away a "dangerous criminal" who the officer "knows" is guilty but against whom evidence is lacking.

See also Goings v. United States, 377 F.2d 753, 762 n.13 (8th Cir. 1967):

> Today the art of statement taking is a recognized science. Inbau & Reid, Criminal Interrogation & Confessions (1962); Schwartz, Trial of Automobile Accident Cases, Vol. I, § 4, pp. 5, 6, "Requisites of Witnesses Statements," 3rd ed. (1965); Smithson, Insurance Law Journal, June, 1958, "Liability Claims and Litigation," pp. 375-403; Schweitzer, Cyclopedia of Trial Practice, Vol. I, § 30, p. 58, "Securing Statements from Witnesses" (1954); Donaldson Casualty Claims Practice, "Richard D. Erwin Series in Risk & Insurance"(1964), pp. 481-500; Averbach, Handling Accident Cases, Vol. 2 p. 269, (1958). Whether the problem be one of fault in communication to a good faith interrogator or culpable strategy of the examiner is immaterial. The fact remains, most ex parte statements reflect the subjective interest and attitude of the examiner as well.

51. *See* Illinois Supreme Court Committee on Evidence, *Majority Report on the Use of Prior Inconsistent Statements of Witnesses as Substantive Proof* 16 (1971).

52. *See* Chapter 6, Section B1 *infra*.

53. 56 F.R.D. 183, 293 (1973). *See also* Preliminary Draft of Proposed Rules of

Evidence for the United States District Court and Magistrates, 46 F.R.D. 161, 331 (1969).

54. 56 F.R.D. at 296. *See* Cal. Evid. Code § 1235 (St. Paul: West, 1966), and the California Law Revision Commission's Comment on § 1235, *reprinted in* 29B Cal. Evid. Code 221.

55. 56 F.R.D. at 295.

56. *See* H.R. Rep. No. 650, 93d Cong., 1st Sess. 13 (1973).

57. United States v. De Sisto., 329 F.2d 929 (2d Cir. 1964).

58. Hearings on Proposed Rules of Evidence Before the Subcomm. on Criminal Justice of the House Comm. on the Judiciary, 93rd Cong., 1st Sess., Supp. 170 (1973).

59. *See* H.R. Rep. No. 650, 93d Cong., 1st Sess. 13 (1973).

60. H.R. Rep. No. 650, *id.* Thus the House believed that the rule would both ensure reliability and help neutralize the effect of any coercion, deception, or subtle influence directed at the witness.

61. *See, e.g.*, letter from James F. Schaefer, Chairman of the Committee on Federal Evidence and Procedure, Trial Lawyers of America, to Rep. William L. Hungate (June 22, 1973) and accompanying material, in Hearings on Proposed Rules of Evidence Before the Subcomm. on Criminal Justice of the House Comm. on the Judiciary, 93d Cong., 1st Sess., Supp. 127-29 (1973); Hearings on H.R. 5463 (Fed. R. Evid.) Before the Senate Comm. on the Judiciary, 93d Cong., 2d Sess. 50-52 (1974) (statement of Edward W. Cleary). *But see* letter from Edward W. Cleary to Herbert E. Hoffman, Counsel, Subcommittee on Reform of Federal Criminal Laws, House Committee on the Judiciary, May 31, 1973, in Hearings on Proposed Rules of Evidence Before the Subcomm. on Criminal Justice of the House Comm. on the Judiciary, 93d Cong., 1st Sess., Supp. 98-99 (1973) (rejecting exclusion of such evidence). *See also* letter from Hon. Albert B. Maris to Herbert E. Hoffman, May 30, 1973, in Hearings on Proposed Rules of Evidence Before the Subcomm. on Criminal Justice of th House Comm. on the Judiciary, 93d Cong., 1st Sess., Supp. 98 (1973).

62. Edward W. Cleary, in testimony before the Senate subcommittee discussing the limitations placed by the House upon the admissibility of substantive evidence, stated: "Their effect is for all practical purposes virtually to destroy the utility of the rule as a solution for the problems it was designed to meet, such as fading memories, bribery, intimidation, and other influences which cause witnesses to change their stories." Hearings on H.R. 5463 (Fed. R. Evid.) Before the Senate Comm. on the Judiciary, 93rd Cong., 2d Sess. 51 (1974).

Cleary had earlier stated:

> The redraft would virtually destroy the utility of provision (A), which deals with prior inconsistent statements. If the witness has made a prior statement under oath, the threat of a perjury charge makes it highly unlikely that he will subsequently relate a different story again under oath. Hence the instances in which the rule would operate under the suggested redraft would be greatly curtailed. The problem area consists of cases in which the prior statement was not under oath, whether in the course of a judicial proceeding or not, and a rule which does not deal with these cases is of no practical significance.

Letter from Edward W. Cleary to Herbert E. Hoffman, May 31, 1973, in Hearings on Proposed Rules of Evidence Before the Subcomm. on Criminal Justice of the House Comm. on the Judiciary, 93d Cong., 1st Sess., Supp. 98-99 (1973).

63. S. Rep. No. 1277, 93d Cong., 2d Sess. 16 n.21 (1974).

64. S. Rep. No. 1277, 93d Cong., 2d Sess., 15-16 (1974). The Senate committee first noted that of all traditional hearsay exceptions only the former testimony exception requires that the prior statement be made under oath. The committee then asserted that the jury has sufficient demeanor evidence to judge the credibility of the prior statement if the declarant was presently testifying in court. Finally, the committee thought that its rule was superior because the prior statements, having been made closer in time to the events they describe, would have been subject to less improper influence and would have been made when the witness's memory was relatively fresh.

65. S. Rep. No. 1227, 93d Cong., 2d Sess., 16 n.21 (1974). For discussion of burden of proof as it affects substantive admission of prior inconsistent statements, *see* Comment, *Prior Inconsistent Statements and the Rule Against Impeachment of One's Own Witness: The Proposed Federal Rules*, 52 Tex. L. Rev. 1383, 1389, 1395-96 (1974).

66. S. Rep. No. 1227, *id. But compare* People v. Green, 3 Cal.3d 981, 479 P.2d 998, 92 Cal. Rptr. 494 (1971) (jury conviction based upon substantive admission of prior inconsistent statement without a motion directed to insufficiency of evidence). A court might be reluctant to grant a defendant's motion for acquittal pursuant to Federal Rule of Criminal Procedure 29 when the only evidence was a prior inconsistent statement. Disregarding the statement would certainly not be construing all of the evidence most favorably to the government. *See* Crawford v. United States, 375 F.2d 332 (D.C. Cir. 1967). The Supreme Court, however, observed in California v. Green, 399 U.S. 149 (1970), that "considerations of due process, wholly apart from the Confrontation Clause, might prevent convictions where a reliable evidentiary basis is totally lacking." *Id.* at 163 n.15. In United States v. Schwartz, 390 F.2d 1 (3d Cir. 1968), the court reversed a conviction when a prior inconsistent statement had been given substantive effect, but it noted that "[e]ven if this testimony were in the record, we conclude that there is insufficient evidence against defendant." *Id.* at 7. In most instances, the government's case could withstand the motion for acquittal without relying upon evidence of a prior inconsistent statement.

67. Conf. Rep. No. 1597, 93d Cong., 2d Sess. 10 (1974).

68. *See* J. Stalmack, *Prior Inconsistent Statement: Congress Takes a Compromising Step Backward in Enacting Rule 801(d)(1)(A)*, 8 Loy. Chi. L. J. 251, 267 (1977).

69. If the witness admits the truth of his or her prior inconsistent statement, the statement is received substantively as adopted testimony. *See, e.g.*, United States v. Taveres, 512 F.2d 872 (9th Cir. 1975); Stevens v. United States, 256 F.2d 619 (9th Cir. 1958). *See also* United States v. Borelli, 336 F.2d 376, 391 (2d Cir. 1964) ("When a witness . . . affirms the truth of a prior statement, [it] is to be considered 'not only as bearing on the credibility of the witness but as affirmative evidence.' . . . [T]he trier of fact has 'two conflicting statements . . . of equal force as evidence.' ").

70. 4 *Weinstein's Evidence* ¶ 801(d)(1) (A)[01] at 801-109 (1984) (the "better view" of Wigmore and McCormick, followed by federal courts in impeachment cases, should also be the approach to determining inconsistency under Rule 801).

71. *See, e.g.*, Sanger v. Brown, 180 Ind. 322, 202 N.E. 1001 (1913). Dean Mason Ladd, *Some Observations on Credibility: Impeachment of Witnesses*, 52 Cornell L. Q. 239, 253 (1967), articulated the following standard:

> [T]he degree of inconsistency must be real. When the statements are placed side by side, it must be possible to say that both cannot be true. Only in this circumstance will the triers have reason to nullify the testimony given in court, which is the only justification for the admissibility of the out-of-court statement.

72. C. McCormick, *Evidence* § 34 at 64 (1954).

73. 3A J. Wigmore, *Evidence* § 1040 at 1048 (Chadbourn Rev. 1970).

74. 539 F.2d 244, 254 (1st Cir. 1976).

75. United States v. Barrett, 539 F.2d 244, 254 (1st Cir. 1976) ("Furthermore, the fact that [the witness'] belief that [the defendant] was not involved might be called an 'opinion' is immaterial. . . . The important point is the clear incompatibility between [the witness'] direct testimony and the alleged statement."). *See also* 3A J. Wigmore, *Evidence* § 1041 at 1052 (Chadbourn Rev. 1970).

76. Felice v. Long Island R.R., 426 F.2d 192 (2d Cir. 1980); United States v. Rice, 550 F.2d 1364 (5th Cir. 1977). *See also* 4 J. Wigmore, *Evidence* § 1129 at 270 (Chadbourn Rev. 1972). Thus if the defendant waives the right to remain silent and makes a statement without then reasserting his or her rights, failure to include matters naturally expected to be included within the statement may be employed for impeachment purposes provided the omission is clearly inconsistent with the witness's in-court testimony.

77. Jenkins v. Anderson, 447 U.S. 231, 239 (1980) ("Common law traditionally has allowed witnesses to be impeached by their previous failure to state a fact in circumstances in which that fact naturally would have been asserted. 3A Wigmore, *Evidence* § 1042, at 1056 (Chadbourn Rev. 1970)"; prearrest silence on the part of a criminal defendant not induced by government action admissible to impeach); Anderson v. Charles, 447 U.S. 404, 407-408 (1980) ("*Miranda* warnings inform a person of his right to remain silent and assure him, at least implicitly, that his silence would not be used against him. . . . *Doyle* bars the use against a criminal defendant of silence maintained after receipt of governmental assurances."); Fletcher v. Weir, 455 U.S. 603 (1982) (silence postarrest but before the giving of *Miranda* warnings may be employed to impeach).

78. *See* People v. Johnson, 109 Ill.App.3d 511, 65 Ill. Dec. 137, 440 N.E.2d 992 (1982).

79. *See* People v. Sam, 71 Cal.2d 194, 454 P.2d 700, 77 Cal.Rptr. 804 (1969); Corsick v. Boston Elevated Ry., 218 Mass. 144, 105 N.E. 600 (1914). *See also* 4 *Weinstein's Evidence* ¶ 801(d)(1)(A)[04] 801-88-801-99 (1979). In People v. Green, 3 Cal.3d 981, 988, 479 P.2d 998, 1002, 92 Cal.Rptr. 494, 498 (1971), the California Supreme Court explained that "[i]n normal circumstances, the testimony of a witness that he does not remember an event is not 'inconsistent' with a prior statement by him describing that event." The court then proceeded, however, to find that the witness's lack of recollection at trial was inconsistent with his prior statement that the defendant was a participant in a drug transaction. The court departed from the general rule because it concluded that the witness's lack of recollection was feigned. *Id.* at 988-89, 479 P.2d at 1002, 92 Cal.Rptr. at 498-99. *See also* Chapter 6, Section C *infra.*

80. 56 F.R.D. 183, 296 (1973).

81. The witness can only be asked about the circumstances surrounding the making of the prior statement, which he or she may or may not recall.

82. In addition, the witness who asserts lack of recollection may not have testified at trial within the meaning of Rule 801(d)(1), because the witness's assertion is not relevant evidence, *see* Fed. R. Evid. 401, and is therefore inadmissible, Fed. R. Evid. 402.

83. *Accord* 4 *Weinstein's Evidence* ¶ 801 (d)(1)(A)[04] at 801-98-801-99 (1979):

> [I]t would seem that the prior statement should not be included under 801(d)(1)(A) if the judge finds that the witness genuinely cannot remember, and the period of amnesia or forgetfulness is crucial as regards the facts in issue. This result would be compatible with case law which suggests that a statement of no recollection is not inconsistent with a former statement about the now forgotten matter. It would also be in keeping with Rule 804(a)(3) which includes among the situations in which a witness is unavailable that arising when he "testifies to a lack of memory of the subject matter of his statement." Although the rules nowhere state that Rule 804 refers back to Rule 801, the reasoning of Rule 804(a)(3) would mean that declarant was not available at trial—a precondition for the exclusion of Rule 801 statements from hearsay. Finally, excluding prior statements where the witness has no recollection of their subject matter would seem to accord with the Supreme Court's emphasis on cross-examination opportunity in at least some of its recent confrontation cases.

84. 3A J. Wigmore, *Evidence* § 1043 at 1061 (Chadbourn Rev. 1970). *Accord* United States v. Thompson, 708 F.2d 1294 (8th Cir. 1983).

85. With respect to the waiver argument, *see* Chapter 4, Section I *infra*.

86. 423 F.2d 1165 (2d Cir. 1970).

87. 3 Cal.3d 981, 479 P.2d 998, 92 Cal.Rptr. 494 (1971).

88. 423 F.2d at 1167. The circuit court quoted the following observations of the trial judge:

> "It must be clear to everybody who looks at this witness that he is faking and he is attempting to avoid giving answers.
>
> * * *
>
> "It is quite evident, in other words, that this witness has in mind avoiding testifying because he believes it is very likely to involve the defendant.
>
> "We are here to get the truth and I do not think it lies in the lips or the mind of any witness to thwart the truth purposely. This is a piece of hypocracy [sic] which is as plain as the nose on your face, and I don't think we ought to allow a mockery of justice to be displayed so openly and so indifferently."

Id. at 1167, n.1.

89. *Id.* at 1169-70 (emphasis added).

90. *See e.g.*, United States v. Davis, 487 F.2d 112 (5th Cir. 1973); United States v. Borelli, 336 F. 2d 376 (2d Cir. 1963).

91. The rationale of *Insana* has found little if indeed any support in subsequent federal decisions. *Cf.* United States v. Rogers, 439 F.2d 490, 496 (8th Cir. 1976) (quoting extensively from *Insana* in support of finding that prior statement is

inconsistent with witness's claim of lack of recollection at trial); United States v. Klein, 488 F.2d 481 (2d Cir. 1973) (citing *Insana* for the proposition that prior testimony is *inconsistent* with claim of lack of recollection at trial).

92. 329 F.2d 929 (2d Cir. 1964).

93. 423 F.2d at 1169.

94. *Id.* at 1170.

95. This is similar to a court's admitting a hearsay declaration under the excited utterance hearsay exception, Fed. R. Evid. 803(2), and then permitting counsel to argue that the jury should give great weight to the statement because of its spontaneous nature.

96. 3 Cal.3d 981, 479 P.2d 998, 92 Cal.Rptr. 494 (1971).

97. California v. Green, 399 U.S. 149 (1970).

98. 3 Cal.3d at 988, 479 P.2d at 1002, 92 Cal.Rptr. at 498.

99. 3 Cal.3d at 989, 479 P.2d at 1002, 92 Cal.Rptr. at 498 (emphasis added). Although the court found that Porter impliedly denied his earlier statements, the circumstances of the case indicated that he feigned lack of recollection to protect the defendant and thus tacitly admitted the truth of his prior statements. The court stated that "Porter unmasked his apparent motive when he protested, 'Like I already said, I mean I've got a conscience, and I don't want to.' " *Id.* at 988, 479 P.2d at 1002, 92 Cal.Rptr. at 498. *Accord* United States v. Thompson, 708 F.2d 1294 (8th Cir. 1983).

100. People v. Green, 3 Cal.2d 981, 988, 479 P.2d 998, 1002, 92 Cal.Rptr. 494, 498 (1971).

101. United States v. Insana, 423 F.2d 1165, 1167 (2d Cir. 1970).

102. Federal Rule of Evidence 104(b) (relevancy conditioned on fact) would govern the procedure for such admission. The judge would admit the statements upon making a preliminary determination that the foundation evidence was sufficient to support a finding of an adoption of truth by the witness.

103. Prior statements have, however, been held admissible under Rule 801(d)(1)(A) when the trial court found that the witness "was fully aware of the content of his prior statement and was simply attempting [through claiming an inability to recall] to avoid implicating [the defendant]," United States v. Rogers, 549 F.2d 490, 496 (8th Cir. 1976); or that his claimed failure to recollect was a mere "contrivance," United States v. Collins, 478 F.2d 837, 838 (5th Cir. 1973); or "when a witness remembers events incompletely or with some equivocation at trial," United States v. Distler, 671 F.2d 954, 958 (6th Cir. 1981). *See generally*, United States v. Shoupe, 548 F.2d 636, 643 (6th Cir. 1977) (when government witness testified at trial as to a lack of memory so selective that the court found it "incredible," the witness could be impeached with his prior statement).

104. When a witness testifies to a lack of recollection, whether real or feigned, admissibility of the witness's prior statements should ordinarily be determined by applying Rule 804(b)(5). *See* Chapter 4, Section E infra.

105. United States v. Iaconetti, 406 F. Supp. 554, 559 (E.D.N.Y.), aff'd, 540 F.2d 574 (2d Cir. 1976) ("What is probably meant is that the exception should not be used for trivial or collateral matters.").

106. de Mars v. Equitable Life Assurance Society of the United States, 610 F.2d 55, 61 (1st Cir. 1979) ("The requirements of part (B) of the rule cannot be ignored.

See, e.g., United States v. Kim, 193 U.S. App.D.C. 370, 379-81, 595 F.2d 755, 764, 66 (D.C. Cir. 1979) (telex excluded because, inter alia, it did not meet the requirements of part (B) of Rule 803(24)); United States v. Reese, 183 U.S.App.D.C. 1 n.18 at 10-11, 56 F.2d 894 n.18 at 903-04 (D.C. Cir. 1977) (no claim or showing that agreement was more probative than any other evidence defendant could procure through reasonable means); Matter of Sterling Nav. Co., Lit., 444 F. Supp. 1043, 1047-48 (S.D.N.Y. 1977) (no effort made to depose or produce other witnesses); Workman v. Cleveland Cliffs Iron Company, 68 F.R.D. 562 (N.D. Ohio, E.D. 1975) (other witnesses to the accident available)."). *See also* 4 *Weinstein's Evidence* ¶803(24)[01] at 803-293-803-294 (1979) ("What is 'reasonable' depends upon such matters as the importance of the evidence, the means of the command of the proponent and the amount in controversy. The good sense of the trial judge must be relied upon. It should not be necessary to scale the highest mountains of Tibet to obtain a deposition for use in a $500 damage claim arising from an accident with a postal truck. Even though the evidence may be somewhat cumulative, it may be important in evaluating other evidence and arriving at the truth so that the 'more probative' requirement cannot be interpreted with case iron rigidity.").

107. 444 F.2d 152 (5th Cir. 1971).

108. *Id.* at 156.

109. 547 F.2d 1346 (8th Cir. 1976).

110. 406 F. Supp. 554, 558-60 (E.D.N.Y. 1976). The other bases were that the statements were authorized admissions by a party-opponent under Rule 801(d)(2)(C) and that they were prior consistent statements offered to rebut a charge of recent fabrication under Rule 801(d)(1)(B). *Id.* at 558. Because the Second Circuit approved the lower court's decision under Rules 803(24) and 801(d)(2)(C), it did not reach the question whether the statements were also admissible under Rule 801(d)(1)(B). 540 F.2d at 577.

111. *Id.* at 556. Defendant also explained that "he was 'leading . . . on' Mr. Lioi in order to 'gather evidence.' " *Id.*

112. *Id.* at 560 ("[A]llowance must be made for situations like this in which the need did not become apparent until after the trial had commenced. Since it was not the proponent's fault that notice could only be given after the trial began, and since the defendant was not prejudiced by the mid-trial notice, the evidence was properly admitted under Rule 803(24).").

113. 542 F.2d 285 (5th Cir. 1976).

114. The prosecution introduced the prior statements to impeach the credibility of the witnesses, and the district court gave an appropriate limiting instruction. On appeal, the Fifth Circuit overruled defendant's challenge to the adequacy of the limiting instruction, holding that the prior statements met all the requirements of Rule 803(24) and therefore could properly have been considered as substantive evidence. *Id.* at 289.

115. *Id.* at 290. The witnesses also admitted voluntarily signing forms waiving the right to remain silent. *Id.*

116. *Id.* at 291.

117. *See also* United States v. Bailey, 581 F.2d 341 (3d Cir. 1978). United States v. Muscato, 534 F. Supp. 969 (E.D.N.Y. 1982). *See generally*, 4 *Weinstein's Evidence* ¶ 803(24)[01] at 803-292 (1979).

118. In *Iaconetti* Judge Weinstein simply stated that "[t]he fact that the statement was made close on the heels of the criminal event and to persons with whom it was appropriate and even necessary to communicate would seem to mitigate the risks of insincerity and faulty memory." 406 F. Sup. at 559. In *Leslie*, however, the court emphasized that the witnesses admitted making the statements, 542 F.2d at 290. In a footnote *Leslie* distinguished United States v. Sisto, 534 F.2d 616 (5th Cir. 1976), on the certainty-of-making point, observing that in *Sisto* the only evidence that the statement was made was the testimony of a government agent and the declarant had "categorically denied having made the statements." *Id.* at 291 n.6.

119. The Advisory Committee's Note to Proposed Rule 803, 56 F.R.D. 183, 300, 303 (1973), made applicable to both Rules 803 and 804 the personal knowledge requirement of Rule 602.

120. If a court is admitting a statement under Rule 804(b)(5), this criterion will not be met because of the declarant's unavailability. The court should thus demand greater circumstantial indications of trustworthiness before admitting a statement under Rule 804(b)(5) than it would if it were applying Rule 803(24) to the same statement and the declarant were available for effective cross-examination at trial.

121. *See* Chapter 7, Section C2(b)(1) *infra* for further discussion of the concept of unavailability under Rule 804(a).

122. 547 F.2d 1346 (8th Cir. 1976).

123. *See, e.g.*, United States v. Garner, 574 F.2d 1141 (4th Cir. 1978) (testimony corroborated by testimony of other witnesses that they accompanied one defendant and a coconspirator on European trips for the purposes of serving as a courier in a drug-related offense); United States v. West, 574 F.2d 1131 (4th Cir. 1978) (slain witness's grand jury testimony corroborated by federal agents who surveyed the events and by photographs of the witness's movement and tape recordings of conversations during drug sales); United States v. Barlow, 693 F.2d 964 (6th Cir. 1982) (grand jury testimony that witness had not been with the defendant after 11:30 P.M. corroborated by the fact that witness was the defendant's girlfriend, that she had been given immunity, and that no motive to fabricate was suggested); United States v. Murphy, 696 F.2d 282, 286-87 (4th Cir. 1982) ("There are abundant indicia of the reliability and trustworthiness of Lattisaw's grand jury testimony. Gantt's credibility may have been subject to question, but her testimony was entirely consistent with Lattisaw's grand jury testimony. So was the testimony of the other witnesses at the scene, including such details as the fact that when Waddell left the bank his mask was partially rolled up so that some of his hair and skin could be seen. There was confirmation in the identification of the Cadillac, the first getaway car, in which Gantt was arrested before reaching Washington and in which the black and gold ski mask was found. That automobile was registered in Waddell's name, just as Lattisaw testified. Conviction did not rest alone upon the grand jury testimony of Lattisaw but upon that together with other strongly corroborative testimony and proof, some of which was unimpeachable. The circumstances fully justified receipt in evidence of the grand jury testimony and our conclusion that its receipt violated neither the Rules of Evidence nor the Confrontation Clause."); United States v. Walker, 696 F.2d 277, 280-81 (4th Cir. 1982) ("Looking to all of Parker's grand jury testimony, one discovers very solid indicia of trustworthiness. He testified to the Coast Guard boarding, his arrest and transfer to the Coast Guard cutter. These were

known facts and undeniable. He was a member of the crew at the time of the vessel's arrest, and from that there would arise a strong inference that he had been a member of its crew from the beginning of the venture. His recital of the events and circumstances that led to his being there derives color from his verified testimony about the Coast Guard boarding and the arrest. Of course, the trustworthiness of his testimony derives further suport from its consistency with that of Thompson, but it rests primarily upon that portion of Parker's testimony that was verified and which is undeniable by these defendants.'').

124. *See, e.g.*, United States v. Gonzales, 559 F.2d 1271 (5th Cir. 1977) (grand jury statements untrustworthy when witness faced confinement for contempt and Government led witness to ''finger'' Gonzales by leading questions).

125. 677 F.2d 586 (7th Cir. 1982).

126. *Id.* at 587-88.

127. The appellants presumably did not appeal the introduction of the tape recording because the tape recording contained their voices and was therefore an admission of a party-opponent. The Federal Rules of Evidence deems party admissions as ''not hearsay' pursuant to Rule 801(d)(2)(A).

128. 677 F.2d at 588.

129. *Id.*

130. *Id.* at 589.

131. *Id.*

132. 581 F.2d 341 (3d Cir. 1978).

133. Fed. R. Evid. 804(b)(3) provides for the admission of statements made against penal interest. The trial court rejected introduction of the statement pursuant to this rule and the appellate court affirmed. Stewart gave the statement in order to receive leniency and thus motivation other than telling the truth was present. 581 F.2d at 345 n.4.

134. 581 F.2d at 348.

135. The court mentioned that Stewart could have borrowed the car from Bailey and robbed the bank with another. Then Stewart could finger Bailey and protect his accomplice. Id. at 349.

136. *Id.*

137. 557 F.2d at 309 (2d Cir. 1977).

138. *Id.* at 315-16.

139. 559 F.2d 1271 (5th Cir. 1977).

140. *Id.* at 1272 (''First, as we have observed, the pressure of the prosecutor and the members of the grand jury on the witness was such that it was incumbent upon him to come up with an answer, whether or not it was true. Second, Guerrero's answers were given to leading questions which would not have been permitted at trial. Fed. R. Evid. 611(c). Such questions are prohibited on the rationale that they might possibly distort the truth of the answers. Third, the fact that the witness was under oath, and subject to the penalties of perjury, loses any significance it might have in view of the threats made by the prosecutor that if the witness remained silent after being given immunity he could be repeatedly called before successive grand juries and given an unlimited number of repeated six-month contempt sentences if he did not testify. Fourth, being under fear that if he told the truth about who hired him physical harm might come to him and his family, Guerrero would have some incentive not to tell the truth. Fifth, the testimony was not cross-examined, was

readily accepted at first telling, and was unsupported by detailed facts concerning Gonzalez.'').

141. *See also* United States v. Barlow, 693 F.2d 954, 962 (6th Cir. 1982) (''[T]he trial court must determine whether the substance of the grand jury testimony possesses 'circumstantial guarantees of trustworthiness' equivalent to the other exceptions included in Rule 804. In making this determination the trial court should consider the declarant's motiviation to testify before the grand jury, the extent to which the testimony reflects the declarant's personal knowledge, whether the declarant has ever recanted the testimony, and the existence of corroborating evidence available for cross-examination.'').

142. The strongest argument for the prosecutor under Rule 804(b)(5) is simply the fact that there are three unavailable and one available witness who can be shown at one time to have identified Sam Smith as the killer or at least as having been at the apartment house when the murder occurred. Whether strength in numbers corroboration would or should carry the day is unlikely but clearly not impossible or even improbable.

John Goodfellow's identification of Sam Smith at the lineup is discussed in the Section that follows.

143. The statement of identification need not occur ''soon'' after the perception. The word *soon* appearing in early drafts of Rule 801(d)(1)(C) was stricken on the basis of a comment of the Justice Department quoted in 4 *Weinstein's Evidence* ¶ 801(d)(1)(C)[01] at 801-25 (1979).

> *Problem*: The qualification that the statement of identification must have been given ''soon'' after the declarant perceived the person whom he identifies, injects into the suggested rule a possible limitation upon which no court has passed. We understand the rule to mean that the identifiction must take place soon after the offense. There has been no decision requiring that lineups be held within a particular period of time after the commission of the offense.
>
> Practical considerations militate against such a restrictive approach. The offender may not be apprehended or otherwise be subject to a lineup until a considerable time after the offense. The victim may be hospitalized as a result of an attack upon him and may not be able to attend a lineup until a considerable period after the event. Even if the proposed rule is read as implying that the statement of identification must have been made ''soon'' after commencement of the identification procedure, we regard it as unduly restrictive. Through fear of retribution, a complaining witness may not make a statement of identification until shortly before he actually testifies at trial, a considerable period of time after the identification procedure, as for instance in United States v. Hinle, D.C.Cir. No. 24, 273 (July 19, 1971) [448 F.2d 1157 (D.C. Cir. 1971)]. Yet even such a statement has some probative value in corroborating the in-court identification.
>
> Recommendation: We suggest deletion of the word ''soon'' from the rule.

144. In United States v. Moskowitz, 581 F.2d 14 (2d Cir. 1978), the majority held that a sketch made by an artist from the description of eyewitness is not a ''statement'' under Rule 801(a) and therefore, not hearsay, Relevancy is established by evidence that the witness previously identified the sketch as correctly depicting the person committing the offense. The sketch is thus treated exactly as if it had been a photograph. *Compare* Friendly, J., concurring, regarding the sketch as an integral

part of the witness's statement to the police artist enabling him to draw and stating that the sketch as drawn accurately depicts the perpetrator of the offense. Under this analysis, the sketch is a statement under Rule 801(a) declared "not hearsay" under Rule 801(d)(1)(C). It is suggested that Judge Friendly has the best of this argument. Since both approaches require that the identifying witness testify at trial, as Judge Friendly pointed out, the practical result is the same.

145. United States v. Lewis, 565 F.2d 1248, 1251 (2d Cir. 1977) ("We agree with the observation there made that Congress has recognized, as do most trial judges, that identification in the courtroom is a formality that offers little in the way of reliability and much in the way of suggestibility.").

146. United States v. Marchand, 564 F.2d 993, 996 (2d Cir. 1977). *See also* Gilbert v. California, 388 U.S. 263, 272 n.3, (1967) ("[T]he earlier identification has greater probative value than an identification made in the courtroom after the suggestions of others and the circumstances of the trial may have intervened to create a fancied recognition of the witness's mind.").

147. *See, e.g.*, United States v. Elemy, 656 F.2d 507 (9th Cir. 1981); United States v. Cueto, 611 F.2d 1056 (5th Cir. 1980); United States v. Fritz, 580 F.2d 370 (10th Cir. 1978); United States v. Lewis, 565 F.2d 1248 (2d Cir. 1977).

148. United States v. Lewis, 565 F.2d 1248, 1252 (2d Cir. 1977) ("If appellant is suggesting that under the new Rules testimony like Agent Farrell's may only be used to bolster an accurate in-court identification, we disagree. It seems clear both from the text and the legislative history of the amended Rule that testimony concerning extra-judicial identifications is admissible regardless of whether there has been an accurate in-court identification. The Senate Report recognizes the possibility that there may be a 'discrepancy . . . between the witness's in-court and out-of-court testimony,' and the House Report praises the amended Rule as a means of ensuring that 'delays in the criminal justice system do not lead to cases falling through because the witness can no longer recall the identity of the person he saw commit the crime.' The occurrence of the very contingency foreseen by the Congress will obviously not serve, of itself, to bar the Farrell testimony."); United States v. Irby, 517 F.2d 506, 507 (4th Cir. 1975) (proper to admit "testimony of the F.B.I. agent who conducted the photographic lineup that he observed one witness identify one defendant in the photographic lineup even though the witness could not identify him in court").

Weak or hesitant in-court identifications have also been held to have been properly bolstered by out-of-court identification testimony. United States v. Fosher, 568 F.2d 207 (1st Cir. 1978); United States v. Watts, 532 F.2d 1215 (8th Cir. 1976); United States v. Scott, 494 F.2d 298 (7th Cir. 1974).

149. *See* M. Graham, *The Confrontation Clause, the Hearsay Rule, and the Forgetful Witness*, 56 Tex. L. Rev. 151 (1978).

150. *See* the Legislative History and Congressional Debate, Cong. Rec. H9654-9655 (daily ed. Oct. 6, 1975) quoted in 4 *Weinstein's Evidence* at 801-9-801-11 (1979).

151. *See* United States v. Elemy, 656 F.2d 507, 508 (9th Cir. 1981):

> Elemy contends that the rule refers only to testimony by a witness to previous identifications made by that witness. In his view, the rule does not permit a witness to testify regarding identifications made by another witness.
>
> The plain words of rule 801(d)(1)(C) do not contain the limitation urged by Elemy, and we decline to read it into the rule. The reasons for admitting identi-

fication statements as substantive evidence are that out-of-court identifications are believed to be more reliable than those made under the suggestive conditions prevailing at trial, and the availability of the declarant for cross-examination eliminated the major danger of hearsay testimony. See Fed. R. Evid. Advisory Committee Note to rule 801(d)(1)(C); Gilbert v. California, 388 U.S. 263, 272-73 n.3, 87 S.Ct. 1951, 1956-57 n.3, 18 L.Ed.2d 1178 (1967). These reasons remain fully applicable when the person who testifies to the statement of identification is not the person who uttered it, so long as the latter also testifies and is available for cross-examination.

In the present case the declarant, Hines, did testify and Elemy's counsel was permitted to cross-examine him at great length. Nor is there anything in the record to suggest that she was not available for reexamination after Agent McNeal testified. The requirement of availability for cross-examination having been met, we conclude that rule 801(d)(1)(C) encompasses the testimony of Agent McNeal concerning the identification statements of witness Hines, and that this testimony was consequently not hearsay.

Our interpretation of the rule is supported by its legislative history. That history indicates that Congress enacted the provision to remedy two perceived problems: (1) the typical situation where the witness's memory no longer permits a current identification and he therefore can only testify as to his previous identification; and (2) the instance where before trial the witness identifies the defendant and then because of fear refuses to acknowledge his previous identification 1121 Cong. Rec. 31, 866-67 (Congressmen Hungate and Wiggins). It is plain that in the second situation the witness's prior identification can only be introduced into evidence by a third party who was present at the original identification.

152. Statement of Rep. Hungate on floor of House of Representatives reported in 4 *Weinstein's Evidence* 801-9 (1979):

We are into the subject matter, and to highlight what I think the facts are. We have a robbery or a burglary, or some crime committed, and they are trying to decide who did it. They bring the victim down to the police station, and they put several people across the line-up, and the victim says, "This is the guy who did it. That is the one."

So then they proceed on the basis of this, and when they get to trial, they call the same fellow who made positive identification within a week of the offense and ask him, "Is this the man? Is this the defendant?"

"Oh, I don't know. I don't know. I don't recognize him."

What is suggested here is that in the field of organized crime—and in some of the even more unorganized crime—there are people of a more vicious nature who suggest to these witnesses that if they would ever like to see their children or their wives again, they had better not recognize this fellow. Or there may be financial reward.

The feeling of those who press for the law the way it came to the House and the way it would be now written is that this is protection for the public against the changing testimony of witnesses.

153. United States v. Irby, 517 F.2d 506, 507 (4th Cir. 1975) (Widener, J., concurring):

The hearsay rule has not been abandoned. See Federal Rules of Evidence, P.L. 93-595, January 2, 1975.

This case is a perfect example of the justification of the statement of Chief Justice Marshall in Queen v. Hepburn, 7 Cranch 290, 3 L.Ed. 348 (1813), that hearsay evidence is, in its own nature, inadmissible.

In our case, the identifying witness, at the trial, identified one of the defendants but could not identify the other. Indeed, as a second defendant, the nearest she came to identification was that of a spectator, one Emmet Hamilton, although the second defendant was in the courtroom. Then, when asked what she did in making the photographic identification, she said: "Well, I looked through the photographs and I picked out a picture, and I *said* this, I believe, is the man that was in the robbery." (Italics added.)

When the FBI agent took the stand, his testimony was that she "selected" the two exhibits. This selection of the two exhibits has been construed in the opinion of the court that "he observed one witness identify one defendant in the photographic lineup."

Thus, allowing the testimony of the FBI agent that the witness "selected" a photograph of the defendant, when the FBI agent's testimony depends on the statement of the witness, is admitting into evidence a conclusion based on an out of court statement, even less reliable than the statement of the witness because a step further removed, and equally objectionable under the hearsay rule. For a good discussion, see Wharton's Criminal Evidence, 13th Ed. (1972), Torcia, §§ 186, 187.

154. The admissibility of prior consistent statements is governed by Rule 801(d)(1)(B) of the Federal Rules of Evidence:

(d) Statements which are not hearsay. A statement is not hearsay if—

(1) Prior statement by witness. The declarant testifies at the trial or hearing and is subject to cross-examination concerning the statement, and the statement is . . . (B) consistent with his testimony and is offered to rebut an express or implied charge against him of recent fabrication or improper influence or motive.

For further discussion of Rule 801(d)(1)(B), *see* M. Graham, *Handbook of Federal Evidence* § 801.12 (St. Paul: West, 1981).

155. *See* Chapter 6, Section B *infra.*

156. *See* Chapter 4, Section C1 *supra.*

157. *See* Chapter 4, Section D *supra.*

158. The contrary position was adopted in United States v. Lewis, 565 F.2d 1248, 1252 (2d Cir. 1977) ("Appellant's final point seems to be that subsection (C) does not apply at all when the identifier has made a erroneous in-court identification because the prior identification is inconsistent with it and was not given under oath, as required by subsection (a). The Government responds that since appellant's appearance had changed significantly by the time of trial, there was inconsistency. More significantly, even though rule 801(d)(1) embraces subsection (C), the latter is not limited by the earlier subsections. Subsection (C) represents a legislative decision to admit statements of identification provided that declarant 'testifies at . . . trial . . . and is subject to cross-examination concerning the statement.' These conditions were met here, and we do not think that subsection (C) is rendered inoperative by

Mrs. Sharpe's misidentification in court."). *But see* United States v. Jenkins, 496 F.2d 57, 68-69 (2d Cir. 1974):

> The trial court's refusal to permit Jenkins, after eliciting from Elmer Evans, a bank customer called by him, that Evans could not recall which photographs had been selected by him from a spread seen shortly after the robbery, to introduce testimony of Agent Batt concerning the photographic selections made by Evans, raises a more serious question. Evans, unlike Green, was in the bank during the robbery, and, at the time he made the selections, Evans was attempting, like Abdella and Leiss, to identify the floorman during the robbery. Evans' prior photographic identification of Wilcox and his non-identification of Jenkins' photo might have been helpful to Jenkins, not as an impeachment of Evans, who was bereft to any recollection on the issue, but as affirmative evidence contradicting the in-court identifications of Jenkins as the floorman of Abdella and Leiss. However, a formidable stumbling block as to the admissibility of Evans' photographic identification of Wilcox arises from the fact that it clearly was hearsay, since it was never made under oath or subject to cross-examination. See 5 J. Wigmore, Evidence §§ 1361, 1362 (3d ed. 1940).
>
> It is true that we have been rather liberal in admitting a witness' prior photographic identification as affirmative evidence, at least where the witness could not presently make an identification. See, e.g., United States v. DeSisto, 329 F.2d 929, 932-934 (2d Cir. 1964), cert. denied, 377 U.S. 979,. 84 S.Ct. 1885, 12 L.Ed.2d 747; United States v. Cunningham, 446 F.2d 194, 197-198 (2d Cir. 1971), cert. denied, 404 U.S. 950, 92 S.Ct. 302, 30 L.Ed.2d 266. But in each case where this has been permitted the requirements of the hearsay rule, while perhaps stretched a bit, were satisfied. In *DeSisto*, for instance, the prior identifications were either made under oath and subject to cross-examination or were adopted by testimony subject to those safeguards on 'which our law places prime reliance for the ascertainment of truth.' 329 F.2d at 934. None of these conditions existed here. Evans' photographic identification of Wilcox was made initially five days after the robbery in Evans' own office with no defense counsel present and it was never repeated, either before the grand jury, at the pretrial suppression hearing or at appellants' trial. Under these circumstances requiring the admission, through testimony of Agent Batt, of Evans' prior photographic identification would depart farther from the traditional hearsay principle than we have yet gone. See United States v. Cunningham, 446 F.2d 914, 197-198 (2d Cir. 1971), cert. denied, 404 U.S. 950, 92 S.Ct. 302, 30 L.Ed.2d 266; United States v. Mingoia, 424 F.2d 710, 713 (2d Cir. 1970); United States v. Insana, 423 F.2d 1165, 1170 (2d Cir. 1970), cert. denied, 400 U.S. 841, 91 S.Ct. 83, 27, 446 F.2d 194, 197-98 (2d Cir. 1970, L.Ed.2d 76).

It should be noted that *Jenkins* is a pre-Federal Rules of Evidence decision.

159. Rule 803(24) may also come into play. *See* 4 *Weinstein's Evidence* ¶ 801(d)(1)(C)[01] at 801-32 (1979) ("The provisions of rule 803(24) may prove helpful. For example, if the witness to a bank robbery testified that he observed the defendant at the time of the event and shortly thereafter positively identified a person in a lineup, but that he could not remember who it was that he then picked out, this testimony plus that of another witness present should suffice and be

admitted, provided that notice is given under Rule 803(24) and a prior hearing was afforded defendant on the issue. The second witness might then testify that the person identified was immediately arrested and fingerprinted and that it was the defendant. By contrast, if the identifying witness claims no memory of the events defendant is charged with and can not testify to the basis for the identification, his cross-examination is of no value since there will be no way of evaluating the probative force of the identification.'').

160. 388 U.S. 218 (1967).

161. 388 U.S. 263 (1967).

162. United States v. Ash, 413 U.S. 300 (1973).

163. Stovall v. Denno, 388 U.S. 293 (1967) (victim in hospital who might not live properly shown accused singly).

164. *See, e.g.*, Simmons v. United States, 390 U.S. 377 (1968); Neil v. Biggers, 409 U.S. 1288 (1972); Manson v. Braithwaite, 432 U.S. 98 (1977); Foster v. California, 394 U.S. 440 (1968).

165. 571 F.2d 344 (6th Cir. 1978).

166. *See* C. McCormick, *Evidence* § 303 at 716 (Cleary ed. 1972) (''This may be accomplished by a statement that he presently remembers that he correctly recorded the fact or that he recognized the writing as accurate at the time he read it. But if his present memory is less effective, it is sufficient if he testifies that he knows it is correct because it was his habit or practice to record such matters accurately or to check them for accuracy. At the extreme, it is even sufficient if he testifies that he recognizes the signature on the statement as his and he believes it correct because he would not have signed it if he had not believed it true at the time.'').

167. *See* Note, *Past Recollection Recorded*, 28 Iowa L. Rev. 530, 533-34 (1943) (''Personal perception of the event recorded is basic to the admissions of the memorandum since the witness is placed on the witness stand only because he has seen the event now sought to be related to the court.'').

168. *See, e.g.*, United States v. Riley, 657 F.2d 1377, 1386 (8th Cir. 1981) (''The record indicates that Ms. Richmond had no present memory or knowledge of the matter recorded; she simply no longer remembered. Ms. Richmond testified that she had no clear present memory of the events in question, even after listening to the tape and reviewing the written statement. She stated that she remembered talking to the law enforcement officers, taping the interview, talking with the FBI agent, reading the written statement in part ('looking it over'), and signing it. She further testified that, at the time of the interviews, she remembered what had happened. The interview and the written statement were both prepared on April 27, 1979, the morning after she sought the assistance of the police and very soon after the events in question. Ms. Richmond did not repudiate either statement.''); United States v. Civella, 666 F.2d 1122, 1129 (8th Cir. 1971) (''At trial, two Government witnesses testified as to the door income at Mother's. The witnesses were Charles Carpenter, an undercover informant who worked as a doorman and manager at Mother's, and Beth Ruona, an IRS special agent who worked as a waitress and 'hat check girl.' Carpenter periodically transmitted door income counts to an IRS agent, who recorded the counts in memoranda. Carpenter routinely reviewed the memoranda to ensure that the information was properly recorded. Ruona gave the IRS memoranda which contained her door income counts. Summaries of the door income counts were admitted into evidence as recorded recollection.'').

169. U.S. Const., Amend. VI. In Pointer v. Texas, 380 U.S. 400, 403 (1965), the Supreme Court held "that the Sixth Amendment's right of an accused to confront the witnesses against him is . . . a fundamental right and is made obligatory on the States by the Fourteenth Amendment."

170. 399 U.S. 149 (1970).

171. Substantive admissibility of Porter's preliminary hearing testimony is described in the following section.

172. *Id.* at 158.

173. *Id.* at 158-60. In *Green* the witness, Porter, admitted at trial making the prior statements. *Id.* at 152. Nelson v. O'Neil, 402 U.S. 622 (1971), concerned a witness who denied making the prior statements admitted into evidence. Defendants O'Neil and Runnels were convicted of kidnapping, robbery, and vehicle theft. *Id.* at 623. At their joint trial, the judge admitted against defendant Runnels an oral confession Runnels allegedly made to a police officer, but the judge instructed the jury it could not consider the confession against O'Neil. *Id.* at 624-25. Runnels flatly denied having made the statement and testified favorably to both himself and O'Neil. *Id.* at 624, 628-29.

In considering defendant O'Neil's confrontation challenge, the Supreme Court recognized that under *Green* and Bruton v. United States, 391 U.S. 1233 (1968). the Sixth Amendment guaranteed O'Neil the right to cross-examine effectively the witnesses whose hearsay statements might be considered as substantive evidence against him. 402 U.S. at 626-28. That Runnell's testimony was favorable to defendant O'Neil, however, precluded a finding that O'Neil was deprived of his right of confrontation.

> The short of the matter is that, given a joint trial and a common defense, Runnels' testimony respecting his alleged out-of-court statement was more favorable to the respondent than any that cross-examination by counsel could possibly have produced, had Runnels "affirmed the statement as his." It would be unrealistic in the extreme in the circumstances here presented to hold that the respondent was denied either the opportunity or the benefit of full and effective cross-examination of Runnels.

Id. at 629.

174. *Id.* at 168-70. Justices Harlan and Brennan would have decided the question reserved by the majority but would have decided it differently. Harlan, concurring, would have overruled the defendant's confrontation challenge on the ground that the Confrontation Clause requires only that the prosecutor physically produce available witnesses. *Id.* at 174, 188-89. Under this view the Confrontation Clause prescribes only a rule of preference and is satisfied if either the declarant is truly unavailable or is available and produced at trial. Because Harlan ascribed no confrontation significance to the practical unavailability of a declarant present in court, he argued that the state had satisfied its confrontation burden in *Green* by producing Porter at trial.

Justice Brennan, dissenting, would have held inadmissible the statement Porter made to officer Wade on the ground that the Confrontation Clause was not satisfied by the physical production of a declarant who testified at trial to a lack of recollection. *Id.* at 194.

> For purpose of the Confrontation Clause, there is no significant difference between a witness who fails to testify about an alleged offense because he is unwilling to do so and a witness whose silence is compelled by an inability to remember. . . . [I]n neither instance are the purposes of the Confrontation Clause satisfied, because the witness cannot be questioned at trial concerning the pertinent facts. In both cases, if a pretrial statement is introduced for the truth of the facts asserted, the witness becomes simply a conduit for the admission of stale evidence, whose reliability can never be tested before the trial factfinder by cross-examination of the declarant about the operative events, and by observation of his demeanor as he testifies about them.

Id. Thus while Justice Harlan's interpretation of the Confrontation Clause in *Green* would always permit the substantive admission of a prior statement by a witness professing lack of recollection at trial, Justice Brennan's view of the requirement of confrontation would always prohibit the use of such a statement.

175. *Id.* at 168-70.

176. People v. Green, 3 Cal.3d 981, 991, 479 P.2d 998, 1004, 92 Cal.Rptr. 494, 500 (1971).

177. *Id.* at 989, 479 P.2d at 1003, 92 Cal.Rptr. at 499 (quoting California v. Green, 399 U.S. 149, 159 (1970)). In considering this purpose of the Confrontation Clause the United States Supreme Court discussed indicia of certainty of making as well as the assurance of truthfulness fostered by the presence of an oath. Because Porter had admitted making the prior statement to police officer Wade, the California Supreme Court also quoted the following from the Supreme Court opinion: " 'If the witness admits the prior statement is his, or if there is other evidence to show the statement is his, the danger of faulty reproduction is negligible and the jury can be confident that it has before it two conflicting statements by the same witness.' " *Id.* (quoting California v. Green, 399 U.S. 149, 158 (1970)).

178. *Id.* at 479 P.2d at 1003, 92 Cal.Rptr. at 499 (quoting California v. Green, 399 U.S. 149, 160 (1970)). The court added in a footnote:

> Moreover, as the United States Supreme Court explains, "The most successful cross-examination at the time the prior statement was made could hardly hope to accomplish more than has already been accomplished by the fact that the witness is now telling a different, inconsistent story, and—in this case—one that is favorable to the defendant."

Id. at 990 n.9, 479 P.2d at 1004 n.9, 92 Cal.Rptr. at 500 n.9 (*quoting* California v. Green, 399 U.S. 149, 59 (1970)). The conclusion that a witness's lack of recollection of the underlying event is inconsistent with a prior statement about the event requires acceptance of the "implied denial" theory developed by the California court earlier in its opinion. *See* Chapter 4, Section C3(b) *supra*.

179. *Id.* at 990, 479 P.2d at 1004, 92 Cal.Rptr. at 500.

180. 399 U.S. at 169-70 (1970).

181. For other cases tackling the question without success, *see, e.g.*, United States v. Payne, 492 F.2d 449 (4th Cir. 1974); Johnson v. State, 338 A.2d 124 (Del. 1975).

182. *See* California v. Green, 399 U.S. 149, 194 (1970) (Brennan, J., dissenting). This situation arises regardless of whether a witness admits, denies, or cannot recall making the prior statement. If a witness has only partial lack of recollection and

remembers crucial segments of the underlying event, an overall ability to cross-examine effectively may be present.

183. *See* Chapter 4, Section C3 *supra.*

184. 399 U.S. at 165-68.

185. People v. Horton, 65 Ill.2d 413, 417, 58 N.E.2d 1121, 1124 (1976).

186. *See, e.g.*, People v. Haywood, 60 Ill.App.3d 236, 376 N.E.2d 328 (1978) (defense not denied adequate opportunity where magistrate barred various defense questions as designed to obtain discovery, but cross-examination still went beyond the scope of the direct examination); People v. Chism, 65 Ill.App.3d 33, 382 N.E.2d 377 (1978) (cross-examination opportunity not rendered inadequate simply because defense was "unable to secure discovery materials prior to the preliminary hearing"); Nabbefeld v. State, 83 Wis.2d 515, 266 N.W.2d 292 (1978) (key factors are the similarity of the issues presented at the preliminary hearing to the issues presented at trial and the competency of the counsel at the preliminary hearing).

187. *See, e.g.*, People v. Wittebort, 81 Mich.App. 529, 265 N.W.2d 404 (1978) (where defense counsel's failure to cross-examine witness was explainable by the likelihood that cross-examination would have been "counter-productive," rather than by the alleged incompetency of counsel appointed just before the hearing started, trial court did not abuse its discretion in admitting the preliminary hearing testimony); Nabbefeld v. State, 83 Wis.2d 515, 266 N.W.2d 292 (1978) (it is contrary to the interests of justice to prohibit the use of the preliminary hearing testimony of an unavailable witness when the circumstances reveal that cross-examination was declined as a matter of strategy to protect the interest of the defendant).

188. 448 U.S. 56 (1980).

189. *Id.* at 70 (passages "in the *Green* opinion suggest that the opportunity to cross-examine at the preliminary hearing—even absent actual cross-examination—satisfies the Confrontation Clause. Yet the record showed, and the Court recognized, that defense counsel in fact had cross-examined Porter at the earlier proceeding. * * * We need not decide whether . . . the mere opportunity to cross-examine rendered the prior testimony admissible. * * * Nor need we decide whether de minimus questioning is sufficient, for defense counsel in this case tested [the currently unavailable witness's] testimony with the equivalent of significant cross-examination.").

190. 400 U.S. 74 (1970).

191. Evans v. Dutton, 400 F.2d 826 (5th Cir. 1968).

192. Dutton v. Evans, 400 U.S. 74 (1970).

193. Chief Justice Burger, Justice White, and Justice Blackmun joined Stewart's opinion. *Id.* at 76. Justice Blackmun also authored a separate concurring opinion in which he offered as an additional ground for the Court's decision that any error was harmless beyond a reasonable doubt. *Id.* at 90-93.

194. *Id.* at 80-83.

> "While it may readily be conceded that hearsay rules and the Confrontation Clause are generally designed to protect similar values, it is quite a different thing to suggest that the overlap is complete and that the Confrontation Clause is nothing more or less than a codification of the rules of hearsay and their exceptions as they existed historically at common law. Our decisions have never established such a congruence."

Id. at 81-82 (quoting California v. Green, 399 U.S. 149, 155 (1970)).

195. *Id.* at 89.

196. *Id.*

197. In Park v. Huff, 493 F.2d 923, 931, rev. en banc, 506 F.2d 849 (5th Cir. 1974), the Fifth Circuit summarized the various tests of *Evans* for trustworthiness.

> (1) Does the trier of fact have "a satisfactory basis for evaluating the truth of the prior statement?" (2) How "real" is the possibility that cross-examination "could conceivably have shown the jury that the statement, though made, might have been unreliable?" (3) What "indicia of reliability" were present to permit the testimony to be placed before the jury although there was no confrontation of the declarant?

198. 400 U.S. at 89. The Fifth Circuit described Shaw's testimony as "incredible," 400 F.2d at 828 n.4, and Justice Blackmun, in his separate concurrence, argued that Shaw was cross-examined so effectively that no normal jury could have believed his testimony, 400 U.S. at 91. Shaw's account on cross-examination was that he conversed with Williams through a closed door, solid except for a ten-square-inch pane of steel-meshed glass. *Id.* at 90-91.

199. *Id.*

200. California v. Green, 399 U.S. 149, 158 (1970).

201. 400 U.S. at 89.

202. 448 U.S. 56 (1980).

203. *Id.* at 59, quoting Ohio Rev. Code Ann. § 2945.49 (1975). The statute reads:

> Testimony taken at an examination an examination or preliminary hearing at which the defendant is present, or at a former trial of the cause, or taken by deposition at the instance of the defendant or the State, may be used whenever the witness giving such testimony dies, or cannot for any reason be produced at the trial, or whenever the witness has, since giving such testimony, become incapacitated to testify. If such former testimony is contained within a bill of exceptions, or authenticated transcript, otherwise by other testimony.

204. *Id.* at 61.

205. The Ohio Supreme Court reasoned that there was little incentive to cross-examine at a preliminary hearing when the ultimate issue was only probable cause. The crucial consideration as thus presented became whether there had been cross-examination. In this case defense counsel did not request at the preliminary hearing that Anita be declared hostile and subject to cross-examination. 55 Ohio St.2d 191, 196, 378 N.E. 492, 496 (1978).

206. 448 U.S. at 66.

This quotation contains the disturbing indication that any hearsay statement falling within a hearsay exception contained in Rule 803 may be admitted against the criminal defendant in the normal case *only* if the government produces the declarant so he or she can be subjected to cross-examination at trial or, if not produced, the government has made a sufficient showing that the declarant is not available to testify. Presumably, production at times could include making the declarant available to be called at the option of the accused and subjected to cross-examination concerning the hearsay statement. In addition, if the declarant is not available for cross-examination at trial, the hearsay statement may be admitted only if it bears adequate "indicia of reliability." However, indicia of reliability "can be inferred without more is a case where the evidence falls within a firmly rooted hearsay exception." U.S. at 66. Taken literally, all hearsay exceptions in Rule 803 would require a showing of unavailability or the production of an available declarant when offered against the accused.

Several factors indicate that the Supreme Court had no such intention in mind. First, the foregoing indicia in *Roberts* was made in the context of a discussion of the former testimony hearsay exception, Rule 804(b)(1), a hearsay exception that itself requires unavailability. Moreover, the casualness displayed in making the comment with respect to unavailability generally in the context of a hearsay exception requiring unavailability belies any intention to make a radical change in the law. As *Roberts* itself states, although the Confrontation Clause "normally requires" a showing of unavailability, *id.*, "competing interests . . . may warrant dispensing with confrontation at trial," *id.* at 64, and further relaxation of the hearsay rule in some cases depending on " 'considerations of public policy and the necessities of the case.' " *Id.* at 64, quoting Mattox v. United States, 156 U.S. 23, 243 (1895). The opinion also indicates that a demonstration of unavailability or production of the declarant is not required when the utility of confrontation is remote. *Id.* at 65 n.7. In this context it is interesting to note that, generally, neither the state courts, the United States Courts of Appeals, nor the leading commentators on the Federal Rules of Evidence have construed *Roberts* as ushering such a radical change. *See, e.g.*, United States v. Hans, 684 F.2d 343, 346 (6th Cir. 1982) ("The district court acknowledged that the checks were exceptions to the hearsay Rule under Rule 803(6) and Rule 803(8), both of which could be utilized 'even though the declarant is available as a witness.' Clearly *Roberts* does not support exclusion of the instant checks."). Finally, it is suggested that any reading of *Roberts* as mandating a requirement of unavailability or production with respect to all hearsay statements admissible pursuant to Rule 803 offered against the criminal defendant is completely out of character with other recent decisions of the Supreme Court including *Evans* itself.

207. *Id.* at 64, 65 (quoting California v. Green, 399 U.S. at 162).

208. *See* Chapter 4, Section C3 *supra.*

209. 547 F.2d 1346 (8th Cir. 1976).

210. *Carlson* looked to *Evans* because it was decided before *Roberts.*

211. *Id.* at 1358. *Accord* United States v. Balano, 618 F.2d 624 (10th Cir. 1979).

212. 665 F.2d 616 (5th Cir. 1982).

213. The Fifth Circuit expressed severe doubt about whether grand jury testimony constitutes evidence admissible pursuant to Rule 804(b)(5) for two reasons. First, treating corroborated grand jury testimony as trustworthy is not rare or exceptional and thus not admissible because Congress indicated that admission under Rule 804(b)(5) is exceptional. Second, grand jury testimony is not subject to rigorous truth testing by cross-examination such as is former testimony. 665 F.2d at 629. Two Supreme Court Justices in a dissent to a denial of certiorari have also strongly implied that grand jury testimony does not meet the trustworthiness standards of Rule 804(b)(5). United States v. Garner, 439 U.S. 936 (1978) (Stewart and Marshall).

214. 665 F.2d at 632. Relying on Ohio v. Roberts, the court held that although the hearsay rule and the Confrontation Clause are not coterminous, they protect the same values. Both involve the defendant's interest in confrontation. Once the right to

confront is waived, the balance falls in favor of permitting the evidence.

215. *Id.* at 630 ("[W]hen confrontation becomes impossible due to the actions of the very person who would assert the right, logic dictates that the right has been waived. The law simply cannot countenance a defendant deriving benefits from murdering the chief witness against him. To permit such subversion of a criminal prosecution 'would be contrary to public policy, common sense, and the underlying purpose of the confrontation clause,' United States v. Carlson, 547 F.2d 1346, 1359 (8th Cir. 1976), cert. denied, 431 U.S. 914, 97 S.Ct. 2174, 53 L.Ed.2d 224 (1977), and make a mockery of the system of justice that the right was designed to protect."). *See* C. McCormick, *Evidence* § 273 at 661 (Cleary ed. 1972) ("It may well be that the real underpinning of the rule of admissibility is a desire to impose swift punishment, with a certain poetic justice, rather than concern over niceties of proof.").

With respect to waiver by reason of witness intimidation, *see also* United States v. Mastrangelo, 693 F.2d, 272 (2d Cir. 1982) ("If Mastrangelo was involved in Bennett's death, his involvement waived his confrontation clause objections to the admission of Bennett's testimony. Because a waiver, if factually supported, will allow us to avoid resolution of the difficult legal and constitutional issues arising under the confrontation clause and rule 804(b)(5), we remand the case to the District Court for an evidentiary hearing on the question of Mastrangelo's involvement in the murder of Bennett."). *Compare* Steele v. Taylor, 684 F.2d 1193, 1201 n.8 (6th Cir. 1982) ("It should be noted that the 'waiver' concept is not applicable, strictly speaking, to procurement, and its use is somewhat confusing. It is a legal fiction to say that a person who interferes with a witness thereby knowingly, intelligently and deliberately relinquishes his right to exclude hearsay. He simply does a wrongful act that has legal consequences that he may or may not foresee. The connection between the defendant's conduct and its legal consequence under the confrontation clause is supplied by the law and not by a purposeful decision by the defendant to forego a known constitutional right. But see United States v. Thevis, 665 F.2d 616 (5th Cir. 1982) holding that procurement of witness unavailability is a 'waiver question.' ").

216. 618 F.2d 624 (10th Cir. 1979).

217. 665 F.2d 616, 631 (5th Cir. 1982).

218. The Second Circuit follows *Balano* and not *Thevis.* United States v. Mastrangelo, 693 F.2d 269, 273 (2d Cir. 1982) ("We see no reason to impose upon the government more than the usual burden of proof by a preponderance of the evidence where waiver by misconduct is concerned. Such a claim of waiver is not one which is either unusually subject to deception or disfavored by the law. *Compare* C. McCormick, *Handbook of the Law of Evidence* § 340 (2d ed. St. Paul: West, 1972). To the contrary, such misconduct is invariably accompanied by tangible evidence such as the disappearance of the defendant, disruption in the courtroom or the murder of a key witness, and there is hardly any reason to apply a burden of proof which might encourage behavior which strikes at the heart of the system of justice itself.").

219. 665 F.2d at 631 *citing* United States v. Wade, 388 U.S. 218, 240 (1967).

220. *See, e.g.,* United States v. West, 574 F.2d 1131 (4th Cir. 1978) (killing suggestive of contract killers but there was no evidence that the defendant was involved in the killing); United States v. Gardner, 574 F.2d 1141 (4th Cir. 1978) (no evidence showing witness's unwillingness due to defendant's intimidation rather

than a code among prisoners not to testify against former coconspirators).

221. In *Thevis*, 665 F.2d at 633 n.17, the court did recognize the possibility that untrustworthy evidence may be being offered, suggesting that Rule 403 concerns and due process considerations may be applied to forestall admissibility. However, neither Rule 403 nor due process considerations would serve as a viable procedural constraint on the admissibility of evidence offered under the *Thevis* waiver doctrine. Rule 403 is ineffective in that application of the balancing test occurs after the trial court first assumes that the evidence is reliable. Ballou v. Henri Studios, Inc., 656 F.2d 1147 (5th Cir. 1981). Due process considerations are helpful to the extent that they focus attention upon the trustworthiness of the evidence. Unfortunately, as indicated in *Thevis* itself, *id.*, the due process test of trustworthiness is even more permissive than the test of trustworthiness imposed upon the Confrontation Clause by *Roberts*.

222. 448 U.S. 56, 66 (1980).

223. *See* Chapter 4, Section B1 *supra*.

224. 448 U.S. at 66.

225. *Id.*

226. For a discussion of Rule 804(b)(5), *see* chapter 4, Section E *supra*.

227. United States v. Gonsalves, 668 F.2d 73, 75 (1st Cir. 1982). *See also* C. McCormick, *Evidence* §§ 271, 273 (Cleary ed. 1972); D. Louisell and C. Mueller, *Federal Evidence* ¶ 97 (Rochester: Lawyers Cooperative, 1977).

228. *See* Chapter 4, Section D *supra*.

229. Under the waiver theory, the jury would never be presented with the evidence of witness intimidation; only the admitted statement would be presented for their consideration.

230. *See generally*, United States v. Cheek, 582 F.2d 668 (2d Cir. 1978); United States v. Monahan, 632 F.2d 984 (1st Cir. 1980); United States v. Gonsalves, 668 F.2d 73 (1st Cir. 1982). *See also* C. McCormick, *Evidence* § 273 at 661 (Cleary ed. 1972); J. Maguire and R. Vincent, *Admissions Implied from Spoliation and Related Conduct*, 45 Yale L. J. 226 (1935).

231. United States v. Gonsalves, 668 F.2d 73, 75 (1st Cir. 1982) ("While probative for this purpose, however, such evidence should not be admitted if its probative value 'is substantially outweighed by the danger of unfair prejudice.' Fed. R. Evid. 403. Other courts have held that evidence of inflammatory threats which tend to paint a picture of the defendant as an unusually violent person—or as a cold-blooded killer—may cause 'severe prejudice' to the defendant and, in a proper case, should be excluded. *See, e.g.*, United States v. Cheek, 582 F.2d 668, 685-86 (2d Cir. 1978); United States v. Weir, 575 F.2d 668, 669-71 (8th Cir. 1978). In United States v. Monahan, 633 F.2d 984, 985 (1st Cir. 1980), we reserved the question whether 'inflammatory or macabre' threats should be excluded under rule 403.").

Chapter 5

Refreshing Recollection

When an occurrence witness testifies at trial on direct examination to a lack of recollection of the subject matter of the witness's prior statement, whether true or feigned, counsel for the government may attempt to refresh the recollection of the witness either by posing a leading question or by showing a writing to the witness. Thus a witness who testifies that he or she cannot recall anything else discussed during a particular conversation may either (1) be asked the leading question "Do you recall whether you discussed Bob's plans for the evening?" or (2) be shown a document that might refresh the witness's recollection regarding any discussion concerning Bob's plans for the evening and then be questioned again whether the witness recalls anything else discussed during the conversation. If the witness states that his or her recollection has been refreshed, the witness may testify about what is then recalled. Use of leading questions to refresh recollection falls within Rule 611(c) of the Federal Rules of Evidence, which provides for the use of leading questions on direct examination of a witness when necessary to develop the witness's testimony.[1] Rule 612 of the Federal Rules of Evidence addresses employment of a writing to refresh recollection.[2]

With respect to refreshment of recollection generally, it is sometimes stated that a party may seek to refresh the recollection of a witness only if the witness testifies that his or her recollection is exhausted and that the witness cannot recall the matter forming the subject of the inquiry.[3] Under such authority, if a witness replies in an absolute fashion, for example, that nothing else was said or nothing else happened, refreshment of recollection would not be permitted.[4] Other decisions, however, reach the sensible position that refreshing recollection is proper even if the witness gives a positive albeit unanticipated answer.[5] As C. McCormick stated, "The witness may believe that he remembers completely but on looking at the memorandum he would be caused to recall additional facts."[6] Counsel can sometimes avoid having to face the issue by incorporating lack of recollection in the question asked, such as "Do you recall whether anything else was said?" When such a question would be inconvenient as a matter of form, counsel must fall back on a general instruction to the witness to respond to questions such as "Was anyone else present?" with the answer "I don't recall."

The process of refreshing recollection must be conducted pursuant to Rule 103(c) of the Federal Rules of Evidence "so as to prevent inadmissible evidence from being suggested to the jury by any means, such as . . . asking questions in the hearing of the jury." When refreshment of recollection is through a writing, this mandate is accomplished easily by counsel handing the writing to the witness accompanied by a request to the witness to read the writing to himself. The witness is then asked whether his or her recollection has been refreshed. If the answer is yes, counsel repeats the initial question. If the witness states that recollection has not been refreshed, it is improper for counsel to read the writing aloud before the trier of fact.[7]

When refreshing recollection is by means of a leading question, counsel may not employ a leading question incorporating the content of the anticipated testimony before the trier of fact if the matter under consideration is of significance in the litigation. For example, when the government seeks to refresh the recollection of a witness it has called regarding a statement bearing directly on the guilt of the defendant, the prosecutor may not use the substance of the statement in his or her question.[8] Accordingly, a question to John Goodfellow in our hypothetical case in Chapter 4 such as "Didn't you see the defendant Sam Smith leaving 709 Maple Avenue on the evening of July 14?" propounded in open court to refresh recollection, is objectionable.[9] The proper procedure is either to reduce the oral statement to writing and proceed as set out above or to excuse the jury and attempt to refresh the witness's recollection by means of the leading question. Only if the witness states that his or her recollection has been refreshed may the witness be once again asked what, if anything, the witness recalls seeing on the evening of July 14. As stated in Goings v. United States:

> [I]f a party can offer a previously given statement to substitute for a witness's testimony under the guise of "refreshing recollection," the whole adversary system of trial must be revised. *The evil of this practice hardly merits discussion. The evil is no less when an attorney can read the statement in the presence of the jury and thereby substitute his spoken word for the written document.*[10]

On the other hand, when the witness cannot recall a preliminary or relatively unimportant matter, such as which direction Maple Avenue runs, a leading question in open court incorporating the answer may be employed.

Similarly, leading questions are also proper to refresh recollection that suggest that something else may have occurred, without directly stating the substance of the occurrence. Thus following the answer "Not that I now recall" to the question "Was anything else said?" the question "Was anything said concerning Bob's plans for the evening?" is proper.

When a party uses a writing to refresh the recollection of a witness while testifying, if the witness states that his or her recollection has been refreshed, the witness may testify to what is then recalled. The writing need not be admissible in evidence. The writing need not have been prepared by the witness, or at the witness's direction. The writing need not have been made at or near the time of the event recorded. Moreover, the original writing rule,[11] also known as the "best evidence rule," does not apply. In short, any writing may be used for this purpose, with the only question being whether the writing is genuinely calculated to revive the witness's recollection.[12] There is a real possibility that the witness will testify from what purports to be a refreshed present memory, when witness's testimony is actually a reflection, conscious or unconscious, of what the witness has read rather than what is remembered.[13] The court may reject such testimony by finding that the writing did not in fact refresh the witness's recollection. In reaching this determination, the court may initially require the witness to read the writing to himself, and surrender possession of it before responding to any questions. To protect against abuse, Rule 612 confers upon opposing counsel the absolute right to inspect the writing referred to by the witness while testifying, to cross-examine regarding it, and to introduce into evidence for the purpose of impeachment those portions of the writing that relate to the testimony of the witness. A finding that the witness's memory is not refreshed may, however, pave the way for admission of the writing under the hearsay exception for past recollection recorded.[14]

Notice that a witness who has been intimidated to claim lack of recollection by definition actually already recalls the subject matter of counsel's inquiry. Refreshing the recollection of such an intimidated witness will thus result in the witness testifying consistent with the witness's prior statement only if the process of refreshing recollection itself somehow instills upon the witness the obligation and courage to speak the truth. Such an eventuality is unlikely to occur.

NOTES

1. Fed. R. Evid. 611(c) provides:

> (c) Leading questions. Leading questions should not be used on the direct examination of a witness except as may be necessary to develop his testimony. Ordinarily leading questions should be permitted on cross-examination. When a party calls a hostile witness, an adverse party, or a witness identified with an adverse party, interrogation may be by leading questions.

2. Fed. R. Evid. 612 provides:

Except as otherwise provided in criminal proceedings by section 3500 of title 18, United States Code, if a witness uses a writing to refresh his memory for the purpose of testifying, either—

(1) while testifying, or

(2) before testifying, if the court in its discretion determines it is necessary in the interests of justice,

an adverse party is entitled to have the writing produced at the hearing, to inspect it, to cross-examine the witness thereon, and to introduce in evidence those portions which relate to the testimony of the witness. If it is claimed that the writing contains matters not related to the subject matter of the testimony the court shall examine the writing in camera, excise any portions not so related, and order delivery of the remainder to the party entitled thereto. Any portion withheld over objections shall be preserved and made available to the appellate court in the event of an appeal. If a writing is not produced or delivered pursuant to order under this rule, the court shall make any order justice requires, except that when the prosecution elects not to comply, the order shall be one striking the testimony or, if the court in its discretion determines that the interests of justice so require, declaring a mistrial.

3. Goings v. United States, 377 F.2d 753 (8th Cir. 1967). *See also* United States v. Jimenez, 613 F.2d 1373 (5th Cir. 1980).

4. *See, e.g.*, NLRB v. Hudson Pulp & Paper Corp., 273 F.2d 660 (5th Cir. 1960); Thompson v. United States, 342 F.2d 137 (5th Cir. 1965); NLRB v. Federal Dairy Co., 297 F.2d 487 (1st Cir. 1962).

5. *See, e.g.*, United States v. Thompson, 708 F.2d 1294 (8th Cir. 1983); United States v. Kenny, 462 F.2d 1205 (3d Cir. 1972); Branizza v. Grayhound Corp., 394 F.2d 33 (5th Cir. 1968); Cox v. United States, 284 F.2d 704 (8th Cir. 1960).

6. C. McCormick, *Evidence* § 9 at 18 (Cleary ed. 1972).

7. Gaines v. United States, 349 F.2d 190 (D.C. Cir. 1965) (prior statements used to refresh may be read aloud only out of presence of jury); Westinghouse Elec. Corp. v. Wray Equip. Corp., 286 F.2d 491 (1st Cir. 1961) (jury improperly permitted to hear deposition read aloud); United States v. McKeever, 271 F.2d 669 (2d Cir. 1959) (if tape recording is to be used to refresh recollection of witness, jury may not hear recording).

8. United States v. Shoupe, 548 F.2d 636, 641 (6th Cir. 1977) ("[W]e find no precedent sanctioning the recitation in the presence of the jury of extended unsworn remarks, attributed to a Government witness, which were allegedly recorded in an unverified document and which inculpate the defendant.").

9. United States v. Socony-Vacuum Oil Co., 310 U.S. 150, 234 (1940) ("[T]here would be error where under the pretext of refreshing a witness' recollection, the prior testimony was introduced as evidence.").

10. 377 F.2d 753, 760 (8th Cir. 1967) (emphasis in original).

11. Fed. R. Evid. 1002 provides:

To prove the content of a writing, recording, or photograph is required, except as otherwise provided in these rules or by Act of Congress.

With respect to the operation of the original writing rule, see M. Graham, *Handbook of Federal Evidence*, §§ 1001.0-1008.1 (St. Paul: West, 1981).

12. United States v. Rappy, 157 F.2d 964, 967 (2d Cir. 1946) ("[A] song, a scent, a photograph, an allusion, even a past statement known to be false."); Johnston v. Earle, 313 F.2d 686 (9th Cir. 1962) (copies of notes prepared by another); Thompson v. United States, 342 F.2d 137, 140 (5th Cir. 1965) ("The fact that a government agent instead of the witness prepared the statement is inconsequential."); Williams v. United States, 365 F.2d 21, 22 (7th Cir. 1966) (memorandum of conversation); United States v. Ricco, 566 F.2d 433 (2d Cir. 1977) (illegal wiretap tapes used before trial to refresh witness's recollection).

13. Jewett v. United States, 15 F.2d 955 (9th Cir. 1926). *See also* United States v. Scott, 701 F.2d 1340, 1346 (11th Cir. 1983) ("Under Fed. R. Evid. 612, refreshing one's recollection is permitted. The trial court carefully instructed the witnesses that they were permitted to testify only as to what they independently remembered. They were instructed not to testify as to any statement contained in the applications for which they did not have an independent recollection.").

14. *See* Chapter 4, Section G *supra.*

Chapter **6**

Prior Inconsistent Statement Impeachment

As developed in Chapter 4, the prior statements in our hypothetical case are not likely to be admissible as substantive evidence. At common law and under the Federal Rules of Evidence, however, prior statements may be admitted for the purpose of impeaching a witness's in-court testimony without regard to whether the statement was made in a formal proceeding as required for substantive admission pursuant to Rule 801(d)(1)(A). The out-of-court statement need only be inconsistent with the in-court testimony of the declarant to be admissible to impeach. The rationale is that a witness who testifies one way at trial while speaking inconsistently before trial is blowing hot and cold, thereby raising doubts about the truthfulness of both statements.[1] Although the prior out-of-court statement is not admitted for its truth, impeachment provides a vehicle for placing the prior statement before a jury that will often, if not almost always, consider it for its truth even though instructed not to do so.[2] Employment of a prior inconsistent statement to impeach in the hope that the jury will give the statement substantive effect in spite of the limiting instruction often arises with respect to impeachment of a witness called by an opponent. It is, however, a far more serious and difficult occurrence when the government seeks to impeach a witness it has itself called to the stand by means of a prior inconsistent statement.[3] The situation in which the government is faced with a witness who has changed testimony at trial as a result of intimidation having in hand a prior inconsistent statement that is not substantively admissible is of immediate concern.

A. THE PREREQUISITES

1. Prior Disclosure of Content

Rule 613(a)[4] of the Federal Rules of Evidence abolishes the requirement emanating from Queen Caroline's Case (1820),[5] also referred to as the "Queen's Case," that cross-examining counsel show or disclose to the witness an inconsistent writing before examination concerning its content. This requirement was abolished in England many years ago by statute. Commentators in this country have for a long time strongly criticized imposing a requirement that the witness must be shown his or her prior written statement before any cross-examination commences concerning its content.[6] Although the federal courts accepted in principle the foundation rule established in the Queen's Case, in practice they never considered themselves bound by its technical requirements. The Supreme Court in The Charles Morgan (1885)[7] noted with approval the traditional foundation requirements applicable to prior inconsistent oral and written statements. The Supreme Court suggested, however, that although the requirement that a witness be shown a prior inconsistent written statement before any cross-examination can begin concerning its content was "ordinarily" applicable, the rule might be ignored in certain situations. "Circumstances may arise, however, which will excuse [the document's] production. All the law requires is, that the memory of the witness shall be so refreshed by the necessary inquiries as to enable him to explain, if he can and desires to do so."[8] Over the years, most federal and state courts came to accept the exception as the ordinary rule. Counsel was not required to show the witness his or her prior written statement in advance of examination as to its content. All that was required was that the witness be provided an opportunity to admit, deny, or explain the inconsistency. The requirement of prior disclosure of the statement to the witness, "everywhere more honored in the breach than in the observance,"[9] is discarded officially by the Federal Rules of Evidence in favor of surprise. The truth-seeking process is better served by cross-examination without first providing the witness a warning. The provision in Rule 613(a) for disclosure upon request to opposing counsel is designed to curtail unwarranted insinuation about the existence of a prior statement.

2. Inconsistency

Prior inconsistent statements are not limited to those that are directly contradictory. As previously discussed, it is sufficient if the inconsistency has a reasonable tendency to discredit the testimony of the witness.[10] This liberal view of inconsistency has generally been applied in the federal courts.[11] The prior inconsistent statement may consist of a previously expressed opinion, regardless of whether the subject matter would be a proper one for opinion evidence if offered at trial.[12] The inconsistency may also consist of the omission from a prior statement of a matter that would reasonably be expected to have been mentioned if true or the failure to speak at all of a matter asserted at trial under circumstances in which it would have been natural to do so.[13] In a similar vein, under circumstances that would normally call for a denial if untrue, the failure to respond to the statement of another may be treated as an adoption by silent acquiescence.[14]

3. The Foundation

At common law a proper foundation must be laid during cross-examination[15] of the witness before introducing extrinsic proof of the existence of a prior inconsistent statement. This traditional foundation consists of directing the attention of the witness to the time, place, and circumstances of the statement, sometimes called "persons present," along with the content of the statement. The traditional foundation focuses the witness's attention on the alleged prior inconsistent statement, thereby placing the witness in the position of being able to admit, deny, or explain the prior statement's existence.[16]

The foundation requirement serves several purposes, including: (1) saving time, since an admission by the witness that the statement was his or her own statement would make unnecesssary the introduction of extrinsic evidence about the making of the statement; (2) avoiding unfair surprise to the adversary by alerting him or her to the possible existence of a prior inconsistent statement and thus enabling the adversary to prepare to meet the issue; and (3) preventing unfairness to the witness by permitting him or her to deny or explain an apparent inconsistency at the time it is first suggested. Accomplishing these objectives does not require strict enforcement of the "time, place, and persons present" aspect of the traditional rule. Courts generally require only that the witness's attention be sufficiently directed to the circumstances surrounding the making of the prior inconsistent statement so that the witness can admit, deny, or do either and explain. On the other hand, the content of the alleged prior inconsistent statement must be presented to the witness with particularity.[17]

Courts applying the common law foundation requirement strictly enforce the requirement that the opportunity to admit, deny, or explain must occur before the introduction of extrinsic evidence. Failure to lay a proper foundation on cross-examination of the witness will bar introduction of extrinsic evidence, that is, evidence offered other than through the witness, about the making of the prior inconsistent statement.[18] The impeaching cross-examiner does not actually have to provide the opportunity for explanation. The cross-examiner may usually require the witness to answer yes or no to the question whether he or she made a particular statement. As long as counsel on redirect is permitted to elicit an explanation, the foundation requirement is deemed satisfied. On redirect examination, the party calling the witness is entitled to have the witness explain, modify, qualify, limit, or otherwise shed light upon the alleged inconsistency by testifying to what the witness claims actually occurred when the prior statement was alleged to have been made and the circumstances surrounding the alleged making of the prior statement.[19] Additional portions of the prior conversation, document, or testimony of the witness that are relevant to explain, modify, qualify, limit, or otherwise shed light upon the alleged inconsistency may also be introduced.[20]

Although the traditional foundation is still generally laid in cases tried in the federal court, formal insistence that the attention of the witness must first be directed to the statement is relaxed by the Federal Rules of Evidence. Rule 613(b) merely requires that the witness be afforded an opportunity to explain or deny and that the opposite party be afforded an opportunity to examine the witness concerning the statement; a particular time or sequence is not mandated. Federal Rule of Evidence 613(b) provides as follows:

Prior Statements of Witnesses

* * *

(b) Extrinsic evidence of prior inconsistent statement of witness. Extrinsic evidence of a prior inconsistent statement by a witness is not admissible unless the witness is afforded an opportunity to explain or deny the same and the opposite party is afforded an opportunity to interrogate him thereon, or the interests of justice otherwise require. This provision does not apply to admissions of a party-opponent as defined in rule 801(d)(2).

Pursuant to Rule 613(b), extrinsic proof may thus be introduced before the witness is allowed to admit, deny, or explain the prior statement.[21] Moreover, what is important under Rule 613(b) is the opportunity to deny or explain, not whether any denial or explanation actually occurs. The foundation requirement is satisfied if the witness remains available for recall by the calling party later during the trial, even if that party chooses not to recall the witness. Rule 613(b), in addition, provides that the opportunity to explain or deny may be refused altogether to a witness when the interests of justice so require. Thus, for example, if counsel does not learn of an inconsistent statement until after a witness ceased being amenable to the court's jurisdiction, the court has discretion to allow the impeachment absent the foundation. The provision of Rule 613(b) relating to an opportunity to explain or deny does not apply to statements admitted not only to impeach but also as substantive evidence, such as, for example, an admission of a party-opponent pursuant to Rule 801(d)(2), with the exception of those statements admitted as substantive evidence solely by virtue of operation of Rule 801(d)(1)(A).

As the Advisory Committee's Note to Rule 613(b) indicates, under Rule 613(b) "[t]he traditional insistence that the attention of the witness be directed to the statement on cross-examination is relaxed in favor of simply providing the witness an opportunity to explain and the opposite party an opportunity to examine on the statement, with no specification of any particular time or sequence."[22] The Advisory Committee's Note suggests that Rule 613(b) facilitates the questioning of collusive witnesses by permitting several such witnesses to be examined before disclosing a joint prior inconsistent statement. One may strongly question whether such a benefit accurately explains dispensing with the requirement that a foundation be laid on cross-examination. It is suggested that the rationale for Rule 613(b) derives from a combination of two factors: (1) rule 801(d)(1)(A), as proposed by the Advisory Committee and the Supreme Court, which made all prior inconsistent statements substantive evidence; and (2) lawyer incompetence as perceived by the Advisory Committee.

To understand why the Advisory Committee recommended Rule 613(b), one must keep in mind that if prior inconsistent statements are admissible only for purposes of impeachment, the foundation requirement fosters the use of such statements to affect credibility while discouraging the trier of fact from giving them substantive consideration. In practice, the foundation requirement serves to place a prior statement in juxtaposition with the testimony at trial of the witness sought to be impeached. In addition, by enabling the witness to admit that a prior statement is his or her own statement, the foundation requirement reduces the likelihood that extrinsic evidence of the prior inconsistent statement will be introduced, evidence that is much harder for the jury not to accept substantively. Under the scheme of the proposed federal evidence rules, however, all prior inconsistent statements were to be admissible as substantive evidence pursuant to rule 801(d)(1)(A). With the substantive admissibility of all such prior statements, this objective fostered by the foundation requirement was no longer relevant, and a practical consideration became paramount. For some unknown reason, trial lawyers often forget, or in some cases never learn, how to lay a proper foundation for extrinsic evidence.[23] The Advisory Committee politely referred to such forgetfulness or incompetence as the "dangers of oversight."[24] With substantive admissibility, these "oversights" could be legitimized by permitting introduction of prior inconsistent statements at any time, as long as the witness was eventually given an opportunity to deny or explain.

As enacted by Congress, however, Rule 801(d)(1)(A) does not permit the substantive admission of all prior inconsistent statements.[25] Thus the traditional foundation requirement's utility in encouraging the jury to consider the prior inconsistent statement solely as an indication of credibility, and not as substantive evidence, remains relevant. Nevertheless, Rule 613(b) as enacted encourages rather than discourages the statement's acceptance by the trier of fact as substantive evidence by permitting extrinsic evidence of a prior statement to be placed before the jury before the witness is provided an opportunity to deny or explain.[26] The government faced with a witness who has changed his or her testimony as a result of intimidation can be expected to take advantage of every opportunity the law provides that encourages the jury to give substantive effect to the witness's out-of-court statement.

Because under Rule 801(d)(1)(A) all prior inconsistent statements are not substantively admissible, the better approach is that counsel should not be given the unfettered right under Rule 613(b) to introduce extrinsic evidence of a statement admitted solely to impeach before the witness has an opportunity to admit, deny, or explain the statement. The court under Rules 403[27] and 611(a)[28] should require that the traditional foundation be laid on cross-examination before the introduction of extrinsic evidence of prior inconsistent statements admissible solely to impeach, unless the interests of justice otherwise require. This would occur, for example, if the witness after testifying became unavailable before the prior statement was discovered or if counsel wants to examine several collusive witnesses before disclosing a joint prior inconsistent statement.

In practice, the traditional foundation is generally laid by counsel during initial examination of the witness. Juxtaposition is the most effective form of impeachment. Counsel wanting primarily to impeach and not to highlight the prior statement to encourage substantive use by the trier of fact therefore opts in favor of confronting the witness with the prior inconsistent statement at the first opportunity. Inertia and lack of appreciation of the change brought about by Rule 613(b) undoubtedly also play their part in maintaining the status quo.

4. Good Faith Basis

Impeachment by means of a prior inconsistent statement is proper only if examining counsel possesses a good-faith basis about the existence of the prior statement. Innuendoes or insinuations of a nonexistent statement are improper. Protection against unwarranted insinuation is provided in part by Rule 613(a)'s requirement of disclosure of the content of the statement on request to opposing counsel. In addition, the court in its discretion may demand before any examination upon the statement an on the record assurance of counsel that, if required, counsel can support the foundation question about whether the witness had made the prior statement with extrinsic evidence establishing the alleged statement's existence.[29]

5. Extrinsic Evidence

If a witness denies making a statement relating to a noncollateral matter, states that he or she cannot remember making it, or otherwise equivocates, not only is extrinsic evidence establishing the making of the statement admissible, extrinsic evidence must later be introduced by counsel conducting the impeachment.[30] If, on the other hand, a witness unequivocally admits having made a prior inconsistent statement relating to a noncollateral matter, whether the prior statement may, not must, be proved by extrinsic evidence is the subject of dispute among the courts and commentators.[31] In practice, extrinsic evidence is rarely offered when a witness unequivocally admits making the prior inconsistent statement. Extrinsic evidence establishing the existence of the prior inconsistent statement is never admissible when the subject matter of the alleged impeaching statement relates to a collateral matter. The cross-examiner must accept the witness's answer.

A matter is noncollateral if the subject matter of the prior inconsistent statement is relevant in the litigation for some purpose other than merely as self-contradiction of the in-court testimony of the witness.[32] The prior statements of each of the four witnesses in our hypothetical case in Chapter 4 identifying Sam Smith as the murderer are noncollateral. In fact, it is hard to imagine a defendant intimidating a witness about a matter that is collateral, a matter by definition not relevant to establishing the offense for which he or she is charged.

When the traditional foundation is required, failure to lay a proper foundation precludes the introduction of extrinsic evidence to impeach.

6. Limiting Instructions

When a prior inconsistent statement is admitted solely to impeach the witness, upon request the jury will be cautioned at the time the statement is introduced, and/or receive a limiting instruction when the court charges the jury about the law, that they are to consider the statement as only affecting the credibility of the witness.[33] When neither a cautionary nor limiting instruction is requested by counsel, if the prior inconsistent statement is extremely damaging if considered by the jury as substantive evidence and the proponent of such evidence has a weak case, the court to avoid plain error must *sua sponte* give such an instruction, but not otherwise.[34] If the jury is not advised that the prior inconsistent statement was admitted solely to impeach, the statement may be considered by the jury as substantive evidence.[35]

B. THE VOUCHER RULE

At common law the traditional voucher doctrine—a party vouches for the credibility of his or her own witness—prevented the party calling the witness from impeaching the witness by means of a prior inconsistent statement.[36] Federal courts, however, long ago developed an important exception: testimony that both surprised and affirmatively damaged a calling party justified impeachment by prior inconsistent statement.[37] The requirement of surprise and affirmative damage permitted a party to impeach his or her own witness when truly necessary. At the same time the twin prerequisites prevented a party from calling a witness solely to place before a jury a substantively inadmissible prior inconsistent statement in the hope that the jury would disregard a limiting instruction and consider the statement as substantive evidence.[38]

In the absence of both surprise and affirmative damage, impeachment of one's own witness was considered inappropriate. If the witness did not give affirmatively damaging testimony, that is, testimony of positive aid to the defendant and not merely disappointing to the prosecution, the prosecution simply did not need to attack the witness's credibility. If the witness's testimony did not surprise the prosecution, it should not be permitted to impeach the witness's testimony by placing before the jury the witness's prior statement, because it could have refrained from eliciting the statement it seeks to impeach.[39] The requirement of surprise served to prevent the prosecution from consciously introducing affirmatively damaging testimony under the only circumstances in which it would do so—when the potential effect on the jury of the prior inconsistent statement outweighed the affirmatively damaging effect of the elicited testimony.[40]

The Federal Rules of Evidence, as originally proposed, would have eliminated any problem of a party's impeachment of his or her own witness by prior inconsistent statements. Proposed rule 801(d)(1)(A) provided that all prior statements inconsistent with testimony given by a witness during trial were defined as "not hearsay." Accordingly, proposed rule 607 provided only that "[t]he credibility of a witness may be attacked by any party, including the party calling him."[41] Since courts were to admit all prior inconsistent statements as substantive evidence, there was no need for a requirement of surprise and affirmative damage to prevent a calling party from using impeachment as a technique to place before the jury statements that are not substantively admissible.[42] Congress, however, amended proposed rule 801(d)(1)(A) to limit the prior inconsistent statements denominated "not hearsay" to those "given under oath subject to the penalty of perjury at a trial, hearing, or other proceeding, or in a deposition." At the same time Rule 607 was enacted as proposed. Restricting prior inconsistent statements that are admissible as substantive evidence without any corresponding restriction of the right of a calling party under Rule 607 to impeach his or her own witness again raised the problem of a calling party's potential misuse of impeachment by prior inconsistent statements. Thus although Rule 607 read literally supports such impeachment, court-imposed restrictions are necessary to prevent abuse. Several suggestions have been offered.

1. Surprise and Affirmative Damage

In considering Rule 801(d)(1)(A), Congress expressed its unwillingness to permit the admission of all prior inconsistent statements as substantive evidence, in major part because of a concern that juries might convict criminal defendants in substantial reliance on unreliable prior inconsistent statements.[43] It certainly follows that Congress did not intend to expand the range of prior inconsistent statements not falling within Rule 801(d)(1)(A), as revised, that are receivable in evidence for the limited purpose of impeachment of a witness called by the impeaching party.[44] Permitting the prosecution without limitation to impeach its own witness by introducing prior inconsistent statements that do not meet the requirements of Rule 801(d)(1)(A) designed to insure reliability would promote the very evil Congress sought to avert by amending proposed rule 801(d)(1)(A). Therefore, congressional intent would be implemented by an interpretation of Rule 607 as requiring surprise and affirmative damage before the government is permitted to impeach its own witness by means of prior inconsistent statements that are neither within Rule 801(d)(1)(A) nor otherwise admissible as substantive evidence.[45]

A Fifth Circuit decision illustrates how disregard of the common law prerequisites of surprise and affirmative damage in favor of a literal interpretation of Rule 607, that is, "the credibility of a witness may be attacked by any party, including the party calling him," nullifies the safeguards that Congress intended to place on the use of prior inconsistent statements under Rule 801(d)(1)(A). In United States v. Alvarez,[46] the defendant was prosecuted for attempting to smuggle 1,600 pounds of marijuana across the Rio Grande. At trial, the government called as a witness Israel Villareal, who had previously confessed his participation in the scheme and had allegedly given a statement to government agents placing defendant Margarito Alvarez at the scene of the crime. Before the trial Villareal had denied making that statement, and he reiterated his denial in his subsequent testimony at trial. Although there was no question that the government was not surprised by the testimony it elicited from Villareal, it was permitted to call the narcotics agents in whose presence Villareal had allegedly incriminated Alvarez to testify about Villareal's purported statement. The jury, which had been instructed to consider the agent's testimony only as evidence of Villareal's credibility, subsequently found Alvarez guilty. Upon Alvarez's appeal, the Fifth Circuit summarily rejected the contention that the government's impeachment of Villareal was improper, ruling that the issue was "foreclosed by Rule 607."[47]

Given the notorious inability of juries to ignore substantively evidence introduced solely for purposes of impeachment, the Fifth Circuit's application of Rule 607 creates the precise danger Congress feared when it limited the substantive admissibility of prior inconsistent statements under Rule 801(d)(1)(A)—namely, that a defendant might be convicted in substantial reliance on an untrustworthy out-of-court statement. Permitting the government freely to impeach its own witnesses with evidence not otherwise admissible subverts without justification congressional intent to have the hearsay rules exclude untrustworthy out-of-court statements from the jury.

2. Federal Rule of Evidence 403

Weinstein's Evidence suggests a different approach to the problem of preventing abusive practice under Rule 607:

> Instead of placing so much emphasis on the motive of the proferror, an approach more consistent with the underlying policy of the federal rules of evidence would be to analyze the problems in terms of rule 403—is the probative value of the impeaching evidence out-weighed by its prejudicial impact?[48]

In practice, the balancing test of Rule 403[49] would prove inferior to the simple surprise and affirmative damage prerequisites for several reasons. Initially, it is questionable in light of the clear language of Rule 607 whether many judges would even consider balancing pursuant to Rule 403. Moreover, ad hoc balancing requires a judge under the pressures of a trial situation to sort out and weigh the probative value of evidence upon witness credibility against the possibility of unfair prejudice, confusion of the issues, and misleading the jury. Accordingly, balancing is unlikely to produce either uniform or predictable results. In addition, two of the key factors suggested by *Weinstein's Evidence*, probative value and prejudicial impact, will often vary directly: the more probative a prior statement is of credibility, the greater the likelihood that the jury will improperly view it as substantive evidence; the less probative of credibility, the less the risk that the statement will be improperly considered.[50] Balancing pursuant to Rule 403 is also likely to be time-consuming and of limited effectiveness in screening the jury from potentially prejudicial prior statements. As *Weinstein's Evidence* apparently envisions the process, the judge would make a Rule 403 decision only after the witness had been confronted with his or her alleged prior statement in the presence of the jury.[51] To determine the probative value of the alleged prior statement, the judge would then inquire into the degree of certainty that the statement was made. This inquiry, which would take place initially outside the jury's presence, could cause substantial delay, for unless extrinsic evidence could be presented on the existence of the prior statement, the application of Rule 403 balancing would be ineffective. Most importantly, it is not clear that such procedures would adequately prevent prejudice. First, the jury could become aware of the prior inconsistent statement before the court initiated its inquiry. Second, the court would most likely find, given the availability of a limiting instruction, that the probative value of the impeaching evidence upon credibility is not substantially outweighed by any potential of unfair prejudice. Third, impeachment of a witness who testifies to a matter that merely disappoints the calling party will frequently be permitted by a trial judge impressed by the apparent trustworthiness of the prior inconsistent statement and sympathetic to the plight of the embarrassed examiner. Impeachment will frequently be permitted for the same reasons even when the examining attorney knew in advance that the witness would not testify consistent with his or her prior statement. Thus impeachment of a party's own witness by means of a prior inconsistent statement will frequently be permitted under Rule 403 in spite of the fact that no legitimate purpose is served by an attack upon the credibility of a witness called by the party in the absence of affirmative damage and that it was not necessary to place the jury in the position of hearing an incriminating prior statement of the witness with an instruction to employ the statement only in assessing credibility in the absence of surprise.

In theory, a proper interpretation of Rule 403 would exclude all impeachment evidence of an intimidated witness's prior statement absent surprise and affirmative damage. If the prosecution intentionally calls a witness knowing the witness will state neutral facts, will claim to know nothing, or will purport to recall nothing, the prosecution is eliciting meaningless testimony from the start. There is no legitimate reason to discredit an intimidated witness who testifies to neutral facts, knows nothing, or remembers nothing. On the other hand, the prejudicial effect of the prior statement's content being given substantive effect in spite of a contrary limiting instruction will be great. Even if the prosecution intentionally elicits affirmatively damaging testimony, prejudice will always substantially outweigh probative value, because the prosecution would not intentionally elicit testimony more damaging than the prior statement is prejudicial. Only if the prosecution is surprised by the witness's affirmatively damaging testimony at trial will probative value upon credibility not be substantially outweighed by the danger of unfair prejudice.

Unfortunately, in practice, for the reasons previously suggested, balancing as a restriction to Rule 607 does not work. In our hypothetical case in Chapter 4, application of Rule 403 will almost surely result in Mary Mahoney being impeached with her prior statement in which she identifies Sam Smith. In short, faced with a witness who has changed her story, most probably as a result of being intimidated, the inclination on the part of the court, as demonstrated by reported decisions, to let the jury know about the witness's signed statement given to the police the day of the incident is just too strong to be denied. The temptation to apply the balancing test Rule 403 to permit what cannot be done directly to be done indirectly in the pursuit of justice in the given case is simply overwhelming. No one wants to see a guilty person go free because he or she has successfully intimidated a witness. Only the imposition of the prerequisites of surprise and affirmative damage will prevent the court from permitting impeachment of a party's own witness employing a prior inconsistent statement that was not considered sufficiently trustworthy by Congress to be admitted as substantive evidence in the hope and with the knowledge that the jury will give the prior statement substantive effect in spite of a specific jury instruction not to do so.

3. "Mere Subterfuge" or "Primary Purpose"

Although no clear pattern has developed in the cases, not surprisingly, on balance, a literal interpretation of Rule 607, that is, no restriction imposed upon impeachment by a party of his or her own witness, appears to predominate over either surprise and affirmative damage or Rule 403 balancing.[52] Sometimes, but not always, the literal interpretation is accompanied by the caveat that impeachment of a party's own witness by means of a prior statement may not be employed as a "mere subterfuge"[53] or for the "primary purpose of placing before the jury substantive evidence which is not otherwise admissible."[54] Application of the "mere subterfuge" or "primary purpose" caveat focuses upon the content of the witness's testimony as a whole. Thus if the witness's testimony is important in establishing any fact of consequence significant in the context of the litigation, the witness may be impeached as to any other matter testified to by means of a prior inconsistent statement. Contrast the requirements of surprise and affirmative damage that focus upon each segment of the witness's testimony rather than the witness's testimony taken as a whole. It is suggested that the mere fact that a witness called by the prosecution testifies in a manner of help to the prosecution as to one aspect of the prosecution's case provides no justification for impeachment of another segment of that witness's testimony that is not both of surprise and affirmatively damaging to the prosecution.

C. LACK OF RECOLLECTION

Questions concerning the requirement of inconsistency arise with respect to impeachment by means of a prior statement of a witness who claims lack of recollection. A witness who testifies to a fact at trial may be impeached with a prior statement of the witness claiming a lack of recollection about the fact; current recollection and prior lack of recollection are inconsistent. When, however, a witness claims lack of recollection on the stand about the existence of an earlier event, a prior statement describing that event is not inconsistent with the witness's current lack of recollection.[55] The establishment of a prior statement describing the event that the witness claims at trial not to recall does, however, bring into question the weight to be afforded the witness's overall ability to recall. Since adversely affecting the credibility of a witness called by an opponent is one of the purposes of cross-examination, inquiry with respect to the prior statement on cross-examination may be permitted in the discretion of the court.[56] Conversely, since counsel on direct examination presumably has no legitimate interest in adversely affecting the overall credibility of a witness he or she has called, impeachment by prior statement about a matter not recalled by a witness on direct examination is normally not permitted.[57] Thus in our hypothetical case in Chapter 4, whether John Goodfellow truly cannot recall or is merely feigning his lack of recollection is irrelevant to the prosecution's right to impeach. Current lack of recollection of a particular fact and prior recollection of the same fact are not inconsistent. Moreover, since the testimony of John Goodfellow at trial that he does not recall is not affirmatively damaging, the prosecution has no need to impeach. The government simply wants to place an otherwise inadmissible statement before the jury under the guise of impeachment. This should not be permitted.

D. HOSTILE WITNESSES AND LEADING QUESTIONS

As a technical evidence question it is clear that the fact that a witness is hostile and may thus be asked leading questions on direct examination has no bearing on the propriety of impeachment of the witness by means of a prior inconsistent statement. Unfortunately, attorneys and judges sometimes fail to appreciate the foregoing point. On other occasions, prosecutors wanting to place a prior inconsistent statement before the trier of fact, while knowing better, simply latch on to the witness's hostility as a justification. When no objection is interposed or when the court itself wants to let the trier of fact hear the witness's prior inconsistent statement, impeachment proceeds.

The process sometimes permitted, albeit incorrectly, of impeachment of a witness called by the party by means of a prior inconsistent statement because the witness is declared hostile by the court is fostered by a certain amount of confusion surrounding the term *cross-examination*.

Cross-examination in common parlance refers to the right of opposing counsel following direct examination to ask leading questions of a witness and to employ modes of impeachment, such as prior conviction, partiality, and prior inconsistent statement, in an attempt to "destroy" the testimony of the witness. Cross-examination is a matter of right. Cross-examination constitutes an important aspect of due process and, in criminal cases, of the right of confrontation.[58] Cross-examination of a particular witness may well be destructive, with the examining counsel employing leading questions and modes of impeachment in an attempt to minimize the trier of fact's assessment of the weight to be accorded the witness's testimony.[59] Questions may be propounded to the witness on cross-examination designed to probe whether the witness possesses the capacity and actually employed the possessed capacity to observe through any of the five senses each of the matters related on direct examination; whether the witness accurately recorded and recollects these firsthand sense impressions; whether the witness possesses the capacity and is employing that capacity to express accurately that which the witness perceived, recorded, and recollects; and whether the witness is being sincere or conversely is fabricating the matters related on direct examination. In addition, questions may be propounded to the witness designed to elicit responses that tend to explain, modify, qualify, limit, or otherwise shed light upon the matters related by the witness on direct examination.

Cross-examination, however, is also in fact much more. Counsel on cross-examination may among others (1) attempt to elicit disputed facts from the witness favorable to his or her case, (2) have the witness repeat those facts testified to on direct favorable to the cross-examiner, (3) have the witness testify to nondisputed facts essential to presentation of his or her theory of the case, (4) establish that the witness's testimony is not harmful to the advocate's case on the critical points under dispute, and/or (5) ask questions to the witness designed primarily to keep the cross-examiner's theory of the case before the trier of fact. Cross-examination is also sometimes much less. It is less in that on cross-examination leading questions are sometimes prohibited and certain kinds of impeachment will not always be allowed.

Leading questions are ordinarily permitted on cross-examination. The reason for prohibiting leading questions, that is, the witness will be responsive to the suggestions of counsel, generally does not apply to the witness under cross-examination. However, if the particular witness is partial to the party cross-examining, there is the same danger in leading questions as on direct examination, and the court has discretion to prohibit their use. One circumstance in which the use of leading questions on cross-examination is inappropriate is when a witness called by an opposing party is with respect to that party a "hostile witness, an adverse party, or a witness identified with an adverse party." Rule 611(c).[60] In such case the witness may be examined on direct examination by means of leading questions and should then be cross-examined without the use of leading questions by his or her own or other friendly counsel. Cross-examination under such circumstances is in reality redirect examination. Another such circumstance arises when, in the court's discretion, a party is permitted on cross-examination to exceed the scope of direct examination. Permission to exceed the scope of direct examination is frequently granted for the convenience of the witness.[61] When inquiry is permitted beyond the scope of direct examination, "inquiry into the additional matters [is conducted] as if on direct examination," Rule 611(b).[62] Therefore, use of leading questions is improper and impeachment, including by means of an inconsistent statement, is governed by Rule 607.[63] Under such circumstances, the party originally calling the witness may proceed to cross-examine the witness by means of leading questions with respect to those matters raised beyond the scope of direct examination.

In contrast, a party calling a witness to testify at trial ordinarily must elicit testimony from the witness on direct examination in response to questions that are nonleading.[64] Nonleading questions do not suggest the desired response to the witness. Specific nonleading questions such as "How many lanes of traffic are there on Main Street at the point of the accident?" tend to keep the witness within the bounds of relevancy and admissibility. They also allow the opponent an opportunity to object to inadmissible evidence before it is given. A narrative answer in response to a general nonleading question, such as "Please tell the jury what you observed at the time of the robbery," possesses the advantages of naturalness and freedom from interruption. The extent to which testimony tends to be confined or free flowing depends largely on the extent to which the nonleading question is specific or general, a matter largely left to the discretion of the examining attorney and, if an objection is made, the trial judge. This discretion sensibly permits the adoption of a course best suited to the particular witness's characteristics, considered in light of testimony to be given in the context of the litigation. In either case the testimony is that of the witness, not a mere assent to the suggestion of the attorney who called the witness to the stand.

A question is leading if it suggests the answer desired by the examiner. The vice of such a question lies in substituting the suggestions of counsel for the actual testimony of the witness.[65] A question may be leading because of its form (for example, "Didn't he . . . ?"), its detail, the examiner's emphasis on certain words, the tone used by the examiner in asking the question, or by the examiner's nonverbal conduct. Generally, questions that may be answered either yes or no are considered leading. Merely using the term *whether or not*, or another form of alternative, does not of itself keep a question from being leading.[66] However, a witness can scarcely be examined without calling the witness's attention to the subject matter on which his or her testimony is sought, and a question so doing is not considered leading.

A judge who sustains an objection to a leading question may be making an empty gesture. Effective enforcement of the rule against leading questions requires foreclosing all further inquiry into the subject, permitting counsel to return to the topic only after an exploration of other matters has reduced the effect of communicating the answer to the witness. These measures are available to the trial judge. The fact that they seldom are invoked may imply that the rule against leading questions is lacking in true substance and operates merely to create a false sense of spontaneity that the examiner might otherwise destroy by use of leading questions.[67] Counsel generally refrain from propounding leading questions on direct examination not only because of a desire to avoid having opposing counsel's objections sustained before the jury but also from a desire to enhance the witness's persuasiveness by having the witness testify in a natural manner in response to nonleading questions.

Counsel may employ leading questions on direct examination of a witness when necessary to develop his or her testimony or when calling a hostile witness, an adverse party, or a witness identified with an adverse party.[68] Leading questions are considered necessary to develop the witness's direct testimony in the following situations:

(a) Undisputed preliminary or inconsequential matters. Leading questions focus the witness's attention upon a topic. Leading a witness on a point about which no controversy exists is harmless and saves time.[69]

(b) A child witness or an adult with communication problems either physical or mental.[70]

(c) A witness whose recollection is exhausted.[71]

(d) A witness who is being impeached by the party who called him or her. The party calling a witness may impeach that witness to the extent provided by Rules 607[72] and 403.[73] Leading questions may be addressed to the witness as part of the process of impeachment.

(e) A witness who is hostile, unwilling, frightened, or biased. A witness who demonstrates recalcitrance at trial by giving damaging testimony or by answering unsurely, reluctantly, obstinately, or belligerently, that is, a witness hostile in fact, may be led.

Notice that merely giving damaging answers in the absence of recalcitrance does not permit counsel to lead. A witness may be recalcitrant because he or she is (1) aligned in interest with the adverse party, (2) antagonistic to the calling party, (3) antagonistic to the court process or the notion of testifying, or (4) for personal reasons unrelated to either party or the judicial process, or for no reason at all, disposed not to disclose relevant facts. The court may permit leading questions when it appears that a witness while testifying is being recalcitrant for whatever reason. A witness, such as Mary Mahoney in our hypothetical case in Chapter 4, demonstrating recalcitrance brought on by intimidation may be asked leading questions. Witnesses who are nervous or upset may also be led when necessary to develop their testimony.

Some witnesses, such as an adverse party, are automatically considered hostile, so leading questions are permitted on direct examination without a prior in-court showing that leading questions are necessary to develop the witness's testimony. Rule 611(c) defines hostile in law witnesses to include "a hostile witness, an adverse party or a witness identified with an adverse party."[74] Because such a witness will not respond to the suggestions of counsel, leading questions are permitted. Hostility in law may be based upon status of the witness alone or status plus pretrial behavior.[75] In determining hostility, the most important single factor is often whether the calling party has been able to prepare the witness to testify at trial. Whether a witness is considered automatically hostile is determined at the time of his or her examination. Thus an occurrence witness who advises the prosecution that he or she does not want to testify against the defendant and will no longer cooperate is a hostile witness.[76] Ordinarily, a current employee, officer, director, managing agent of a party, and a relative of a party will be considered a "witness identified with that" party, and thus subject to leading questions by the opponent.[77] Following the examination of a witness hostile in law, the side to which the witness is favorable is entitled to examine the witness as if on redirect, that is, to explain, modify, qualify, limit, or otherwise shed light on the testimony attacked. Leading questions may be employed in this effort only to the extent normally permitted on redirect examination.[78]

The pattern of leading questions being generally permitted on cross-examination but not direct examination of a witness sometimes creates confusion when the term *cross-examination* is employed in the context of a party's examination of a hostile witness called by that party. Consider, for example, Illinois Supreme Court Rule 238:

Impeachment of Witnesses; Hostile Witnesses

(a) The credibility of a witness may be attacked by any party, including the party calling him.

(b) If the court determines that a witness is hostile or unwilling, he may be examined by the party calling him as if under cross-examination.[79]

Illinois Supreme Court Rule 238(a) is verbatim Rule 607 of the Federal Rules of Evidence.[80] Illinois Supreme Court Rule 238(b) provides that a "hostile or unwilling" witness may be examined by the party calling him or her as if under cross-examination. On cross-examination a witness may be asked leading questions and impeached employing any of the permissible modes of impeachment including impeachment by means of a prior inconsistent statement. Thus under Rule 238(b) one may argue that a witness who is either hostile, that is, hostile in law, or unwilling, that is, hostile in fact, may be impeached by means of a prior inconsistent statement. However, Rule 238(a) already provides that any party including the party calling the witness may impeach and may do so without first establishing hostility or unwillingness. Moreover, hostility and unwillingness relate to the need to employ leading questions to develop the witness's testimony on direct examination and conversely to the fact that the witness will not be responsive to any suggestions contained in the leading questions, the vice against which the bar to leading questions on direct examination is directed. Hostility and unwillingness do not relate at all to the need of the calling party to impeach the witness by means of a prior inconsistent statement based upon the presence of surprise and affirmative damage, nor do they address the concern that the jury will give a prior inconsistent statement employed solely to impeach substantive effect in spite of a jury instruction not to do so.[81] Rule 238(b) should be amended to provide that "If the court determines that a witness is hostile or unwilling, the party calling him may interrogate by leading questions."

E. THE COURT'S WITNESS DOCTRINE

At common law and under Rule 614(a)[82] of the Federal Rules of Evidence, the court may on its own motion or at the suggestion of a party call a witness not previously called by a party. All parties may cross-examine witnesses called to testify by the court, that is, lead and impeach. The court's right to call witnesses derives from the court's basic responsibility to administer justice for the purpose of ascertaining the truth. Exercise of the right rests in the court's discretion.[83] In practice, however, this discretion to act on its own motion is rarely exercised in favor of calling a lay witness.[84] The calling of lay witnesses by the court is generally considered to be an unwarranted intrusion into the adversary system and thus should be undertaken only when clearly required in the interests of justice.[85] Instances in which the action may be warranted arise in situations such as custody matters in which a special obligation is placed upon the court to protect the interests of a nonparty. When a lay witness is called by the court, the court should advise the jury about why the witness was called as a court's witness and instruct them that the witness's testimony is entitled to no greater weight simply because he or she has been called by the court.[86]

At common law the power of the court to call a witness at the suggestion of a party has most often been exercised when the government expects that a witness will be perceived by the jury as untrustworthy and wants to escape the necessity of calling him or her, thereby avoiding any apparent association with the witness before the jury.[87] Calling a witness as a court's witness also serves to circumvent the common law rule against impeachment of a party's own witness.[88] If a witness is called at common law at the request of the government as a court's witness, as is true under Rule 614(a), either party may then cross-examine the witness, that is, lead and impeach.[89]

To illustrate the operation of the court's witness doctrine at common law, consider the approach assumed in criminal cases in Illinois. Returning to our hypothetical case in Chapter 4, Mary Mahoney before trial advised the prosecuting attorney that the description she had previously given was incorrect. Her current description of the man fleeing the building does not correspond to the accused. Faced with prior knowledge that Mary Mahoney is a "flipped" witness, the prosecuting attorney is barred by the common law voucher rule from placing Mary Mahoney on the witness stand, eliciting her current description of the man fleeing the building and then impeaching her with her prior inconsistent description of the culprit. However, the prosecuting attorney could advise the court that Mary Mahoney has flipped and that for that reason he doubts her veracity as a witness. Such fact coupled with a showing that the testimony of the witness whose veracity can no longer be vouched relates to direct, that is, crucial, issues in the case and is necessary to prevent a miscarriage of justice permits an Illinois trial judge to call the witness as a court's witness.[90] Once called as a court's witness, the prosecution is free to lead and impeach the witness including impeachment by means of a prior inconsistent statement. In short, the court's witness doctrine often serves as a mechanism to permit impeachment of a witness called by the prosecution with a prior inconsistent statement without having to satisfy the tests otherwise applicable to prevent unwarranted impeachment of a party's own witness for the purpose of placing prior statements of the witness not substantively admissible before the jury.

Under the Federal Rules of Evidence, a party who does not want to vouch for the veracity of a witness possessing crucial testimony will almost invariably be able to have the witness declared hostile under Rule 611(c)[91] A party calling such a witness will thus be permitted to propound leading questions. The impeachment of such a witness is conducted according to Rule 607, which provides generally that the party calling the witness may impeach. Whether the party calling a particular witness will be entitled to impeach with a prior inconsistent statement is a matter that should be approached squarely and not circumvented by the simple expedient of having the witness declared a court's witness.[92] Difficulties accompanying witness association with a party can be ameliorated, if not totally removed, by the court advising the jury when the witness is called that the witness has been declared hostile to the calling party. Accordingly, under the Federal Rules of Evidence trial courts should rarely exercise their discretion in favor of calling a lay witness to testify at trial and should never do so to avoid addressing those considerations properly bearing upon the question of whether the prosecution should be permitted to impeach a particular witness it wants to call by means of a prior inconsistent statement.[93]

F. SUMMARY

Regardless of whether a court adopts a literal reading of Rule 607, or addresses the concerns that arise when the government attempts to impeach a witness it has called with a nonsubstantively admissible prior inconsistent statement by resorting to either surprise and affirmative damage, Rule 403 balancing, or the mere subterfuge-primary purpose limitation, Rule 607 remains inapplicable in any case involving a murdered or otherwise unavailable witness as defined in Rule 804(a). Thus in our hypothetical case in

Chapter 4, Rule 607 may not be employed to place before the jury a statement by Bob Williams, who was murdered, or statement of Jim James, who refused to testify. Impeachment in both cases by prior statement is simply not possible since there is not testimony to impeach. Similarly, when John Goodfellow testifies to a lack of recollection, his prior out-of-court statement detailing the fact no longer recalled is not inconsistent and may not be employed by the government to impeach.

In the case of an intimidated witness who at trial tells a different story, the dual prerequisites of surprise and affirmative damage as proper restrictions on Rule 607, whether applied directly or in conjunction with Rule 403 balancing, severely restrict the government's ability to impeach a witness called by the government by means of a prior inconsistent statement. Surprise and affirmative damage do not often occur. The prosecution will on most occasions know in advance of trial that the witness will not testify against the defendant in accordance with the witness's prior statement. Thus surprise is absent. Moreover, witnesses who do not want to testify against a defendant will often testify to neutral facts or feign a lack of recollection, rather than provide testimony of positive assistance to the accused. In either case there is no affirmative damage. Permitting impeachment under such circumstances would be permitting the use of impeachment by means of a prior inconsistent statement as a subterfuge in the hope that and with the knowledge that the jury will give the prior statement substantive consideration in spite of the fact that they are instructed by the court not to do so.

Impeachment by means of a prior inconsistent statement is not a proper response of the law to the problem of witness intimidation. When a witness has been successfully intimidated resulting in the witness not testifying at the trial consistently with a prior statement made to the authorities, the proper response of the law should be to provide for the maximum breadth of substantive admissibility for the prior statements of the witness warranted by considerations of trustworthiness. Suggestions to that end are put forth in the next chapter. However, once it is determined that the prior statement of the witness does not warrant receipt as substantive evidence, the law should not permit the jury to be advised about the prior statement of the witness unless clearly necessary for the purpose of impeachment. A prior inconsistent statement is only necessary for the purpose of impeachment of an intimidated witness called by the government when the dual prerequisites of surprise and affirmative damage are present.

NOTES

1. C. McCormick, *Evidence* § 34 at 68 (Cleary ed. 1972).
2. *See* Chapter 6,Section 5 *infra.*
3. *See* C. McCormick, *Evidence* § 38 at 75 (Cleary ed. 1972); 3A J. Wigmore, *Evidence* §§ 896-908 (Chadbourn Rev. 1970).

4. Fed. R. Evid. 613(a) provides:

(a) Examining witness concerning prior statement. In examining a witness concerning a prior statement made by him, whether written or not, the statement need not be shown nor its contents disclosed to him at that time, but on request the same shall be shown or disclosed to opposing counsel.

5. 129 Eng. Rep. 969 (1820).

6. 4 J. Wigmore, *Evidence* § 1259 at 610 (Chadbourn Rev. 1972) ("[A] rule which for unsoundness of principle, impropriety of policy, and practical inconvenience in trials [is] the most notable mistake that can be found among the rulings upon the present subject."); L. Stern and D. Grosh, *A Visit with Queen Caroline: Her Trial and Its Rule*, 6 Cap. U. L. Rev. 165, 198 (1976) ("Grant the argument of the judges that a letter or other writing is the best evidence of its contents and that therefore a witness should not be questioned to give his version of the letter's contents from memory, if it is desired to prove what the letter says. But there are nevertheless many cases in which the purpose of the questioning is not to prove the contents of the letter, but rather to test the credibility of the witness. If a witness has claimed to remember the details of an event, but relates falsely what he wrote in a letter associated with the event, that fact diminishes the trust which might be attached to his memory. Similarly, if the witness falsely denied writing a particular letter, or lies about what he wrote, that fact obviously is evidence that he is likely to be lying in other parts of his testimony about related matters. But if the rule in the Queen's Case is followed, and it is required that the witness first be shown or read the letter, this valuable chance to test his memory and veracity is lost. A forgetful witness will have his memory of the letter refreshed or corrected, though his memory for the rest of his testimony remains faulty. A lying witness will discover the matters on which he may safely lie and those in which he must equivocate, thus guarding the lie from discovery.").

7. The Charles Morgan, 115 U.S. 69 (1885).

8. *Id.* at 77-78.

9. United States v. Dillyard, 101 F.2d 829, 837 (2d Cir. 1938), quoted in United States v. Williamson, 516 F.2d 390, 392 (2d Cir. 1975).

10. C. McCormick, *Evidence* § 34 at 68 (Cleary ed. 1972) ("[C]ould the jury reasonably find that a witness who believed the truth of the facts testified to would have been unlikely to make a prior statement of this tenor?"); 3A J. Wigmore, *Evidence* § 1040 at 1048 (Chadbourn Rev. 1970) ("Do the two expressions appear to have been produced by inconsistent beliefs?").

11. *See, e.g.*, United States v. Barrett, 539 F.2d 244, 254 (1st Cir. 1976) ("To be received as a prior inconsistent statement, the contradition need not be in plain terms. It is enough if the proferred testimony, taken as a whole, either by what it says or by what it omits to say, affords some indication that the fact was different from the testimony of the witness whom it is sought to contradict.").

12. United States v. Barrett, 539 F.2d 244, 254 (1st Cir. 1976) ("Furthermore, the fact that [the witness's] belief that [the defendant] was not involved might be called an 'opinion' is immaterial. . . . The important point is the clear incompatibility between [the witness's] direct testimony and the alleged statement.").

13. Jenkins v. Anderson, 447 U.S. 231, 239 (1980) ("Common law traditionally has allowed witnesses to be impeached by their previous failure to state a fact in cir-

cumstances in which that fact naturally would have been asserted. 3A Wigmore, *Evidence* § 1042, at 1056 (Chadbourn rev. 1970)."); United States v. Rice, 550 F.2d 1364, 1373 (5th Cir. 1977):

> While Kilgore was being cross-examined, the government turned over to the defendants a hand-written statement, prepared by Kilgore at an undetermined date, which was a summary of the events to which he had testified. The statement related various aspects of the conspiratorial operations. Massler's name did not appear in the account but the names of the other defendants were included.
>
> Alvarez had the exhibit marked for identification and cross-examined Kilgore about it, as did Massler's attorney. Several days later, Massler informed the Court that he intended to offer Kilgore's written statement into evidence as exculpating Massler by failure to mention his name. The Court reserved its ruling. After several discussions about the admissibility of the exhibit, the government withdrew its objections and the statement was admitted.

14. With respect to the concept of inconsistency, *see also* Chapter 4, Section C2 *supra*.

15. When a witness called by the party is being impeached, the foundation would be laid on direct examination.

16. Robertson v. M/S Sanyo Maru, 374 F.2d 463, 465 (5th Cir. 1967) ("[T]he cross-examiner should ask the witness whether he made the statement, giving its substance, naming the time, the place, and the person to whom made."); Sylvester v. Meditz, 278 F. Supp. 810, 813 (E.D. Wis. 1968) ("The proper procedure for laying a foundation for impeachment by prior inconsistent statements made orally is to call the attention of the witness to the particular time and occasion when the witness purportedly made the statement. The witness should be informed 'what the statements were and the conditions and circumstances under which they were made.' ").

17. Brooks v. United States, 309 F.2d 580, 582 (10th Cir. 1962) ("[I]t is necessary that the prior statements be called to his attention, and that he be given an opportunity to admit, deny, or explain them.").

18. United States v. Wright, 489 F.2d 1181, 1187 (D.C. Cir. 1973) ("[B]efore introducing extrinsic proof of a witness' prior inconsistent statement, the witness must be asked whether he or she made the statement and must be given an oppportunity to explain it.").

19. When a party is impeaching a witness he or she has called, the explanation may be elicited by opposing counsel during cross-examination.

20. United States v. McPartlin, 595 F.2d 1321, 1354 (7th Cir. 1979) ("The Government also points out that pursuant to Rule 613(b), the witness was permitted . . . to explain the impeaching grand jury testimony by stating that he had been unfamiliar with the geography of Liechtenstein and because of that he had not understood the question at the time of his first grand jury appearance."); United States v. Franzese, 392 F.2d 954 (2d Cir. 1968) (witness explained that he feared death or bodily harm); United States v. Scandifia, 390 F.2d 244 (2d Cir. 1968) (witness testified that his family had received threatening phone calls).

21. United States v. Praetorius, 622 F.2d 1054, 1065 (2d Cir. 1979) ("Lebel, however, correctly points out that the trial judge was misinterpreting the rule in requiring that Laws be confronted with the 'statement' immediately. The rule does not specify any particular order of calling witnesses, and so the defense should have been able to introduce the evidence during the examination of Agent Yaniello.").

22. 56 F.R.D. 183, 279 (1973).

23. C. McCormick, *Evidence* § 37 at 74 (Cleary ed. 1972) ("When [the foundation] is overlooked by the impeacher, as it often is . . . .").

24. 56 F.R.D. 183, 279 (1973).

25. Fed. R. Evid. 801(d)(1)(A) provides:

> (d) Statements which are hearsay. A statement is not hearsay if—
>
> (1) Prior statement by witness. The declarant testifies at the trial or hearing and is subject to cross-examination concerning the statement, and the statement is (A) inconsistent with his testimony, and was given under oath subject to the penalty of perjury at a trial, hearing, or other proceeding, or in a deposition, or . . . .

26. M. Graham, *Employing Inconsistent Statements for Impeachment as Substantive Evidence: A Critical Review and Proposed Amendments of Federal Rules of Evidence 801(d)(1)(A), 613, and 607*, 75 Mich. L. Rev. 1565, 1605-7 (1977):

> As pointed out in the Advisory Committee Note, rule 613(b) permits extrinsic proof to be introduced before the witness is allowed to admit, deny, or explain the prior statement.
>
> * * *
>
> [I]f opposing counsel does recall the witness for denial or explanation followed by cross-examination relating hereto, the prior statement in one form or another will have been placed before the jury on as many as five separate occasions—cross-examination, extrinsic evidence, cross-examination upon the extrinsic evidence, recall of the witness for explanation, and cross-examination again.
>
> Rule 613(b) not only enables examining counsel to place the prior inconsistent statement before the trier of fact on multiple occasions, but it also permits the party impeaching the witness to delay the witness' denial or explanation. For example, if the content of the prior inconsistent statement is first introduced through extrinsic evidence as part of defendant's case-in-chief, plaintiff will in all likelihood be foreclosed from presenting the witness' explanation or denial until rebuttal. This delay, which may well be substantial, could seriously impair the plaintiff's ability to rehabilitate the witness. Moreover, in addition to the fact that the mere mention of the statement in rebuttal permits it to be scrutinized yet another time upon further cross-examination of the witness, it seems clear that even if plaintiff's counsel does choose to offer an explanation,
>
>> [g]iven such time to crystallize, it is questionable whether the jury's estimation of the witness can be restored to its former status by his belated explanation. Conceivably, the jury may be even more prone to discount the belated explanation knowing that the witness has had the opportunity to confer with counsel after the evidence of the inconsistent statement was presented.
>
> Cross-examining counsel wishing to highlight a prior inconstency in this manner may now do so, for Rule 613(b) provides that the witness need no longer be given the chance to deny or explain his prior statement before admission of extrinsic evidence. Moreover, under ruled 613(b) a party wishing to emphasize an inconsistent statement he believes the witness will admit making may avoid the danger that a court will exclude extrinsic evidence of the prior statement by simply introducing the extrinsic evidence before the witness is provided an opportunity to admit, deny, or explain.

27. *See* note 49 *infra.*

28. Fed. R. Evid. 611(a) provides:

> (a) Control by Court. The court shall exercise reasonable control over the mode and order of interrogating witnesses and presenting evidence so as to (1) make the interrogation and presentation effective for the ascertainment of the truth, (2) avoid needless consumption of time, and (3) protect witnesses from harassment of undue embarrassment.

29. United States v. Bohle, 445 F.2d 54, 74 (7th Cir. 1971) ("Where a trial judge is aware of the possibility that counsel intends to ask an impeaching question having prejudicial implications, it is proper and advisable, in the interests of avoiding abuse and of insuring a fair trial to both the prosecution and the defendant, that the judge inquire of counsel whether the question on which he is about to embark is for the purpose of impeachment and whether and how counsel intends to follow up the question with impeaching proof. If there is no intention to introduce such impeaching proof, the question may, in the court's discretion, be properly excluded.").

30. Robertson v. M/S Sanyo Maru, 374 F.2d 463, 465 (5th Cir. 1967) ("If the witness denies the making of the statement or fails to admit it, the cross-examiner must prove the making of the alleged statement at his next stage of giving evidence."); United States v. Bohle, 445 F.2d 54, 74 (7th Cir. 1971) ("[I]n civil litigation and in the case of the prosecution in a criminal case, the duty to follow up foundation with evidence is breached at the risk of reversal of any tainted victory.").

31. *Compare* Gordon v. United States, 344 U.S. 414, 420 (1953) ("[A]n admission that a contradiction is contained in a writing should not bar admission of the document itself in evidence."), with Dilley v. Chesapeake & Ohio Railway Company, 327 F.2d 249, 251 (6th Cir. 1964) ("Where a witness admits a statement attributed to him there is no necessity to prove it and the statement is not admissible in evidence."). *See also* C. McCormick, *Evidence* § 37 at 72-73 (Cleary ed. 1972) ("If, however, the witness unequivocally admits the making of the supposed statement, may the cross-examiner still chooe to prove it again by another witness? Wigmore, with some support, suggests that he may, but the prevailing view is to the contrary and in the usual situation this seems the more expedient practice. It saves time and minimizes the calling of witnesses upon what is only a side issue; yet circumstances may be such, especially when the statement is in writing, that the judge's discretion to allow the impeachment to proceed should be recognized.").

32. For a full discussion of collateral and noncollateral, *see* M. Graham, *Handbook of Federal Evidence* § 607.2 (1981).

33. E. Devitt and C. Blackmar, *Federal Jury Practice and Instructions* § 17:08 (3d ed. St. Paul:West, 1977):

Impeachment—Inconsistent Statements or Conduct—Falsus in Uno Falsus in Omnibus

> The testimony of a witness may be discredited or impeached by showing that he previously made statements which are inconsistent with his present testimony. The earlier contradictory statements are admissible only to impeach the credibility of the witness, and not to establish the truth of these statements. It is the province of the testimony of a witness who has been impeached.
>
> If a witness is shown knowingly to have testified falsely concerning any

material matter, you have a right to distrust such witness testimony in other particulars and you may reject all the testimony of that witness or give it such credibility as you may think it deserves.

An act or omission is "knowingly" done, if done voluntarily and intentionally and not because of mistake or accident or other innocent reason.

34. United States v. Lester 491 F.2d 680, 683 (6th Cir. 1974):

Under this Circuit's established rule, it is obvious that the District Court's failure to advise the jury that Bevins' prior inconsistent statement could be received only for impeachment purposes and not for substantive proof of appellant Lester's crime was plain error affecting substantial rights. Fed. R. Crim. P. 52(b).

In United States v. Lipscomb this court stated:

> "We are of the opinion that the failure of the trial judge to limit through cautionary instructions the jury's consideration of these extra-judicial statements to impeachment purposes requires reversal. Although such an instruction was not specifically requested, it has generally been held that failure to give it amounts to plain error where, as here, the government's case is weak and the statement is extremely damaging. Jones v. United States, 128 U.S. App. D.C. 36, 385 F.2d 296 (1967); Newman v. United States, 331 F.2d 968 (8th Cir. 1964); Upham v. United States, 328 F.2d 661 (5th Cir. 1964). Also see Benson v. United States, 402 F.2d 576 (9th Cir. 1968)." United States v. Lipscomb, 425 F.2d 226, 227 (6th Cir. 1970).

35. Diaz v. United States, 223 U.S. 442, 450 (1912) ("[W]hen evidence of [hearsay] is admitted without objection it is to be considered and given its natural probative effect as if it were in law admissible.").

36. *See generally*, C. MCormick, *Evidence* § 38 (Cleary ed. 1972); 3A J. Wigmore, *Evidence* §§ 896-908 (Chadbourn Rev. 1970).

37. *See, e.g.*, Hickory v. United States, 151 U.S. 303 (1894); United States v. Lemon, 497 F.2d 854 (10th Cir. 1974); United States v. Davis, 487 F.2d 112 (5th Cir. 1973); Randazzo v. United States, 300 F.2d 794 (8th Cir. 1924).

38. *See e.g.*, United States v. Lemon, 497 F.2d 854 (10th Cir. 1974); United States v. Coppola, 479 F.2d 1153 (10th Cir. 1973); United States v. Davis, 487 F.2d 112 (5th Cir. 1973); Bushaw v. United States, 353 F.2d 477 (9th Cir. 1965).

39. Randazzo v. United States, 300 F. 794, 797-98 (8th Cir. 1924) ("In its simplest statement it is that, when a party calls a witness and is surprised by affirmative evidence given by the witness, which actually aids the adversary party, the party calling the witness may cross-examine him, and show statements made by him which are contrary to the testimony given by him on the witness stand. But when the witness merely fails, when called, to testify in favor of the party calling him, as he was expected to do, but says nothing which tends to aid the case of the adversary party, he cannot be cross-examined or impeached by the party who calls him.").

40. Wigmore objected to the surprise requirement. He envisioned no harm in allowing a party to show contradiction by calling a witness who will not adhere to a prior statement: the party could have contradicted the witness if the calling party's opponent had called the witness and elicited the same testimony. In addition, Wigmore did not believe that the calling party should be deprived of the witness's remaining testimony. 3A J. Wigmore, *Evidence* § 904 (Chadbourn Rev.

1970). The other party, however, would not seek to elicit the current testimony unless it was affirmatively damaging to the calling party's case. When the current testimony is affirmatively damaging, the requirement of surprise prevents the calling party from eliciting it under the only circumstances in which he or she would do so—when the potential effect of the prior inconsistent statement on the jury outweighs the damaging effect of the current testimony. In most if not all of these cases, the opposing party would reach the same conclusion and not elicit the damaging testimony from the witness. Thus in these circumstances the jury would never be exposed to the prior inconsistent statement. If the adversary does choose to elicit such testimony, impeachment of counsel would be permitted.

The surprise requirement would not prevent the calling party from eliciting favorable testimony from the witness, because the calling party need only avoid inquiring about testimony already known to be adverse. If the witness should give damaging testimony in a nonresponsive answer, the court, in its discretion, may permit impeachment by the prior inconsistent statement. If the opponent elicits the testimony on cross-examination, impeachment on redirect would be proper.

41. 56 F.R.D. 183, 266 (1973).

42. The Advisory Committee's Note to proposed rule 607, in rejecting the voucher doctrine, relied on proposed rule 801(d)(1)(A). The committee pointed out that "if the impeachment is by a prior statement, it is free from hearsay dangers and is excluded from the category of hearsay under [proposed] Rule 801(d)(1)(A)." 56 F.R.D. at 267.

43. *See* Chapter 4, Section C1(b) *supra*.

44. *See* Hearings on H.R. 5463 Before the Senate Comm. on the Judiciary, 93d Cong., 2d Sess. 299, 301-4, 308-19 (1974) (testimony and statement of Herbert Semmel). Semmel stated:

> [W]e would recommend one change [in rule 607] for this reason: Under the rule, a party could call a witness knowing the witness' testimony will be adverse, and then impeach that witness by a prior inconsistent statement. Of course, technically the jury is instructed that the prior inconsistent statement is to be considered only for impeachment purposes. Nevertheless, in practice juries are likely to give the statement weight in determining liability or guilt.
>
> In order to be consistent with the House version of rule 801(d), we think an amendment is necessary to rule 607 to limit the rule to permit impeachment by prior inconsistent statements to cases where the party calling the witness is surprised. This is really the traditional role which is in effect in a majority of jurisdictions today.

Id. at 319.

45. Before enactment of Rule 607, a number of comments questioned whether the rule might lead to government abuse in criminal cases. For example:

> Rule 607. The liberalization of a rule permitting a party to attack the credibility of his own witness has many advantages in a civil case, but may be seriously abused by the prosecution in a criminal case. The most glaring abuse occurred in Douglas v. Alabama, 380 U.S. 415 (1965), in which a prosecutor called a co-defendant who asserted the Fifth Amendment privilege against self-incrimination. The trial judge permitted the prosecutor to "cross-examine" his own witness by reading

the witness' confession to him. This practice was condemned by the Supreme Court, but lesser forms of impeachment by prosecutors of their own witnesses have troubled federal courts. Our Circuit announced a reasonable rule in Bushaw v. United States 353 F.2d 477, 481 (9th Cir. 1965) which holds:

> "a party is not permitted to get before the jury, under the guise of impeachment, an ex parte statement of a witness, by calling him to the stand when there is good reason to believe he will decline to testify as desired, and when in fact he only so declines."

The court then announced a restriction to this type of impeachment: "A party must show both surprise and damage before being permitted to impeach his own witness." For criminal cases, this requirement of both damage and surprise should be required.

Hearings on Proposed Rules of Evidence Before the Special Sub-comm. on Reform of Federal Criminal Laws of The House Comm. on the Judiciary, 93d Cong., 1st Sess., Ser. 2 at 237 (1973) (statement of John J. Cleary on behalf of the National Legal Aid and Defense Association). *See* 3 *Weinstein's Evidence* at 607-3 (1981).

46. 548 F.2d 542 (5th Cir. 1977).

47. *Id.* at 543 n.3.

48. 3 *Weinstein's Evidence* ¶ 607[01] at 607-17 (1981).

49. Fed. R. Evid. 403 provides:

> Although relevant, evidence may be excluded if its probative value is substantially outweighed by the danger of unfair prejudice, confusion of the issues, or misleading the jury, or by considerations of undue delay, waste of time, or needless presentation of cumulative evidence.

50. *See* M. Graham, *The Relationship Among Federal Rules of Evidence 607, 801(d)(1)(A), and 403: A Reply to Weinstein's Evidence*, 55 Tex. L. Rev. 573 (1977).

51. According to Weinstein, "[v]ery seldom are evidence questions ruled upon by a pre-trial judge. Where discretion is involved, it is usual to postpone decision until the trial. . . . Often it is not until the trial that the need for a special type of hearsay becomes apparent." J. Weinstein, *Alternatives to the Present Hearsay Rule*, 44 F.R.D. 375, 380 (1968).

52. *See, e.g.*, United States v. Dennis, 625 F.2d 782, 795 n.6 (8th Cir. 1980) ("At common law, the party calling a witness at trial could not impeach his credibility unless the party could show both surprise and substantial harm. Bushaw v. United States, 353 F.2d 477 (9th Cir. 1965). But Rule 607 of the Federal Rules of Evidence allowed impeachment of one's own witness. So long as prior inconsistent statements are otherwise admissible, they may be used for impeachment; and surprise is no longer a prerequisite to their use. United States v. Long Soldier, 562 F.2d 601, 605 (8th Cir. 1977). The prosecution's ability to impeach its witness with prior inconsistent statements is crucial in cases where the 'turncoat' witness is afraid. United States v. Gerry, 515 F.2d 130, 190-40 (2d Cir. 1975) (loansharking prosecution), or hostile, United States v. Rogers, 549 F.2d 490 (8th Cir. 1976) (charged with the same offense)."); United States v. Palacios, 556 F.2d 1359, 1363 (5th Cir. 1977) ("Under rule 607 the government's impeachment of [the witness] by her prior inconsistent statement was proper without a showing of surprise."); United States v. Long

Soldier, 562 F.2d 601 (8th Cir. 1977) (surprise is no longer a viable requirement for impeaching a party's own witness with an inconsistent statement); Hilyer v. Howat Concrete Co., Inc., 578 F.2d 422 (D.C. Cir. 1978) (irrelevant that appellee called witness since under Rule 607 witness may be impeached by any party); United States v. Inendino, 604 F.2d 458 (7th Cir. 1979) (literal interpretation of Rule 607 sanctioned calling of witness for sole purpose of placing inconsistent statement before jury).

53. United States v. Morlang, 531 F.2d 183, 190 (4th Cir. 1975) ("The overwhelming weight of authority is, however, that impeachment by prior inconsistent statement may not be permitted where employed as a mere subterfuge to get before the jury evidence not otherwise admissible."); United States v. Fay, 668 F.2d 375, 378-79 (8th Cir. 1981):

> Defendant also contends that the trial court erred in excluding testimony concerning an alleged statement by Anita to her mother, Beatrice Traversie, that she was going to Leah's house and "fight like hell." Anita denied making this statement. When defense counsel questioned Beatrice about the statement, the government objected and defense counsel made an offer of proof that Beatrice would have also denied the statement. Counsel then revealed that he intended to call Norma Black Moon to testify that Beatrice repeated this statement to her the morning after the fight. It is defendant's position that the testimony was admissible to impeach Beatrice. . . .
>
> The government correctly characterizes Norma's testimony as hearsay within hearsay, and therefore both Anita's statement to her mother and Beatrice's repetition of the statement to Norma must be independently admissible. Fed. R. Evid. 805. Anita's statement to Beatrice is arguably admissible either under Rule 803(3) as showing her then existing state of mind, or under Rule 613(b) as evidence of a prior inconsistent statement offered to impeach Anita. Beatrice's repetition of Anita's statement to Norma, however, is admissible, if at all, only under Rule 613(b) as a prior inconsistent statement offered to impeach Beatrice. The government argues that the trial court properly excluded the testimony because defendant admittedly called Beatrice knowing she would deny the statement and intending to impeach her with Norma's testimony. Although Rule 607 allows a party to impeach his own witness, "[c]ourts must be watchful that impeachment is not used as a subterfuge to place otherwise inadmissible hearsay before the jury." United States v. Rogers, 549 F.2d 490, 497 (8th Cir.), cert. denied, 431 U.S. 918, 97 S.Ct. 2182, 53 L.Ed.2d 229 (1976), citing United States v. Morlang, 531 F.2d 183, 189 (4th Cir. 1975) ("[I]t has never been the rule that a party may call a witness where his testimony is known to be adverse for the purpose of impeaching him."). We cannot say the trial court abused its discretion in excluding this evidence.

54. United States v. Miller, 664 F.2d 94, 97 (5th Cir. 1981):

> Next, Miller alleges that the impeachment by the Government of Crawford, a Government witness, through the use of his prior statement was improper. Miller admits the statement could be used to impeach Crawford's credibilty, but argues the Government's use of the statement for impeachment was a guise to get the statement, inadmissible as hearsay, before the jury as positive evidence. The

Government argues it used the statement for impeachment purposes only and impeachment was proper since Crawford was a hostile witness whose testimony differed from his prior statement on relevant issues.

Clearly, the Government can impeach its own witness, see Fed. R. Evid. 607, and evidence of a prior inconsistent statement of the witness may be admitted for that purpose even though the statement tends directly to inculpate the defendant. See United States v. Sisto, 534 F.2d 616, 622 (5th Cir. 1976); Williams v. United States, 394 F.2d 821 (5th Cir.), cert. denied, 393 U.S. 890, 89 S.Ct. 211, 21 L.Ed.2d 169 (1968). Of course, the prosecutor may not use such a statement under the guise of impeachment for the primary purpose of placing before the jury substantive evidence which is not otherwise admissible. United States v. DeLillo, 620 F.2d 939, 946 (2d Cir. 1980), cert. denied, 449 U.S. 835, 101 S.Ct. 108, 66 L.Ed.2d 41 (1981); United States v. Rogers, 549 F.2d 490, 497 (8th Cir. 1976), cert. denied, 431 U.S. 918, 97 S.Ct. 2182, 53 L.Ed.2d 229 (1977); United States v. Morlang, 531 F.2d 183, 190 (4th Cir. 1975); United States v. Dobbs, 448 F. 2d 1262 (5th Cir. 1971).

There is nothing in the record to indicate Crawford was called to the stand merely to get his FBI statement before the jury or to establish facts beyond the alleged contradiction. Under the Government's theory of the case, Crawford was the hub of a stolen truck ring in which Miller was involved. In his prior statement, Crawford had detailed Miller's involvement with the stolen trucks and identified him as the trucks' seller. There is nothing in the record to indicate the Government knew Crawford was going to deviate from his prior statement. Indeed, during his testimony at the prior trial of Ward, Miller's alleged coconspirator, Crawford explained Miller's involvement in a manner consistent with his prior statement.

On direct examination during Miller's trial, Crawford said he did not know that Miller had anything to do with the stolen trucks. He identified someone other than Miller as the seller of the stolen trucks. On redirect, he had trouble at times remembering facts and became irritable. During impeachment on redirect he stated he was "just not coherent" and that he had "given up" on himself. His prior statement was used only to indicate those areas where Crawford's present testimony contradicted his earlier statement.

55. People v. Green, 3 Cal. 3d 981, 92 Cal. Rptr. 494, 479 P.2d 998 (1971) ("In normal circumstances, the testimony of a witness that he does not remember an event is not 'inconsistent' with a prior statement by him describing that event.").

If the court finds that the lack of recollection displayed by the witness called by that party is feigned, probably as a result of intimidation by the accused, one court has found the witness's feigned lack of recollection to be an adoptive admission of the prior statement. United States v. Insana, 423 F.2d 1165 (2d Cir. 1970). It is suggested that the better approach is always to treat a prior statement of a witness who claims lack of recollection as not inconsistent and look to Rule 804(b)(5) to determine substantive admissibility. See Chapter 4, Section C3(b) *supra.*

56. M. Graham, *The Confrontation Clause, The Hearsay Rule and the Forgetful Witness*, 56 Tex. L. Rev. 151, 201, 203 (1978):

> When a party proffers a witness whose testimony it desires the jury to credit, the opponent has the right on cross-examination to explore the testimony of the

witness with an eye toward attacking, eroding, and ultimately destroying the witness' credibility in the eyes of the jury. In recognition of this principle the common law permitted the use of prior inconsistent statements for the purpose of impeachment, although it prohibited such statements from being introduced as substantive evidence. The propriety of impeachment by inconsistent statement is clear when the witness testimony on direct examination flatly contradicts what he said before trial. The jury may discount or disbelieve the portion of the witness' testimony that is inconsistent with his prior statements, or it may judge the witness' overall credibility to have been so shaken that it disregards his entire testimony. These principles are less easily applied to the case in which a witness testifies he cannot recall a fact asked of him on cross-examination.

Assume for example, that in a prosecution for reckless homicide a witness called by the Government testifies on direct examination that defendant's truck approached the intersection of the accident at eighty miles per hour, but that he cannot recall the color of the traffic light controlling the intersection. Defendant's investigator has a hand-written statement of the witness that defendant's truck was going no more than the speed limit, forty miles per-hour, and that the traffic light at the intersection was red for the victim and green for the defendant. With proper foundation, defense counsel may impeach the witness with his prior inconsistent statement about the speed of the truck. The jury might also discredit the witness' professed ability to observe and recall the speed of the truck because of his current inability to recall the color of the light. In addition, defense counsel should be allowed to prove that the witness made a prior affirmative statement about the light, without reference to the content of the statement, because the witness' proferred ability to recall the color of the light before trial may impeach the witness' trial testimony about the speed of the truck. For example, if the witness purported to recall the color of the light one year after the accident and only two months before the trial, the jury may doubt the sincerity of his professed lack of recollection at trial. If the jury concludes that the witness is feigning loss of memory about the color of the light, it may properly discount or disregard his testimony about the speed of the truck. Moreover, if the jury believes that the witness has truly forgotten the color of the light only two months after making a statement about the matter, it may properly discredit the witness' professed ability to recall the speed of the truck.

The more difficult question is whether counsel may also impeach the witness with the content of the prior statement. Arguably, a court should not allow proof of the content of the statement beyond a mere identification that it relates to the color of the light because it is the fact that the witness previously professed recollection and not the content of his statement that impeaches. On the other hand, the jury undoubtedly has already deduced from the fact of defense counsel's inquiry that the prior statement indicated the light was green for the truck. In addition, the detail of the prior statement will certainly affect the jury's evaluation whether the witness is feigning lack of recollection, and confronting the witness with the content of the statement may refresh his recollection and prompt him to affirm the truth of the statement. Finally, the jury's ability to judge credibility by the demeanor of the witness as he professes lack of recollection will be aided if the witness is confronted it the content of his prior statement. Because of these considerations, trial courts should have discretion to permit opposing counsel to inquire about both the fact and the content of the prior statement.

The propriety of permitting counsel to impeach a forgetful witness with either the fact or the content of his prior statements ultimately turns on a balancing of the necessity and probative effect of such impeachment against the unfair prejudice that would result if the jury improperly considered the statements as substantive evidence. * * * When an opponent's witness professes lack of recollection, . . . , the balance should generally be struck in favor of permitting impeachment. Given the availability of a limiting instruction, in such case the probative value of impeachment is usually not substantially outweighed by the danger of unfair prejudice.

57. M. Graham, *id.* at 172-73:

If the prior statement of a witness claiming lack of recollection at trial does not meet the requirements of rule 801(d)(1)(A) or qualify for a hearsay exception in rule 803 or 804, the statement is not admissible as substantive evidence, but the proponent might nevertheless offer the statement for the limited purpose of impeaching his own witness. The initial flaw in such an offer is that a prior statement of a party's own witness is not inconsistent with a current lack of recollection. Moreover, when a party seeks to impeach his own witness with a prior inconsistent statement not itself substantively admissible, rules 607 and 403, properly understood, require that the party must first show both surprise and affirmative damage. Affirmative damage refers only to testimony of positive assistance to the opponent. Accordingly, failure of a witness to recall the underlying event is not affirmatively damaging. While the party calling the witness may have been made to appear somewhat foolish to the jury, the witness has not provided evidence of positive assistance to the opponent. Thus, even if a prior statement is somehow deemed inconsistent with lack of recollection at trial and surprise is present, the statement is not admissible solely for the purpose of impeachment because the party calling the witness cannot show the requisite affirmative damage.

Of course, the mere existence of a prior statement may impeach the overall credibility of a witness who testifies to lack of recollection. Since impeachment of such a witness by the calling party serves no legitimate purpose, however, it should be prohibited. For example, if a witness to an accident professes lack of recollection about a particular fact, establishing that the witness should not be believed is of no moment to the party calling the witness. The real motive of the calling party in attempting to impeach the witness with a prior statement would be to create a circumstance in which the jury would likely give substantive effect to the prior statement, a circumstance the prerequisites of surprise and affirmative damage strive to avoid.

Compare United States v. Distler, 671 F.2d 954, 958 (6th Cir. 1981):

The eyewitnesses who testified at appellant's trial were predominantly associated with Highway Wrecking Co., which was carrying on the demolition at the site that we have referred to. This concern was operated by Frank Hornung, who happened to be a close friend of appellant. The eyewitnesses, who testified at appellant's trial in late 1978, had also testified before the grand jury in mid-1977. During the one and one-half year hiatus between the grand jury proceedings and

> appellant's trial many of the witnesses forgot portions of their grand jury testimony or remembered it with less certainty of detail. Accordingly, much of the grand jury testimony was introduced as evidence at appellant's trial and was considered by the jury as substantive evidence of guilt in accordance with Fed. R. Evid. 801(d)(1).
>
> With regard to appellant's assertion that some of the grand jury testimony was erroneously admitted under Rule 801(d)(1)(A) because it was not inconsistent with in-court testimony, our review of the record convinces us that the trial court did not abuse its discretion when it admitted the challenged grand jury testimony. We think it clear that, for purposes of this rule, partial or vague recollection is inconsistent with total or definite recollection. Thus, when a witness remembers events incompletely, or with some equivocation at trial, it is not improper to admit a prior statement that otherwise complies with the limitations of Rule 801(d)(1), if that prior statement indicates that at an earlier time the witness remembered the events about which he testifies with more certainty or in more detail. In such a case, it may well be that some of the prior testimony corroborates the in-court testimony. The admission of this evidence, however, is not error if, as is the case here, the prior statements are predominantly inconsistent with the in-court statement and the corroborative portions are needed to set the whole in context. Determinations such as these are properly left to the discretion of the trial court, and that discretion was not abused here.

It is suggested that the approach taken in *Distler* is incorrect. A witness who lacks recollection about an event related in a prior statement is not, as required by Rule 801(d)(1)(A), "subject to cross-examination concerning the statement." Such a witness is "unavailable" as provided in Rule 804(a)(3) on the bases of having testified "to a lack of memory of the subject matter of his statement." Admissibility of grand jury statements relating to matters not adequately recalled at trial should be determined under Rule 804(b)(5). *See* Chapter 4, Section E *supra*.

58. United States v. Caulde, 606 F.2d 451, 457 (4th Cir. 1979):

> "There are a few subjects, perhaps, upon which [the Supreme] Court and other courts have been more nearly unanimous than in their expressions of belief that the right of confrontation and cross-examination is an essential and fundamental requirement for the kind of fair trial which is this country's constitutional goal." Pointer v. Texas, 380 U.S. 400, 405, 85 S.Ct. 1065, 1068, 13 L.Ed.2d 923 (1965). A full cross-examination of a witness upon the subjects of his examination in chief is the right, not the mere privilege, of the party against whom he is called.
>
> * * *
>
> It may not be an exaggeration to claim, as Wigmore does, that cross-examination "is beyond any doubt the greatest legal engine ever invented for the discovery of truth." 5 Wigmore, Evidence § 1367 (Chadbourn rev. 1976). And, its efficacy in testing the accuracy and completeness of testimony is so well understood that the right of cross-examination is "one of the safeguards essential to a fair trial." Alford v. United States, . . . , 282 U.S. at 692, 51 S.Ct. at 219. Evidence supplied through the lips of witnesses is subject not only to the possible infirmities of falsification or bias; it is also subject to the inaccuracies which inevitably flow from the fallibility of human powers of observation, memory and

description. "The annals of the legal profession are filled with instances in which testimony, plausible when supplied on examination in chief, has by cross-examination been shown to be, for one or more of the reasons mentioned, faulty or worthless." Linsdsey v. United States, 77 U.S. App. D.C. at 2, 133 F.2d at 369; see, e.g., 3 Wigmore Evidence § 782(3), (4) (Chadbourn rev. 1970). Certainly no one experienced in the trial of lawsuits would deny the value of cross-examination in bringing out the truth; indeed, "[c]ross-examination is the principal means by which the believability of a witness and the truth of his testimony are tested." Davis v. Alaska, 415 U.S. 308, 316, 94 S.Ct. 1105, 1110, 39 L.Ed.2d 347 (1974).

The theory of cross-examination supports what has been learned from years of practical experience. On direct examination, a witness, even if completely unbiased, only discloses part of the necessary facts, chiefly because his testimony is given only by way of answers to specific questions, and the attorney producing him will usually ask only for the facts favorable to his side of the case. Someone must probe for the remaining facts and qualifying circumstances, and ensure that the testimony is accurate, complete, and clearly understood. The best person to do this is the one most vitally interested, namely the opponent. 5 Wigmore Evidence § 1368 (Chadbourn rev. 1974). For these reasons, cross-examination is a "right long deemed is essential for the due protection of life and liberty that it is guarded against legislative and judicial action by provisions in the Constitution of the United States and in the constitutions of most if not all the States composing the Union." Pointer v. Texas, 380 U.S. at 404, 85 S.Ct. at 1068, quoting Kirby v. United States, 174 U.S. 47, 55-56, 19 S.Ct. 574, 43 L.Ed. 890 (1899).

59. Davis v. Alaska, 415 U.S. 308, 316 (1974) ("Cross-examination is the principal means by which the believability of a witness and the truth of his testimony are tested. Subject always to the broad discretion of a trial judge to preclude repetitive and unduly harassing interrogation, the cross-examiner is not only permitted to delve into the witness' story to test the witness' perceptions and memory, but the cross-examiner has traditionally been allowed to impeach, i.e., discredit, the witness.").

60. Fed. R. Evid. 611(c) provides:

> (c) Leading questions. Leading questions should not be used on the direct examination of a witness except as may be necessary to develop his testimony. Ordinarily leading questions should be permitted on cross-examination. When a party calls a hostile witness, an adverse party, or a witness identified with an adverse party, interrogation may be by leading questions.

61. Wills v. Russell, 100 U.S. 621. 626 (1879) ("Cases not infrequently arise where the convenience of the witness or of the court or the party producing the witness will be promoted by a relaxation of the rule, to enable the witness to be discharged from further attendance.").

62. Fed. R. Evid. 611(b) provides:

> (b) Scope of Cross-Examination. Cross-examination should be limited to the subject matter of the direct examination and matters affecting the credibility of the witness. The court may, in the exercise of discretion, permit inquiry into additional matters as if on direct examination.

63. *See* Chapter 6, Section B *supra.*

64. Fed. R. Evid. 611(c), note 60 *supra.*

65. G. Denroche, *Leading Questions*, 6 Crim. L. Q. 21, 22 (1963) ("[F]irst, that the witness is presumed to have a bias in favour of the party calling him; secondly, that the party calling a witness, knowing what that witness may prove, might by leading bring out only that portion of the witness' story favourable to his own case; and thirdly, that a witness, intending to be entirely fair and honest, might assent to a leading question which did not express his real meaning.").

66. E. Morgan, *Basic Problems of Evidence* 58 (Philadelphia: ALI-ABA, 1961) ("There is no mechanical test for distinguishing a leading from a nonleading question. Usually a question that may be answered by yes or no is considered as leading, but it is not necessarily so. 'Did you or did you not' and 'state whether or not,' do not permit such an answer but they may be followed by matter that clearly indicates the desired answer. All that can be safely said is that a question so framed, or uttered with such an emphasis, or accompanied by such non-verbal conduct of the questioner as to suggest the desired answer, is leading. One form of leading is by assuming facts not conceded or not yet in evidence; such a question is often misleading as well.").

67. E. Cleary, *Evidence as a Problem in Communicating*, 5 Vand. L. Rev. 277, 287 (1952) ("The witness is protected against suggestion only while on the stand, seemingly on the assumption either that intervening influences are unimportant or that he comes untouched from event to court. The former is directly contrary to the theory upon which leading questions are prohibited. The latter simply is not so. . . . Under the system of party responsibility for the production of witnesses, no competent attorney dreams of calling witnesses who have not previously been interviewed. The preliminary interview affords full play to suggestion and context and evokes in advance of trial a complete verbalization, the importance of which cannot be overlooked. When the witness testifies, are his verbalizations at that time based upon his recall of the event or upon his recall of his former verbalizatons?").

68. Fed. R. Evid. 611(c), note 60 *supra.*

69. 3 J. Wigmore *Evidence*, § 775 at 168 (Chadbourn Rev. 1970) ("When a witness is asked about matters preliminary to the main topics of controversy—matters essential to be brought out and yet not themselves in controversy—such as the witness's name, age, residence, relationship to the parties, and the like it is obvious that there is usually not danger of improper suggestion, simply because there is not motive for it.").

70. United States v. Littlewind, 551 F.2d 244 (8th Cir. 1977) (13- and 14-year-old rape victims properly led after showing reluctance on stand); Litherland v. Petrolane Offshore Const. Services, 546 F.2d 129 (5th Cir. 1977) (leading questions permitted to witness displaying difficulty in communicating by reason of obvious mental deficiency).

71. *See* Chapter 6, Section C *supra.*

72. *See* note 49 *supra.*

73. United States v. Tunnell, 667 F.2d 1182, 1188 (5th Cir. 1982) ("The videotape made it possible for the trial court to gauge Russell's attitude more accurately than would have been possible with just a cold deposition record. This is a very persuasive argument for the use of videotape depositions in lieu of the traditional transcriptions. The trial judge was able to note Russell's attitude reflected by his motions,

facial expressions, demeanor, and voice inflections. As a result, the trial judge concluded that Russell evinced a hostility to the prosecution, which made leading questions appropriate."); United States v. Brown, 603 F.2d 1022, 1026 (1s Cir. 1979) ("The record does not bear out appellant's contention that witness Proulx was not adverse, evasive or hostile. Proulx and appellant were close friends. The evidence strongly suggests that Proulx was a participant in the crime. HIs testimony is replete with lapses of memory attributed to alcohol and drugs. He stressed several times his susceptibility to suggestion by the last person who talks to him. Appellant talked to Proulx at length about the case right up to the trial. While Proulx was not hostile in the sense of being contemptuous or surly, he was both evasive and adverse to the government.").

74. *See* note 60 *supra*.

75. M. Graham, *Examination of a Party's Own Witness Under the Federal Rules of Evidence: A Promise Unfulfilled*, 54 Tex. L. Rev. 917, 925-26 (1976) ("[A] party could establish the hostility of his own witness for the purpose of leading in one of three basic ways. First, a witness could be presumed to be hostile to a criminal defendant if his status closely identified him with the government's interest. For example, a government agent, complaining witness, or, in appropriate cases, the paid informer could be presumed hostile; the Government could rebut this presumption by showing that the witness had cooperated with the defense before trial or that the defendant successfully suggested answers to the witness at trial through leading questions. Second, the defendant could show a witness's hostility through pretrial behavior that alone or with the witness' status indicated an identification of interest with the Government. Last, all courts considered hostile a witness who responded reluctantly or evasively or who gave damaging answers to the calling party's questions.").

76. *See* United States v. Diaz, 662 F.2d 713, 718 (11th Cir. 1981) ("Prior to redirect, defense counsel asked that Gelebert be declared a hostile witness. The prosecutor's objection to this request was sustained. The record clearly reflects, however, that, despite the grant of immunity, Gelebert's hostility was directed to the government, rather than to Diaz. Previously, Gelebert had testified that he was a very good friend of Diaz and that he had known him for approximately five years; and, upon re-direct, Gelebert answered defense counsel's questions without hesitation, admitting the conversations about marijuana. * * * Accordingly, the trial court's refusal to declare Gelebert a hostile witness was entirely proper. "); Esco Corporation v. United States, 340 F.2d 1000, 1005 (9th Cir. 1965) ("[T]he trial court correctly concluded that the witnesses . . . were in truth not favorable to the party calling them . . . and hence could properly be considered hostile witnesses. As such they were properly and lawfully subjected to leading questions.").

77. Ellis v. City of Chicago, 667 F.2d 606, 613 (7th Cir. 1981) ("We agree with plaintiffs that the district court should have permitted leading questions during plaintiffs' direct examinations of Officer Clandra and Sergeant Holub. These police officers were employees of defendant City of Chicago at all times during the litigation and were each present during portions of the incident which gave rise to this lawsuit. Moreover, the record indicates that both officers had worked closely with defendant Frank Kusar during the period of their employment. Officer Clandra and Sergeant Holub thus clearly qualified as 'witness[es] identified with an adverse party' for purposes of Rule 611(c).").

78. M. Graham, *Handbook of Federal Evidence* § 611.12 at 546 (1981):

> In order to accomplish [the objectives of redirect], it is frequently necessary to direct the witness's attention to the exact subject matter of the testimony sought. Hence, some questions which might be objectionable as leading if asked during direct examination will often be permitted on redirect examination as necessary to the development of the witness's testimony. It is also generally proper to employ a leading question incorporating particular factual matters where refutation takes the form of a denial. However, where refutation takes another form such as explanation, it is improper to incorporate the explanation or other testimony desired into the question itself.

79. Ill.R.S. 1983, c.110A, § 238.

80. *See* text accompanying note 41 *supra*.

81. With respect to determining when such impeachment is proper, *see* Chapter 6, Section B *supra*.

82. Fed. R. Evid. 614(a) provides:

> (a) Calling by court. The court may, on its own motion or at the suggestion of a party, call witnesses, and all parties are entitled to cross-examine witnesses thus called.

83. Smith v. United States, 331 F.2d 265, 273 (8th Cir. 1964) ("The exercise of the right or rule [to call witnesses] is a discretionary matter with the trial court and only for an abuse of that discretion resulting in prejudice to the defendant will the trial court be judged in error and a conviction reversed.").

84. United States v. Oster, 422 F. Supp, 93, 103 n.11 (S.D.N.Y. 1976) ("Although rarely invoked, the Court, in its discretion, may call a person as a court witness."); United States v. Marzano, 149 F.2d 923 (2d Cir. 1945) (the calling of a witness by the court is seldom desirable).

85. 3 *Weinstein's Evidence* ¶ 614[01] at 614-4 (1981) ("Judges are reluctant to call witnesses without a request from a party because they know little of what lies below the surface of a case and they can blunder into serious problems by not relying on counsel's intimate knowledge of the facts.").

86. United States v. Karnes, 531 F.2d 214 (4th Cir. 1976).

87. United States v. Leslie, 542 F.2d 285, 289 (5th Cir. 1976) ("Rules 607 and 611 would appear to allow the government to lead, cross-examine, and impeach its own witness in cases like the instant one. Yet given the asserted likelihood that Gayle, Lynch and Rogers would testify adversely to the government, leading to the inevitable government attempt to impeach, the court could properly protect the prosecution from whatever tendency the jury might have had to associate the witnesses with the calling party.").

88. Advisory Committee's Note to Rule 614(a) ("While exercised more frequently in criminal than in civil cases, the authority of the judge to call witnesses is well established. McCormick, § 8, p. 14; Maguire, Weinstein, et al., Cases on Evidence 303-304 (5th ed. 1965); 9 Wigmore § 2484. One reason for the practice, the old rule against impeaching one's own witness, no longer exists by virtue of Rule 607.").

89. Chalmette Petroleum Corp. v. Chalmette Oil Dist. Co., 143 F.2d 826, 829 (5th Cir. 1944) ("If neither party will risk calling a witness who knows important facts,

it is in the power of the court to call and examine such a witness . . . allowing both parties the right of cross-examination and impeachment.''); United States v. Browne, 313 F.2d 197, 199 (2d Cir. 1963) (with respect to witnesses called by the court, ''either of the parties is entitled to impeach him by the usual methods, including proof of prior inconsistent statements.'').

90. People v. Dennis, 47 Ill.2d 120, 265 N.E.2d 385 (1970); People v. Marino, 44 Ill.2d 562, 256 N.E.2d 770 (1970); People v. Siciliano, 4 Ill.2d 581, 123 N.E.2d 725 (1955); Carle v. People, 200 Ill. 494, 66 N.E. 32 (1902).

91. *See* Chapter 6, Section D *supra*.

92. M. Graham, *Examination of a Party's Own Witness Under the Federal Rules of Evidence: A Promise Unfulfilled*, 54 Tex. L. Rev. 917, 991 n.345 (1976) (''Having the court call the witness, moreover, does not directly serve the principles governing the propriety of leading questions, refreshing recollections, cross-examination, and impeachment in civil and criminal cases.'').

93. United States v. Karnes, 531 F.2d 214, 217 (4th Cir. 1976) (''We have no doubt that, failing to appreciate that the government could not prove its case without them, the district court's motive in calling the witnesses was to get at the truth and to enable the government to cross-examine and perhaps to impeach them with regard to any testimony unfavorable to the government which was inconsistent with their prior statements. But the same result could have been achieved by an accepted means. The government must, of course, use its witnesses as it finds them. In many cases the prosecution must depend upon the testimony of persons who are co-defendants, co-conspirators, felons, accomplices, etc., and such witnesses often evidence hostility, are impeachable from their past or current activities, or change or slant their testimony from what, based upon prior statements, the government expects them to say. Under such circumstances, a district judge may afford wide latitude to the government to lead, to cross-examine, and particularly to impeach such witnesses.'').

Chapter 7

Expanding Substantive Admissibility

The discussion so far has demonstrated that the concern for trustworthiness at common law precludes the introduction as substantive evidence of prior statements of prosecution witnesses not meeting the requirements of a traditional hearsay exception. The Federal Rules of Evidence retain this concern while expanding to a limited extent the breadth of prior statements thought sufficiently trustworthy to be admitted as substantive evidence. Rule 801(d)(1)(A) in defining certain prior statements as "not hearsay" requires that the prior statement be made at a formal proceeding and that the declarant be subject to meaningful cross-examination at trial regarding the subject matter of the statement. In our hypothetical case in Chapter 4 only Bob Williams's prior statement was made at such a proceeding, but his murder renders him unavailable for meaningful cross-examination concerning the subject matter of the statement. Rule 803(24), "other [hearsay] exception," permits the introduction of out-of-court statements provided certainty of making, necessity, substantial importance, and trustworthiness are adequately established. Rule 803(24) also envisions that the declarant be available to be called in order to deny or explain the statement. In the hypothetical case John Goodfellow, Jim James, and Bob Williams are all unavailable because of forgetfulness, refusal to testify, and death, respectively. However, Rule 804(b)(5) permits admission of a hearsay statement not meeting a traditional hearsay exception when the declarant is unavailable provided that a sufficient showing of certainty of making, necessity, substantial importance, and trustworthiness is made. In this regard, statements given to police investigators are generally viewed as questionable, especially when the statement, such as occurred with Jim James, is made while the declarant is under investigation. Even grand jury testimony will be found inadmissible when equivalent circumstantial guarantees of trustworthiness are absent such as when either untrustworthy partiality such as bias, interest, or prejudice or undue governmental influence through the use of leading questions or otherwise is involved.

Since most prior out-of-court statements of witnesses are not admissible, defendants have an incentive to intimidate witnesses by any means possible including even killing them. Witness protection programs can be of only limited assistance in preventing such intimidation. Making intimidation a crime and providing a civil damage recovery is more an expression of concern than a real solution. Denying the accused discovery of the names of witnesses until trial is only preventative when the defendant does not already know and cannot easily otherwise discover the witnesses' identities. In most cases the defendant already knows or can easily obtain through investigation the names of the key witnesses against him. Moreover, denial of discovery of the names of witnesses in advance of trial as practiced in the federal court has adverse implications at trial as to the ability of defense counsel to represent the accused effectively. Disclosure of witness statements only after direct examination also causes delays. The net result is that in many cases, the government, although not so required, voluntarily discloses in advance of trial the identity of witnesses it intends to call and provides copies of any prior statements. Nor is the waiver doctrine the appropriate solution. Sufficient evidence establishing intimidation is most often lacking. More importantly, the concept of waiver fails to address adequately legitimate concern about the trustworthiness of the prior statement.

Our criminal justice system must simultaneously address both the concern for the trustworthiness of hearsay admitted at trial and the need to reduce incentives for defendants to harm witnesses before trial. Three avenues of response are suggested. First, the scope of prior inconsistent statements of an available witness admitted as substantive evidence should be expanded to the full breadth consistent with the concern for certainty of making, necessity, substantial importance, and guarantees of trustworthiness. Second, greater resort may be had to those procedures providing for the preservation of testimony of witnesses following formal charge, including production of the witness at a preliminary hearing and the taking of depositions to perpetuate testimony. Finally, a new proceeding should be created for the preservation of the testimony of witnesses when a potential threat of intimidation is suspected. This preservation proceeding would insure certainty of making while facilitating the determination of trustworthiness should the witness in fact prove unavailable at trial. Preservation of testimony in the manner proposed and substantive admissibility at trial when warranted if the witness's testimony proves unavailable will not only assist in obtaining just convictions but will go a long way toward reducing the incentives now present for defendants to intimidate witnesses.[1]

A. PRIOR INCONSISTENT STATEMENTS

The previous review of the common law restrictions on the admission of prior inconsistent statements as substantive evidence and the debate surrounding the adoption of Rule 801(d)(1)(A)[2] make apparent that the dispute over the substantive admissibility of prior inconsistent statements involves the question of what circumstances will provide sufficient assurance that a prior statement was indeed made and that coercion, deception, or subtle influence has not impaired its trustworthiness. One should observe that concern with fabrication, coercion, deception, and subtle influence is an implicit rejection of the orthodox rule's contentions with respect to the importance of contemporaneous cross-examination. More importantly, such concerns are a recognition of the limited effectiveness of cross-examination, whenever conducted, in discovering the truth at a modern trial. Concern with the risk of fabrication acknowledges the difficulty inherent in the trier of fact's task in determining whether to believe the witness who denies making a prior inconsistent statement[3] or the witness who offers extrinsic evidence of the statement's existence.[4] Rather than entrust that responsibility solely to the trier of fact, Congress, with an eye toward criminal cases, chose to limit substantive admissibility of prior inconsistent statements to situations in which the likelihood of total fabrication is practically nonexistent and, as a helpful but as will be argued later unessential byproduct, the risk of coercion, deception, or subtle influence is significantly reduced.

Acknowledging the legitimacy of congressional concerns regarding Rule 801(d)(1)(A), it nevertheless appears that the rule's safeguards designed to ensure that a prior inconsistent statement was actually made and accurately recorded are overly strict. Why should the rule exclude a signed or handwritten statement that is acknowledged by the witness or proved to be the witness's by other evidence? Why should it exclude an oral statement not made under oath when the witness during testimony admits that he or she made it?[5] Why should the rule exclude an affidavit prepared by the witness's attorney that was executed under oath and submitted to the court in the same or another proceeding?[6]

Alternative proposals have been advanced that would authorize substantive admission of prior inconsistent statements when it is sufficiently established that they were made. These proposals assert that substantive admissibility should extend to all prior inconsistent statements for which there are substantial guarantees of certainty of making and accuracy of reporting and for which an effective opportunity exists at trial to examine witnesses to expose and counteract any impropriety, such as coercion, deception, or subtle influence, that may have occurred in the taking of the statement. C. McCormick, for example, has suggested the following rule:

A statement made on a former occasion by a declarant having an opportunity to observe the facts stated, will be received as evidence of such facts, notwithstanding the rule against hearsay if,

(1) the statement is proved to have been written or signed by the declarant, or to have been given by him as testimony in a judicial or official hearing, or the making of the statement is acknowledged by a declarant in his testimony in the present proceeding, and

(2) the party against whom the statement is offered is afforded an opportunity to cross-examine the declarant.[7]

McCormick's proposal contains one important qualification: it requires that the declarant have personal knowledge of the facts stated. The English Evidence Act of 1938 contained a similar personal knowledge requirement:

In any civil proceeding where direct oral evidence of a fact would be admissible, any statement made by a person in a document and tending to establish the fact shall, on production of the original document, be admissible as evidence of that fact if the following conditions are satisfied, that is to say—

(i) if the maker of the statement either—

(a) had personal knowledge of the matters dealt with by the statement;

(b) [made the statement as part of a business record]; and

(ii) if the maker of the statement is called as a witness in the proceedings.[8]

Although the effect of the personal-knowledge requirement has not been elaborated by the authors of the proposals that adopt it,[9] the requirement has at least two very important consequences. First, only a witness with personal knowledge of the subject matter of a prior inconsistent statement can be examined about whether the statement is truthful. Second, the requirement excludes from evidence all prior statements of a witness that merely narrate a third person's declaration unless the witness also has personal knowledge of the facts underlying the third person's statement. Thus a witness's prior statement that he or she heard a criminal defendant make an incriminating admission would be inadmissible as substantive evidence unless the witness had personal knowledge of the incriminating conduct itself.[10] The personal-knowledge requirement excludes from evidence those statements most open to fabrication by the declarant while assuring the opportunity for effective cross-examination. Coupled with strong guarantees that the prior inconsistent statement was actually made,[11] cross-examination—here, really redirect examination—of a witness with personal knowledge of the underlying facts can be expected to test effectively the reliability of the prior statement.

The following illustration demonstrates the importance of the requirement of personal knowledge. Assume that in a bank-robbery prosecution the government calls a friend of the accused to the stand. The friend testifies that he saw the defendant at a local bar on the night of the offense, that the defendant did not say anything to him at that time, that he appeared in normal health, and that he was not carrying anything. Assume further that the prosecution possesses a written statement by the friend that concerns the night in question. While on the stand, the friend admits having written and signed the statement, although he denies its factual accuracy. Under the proposals imposing a requirement of personal knowledge, a prior inconsistent statement contained in the friend's written declaration to the effect that the defendant had admitted robbing the bank would not be admissible as substantive evidence, since the friend had no personal knowledge of the underlying subject matter of his prior inconsistent statement, that is, that the defendant in fact robbed the bank. Conversely, a prior inconsistent statement in the friend's out-of-court declaration to the effect that when the defendant entered the bar he was very sweaty and out of breath, was wearing a torn shirt, and was carrying a brown paper bag would be substantively admissible "firsthand hearsay," since the friend's prior inconsistent statement sufficiently demonstrates his personal knowledge of the matters stated.

Both the McCormick recommendation and the English statute would keep the prior inconsistent statement in our example that the defendant admitted robbing the bank from the jury. This type of statement—the "double-level hearsay" statement,[12] typified by the admission-confession of the criminal defendant—is the kind of evidence that has most concerned the judicial system.[13] Such statements raise the greatest risk of total fabrication by the witness and consequently the greatest danger of misapplication by the jury.[14] Under either of the foregoing proposals, only "firsthand hearsay" would be admissible.[15] An admission or confession contained in a witness's prior inconsistent statement, the least reliable and most damaging evidence to the criminal defendant, would not be admitted as substantive evidence unless the declarant also had personal knowledge of the underlying event.[16]

Subject to the requirement of personal knowledge, the suggested modification of the common law would give substantive admission to inconsistent statements of a witness available at trial for cross-examination which the witness acknowledges at trial having made. Thus in the hypothetical case presented in Chapter 4, if Mary Mahoney acknowledges on the witness stand the giving of a prior description to police officers, the prior description inconsistent with her in-court testimony would be admissible. In addition, statements proved to have been written or signed by such a witness would be given substantive effect. Thus if Jim James had not refused to testify at trial but had instead testified inconsistently with his prior written statement to the police, his prior written statement would be available to the jury. Finally, the proposals implicitly recognize that recorded statements of such a witness provide sufficient protection against fabrication to be given substantive effect. Thus if John Goodfellow was available at trial for cross-examination by testifying inconsistently rather than claiming lack of recollection, his prior recorded statement would be admissible.

The foregoing proposals would, however, exclude from substantive evidence an unacknowledged oral statement, the prior statement most likely not to have been made and most likely, if made, to have been unfairly obtained or inaccurately reported.[17] In this context consider the position of the accused's attorney who is attempting to cross-examine a police office about whether an oral inconsistent statement was made by the witness. If the police officer in fact spoke to the witness, such as occurred in the case of Mary Mahoney, cross-examination about time, location, and so on will be unavailing. The situation resolves itself ultimately into a "Yes he did" versus "No I didn't" situation. It is suggested that determination of guilt should not be based upon such evidence.

With respect to written, recorded, and acknowledged statements substantively admissible under each of the proposals when made by a witness possessing personal knowledge of the underlying subject matter, it is undeniable that coercion, deception, or subtle influence may have affected the process of taking and preserving the statement. However, the circumstances surrounding the actual making of the statement may be explained by the swiftness to the trier of fact, and the declarant may provide the trier of fact with a complete explanation of why the statement is misleading, inaccurate, or otherwise incorrect.[18] Others who were present when the statement was made, including persons called to lay a foundation for its admission as a prior inconsistent statement, may be examined and cross-examined on such matters as well. Moreover, and critically important, the witness possessing personal knowledge of the event related is in a position to advise the trier of fact of what he or she now contends actually occurred. The jury may observe the demeanor of the witness throughout. Effective cross-examination by counsel opposing the truth of the prior inconsistent statement can be expected to do no more; it rarely accomplishes as much.

In short, the difficulty with Rule 801(d)(1)(A) is not that it fails to permit substantive admission of all prior inconsistent statements but that it fails to admit many statements that almost certainly were made and for which an effective opportunity exists at trial to examine witnesses to expose and counteract any impropriety, such as coercion, deception, or subtle influences, that may have occurred in the taking of the statement. The McCormick and English proposals broaden admissibility beyond Rule 801(d)(1)(A)'s limitation of statements made at formal proceedings. Yet each, assisted by the requirement of personal knowledge, insures to a sufficient degree of certainty that the statements were made and may be explored for trustworthiness at trial; at the same time, both exclude the most untrustworthy declaration, the unacknowledged oral statement. Accordingly, it is suggested that Rule 801(d)(1)(A) be amended to state:

(d) Statements which are not hearsay. A statement is not hearsay if:

(1) Prior Statement of Witness. The declarant testifies at the trial or hearing and is subject to cross-examination concerning the statement, and

(A) The statement is inconsistent with his testimony, and (i) is proved to have been made under oath subject to penalty of perjury at a trial, hearing, or other proceeding or in a deposition, or (ii) is made by a declarant having personal knowledge of the underlying event or condition the statement narrates, describes, or explains and (1) the statement is proved to have been written or signed by the declarant, or (2) the making of the statement is acknowledged to have been made either (a) by the declarant in his testimony in the present proceeding or (b) by the declarant under oath subject to the penalty of perjury at a prior trial, hearing, or other proceeding or in a deposition, or (3) the statement is proved to have been accurately recorded by a tape recorder, video-tape recorder, or any other similar electronic means of sound recording.[19]

Certain provisions of the proposed rule deserve specific mention. Current Rule 801(d)(1)(A) does not permit substantive admissibility when a witness at trial acknowledges the making but denies the truth of the inconsistent statement; in contrast, 801(d)(1)(A)(ii)(2)(a) of the proposed rule would give substantive admissibility to this inconsistent statement. In addition, 801(d)(1)(A)(ii)(2)(b) of the proposed rule provides the possibility of substantive admissibility for a prior oral statement the making of which the witness had acknowledged while testifying at a prior trial, hearing, other proceeding, or deposition, even if the witness had denied its truth at that proceeding. Thus subject to the requirement of personal knowledge, if a witness at the current trial had earlier appeared at one of these formal proceedings and there had stated that he or she had made a particular oral statement, under the proposal the statement would be admissible substantively in the present trial if it is inconsistent with the witness's present trial testimony, even if the witness now states that he or she never made the prior oral statement or that it was untrue.

The proposal also requires that the statement be "proved" to have been made whenever the witness refuses to acknowledge making it. Introduction of evidence sufficient to support a jury finding that the witness made the out-of-court statement, Rule 104(b), is inadequate. Rather, the litigant seeking to use a prior inconsistent statement that the witness has not admitted making as substantive evidence must initially satisfy the court that it is more probably true than not true that the statement was in fact made, Rule 104(a). Since an in-court declarant who denies making a prior inconsistent statement will necessarily be testifying under oath, the proposal is justified in imposing a greater requirement of certainty that he or she made the statement—accomplished by placing on the proponent of the out-of-court declaration the burden of proof of more probably true than not true—than governs the admission of other disputed writings. Such direct testamentary contradiction is often not present with respect to authentication of writings admitted pursuant to the doctrine of conditional relevance. Given the nature of the prior inconsistent statements that fall within the proposed rule, it is probable that the witness will seldom deny making the statement, although the possibility of forged signatures on or alterations in prior written or recorded statements creates a potential for dispute over whether such statements were made. Ultimately, the decision about whether the statement was made rests with the jury.

Although proposed rule 801(d)(1)(A) requires that the proponent prove that it is more probably true than not true that the statement alleged to be that of the declarant was the exact statement the declarant wrote, recorded, or signed, the proponent of the prior statement should not be required to bear this burden of proof regarding other contested matters relating to the statement. The special problems of distortion through subtle wording variations, complete omissions, or fabricated additions in the preparation of the statement followed by uncritical signing, subtle influence, appeal to the declarant's desire to please another person, and so on are to be resolved and can be adequately resolved by the jury after it has heard such allegations presented by the in-court declarant and explored during the cross-examination of the person who obtained the prior statement. The jury, consistent with its traditonal function, is assigned the task of judging the credibility of each witness and of deciding what in fact occurred when the prior statement was allegedly made. However, if the declarant asserts that a prior statement was made involuntarily, under the proposed rule the proponent of the statement would be required to convince the judge that it is more probably true than not true that the statement had not been the product of coercion.[20]

In summary, proposed rule 801(d)(1)(A) increases to the extent justified by concern for certainty of making and circumstantial guarantees of trustworthiness the breadth of prior inconsistent statements that would be substantively admitted when the declarant is available for cross-examination. The proposed rule also provides police officers and prosecuting attorneys the opportunity easily and promptly to preserve a prior statement of a witness by video or tape recording the witness's oral statement[21] or by having the witness either prepare a handwritten statement or execute a written statement prepared for the witness's signature. The proposed rule does not, of course, address the problem of determining when a prior statement of a witness may be offered as substantive evidence where the declarant of the statement has been intimidated resulting in the total loss of his or her testimony at trial.

B. HEARINGS AND DEPOSITIONS

Presentation of the witness at a hearing offers an opportunity to perpetuate the witness's testify for admission into evidence as former testimony under Rule 804 (b)(1) should the witness prove unavailable at trial because of witness intimidation or otherwise. However, various practical considerations make it less than likely that substantial increased use of available hearings for the purpose of perpetuating testimony will occur. The prosecutor, whether at a suppression hearing or preliminary hearing, is primarily concerned with accomplishing the limited objective at hand such as establishing voluntariness, consent to search, or probable cause, while exposing his or her case to scrutiny by the accused to the least extent possible. Accordingly, hearsay testimony is often employed with only the police officer testifying. Summary conclusionary questions are often asked to the police officer, or an occurrence witness or victim who testifies, by means of leading questions at the suppression or preliminary hearing to the extent permitted by the court over objection. Moreover, even when a witness possessing personal knowledge is called and nonleading questions are asked, only the minimum information needed to accomplish the objective at hand will be obtained from the witness. Testimony elicited in this fashion will be less persuasive if later admitted at trial than testimony taken with the express purpose of perpetuation in mind. Moreover, if the witness proves unavailable, objection can be interposed at trial to the introduction of prior hearing testimony taken in the foregoing manner as former testimony under Rule 804(b)(1), on the basis that similar motive did not exist and an adequate opportunity was not provided for cross-examination at the prior hearing.[22] Although it certainly would be beneficial for prosecutors to keep in mind that testimony elicited from a witness at a hearing may be offered later at trial, it is doubtful that considerations of perpetuation will significantly affect present practice. Too many other competing considerations make it very unlikely that the interest in perpetuation against the contingency of unavailability will be the dog that wags the tail of strategy at pretrial hearings.

The availability of the deposition to perpetuate testimony in the federal court pursuant to Federal Rule of Criminal Procedure 15 and many state courts offers another opportunity to protect against the loss of a witness's testimony at trial due to witness intimidation. Increased resort to perpetuation depositions under appropriate circumstances is undoubtedly both a good idea and a likely result of the current wave of concern over the problem of witness intimidation. However, various impediments stand in the way of the perpetuation proceeding as currently constituted from becoming a truly meaningful tool in the fight against witness intmidation.

Federal Rule of Criminal Procedure 15(a) provides that a perpetuation deposition may be taken by the prosecution "whenever due to exceptional circumstances of the case it is in the interest of justice that the testimony of a prospective witness of a party be taken and preserved for use at trial." As previously developed, "exceptional circumstances" exist whenever it appears that a prospective witness may be unable to attend or be prevented from attending the hearing, that the potential testimony of the witness is material, and that the interests of justice require that his deposition be taken.[23] Florida Rule of Criminal Procedure 3.190(j)(1) is almost identical:

After an indictment or information upon which a defendant is to be tried is filed, the defendant or the State may apply for an order to perpetuate testimony. The application shall be verified or supported by the affidavits of credible persons that a prospective witness resides beyond the territorial jurisdiction of the court or may be unable to attend or be prevented from attending a trial or hearing, that his testimony is material and that it is necessary to take his deposition to prevent a failure of justice. The court shall order a commission to be issued to take the deposition of the witnesses to be used in the trial and that any designated books, papers, documents or tangible objects, not privileged, be produced at the same time and place. If the application is made within ten days before the trial date, the court may deny the application.

Similarly, Uniform Rule of Criminal Procedure 431(a) states:

When taken. At any time after the defendant has appeared, any party may take the testimony of any person by deposition, except:

(1) The defendant may not be deposed unless he consents and his lawyer, if he has one, is present or his presence is waived;

(2) A discovery deposition may be taken after the time set by the court only with leave of court;

(3) A deposition to perpetuate testimony may be taken only with leave of court, which shall be granted upon motion of any party if it appears that the deponent may be able to give material testimony but may be unable to attend a trial or hearing; and

(4) Upon motion of a party or of the deponent and upon a showing that the taking of the deposition does or will unreasonably annoy, embarrass, or oppress the deponent or a party, the court in which the prosecution is pending or the court of the [district] where the deposition is being taken may order that the deposition not being taken or continued or may limit the scope and manner of its taking. Upon demand of the objecting party or deponent, the taking of the deposition shall be suspended for the time necessary to make the motion.

Attendance of witnesses and production of documentary evidence and objects may be compelled by subpoena under Rule 731.

Generally, two major obstacles inhibit the effectiveness of perpetuation depositions as currently constituted in combating witness intimidation. First, a deposition perpetuation proceeding may not be conducted until after the defendant has appeared. Having appeared, the presence of the defendant at the deposition is required unless the defendant waives the right, voluntarily absents himself or herself after the start of the deposition, or the judge orders that the deposition proceed with the accused removed because of his or her disruptive conduct. Even in the event of any of these circumstances, the defendant's counsel must be present. If the defendant is not present at the deposition and his or her absence is not excused, the deposition of the unavailable deponent may not be received at trial as substantive evidence when offered by the government. The requirement that the defendant has appeared, that the defendant receive notice of the perpetuation deposition, that the defendant be present at the deposition, and that the defendant be represented by counsel all result in the passage of time during which the witness may be intimidated. If the defendant did not already know the identify of the witness or the witness's address, the defendant will receive such information in the notice of the perpetuation deposition. Moreover, the perpetuation deposition itself provides the accused an opportunity by virtue of his or her mere presence coupled with the right of cross-examination to place pressure on the witness.

Second, the perpetuation deposition may be taken only if the prosecution on a verified application or by affidavit establishes either that the witness may be unable to attend the trial, usually for reasons of health or location out of the country, or may be prevented from attending the trial. With respect to witness intimidation, the prosecution may not know about attempts at intimidation until too late. Moreover, if the prosecution has merely heard rumors about or only somehow senses the probability of an attempt at intimidation, the prosecution would lack sufficient basis to make an adequate showing by verified application or affidavit that the witness may be prevented from testifying at trial. The problems inherent in satisfying the standard for obtaining a deposition were enumerated in the context of debate on Federal Rule of Criminal Procedure 16 and its then proposed disclosure of potential witness lists.

> Rule 16 as it would be amended by the Supreme Court or House Judiciary Committee versions may seem to offer solutions to our problems, but the solutions are chimerical. There is the provision, first, for the protection order in subdivision (d)(1), under which a court may deny or order any part of the normal discovery "upon a sufficient showing." There are theoretical difficulties in making a showing why the normal rule should not be followed on the basis of the nature of the charges, or an arrest record or even a reputation. Demonstrating that there has been a high incidence of violence and threats of violence in a range of federal criminal cases may seem a little beside the point in determining whether one defendant should be denied what others are accorded. An appreciation of the general problem is a sound argument for keeping the rule as it is, but change the rule and allow an exception for valid reason, and a judge may want a reason peculiar to the case in front of him. The government cannot always be that specific. Our problem is with risks and probabilities, not near certainties. If we had particular reason to expect violence we could guard the witness or take other measures. And pretrial discovery can occur well before the trial; there is no utility in a protective order after giving away the witness's identity.[24]

Assuming arguendo that in a few cases there may be available evidence that a particular witness may be intimidated sufficient to warrant a court-ordered perpetuation deposition, instigation of the procedure may itself serve to aggravate rather than eliminate the threat. A knowledgeable defendant may initiate or intensify wrongful efforts to ensure that he or she is the first to reach the witness and is ultimately successful in suppressing the witness's testimony.

In summary, the absence of hard evidence of witness intimidation makes it impossible for the government in most cases to satisfy the prerequisites to securing an order to conduct a perpetuation deposition. Moreover, in those few instances where sufficient facts are available to satisfy a court of the existence or likelihood of witness intimidation, the delay embodied in the taking of the perpetuation deposition along with the presence of the accused curtails its effectiveness. What remains is to develop an alternative proceeding that will preserve testimony almost immediately after a witness contacts law enforcement officials and do so without imposing a preliminary threshold standard of present or likely intimidation that cannot be met in the great majority of cases. Any such proceeding must insure certainty of making and facilitate the determination of the presence of equivalent circumstantial guarantees of trustworthiness required for substantive admissibility of the preserved testimony should the witness's live testimony prove unavailable at trial.

C. PRESERVATION PROCEEDINGS

Under rule 801(d)(1)(A) a prior statement of a declarant, inconsistent with his or her trial testimony, is admissible as substantive evidence provided the declarant is subject at trial to cross-examination and the prior inconsistent statement was given under oath, subject to the penalty of perjury at a trial, hearing, or other proceeding or in a perpetuation deposition. Such statements are deemed sufficiently established to have been made to meet the concern for certainty of making. A suppression hearing or a preliminary hearing is a "hearing" as employed in rule; grand jury testimony is included within the concept of "other proceeding."[25] However, statements made to law enforcement officials, whether oral, written, recorded, or acknowledged, even if given under oath, fall outside the concept of "other proceeding."[26] Substantive admissibility of prior inconsistent statements made at a suppression or preliminary hearing, at a perpetuation deposition, or before a grand jury is a helpful addition to the common law hearsay exception for former testimony of an unavailable declarant. However, if a witness cannot testify promptly before such a proceeding either because there is no grand jury in session, because practical or tactical considerations preclude the witness's grand jury appearance, because a preliminary hearing is not normally scheduled earlier than ten days following initial appearance, or because the defendant seeks a "reasonable" delay in the holding of a preliminary hearing,[27] a suppression hearing, or a perpetuation deposition set forthwith following initial appearance, the potential or actual defendant will have more than ample time within which to intimidate the witness. A prospective witness who has only spoken with law enforcement officials remains very much a target until the witness can give his or her testimony in a formal proceeding that will preserve the witness's testimony should the witness testify inconsistently at trial.

Proceedings currently available to preserve the witness's testimony for later substantive admissibility as former testimony, Rule 804(b)(1), should the witness's testimony prove unavailable at trial due to witness intimidation are similarly inadequate. Deficiencies caused by the limited purpose of and by delay associated with the preliminary hearing and the suppression hearing were previously explored. Difficulties surrounding establishing "exceptional circumstances" and delay with respect to the perpetuation deposition have also been discussed. In addition, in the federal court and in a minority of state courts, oral statements, written or recorded statements, and grand jury testimony of an unavailable witness may be offered as substantive evidence under Rule 804(b)(5). However, with respect to oral and written or recorded statements, the prosecution is rarely able to convince the court that such statements possess the magnitude of circumstantial guarantees of trustworthiness required for admissibility. Although the situation with respect to grand jury testimony is more promising, the manner in which grand jury testimony is elicited leaves substantial question in any given case whether equivalent circumstantial guarantees of trustworthiness can be shown.

The prosecution should be provided an opportunity to preserve the witness's testimony at a formal proceeding held as near to the event in question as is possible for substantive admissibility against the contingency of the available witness "flipping" and against the witness's testimony being unavailable at trial. The formal proceeding made promptly available to the prosecution must be constituted to insure adequate certainty of making and facilitate any subsequent ascertainment of equivalent circumstantial guarantees of trustworthiness required to determine admissibility at trial should the witness's testimony prove unavailable.[28]

The proposal that follows for the creation of a preservation proceeding is designed to bring up the odds of the prior statement of the unavailable witness being found sufficiently trustworthy to be admitted under Rule 804(b)(5). The components of the preservation proceeding being proposed are (1) the taking of testimony at a hearing before a noninvestigative presiding officer; (2) the taking of testimony with the express purpose of facilitating the later determination of equivalent circumstantial guarantees of trustworthiness required by Rule 804(b)(5) for admissibility; (3) cross-examination by designated counsel provided with full discovery, but in the absence of the defendant, thus permitting the preservation proceeding to be held without delay; and (4) finally, the incorporation of procedural rules relating to the taking of testimony at the preservation proceeding and its subsequent use at trial designed to accomplish the specific objective at hand.

1. The Components

(a) Noninvestigative Presiding Officer

The Ninth Circuit has shed some light on the meaning of "other proceeding" in Rule 801(d)(1)(A) and in the process upon the type of proceeding that insures certainty of making and facilitates the ascertainment of guarantees of trustworthiness. In United States v. Castro-Ayon,[29] the court had to decide whether an immigration proceeding qualified as an "other proceeding." An unarmed border patrol agent stopped a van carrying 11 illegal aliens. The van's registration was in the name of Rafael Castro-Ayon, a United States citizen. At a border patrol station, Agent Pierce, a special inquiry officer, informed the aliens of their rights, placed them under oath, and conducted an interrogation. Each interrogation was recorded on tape.[30] As a result of thee events, Castro-Ayon was indicted for inducing illegal immigration, transporting illegal immigrants, and conspiracy.

At Castro-Ayon's trial the government called three of the aliens and inquired about Castro-Ayon.[31] The testimony of each tended to exculpate the defendant. The aliens admitted making statements to Agent Pierce after their arrest. The government then called Agent Pierce who testified to the prior statements, which were inconsistent with those given at trial.[32] The defendant objected to the admission of the evidence. The trial court permitted the introduction of the statements as substantive evidence under Rule 801(d)(1)(A).

On appeal, the Ninth Circuit upheld the admission of the statements. First the court reasoned that if Congress had intended to limit the reach of "other proceeding" to grand jury testimony, it would have used the term *grand jury*. Second, the court found that the immigration proceeding bore similarities to a grand jury proceeding. The court stated:

> [B]oth are investigatory, ex parte, inquisitive, sworn, basically prosecutorial, held before an officer other than the arresting officer, recorded, and held in circumstances of some legal formality. Indeed, this immigration proceeding provides more legal rights for the witnesses than does a grand jury: the right to remain totally silent, the right to counsel, and the right to have the interrogator inform the witness of these rights.[33]

The opinion was careful expressly to deny that the court's holding made admissible every sworn statement given during a police station interrogation. Recognizing that the border patrol station interrogation bore similarities to a police station interrogation, the court nevertheless concluded that the border patrol interrogation would qualify as an "other proceeding."

Although the court did not specifically state its reasoning about the differences qualifying the immigration proceeding conducted at the border patrol station and not the ordinary witness interrogation conducted at the police station, the critical difference is with respect to an aspect of the immigration proceeding quoted above. A police station interrogation, as well as a grand jury proceeding, can be investigatory, ex parte, inquisitive, and involve sworn statements. Furthermore, if the witness is also being detained by the police, the witness will have been informed of his or her rights. What remains is the presence of a noninvestigative officer. A police station interrogation does not involve the presence of an officer "other than the arresting officer." The immigration proceeding involved in *Castro-Ayon* requires a special inquiry officer to conduct the proceeding, that is, an officer may not conduct proceedings in which he or she has any investigative functions or prosecutorial functions.[34] A special inquiry officer is an immigration official the Attorney General deems qualified to conduct such a proceeding.[35] The special inquiry officer is impowered to receive and adduce relevant evidence, rule upon any objections, and regulate the course of the hearing.[36] Additionally, the hearing must be recorded verbatim except for statements that the special inquiry officer permits to be made off the record.[37]

In summary the immigration proceeding, in comparison to a police station interrogation, is similar to the usual grand jury proceeding in that it is a proceeding conducted by or before a person having no investigative function. The presence of a noninvestigative presiding officer appointed by the Attorney General or the presence of the members of the grand jury provides assurance that the statement was made under conditions not involving coercion, deception, or subtle influence. Verbatim recording assures certainty of making of the prior statement. *Castro-Ayon* thus strongly suggests that the federal government and the states can experiment in the creation of formal proceedings providing adequate assurance of certainty of making while facilitating the ascertainment of circumstantial guarantees of trustworthiness. Such a proceeding designed to preserve testimony should include provision for the presence of a qualified noninvestigative officer, that is, a judge, magistrate, or attorney appointed specially to preside, recording of the proceeding to insure certainty of making, and formal regulation of the taking of evidence.

(b) Facilitating Determining Trustworthiness

Inaugurating proper procedures for the taking of evidence is the linchpin to the critical function of the preservation proceeding of facilitating ascertainment of equivalent circumstantial guarantees of trustworthiness required for admissibility of preservation proceeding testimony should the witness's live testimony be unavailable at trial for any reason including witness intimidation. An assessment of trustworthiness of a statement involves an assessment of credibility of the declarant together with an assessment of corroborative and contradictory evidence bearing on the truth of the matter asserted in the statement considered in light of the totality of surrounding circumstances. Credibility of the witness is dependent upon the willingness of the witness to tell the truth, that is, sincerity, and upon the witness's ability to describe accurately the event of which he or she purports to have personal knowledge. A witness's ability to describe accurately an event of which the witness purports to possess personal knowledge is the product in turn of the nature and extent of the witness's actual employment of his or her particular physical and mental capacity to perceive, record, and recollect the matter described and the witness's ability to narrate. Determining trustworthiness of a statement thus in part involves an assessment of each component of credibility, that is, the declarant's perception, recordation and recollection, narration, and sincerity with respect to the matter asserted in the statement.

In assessing the credibility of a witness the trier of fact looks to the demeanor of the witness, as well as to the content of the witness's testimony on direct examination and the witness's answer to questions asked on cross-examination. Leading questions are not permissible on direct examination except as may be necessary to develop the witness's testimony.[38] A leading question suggests the answer desired by the examiner. The vice of such a question lies in substituting the suggestions of counsel for the actual testimony of the witness. On the other hand, leading questions are ordinarily permitted on cross-examination. The reason for prohibiting leading questions, that is, the witness will be responsive to the suggestions of counsel, generally does not apply to the witness under cross-examination. Examination of the witness at the preservation proceeding should be as if at trial. Thus leading questions by the prosecution to the witness on direct examination would be prohibited except as may be necessary to develop the witness's testimony.

Discrediting a witness on cross-examination concerning the witness's perception, recordation and recollection, or narration may sometimes be accomplished by the simple means of a leading question. For example, a witness may be asked whether it was night when the event occurred or whether the witness was more than 400 feet away at the time. Because a simple leading question will tend to be argumentative when the attack is upon sincerity, resort to a specific mode of impeachment is generally required. Depending upon the circumstances, the modes of impeachment of a witness's sincerity potentially available are (1) reputation for truth and veracity;[39] (2) prior act of misconduct;[40] (3) prior conviction;[41] (4) partiality, that is, interest, bias, corruption, or coercion;[42] (5) contradiction by other evidence, including conduct of the witness;[43] and (6) self-contradiction with one's own prior inconsistent statement.[44] Impeachment by reference to matters of religion is not allowed.[45] Leading questions may be employed in the process of attacking the witness's sincerity in any of the foregoing modes. Illustrative is the question "You are the mother of the defendant, aren't you?" With respect to certain modes of impeachment, particularly, contradiction and prior inconsistent statement, the attack also extends to personal knowledge. To illustrate, if the witness denies being 400 feet away, asserting instead that he or she was only 20 feet from the event, a prior inconsistent statement that the witness was 400 feet away constitutes an attack not only upon sincerity but upon perception and recordation and recollection.

The procedure for the taking of the testimony of the witness must be structured to facilitate to the extent possible an accurate assessment of the credibility of a witness and thus the trustworthiness of his or her preserved testimony should the witness prove unavailable at trial. To accomplish this objective, it is essential that an opportunity for counsel to cross-examine be provided. To enhance the potential for destructive cross-examination, full discovery of then available material is also a must. Finally, the preservation proceedings should be conducted promptly to enhance the likelihood of accurate recollection and reduce the opportunity during which the witness can be subjected to coercion, deception, or subtle influence by the prosecution as well as reduce the time within which the witness can fabricate a credible story. A prompt preservation proceeding also serves to reduce the risk of the witness being intimidated by the accused.

(c) Designated Counsel

In Ohio v. Roberts[46] the United States Supreme Court discussed in the context of the Confrontation Clause and the hearsay rule the role of cross-examination in insuring trustworthiness. The court found that opportunity for detailed exploration of the events was crucial to finding the evidence sufficiently reliable for purposes of satisfying the Confrontation Clause in connection with the admission of preliminary hearing testimony of an unavailable witness.[47] The opportunity for detailed exploration of events would require the presence of a trained attorney representing the defendant. The court, however, rejected the contention that the cross-examination must be conducted by the attorney who later represents the defendant at trial.[48] In *Roberts* the Supreme Court found no substance in the defendant's argument that statements given in a preliminary hearing not conducted by his trial attorney required "a particularized search for 'indicia of reliability.' "[49] The attorney at the preliminary hearing, however, was the defendant's counsel at that time and bore a responsibility to his client. In addition, the accused was available at the preliminary hearing to assist counsel in conducting cross-examination.

Current statutes authorizing the taking of depositions to perpetuate testimony demonstrate that cross-examination *by counsel for the accused* at a special proceeding is sufficient to ensure trustworthiness of the evidence and admissibility as former testimony at trial should the witness's testimony prove unavailable. As stated before, the utility of such depositions in combating witness intimidaton is, however, problematic. The deposition occurs too late; it cannot be held before formal appearance of the accused. The deposition also requires that the defendant be advised in advance of the name of the witness. These aspects of perpetuation deposition procedure inform a defendant whom to intimidate while providing the time for intimidation to take place. Finally, presence of the accused at the perpetuation deposition may itself have an intimidating effect.[50]

The preservation proceeding, to be effective in combating witness intimidation, therefore must be held forthwith, sometimes even before the defendant is identified, and without prior disclosure to the defendant of the identity of the witness. It follows that for the preservation proceeding to be effective it must be held in the absence of the defendant. On the other hand, to facilitate a subsequent determination of equivalent circumstantial guarantees of trustworthiness should the preservation proceeding testimony be offered when the witness's testimony at trial proves unavailable, the witness should be cross-examined at the preservation proceeding. The preservation proceeding must therefore include the presence of an attorney to represent the interests of the person or persons who the witness will incriminate. Accordingly, a court or magistrate must be able to appoint a public defender or other attorney as designated counsel for the express and sole purpose of representing the interests of the person who may be incriminated by the testimony of the witness at the preservation proceeding in such person's absence.

The attorney designated to cross-examine on behalf of the potential defendant at the preservation proceeding should be provided with all of the then available discoverable material. Disclosure in advance of the preservation hearing is essential to the later determination of whether sufficient circumstantial guarantees of trustworthiness are present with respect to the witness's testimony when offered at trial should the declarant prove unavailable. Rule 412(a) of the Illinois Supreme Court Rules[51] illustrates the type of material to be provided:

(a) Except as it otherwise provided in these rules as to matters not subject to disclosure and protective orders, the State shall, upon written motion of defense counsel, disclose to defense counsel the following material and information within its possession or control:

(i) the names and last known addresses of persons whom the State intends to call as witnesses, together with their relevant written or recorded statements, memoranda containing substantially verbatim reports of their oral statements, and a list of memoranda reporting or summarizing their oral statements. Upon written motion of defense counsel memoranda reporting or summarizing oral statements shall be examined by the court in camera and if found to be substantially verbatim reports of oral statements shall be disclosed to defense counsel;

(ii) any written or recorded statements and the substance of any oral statements made by the accused or by a codefendant, and a list of witnesses to the making and acknowledgement of such statements;

(iii) a transcript of those portions of grand jury minutes containing testimony of the accused and relevant testimony of persons whom the prosecuting attorney intends to call as witnesses at the hearing or trial;

(iv) any reports or statements of experts, made in connection with the particular case, including results of physical or mental examinations and of scientific tests, experiments, or comparisons, and a statement of qualifications of the expert;

(v) any books, papers, documents, photographs or tangible objects which the prosecuting attorney intends to use in the hearing or trial or which were obtained from or belong to the accused; and

(vi) any record of prior criminal convictions, which may be used for impeachment, of persons whom the State intends to call as witnesses at the hearing or trial.

In addition, unless the discovered material adequately provides, the prosecution should be required to place the witness's testimony to be preserved in context by providing designated counsel with a copy of the police report or other document sufficient for the purpose. If no such document exists, it is suggested that it would be appropriate to have a police officer or other person testify on personal knowledge and hearsay if necessary to accomplish the same goal. Complete discovery should be provided to designated counsel in advance or at the preservation proceeding even when under the jurisdiction's own discovery rules disclosure would only occur after the conclusion of the witness's direct testimony at trial.

Encouraging detailed exploration on cross-examination of the witness's testimony given on direct examination at the preservation proceeding faces a tactical concern. Above all, an attorney on cross-examination does not want to elicit further damaging responses. To avoid such a possibility, an attorney, subject to certain limited exceptions, wil not ask a potentially damaging question to which the attorney does not already know the answer. Thus for tactical reasons an attorney is most often unwilling to undergo a fishing expedition that may or may not elicit responses discrediting the witness or the testimony of the witness if the risk of eliciting further incriminating evidence instead is substantial. In short, if the witness becomes unavailable at trial, defense counsel does not want to find that he or she has perpetuated testimony more damaging than that which would have existed without the cross-examination.

Concern on the part of designated counsel with perpetuating damaging responses on cross-examination would clearly be warranted given the structure of the preservation proceeding. The promptness of a proceeding will undoubtedly present designated counsel representing the defendant's interest from having adequate time to investigate the facts. Moreover, designated counsel will not have the benefit of having consulted with the defendant or the defendant's witnesses. Thus designated counsel will often be unaware of facts known to the defendant and the defendant's witnesses including the defendant's version of what occurred during the incident forming the crux of the criminal charge itself.

To encourage thorough exploration on cross-examination, a fishing expedition, it is necessary to provide that testimony elicited on cross-examination of the witness at the preservation proceeding may not be employed at trial as substantive evidence by the government if the witness's testimony proves unavailable.[52] The fishing expedition thus sanctioned permits thorough exploration on cross-examination by designated counsel of all aspects of the trustworthiness of the witness's direct testimony. Thorough exploration on cross-examination of the direct testimony of the witness is essential to a determination of equivalent circumstantial guarantees of trustworthiness if the testimony given on direct examination is offered into evidence at trial. To implement the suggestion effectively, the prohibition against admissibility of evidence elicited on cross-examination when offered by the government must also extend to testimony elicited by the government on redirect examination unless the defendant opens the door to admissibility by offering at trial testimony given on cross-examination to which the redirect relates.

An experienced attorney as designated counsel, the encouragement given to designated counsel to conduct an explorative cross-examination, full discovery of available material, and the eliciting of testimony from the witness on direct examination by means of nonleading questions except as may be necessary to develop the testimony together serve to insure that all matters bearing upon the trustworthiness of the witness's testimony will be explored at the preservation proceeding. Combining the foregoing with other elements of what constitute a formal proceeding, the preservation proceeding would encompass the presence of a noninvestigative presiding officer (that is, a judge, magistrate, or attorney appointed specially to preside), the prosecutor, an experienced attorney designated to represent the accused's interest, and the witness, with one or more adequate methods of recording the statement. Use of videotape would not only adequately insure certainty of making but would preserve the witness's demeanor at the preservation proceeding for subsequent consideration.

(d) Procedure at Proceeding

At any time before trial including the period before arrest or even identification of the accused, the prosecution must be able to bring any witness voluntarily or by subpoena[53] before a judge, magistrate, or attorney specifically appointed to conduct the proceedings for the express purpose of preserving the witness's testimony. To initiate a preservation proceeding, the prosecution *should not* have to make any showing whatsoever about the likelihood of the witness being unable to attend or of being prevented from attending the trial. The presiding officer should immediately designate a public defender or a member of the private bar to represent the interests of the person accused or implicated by the witness at the proceeding. The cost of designated counsel should be borne by the state. Designated counsel for the accused must be provided with available discovery. The scope and manner of direct examination and cross-examination should be as permitted at trial.[54] During the proceeding, designated counsel representing the accused's interests should object during direct examination to matters of form in obtaining the witness's testimony including the use of leading questions by the prosecution and matters that can usually be obviated if raised, such as lack of a sufficient foundation.[55] Other objections, such as relevancy, would be automatically reserved for trial.[56] Designated counsel on cross-examination would be expected to ask questions designed to explore matters affecting credibility such as lack of personal knowledge, untrustworthy partiality, inconsistent conduct or statements, and character for untruthfulness. It is anticipated that the designated attorney will thoroughly probe all avenues of impeachment indicated by discoverable material made available before or at the preservation proceeding. Designated counsel should also cross-examine the witness to the extent success may be reasonably anticipated to discover and then develop any other matters bearing upon the trustworthiness of the witness's testimony. Lack of admissibility of answers of the witness to inquiries during cross-examination when offered by the government is designed to encourage broad exploration; a fishing expedition is intended.

Since the purpose of the proceeding is to ensure certainty of making and develop evidence bearing upon the trustworthiness of the testimony, thorough exploration is essential even though to some extent designated counsel will in the process be educating and thus preparing the witness to respond to the line of cross-examination when repeated at trial.[57] The witness at trial may "rehabilitate himself . . . and state that at the hearing he was confused, but that everything is now clear in his mind."[58] Similarly, if the particular prosecution witness is one who otherwise might "soften" his or her view of the facts as time passes and the witness's emotional involvement lessens, extensive cross-examination at the preservation proceeding may only serve to harden the witness's position and make the witness less able to retreat to a more friendly position at trial. On the other hand, many witnesses are more likely to make damaging admissions or contradictory statements at the preservation proceeding, because they will have been less thoroughly briefed for that proceeding than they would be for a trial.[59] Also, with respect to most witnesses, the more they say before trial, the more likely that there will be some inconsistency between their trial testimony and their previous statements. The witness's response to questions asked at the preservation proceeding would be available to impeach any different response by the witness at trial.[60] An inconsistent statement made at a preservation proceeding, being a formal proceeding with the witness under oath, may have a more damaging impact upon the witness's credibility in comparison to prior statements given to the police.[61] Thus, in short, if a tactical disadvantage occurs by virtue of the procedures suggested, it is certainly minor and does not have any affect on the overall fairness of the accused's trial.

The presiding officer must assume an active role in facilitating the subsequent determination about whether the witness's testimony is sufficiently trustworthy to be admitted at trial if the witness proves unavailable. The presiding officer should exercise reasonable control over the mode, order, and form of examination of the witness with an eye toward the ultimate determination of admissibility.[62] The presiding officer should have the right both during and at the conclusion of the witness's testimony to interrogate the witness[63] to develop fully the foundation for the witness's testimony, to bring out needed facts not elicited by the parties, and to clarify those facts to which the witness has already testified bearing on the trustworthiness of the witness's testimony.[64] In addition, the presiding officer may inquire just to give the witness one more opportunity to support, confirm, qualify, change, or otherwise modify or alter his or her prior testimony. The asking of questions to the witness at any time by the presiding officer may very well evoke a different response from the witness than near identical or even identical questions by either counsel. It is suggested that the authority vested in the presiding officer sometimes will strike a more honest chord. Following the taking of the witness's testimony, to the extent not previously explored, the presiding officer should ask a series of questions such as:

1. Did anyone threaten you or force you in any way to give your testimony? If the answer is yes, the presiding officer should ascertain the facts.
2. Did anyone suggest, request, or imply in any manner that you testify to any fact which you testified to today. If the answer is yes, the presiding officer should ascertain the facts.
3. Has there been any plea agreement entered into between you (or your counsel) and counsel for the government?
4. Has there been any grant of immunity entered into between you or your counsel and counsel for the government?
5. (If the answer to 3 or 4 is yes.) What is the substance of that plea agreement or grant of immunity? Do all parties agree that the substance of the plea agreement or grant of immunity has been correctly stated? (If a written plea agreement exists, have the government submit a copy to designated counsel and have one filed for the record.)
6. Have you been under the care of a psychologist or psychiatrist?
7. Are you addicted to narcotics? Were you using narcotics at the time of the event you related?
8. Are you addicted to alcohol? Were you drinking during the event?
9. Ask the witness to state the extent of his participation in the alleged crime, if

any, and advise that if falsely made he will be subject to a prosecution for perjury.

10. Is there anything not covered in your testimony or by the questions which is relevant to a determination of the trustworthiness of your testimony?

At the conclusion of the preservation proceeding, the presiding officer may be requested or required to place a statement on the record setting forth his or her assessment of the trustworthiness of the witness's statement evaluated in light of the witness's testimony and corroborating and contradictory facts as considered together with surrounding circumstances represented in affidavits, reports, or otherwise. This assessment, if made, should also set forth particular factual matters considered significant along with an evaluation of the witness's credibility based upon the examination, any extrinsic evidence otherwise available bearing on credibility,[65] and the witness's demeanor. The initial determination of trustworthiness by the presiding officer could prove of great assistance to the judge asked to determine admissibility at trial if the witness proves unavailable. In addition, such an initial determination may assist the prosecution in determining additional steps to be taken to corroborate or otherwise bolster the witness's testimony. If the assessment of the presiding officer at the preservation proceeding raises substantial doubt about admissibility at trial, the prosecution may choose to take protective measures, or additional protective measures if some had already been taken, to insure the presence and the testimony of the witness at trial or proceed to perpetuate the witness's testimony as former testimony as promptly as possible by means of either a preliminary hearing or perpetuation deposition.

The transcript and, if made, a videotape recording of the preservation proceedings should be sealed. Designated counsel should be under order not to discuss the preservation proceeding with outsiders including the accused or his or her attorney. The press should be barred from the proceeding itself. All of these measures are necessary to ensure the safety of the witness when the identity of the witness as distinguished from the content of the witness's testimony is not known to the actual or potential accused. Disclosure of the name and address of the witness and the testimony that was preserved should be in accordance with the discovery rules of the particular jurisdiction. Thus, for example, in Illinois this information would be made available before the preliminary hearing,[66] and in the federal court the transcript would be made available only after the witness has completed his or her direct examination at trial.[67] The transcript must be disclosed to defense counsel in advance of any determination of admissibility should the witness prove unavailable at trial.

When the identity of the witness is already known to the defendant, it is in the interest of the witness that the defendant through his or her counsel be advised that the witness's testimony has been preserved. A defendant, once advised that intimidation of the witness is unlikely to keep the witness's testimony from the jury, is less likely to undertake the intimidation in the first place. The deterrent effect of the preservation deposition on the conduct of the defendant will not occur unless the defendant is advised through his or her counsel that the witness's testimony has already been preserved.

2. Determining Admissibility

If the witness whose testimony was preserved testifies at trial in a manner inconsistent with his or her preservation proceeding testimony, the preservation testimony would be admissible on behalf of either the prosecution or defense both to impeach and as substantive evidence. The language of Rule 801(d)(1)(A) referring to "other proceeding" is obviously broad enough to include testimony at a preservation proceeding; the preservation proceeding permits adequate assurances of certainty of making and is more conducive to trustworthiness than testimony before a grand jury.

If the witness whose testimony was preserved proves "unavailable at trial," the admissibility of the witness's testimony at the preservation proceeding must be governed by the criteria for "other [hearsay] exception" set forth in Rule 804(b)(5) and not the criteria for former testimony set forth in Rule 804(b)(1).

(a) Former Testimony

Use of Rule 804(b)(1)[68] as a standard of admissibility is inappropriate for a variety of reasons. The hearsay exception for former testimony not only envisions an attorney conducting cross-examination, it at a minimum envisions an attorney assisted by his or her client conducting cross-examination. Although it is true that designated counsel will have had an adequate opportunity and the same basic motive to develop the witness's testimony at the preservation hearing as would the accused's counsel at trial, important differences remain. First, designated counsel was neither selected nor approved by the accused; the style and quality of attorneys do vary. Of greater importance, designated counsel will not have discussed the case with the accused. Thus designated counsel will be in the dark about the accused's defense. The attorney will be unaware of facts about the event in question and the witness whose testimony was preserved known to the accused and others available to the accused. Tactical decisions, while in the reduced-risk form contemplated, will nevertheless be made without input from the defendant. As the Report of the House Committee on the Judiciary indicated in amending Rule 804(b)(1) to include among other notions the requirement that the defendant against whom the testimony is being offered be the defendant in the prior proceeding, it is "generally unfair to impose upon the party against whom the hearsay evidence is being offered responsibility for the manner in which the witness was previously handled by another party."[69] Even putting informational and tactical concerns aside, it is hard to argue that a person who has not been charged, maybe not even arrested, and possibly not even identified, can be considered a party to the preservation proceeding as required by Rule 804(b)(1), when the person is not present, has no contact with anyone who is present, and does not even know of the proceeding.[70] Thus although Rule 804(b)(1) has the distinct advantage that statements meeting its requirements are automatically admissible without an ad hoc search for circumstantial guarantees of trustworthiness, the cross-examination that takes place at the preservation hearing is clearly too divergent from the cross-examination contemplated to bring the preservation proceeding within the hearsay exception for former testimony.

(b) Federal Rule of Evidence 804(b)(5)

Admissibility of the testimony of the witness "unavailable at trial" given at the preservation proceeding should be governed by the criteria set forth in Rule 804(b)(5). Thus the testimony would be admissible as substantive evidence only if the court at trial finds that the statement possesses, among others, equivalent circumstantial guarantees of trustworthiness to the other hearsay exceptions contained in Rule 804(b).

(1) *Unavailability Requirement.* At common law the requirement of unavailability evolved separately in connection with particular hearsay exceptions rather than along general lines. However, as the Advisory Committee's Note to Rule 804(a) points out, "no reason is apparent for making distinctions as to what satisfies unavailability for the different exceptions." Accordingly, Rule 804(a) alters this pattern by treating unavailability as a single concept applicable to each exception. An exception to this unified approach exists only with respect to imposition of a requirement regarding procuring testimony of a witness absent from the hearing applicable solely to Rules 804(b)(1), (3), and (4) when the proponent of the hearsay statement is unable to compel the witness's attendance by process or other reasonable means, Rule 804(a)(5). Since the admissibility of preserved testimony of an unavailable witness is being offered under Rule 804(b)(5), the exception in Rule 804 is inapplicable to the situation at hand. Rule 804(a) provides as follows:

Hearsay Exceptions: Declarant Unavailable

(a) Definition of unavailability. "Unavailability as a witness" includes situations in which the declarant—

(1) is exempted by ruling of the court on the ground a privilege from testifying concerning the subject matter of his statement; or

(2) persists in refusing to testify concerning the subject matter of his statement despite an order of the court to do so; or

(3) testifies to a lack of memory of the subject matter of his statement; or

(4) is unable to be present or to testify at the hearing because of death or then existing physical or mental illness or infirmity; or

(5) is absent from the hearing and the proponent of his statement has been

unable to procure his attendance (or in the case of a hearsay exception under subdivision (b)(2), (3) or (4), his attendance or testimony) by process or other reasonable means.

A declarant is not unavailable as a witness if his exemption, refusal, claim of lack of memory, inability, or absence is due to the procurement or wrongdoing of the proponent of his statement for the purpose of preventing the witness from attending or testifying.

The definition of *unavailability* contained in Rule 804(a) provides five alternatives, each alone sufficient to meet the requirement. The thrust of the alternative definitions of unavailability concerns the unavailability of the testimony of the witness, which includes, but is not limited to, situations in which the witness is not physically present in court.[71] Physical presence on the witness stand does not make a witness available within the meaning of the rule if the witness exercises a privilege, simply refuses to answer, or testifies to a lack of memory about the subject matter of his or her prior statement.

Rule 804(a)(1) provides that a witness exempt from testifying concerning the subject matter of the witness's statement on the grounds of privilege is unavailable. An actual claim of privilege must be made by a witness, other than a criminal defendant,[72] and allowed by the court before the witness will be considered unavailable on the basis of a privilege.[73] Rule 804(a)(2) provides that one who persists in refusing to testify concerning the subject matter of one's statement, despite an order of the court to do so, is unavailable.[74] Silence resulting from misplaced reliance upon a privilege without making a claim, or in spite of a court denial of an asserted claim of privilege, constitutes unavailability under this subsection.[75]

Rule 804(a)(3) provides that a witness who testifies to a lack of memory of the subject matter of his or her statement is unavailable.[76] A witness may either truly lack recollection or, for a variety of reasons, including, as we know all too well, intimidation by the accused, feign lack of recollection.[77] In either event, the witness is unavailable to the extent that he or she asserts lack of recollection of the subject matter of the prior statement even if the witness recalls other events. Rule 804(a)(4) provides that a witness unable to be present or to testify at the hearing because of death or then existing physical or mental illness or infirmity is unavailable. Death is the most obvious basis.[78] Mental illness[79] or physical disability[80] of a serious nature is equally compelling. If the reason for the prosecution's witness's unavailability is only temporary, considerations underlying the Confrontation Clause may require resort to a continuance.[81]

Rule 804(a)(5) provides that a declarant is unavailable if the declarant's presence cannot be secured by process or other reasonable means.[82] In federal criminal cases a subpoena may be served at any place within the United States.[83] In all criminal cases the Confrontation Clause[84] itself requires that before former testimony, Rule 804(b)(1), may be introduced against the accused as a substitute for in-court testimony, the prosecution makes a good faith effort to obtain the presence of the witness at trial. Witnesses who are in state or federal prison can be required to appear in state or federal court pursuant to a subpoena to the individual and a writ of habeas corpus *ad testificandum* issued to the appropriate prison authority.[85] Under both Rule 804(a)(5) and the Confrontation Clause, whether the government has shown good faith in attempting first to locate the witness and second to procure the witness's attendance by process or voluntarily by reasonable means must be determined on a case-by-case basis after careful review of the particular facts and circumstances.[86]

Determination of unavailability is a matter decided by the court; the party offering the statement has the burden of showing unavailability.[87] A witness is not "unavailable" under any of the subdivisions of Rule 804(a) if the circumstances that would otherwise constitute unavailability are due to the procurement or other wrongdoing of the proponent of the statement.[88]

(2) *Specified Criteria.* Statements of an unavailable witness made at a preservation proceeding must satisfy the requirements of Rule 804(b)(5).

Other Exceptions

* * *

(b) Hearsay Exceptions. The following are not excluded by the hearsay rule if the declarant is unavailable as a witness:

(5) Other Exceptions. A statement not specifically covered by any of the foregoing exceptions but having equivalent circumstantial guarantees of trustworthiness, if the court determines that (A) the statement is offered as evidence of a material fact; (B) the statement is more probative on the point for which it is offered than any other evidence which the proponent can procure through reasonable efforts; and (C) the general purposes of these rules and the interests of justice will be best be served by admission of the statement into evidence. However, a statement may not be admitted under this exception unless the proponent of it makes known to the adverse party sufficiently in advance of the trial or hearing to provide the adverse party with a fair opportunity to prepare to meet it, his intention to offer the statement and the particulars of it, including the name and address of the declarant.

Rule 804(b)(5) contains five express requirements, all of which must be determined by the court to have been satisfied before the statement may be admitted. Four of these requirements, that is, materiality, necessity, satisfaction of the rules, and notice, may be disposed of in passing. The final criterion, that is, equivalent circumstantial guarantees of trustworthiness, deserves careful exploration in light of procedures established for the preservation proceeding.

The requirement that the statement be offered as evidence of a material fact means that not only must the fact the statement is offered to prove be relevant but that the fact be of substantial importance in determining the outcome of the litigation. Introduction of the hearsay statement must be necessary by being more probative on the point for which it is offered than any other evidence that the proponent may reasonably procure. Whether a particular effort to procure alternative proof of a matter may reasonably be demanded must depend upon the fact at issue considered in the context of the litigation. The requirement that the general purposes of the rules of evidence and the interest of justice be best served by admission of the statement into evidence is of little practical importance in determining admissibility. Finally, a hearsay statement may not be admitted under the "other exception" exception of Rule 804(b)(5) unless the proponent of it makes known to the adverse party, sufficiently in advance of the trial or hearing to provide the adverse party with a fair opportunity to prepare to meet it, his or her intention to offer the statement and the particulars of it, including the name and address of the declarant.

The requirement of "equivalent circumstantial guarantees of trustworthiness" requires that the court undertake a search for trustworthiness—trustworthiness equivalent to that possessed by statements falling within an enumerated hearsay exception. In evaluating trustworthiness, courts have looked to four criteria: certainty that the statement was made; assurance of personal knowledge of the declarant of the underlying event; practical availability of the declarant at trial for meaningful cross-examination concerning the underlying event; and finally, an ad hoc ascertainment of trustworthiness based upon the totality of the surrounding circumstances including corroborating facts and an assessment of credibility of the declarant, considered in light of the class-type exceptions to the hearsay rule supposed to demonstrate such characteristic. Relevant factors bearing upon the ascertainment of trustworthiness include (1) the declarant's partiality, that is, interest, bias, corruption, or coercion; (2) the presence or absence of time to fabricate; and (3) suggestiveness brought on by the use of leading questions.

Procedures established for the preservation proceeding will facilitate application of these criteria. To begin, one knows that the declarant is unavailable and that the statement of the declarant was in fact made. The eliciting of testimony of the witness at the preservation proceeding by the prosecution by means of nonleading questions with exploration on cross-examination by designated counsel should be helpful in judging the personal knowledge of the declarant. In addition, the witness's response to questions on cross-examination exploring credibility presented to the court on videotape permitting evaluation of demeanor should greatly assist the determination of trustworthiness. Matters bearing on the credibility of the witness not raised at the preservation proceeding may also be brought before the court.[89] Similarly, evidence establishing facts corroborating and those contradicting the statement of the declarant may properly be brought before the court and evaluated in determining whether the government has established the presence of equivalent circumstantial guarantees of trustworthiness.

It is suggested that evidence of intimidation causing physical unavailability or feigned lack of recollection should *not* be considered by the court in determining whether the statement is sufficiently trustworthy to be received in evidence. The defendants, his or her agents, or others have almost as much if not just as much reason to silence a witness who is falsely incriminating the defendant as one who is testifying truthfully. Such evidence, if considered, possesses a substantial tendency to be overvalued.[90]

In applying the foregoing criteria, statements of uninvolved occurrence witnesses are extremely likely to be found sufficiently trustworthy to be admitted. Thus in our hypothetical case in Chapter 4, it is almost certain that if Mary Mahoney and John Goodfellow had repeated their initial statements to the police at the preservation proceeding, each statement would be found to possess equivalent circumstantial guarantees of trustworthiness and be admitted at trial when the respective declarant's testimony proved unavailable. The testimony of Jim James and Bob Williams is more troublesome. Nevertheless, on the facts presented, it is anticipated that both statements would be found sufficiently trustworthy when evaluated in light of the corroborating facts and an assessment of credibility.

Statements of unavailable witnesses satisfying the requirements of Rule 804(b)(5) would not fun afoul of the Confrontation Clause. As stated in *Ohio v. Roberts*:

> In sum, when a hearsay declarant is not present for cross-examination at trial, the Confrontation Clause normally requires a showing that he is unavailable. Even then, his statement is admissible only if it bears adequate "indicia of reliability." Reliability can be inferred without more in a case where the evidence falls within a firmly rooted hearsay exception. In other cases, the evidence must be excluded, at least absent a showing of particularized guarantees of trustworthiness.[91]

"Equivalent circumstantial guarantees of trustworthiness" and "particularized guarantees of trustworthiness" are surely intended to be synonymous.

NOTES

1. No one is asserting that preservation of testimony will stop all intimidation of witnesses. Live testimony accusing the defendant of a crime will be more persuasive to a jury than hearing a prior statement of the witness read by the attorney for the government. Moreover, members of organized crime may believe it is advantageous in the long run to make examples of anyone who testifies even after the damage has been done and the defendant convicted. Assuming some murders will occur, the question remains whether the murders that do occur will be significantly fewer than would have occurred without preservation of testimony. Currently, murders do more than reduce impact or set an example—they also eliminate damaging testimony

that might put the perpetrator in jail. One trusts that a preservation proceeding will create a distinction that amounts to a significant difference.

2. *See* Chapter 4, Section 1(b) *supra.*

3. Notice that in our hypothetical case in Chapter 4 Mary Mahoney refused to go to the police station because her children would be unattended. To deal with such a situation the police should carry a portable tape recorder in their police car. A statute should be enacted requiring not only that occurrence witnesses talk to the police but that police officers take reasonable steps to have witness statements tape recorded or be handwritten by, or at least signed by, the witness either at the scene of the incident, wherever otherwise initially contacted, or at the police station.

4. The same issue arises with respect to admissions of a party-opponent. As experienced trial counsel know, it is not unusual for one party to claim that the opponent said something that the opponent flatly denies having said. Here the rules of evidence say the jury is to decide the issue of credibility, and yet this situation and that regarding the substantive admissibility of prior inconsistent statements would appear to be identical. Moreover, how is fabrication by the in-court declarant of alleged present sense impressions, excited utterances, or other hearsay exceptions prevented? What then distinguishes testimony regarding prior inconsistent statements of an in-court declarant from testimony of a witness relating an alleged admission or statement admitted under a hearsay exception? In what sense do prior inconsistent statements lack the indicia of reliability thought to justify admission of recognized hearsay exceptions? On what ground does the adversary process accept the risk that a party will fabricate a statement of an opponent but reject the same risk regarding statements of a witness unless such statements otherwise fall into a recognized hearsay exception?

5. If the witness also admits that his or her prior inconsistent statement is true, the statement is substantively admissible as adopted testimony. United States v. Tavares, 512 F.2d 872 (9th Cir. 1975); United States v. Ellis, 461 F.2d 962 (2d Cir. 1972); Tripp v. United States, 295 F.2d 418 (10th Cir. 1961); Stevens v. United States, 256 F.2d 619 (9th Cir. 1958).

6. *See* United States v. Schwartz, 252 F. Supp. 866 (E.D. Pa. 1966).

7. C. McCormick, *The Turncoat Witness: Previous Statements as Substantive Evidence*, 25 Tex. L. Rev. 573, 588 (1947). *See also* C. McCormick, *Handbook of the Law of Evidence* § 39 at 82 (St. Paul: West, 1954).

8. Evidence Act, 1938, 1 & 2 Geo. 6, c. 28, § 1, *repealed* by Civil Evidence Act, 1968, c. 64, § 20(2). The personal knowledge requirement was also incorporated in a proposal advanced by J. Falknor. Out-of-court declarations would have been substantively admissible under the Falknor proposal if

> previously made by a person who is present at the hearing and available for cross-examination if the judge finds that (a) the declarant had an adequate opportunity to perceive the event or condition which the statement narrates, describes or explains and (b) the statement was written or signed by the declarant or the making of the statement is acknowledged by the declarant in his testimony in the present proceeding.

J. Falknor, *The Hearsay Rule and Its Exceptions*, 2 U.C.L.A. L. Rev. 43, 54 (1954).

9. Falknor alone discussed the need for a personal knowledge requirement. Falknor, *supra* note 8 at 53-54.

10. It is very easy for someone simply to say that someone told him or her something. It is much more difficult to convincingly fabricate having seen something you did not see. Cross-examination is much more likely to be effective in exposing fabrication in the latter as compared to the former instance.

11. The Fifth Circuit has examined the certainty-of-making factor with respect to the substantive admissibility under Rule 803(24) of prior inconsistent statements not meeting the stricter requirements of Rule 801(d)(1)(A). Rule 803(24) authorizes substantive admission of hearsay statements not included within any specific exception if notice of their intended use is given and they possess "equivalent circumstantial guarantees of trustworthiness" and meet certain additional requirements regarding probative value. In United States v. Leslie, 542 F.2d 285 (5th Cir. 1976), the Fifth Circuit upheld the substantive admissibility of prior written statements of three witnesses who at trial denied the truth of parts of their statements and claimed lapse of memory with respect to other parts. The court, after discussing the various indicia of reliability, stated that "[p]erhaps most significantly, for all practical purposes they admitted making the statements." 542 F.2d at 290. The court distinguished United States v. Sisto, 534 F.2d 616 (5th Cir. 1976), an earlier Fifth Circuit case that denied substantive admission to a witness's prior inconsistent statement as follows:

> These factors distinguish this case from United States v. Sisto, . . . in which we held that the trial court had committed plain error by failing to instruct the jury that prior statements allegedly made by the defendant's accomplice were admissible for impeachment only. In *Sisto* the only evidence that the statements were made was the testimony of a government agent. The alleged declarant categorically denied having made the statements, and there was no evidence of a writing or transcription. The House Judiciary Committee was no doubt concerned about exactly this problem of a possible "manufactured" prior statement being used against a criminal defendant when it rejected rule 801(d)(1) as proposed by the Supreme Court. Once a witness has admitted making the prior statement and only disputes the truth of its contents, however there is no problem of a *contrived* extrajudicial statement getting before the jury for use as substantive evidence.

542 F.2d at 291 n.6 (emphasis in original).

12. Double-level hearsay statements are substantively admissible only if there exists an exception to the hearsay rule at each level. *See* Fed. R. Evid. 805.

13. A confession is a comprehensive acknowledgement of guilt or of facts that necessarily and directly imply guilt. An admission is a statement of fact that when considered in light of other facts may lead to an inference of guilt but from which guilt does not necessarily flow.

14. The practical difficulties faced by the criminal defendant in opposing the use of an alleged oral inconsistent statement are well stated in 4 *Weinstein's Evidence* ¶ 801(d)(1)(a)[05] at 801-101-801-102 n.4 (1979):

> Most instances in federal criminal cases as the rule was adopted by the Supreme Court would have pitted the witness against an FBI agent who interviewed the witness while accompanied by a colleague and made a report on the essentials of the story. In such a swearing contest the witness will almost always be at a dis-

> advantage so far as the jury is concerned. Even should there be some discrepancies between the FBI report and an agent's testimony, the use of the report—available as [§ 18 U.S.C.] 3500 material—will generally tend to support the agent's credibility because it will indicate that a contemporaneous memorandum was made. The agent on redirect will be able to explain that the report did not contain all the details and that the regular Bureau practice is to destroy original notes when the typed report is prepared. The realities of the situation explain why defense counsel and members of Congress were so opposed to the rule as adopted by the Supreme Court. Nevertheless, it is probably true that the jury is more apt to arrive at a sound factual determination if it is given as much available data as possible, including evidence of what a key witness said on prior occasions.

With respect to state court proceedings, the trustworthiness of police officer testimony is even more subject to question.

Moreover, the risk of fabrication and distortion is significantly increased when a witness purports merely to repeat another's out-of-court declaration. It is always easier to say that X said something than to "report" personal observations of an event one did not see. Even if X did in fact tell the witness something, it would not be unusual for the person asserting to have overheard the out-of-court declaration to inject, intentionally or otherwise, additional or different statements into the conversation. Unfortunately, these fabricated or distorted statements will often be highly damaging admissions or confessions not easily discounted by the jury.

The party opposing the truth of the prior out-of-court declaration containing a second-level hearsay declaration is in a particularly difficult position. The witness who is asserted to have repeated the second-level hearsay declaration could deny having made any such statement and deny ever having heard the alleged second-level statement. Such later denial is not particularly forceful, however, especially if the declarant must admit contact with the person to whom the second-level statement is attributed. If, on the other hand, personal knowledge is required, the witness can do much more than offer a simple denial. The witness can testify about what he or she actually perceived or, if nothing was perceived, explain, for example, that it would not have been possible to see anything because he or she was in California on the day of the event. Note the discouragement to the purported hearer of the witness's out-of-court declaration to fabricate the existence of the statement or to add second-level embellishments. One is much less likely to fabricate what the witness out of court allegedly perceived and stated than to fabricate what the witness out of court allegedly heard and repeated. Often a policeman will testify that "[t]he witness told me that John told him that he robbed the store." If the witness knows John, the jury could mistakenly give credibility to the story, since it is far from implausible and extremely difficult for the witness to refute. In sum, the increased risk both of fabrication and of faulty recollection, with the limitations on effective cross-examination, warrant general exclusion of second-level hearsay statements pursuant to Rule 801(d)(1)(A). At the same time, situations may exist in which a prior inconsistent statement not meeting the requirements of Rule 801(d)(1)(A) should be admitted substantively pursuant to Rule 803(24). For example, assume the defendant's mother voluntarily goes to a police station and gives a tape-recorded statement that her son had just told her that he had found his wife in bed with the milkman and that he was going to kill both of them. She asks the police to stop her son. The mother's statement, even though containing second-level hearsay about which the mother lacks personal knowledge, should be found admissible in a murder prosecution against her son pursuant to Rule 803(24), even if she denies making it while testifying in court.

15. Statement of Lord Chancellor on the second reading of the Bill for the Act of Lords, Civil Evidence Act, 1968, c. 64, § 2, whose forerunner was § 1 of Evidence Act of 1938, 288 H. of L. Off. Rep. 1341, 1342. *Compare* Fed. R. Evid. 805, permitting double-level hearsay if an exception exists for each level. The requirement of personal knowledge gives the declarant an opportunity to state either what he or she now alleges to have seen or that, having not even been at the location indicated in the prior inconsistent statement at the time alleged, the declarant saw nothing. This statement is a far more effective rebuttal than a mere denial by the witness that someone else said something to him or her.

16. Pursuant to current Fed. R. Evid. 801(d)(1)(A), a statement by anyone concerning the defendant's confession would be admissible, in spite of the declarant's lack of personal knowledge, if it were given to a grand jury or made at a prior trial. For a discussion of whether the formality of the making of the statement is an adequate reason to dispense with the personal knowledge requirement, *see* note 19 *infra*.

17. Many out-of-court declarations are admissible under the Federal Rules of Evidence without regard to whether they are oral or in writing. Present sense impressions (Fed. R. Evid. 803(1)), excited utterances (Fed. R. Evid. 803(2)), and statements of purposes of medical diagnosis or treatment (Fed. R. Evid. 803(4)) are examples. Moreover, none of these examples require that the declarant be available and thus be subject to cross-examination. Admittedly, these exceptions to the hearsay rule are based at times on certain assumptions about the certainty of making and accuracy of reporting of the matter related.

18. Fed. R. Evid. 613(b) provides:

> Extrinsic evidence of a prior inconsistent statement by a witness is not admissible unless the witness is afforded an opportunity to explain or deny the same and the opposite party is afforded an opportunity to interrogate him thereon, or the interests of justice otherwise require. This provision does not apply to admissions of a party-opponent as defined in rule 801(d)(2).

See also Chapter 6, Section A3 *supra*.

19. The proposal does not extend the personal knowledge requirement to statements now admissible pursuant to Rule 801(d)(1)(A) primarily because such a requirement has never been incorporated as part of the common-law hearsay exception for former testimony, an exception closely paralleling Rule 801(d)(1)A)'s reference to testimony at a trial, hearing, or deposition. Moreover, although the same arguments put forth above are applicable to such prior inconsistent statements, additional indications of reliability are provided by the formality and public nature of the prior proceeding. With respect to statements concededly made, such formality does significantly reduce the effect of coercion, deception, or subtle influence. In any event, application of the personal knowledge requirement to such prior statement would certainly not be unacceptable.

Uniform Rule of Evidence 801(d)(1)(A) permits substantive admissibility of *all* prior inconsistent statements in civil proceedings. Although the proposal made herein does not differentiate between civil and criminal proceedings, the reduced practical effect of blanket substantive admissibility in civil cases, with the simplification such admissibility would accomplish with respect to problems addressed in Rules 613 and 607 of the Federal Rules of Evidence, makes the Uniform Rules' treatment of civil proceedings an acceptable if not preferable alternative.

20. The question of the voluntariness of the prior inconsistent statement was faced in La France v. Bohlinger, 499 F.2d 29 (1st Cir. 1974). The case involved the question of whether a witness's prior out-of-court statement inculpating the defendant could be used solely for purposes of impeachment without a judicial determination that the statement was voluntarily made. The court concluded that a preliminary hearing on voluntariness was constitutionally mandated and that the more-probably-true-than-not-true standard applied, relying in part on Napue v. Illinois, 360 U.S. 264, 269 (1959): "The principle that a State may not knowingly use false evidence, including false testimony, to obtain a tainted conviction, implicit in any concept of ordered liberty, does not cease to apply merely because the false testimony goes only to the credibility of the witness."

The right of confrontation applies to prior inconsistent statements offered as substantive evidence against the criminal defendant. *See generally*, D. Davenport, *The Confrontation Clause and the Co-Conspirator Exception in Criminal Prosecution: A Functional Analysis*, 85 Harv. L. Rev. 1378 (1972); E. Griswold, *The Due Process Revolution and Confrontation*, 119 U. Pa. L. Rev. 711 (1971); F. Read, *The New Confrontation Dilemma*, 45 S. Cal. L. Rev. 1 (1972); E. Semerjian, *The Right of Confrontation*, 55 A.B.A. J. 152 (1969).

For a general discussion of confrontation issues raised when a witness admits, denies, or does not recall either the making or substance of a prior inconsistent statement, *see* 4 *Weinstein's Evidence* ¶¶ 801(d((1)(A)[01]-801(d)(1)(A)[08] (1979). *See also* M. Graham, *The Confrontation Clause, the Hearsay Rule, and the Forgetful Witness*, 56 Tex. L. Rev. 151 (1978). Given the requirements of the proposed rule, it seems very unlikely that a witness will in fact deny making the statement. If the witness does admit making the statement, he or she may either affirm or deny the truth of its contents or deny recollection of the underlying events. If its truth is affirmed, the prior statement has become current testimony and will be given substantive effect. *See* note 5 *supra*. If the statement's truth is denied, the prior statement may also be given substantive effect pursuant to California v. Green, 399 U.S. 149 (1970). If the witness denies knowledge or memory of the underlying event, the court must decide whether the witness's "apparent lapse of memory so affected [the defendant's] right to cross-examination as to make a critical difference in the application of the Confrontation Clause." 399 U.S. at 168. For a full discussion of this issue, *see* Chapter 4, Section C3 *supra*.

21. Although it is hoped that police officers will be encouraged by the proposal, if not required by statute, to carry tape recorders and record witness statements when indicated, it is not intended that the initial recording and every subsequent recording or written statement must be preserved and ultimately disclosed to the defendant. The prosecution has, in my opinion, the right to discuss the case with the witness to appreciate what happened in context and then have the witness give a coherent

statement describing relevant events. Initial tape recordings, like initial officer's notes, need not be retained.

22. *See* Chapter 4, Section B2 *supra.*

23. *See* Chapter 2, Section D5 *supra.*

24. *Federal Rules of Criminal Procedure Amendment Act of 1975*: Hearing Before the Senate Comm. on the Judiciary, 94th Cong., 1st Sess. 165 (1975) (statement of John C. Keeney, Acting Assistant Attorney General, Criminal Division).

25. United States v. Long Soldier, 562 F.2d 601 (8th Cir. 1977); United States v. Mosley, 555 F.2d 191 (8th Cir. 1977).

26. United States v. Livingston, 661 F.2d 239 (D.C. Cir. 1981); United States v. Ragghianti, 560 F.2d 1376 (9th Cir. 1977); Martin v. United States, 528 F.2d 1157 (4th Cir. 1975).

27. The timing of a preliminary hearing following initial appearance appears to vary throughout the country. In Illinois it even varies within the state with Cook County holding a preliminary hearing on certain serious offenses the next day and downstate holding the preliminary hearing within a customary 10-14 day period.

28. Unless the proceeding insures not only certainty of making but, to the extent possible, equivalent circumstantial guarantees of trustworthiness supporting substantive admissibility as well, the witness remains at risk up to trial. Thus the proceeding must not only be prompt but seek to establish trustworthy and thus admissible testimony.

29. 537 F.2d 1055 (9th Cir. 1976).

30. *Id.* at 1056.

31. The opinion does not indicate either the presence or absence of surprise.

32. 537 F.2d at 1056. The court declined to mention the content of the prior statements or the trial testimony.

33. *Id.* at 1058.

34. 8 U.S.C. § 1226(a).

35. 8 U.S.C. § 1101(4).

36. 8 C.F.R. § 236.2(b).

37. 8 C.F.R.§ 236.2(c).

38. Fed. R. Evid. 611(c) provides:

> ***Mode and Order of Interrogation and Presentation***
>
> * * *
>
> (c) Leading questions. Leading questions should not be used on the direct examination of a witness except as may be necessary to develop his testimony. Ordinarily leading questions should be permitted on cross-examination. When a party calls a hostile witness, an adverse party, or a witness identified with an adverse party, interrogation may be by leading questions.

See also Chapter 6, Section D *supra.*

39. Fed. R. Evid. 608(a) provides:

> ***Evidence of Character and Conduct of Witness***
>
> (a) Opinion and Reputation Evidence of Character. The credibility of a witness may be attacked or supported by evidence in the form of opinion or repu-

tation, but subject to these limitations: (1) the evidence may refer only to character for truthfulness or untruthfulness, and (2) evidence of truthful character is admissible only after the character of the witness for truthfulness has been attacked by opinion or reputation evidence or otherwise.

40. Fed. R. Evid. 608(b) provides:

Evidence of Character and
Conduct of Witness

* * *

(b) Specific Instances of Conduct. Specific instances of the conduct of a witness, for the purpose of attacking or supporting his credibility, other than conviction of crime as provided in rule 609, may not be proved by extrinsic evidence. They may, however, in the discretion of the court, if probative of truthfulness or untruthfulness, be inquired into on cross-examination of the witness (1) concerning his character for truthfulness or untruthfulness, or (2) concerning the character for truthfulness or untruthfulness of another witness as to which character the witness being cross-examined has testified.

41. Fed. R. Evid. 609 provides:

Impeachment of Evidence of
Conviction of Crime

(a) General Rule. For the purpose of attacking the credibility of a witness, evidence that he has been convicted of a crime shall be admitted if elicited from him or established by public record during cross-examination but only if the crime (1) was punishable by death or imprisonment in excess of one year under the law under which he was convicted, and the court determines that the probative value of admitting this evidence outweighs its prejudicial effect to the defendant, or (2) involved dishonesty or false statement, regardless of the punishment.

(b) Time Limit. Evidence of a conviction under this rule is not admissible if a period of more than ten years has elapsed since the date of the conviction or of the release of the witness from the confinement imposed for that conviction, whichever is the later date, unless the court determines, in the interests of justice, that the probative value of the conviction supported by specific facts and circumstances substantially outweighs its prejudicial effect. However, evidence of a conviction more than 10 years old as calculated herein, is not admissible unless the proponent gives to the adverse party sufficient advance written notice of intent to use such evidence to provide the adverse party with a fair opportunity to contest the use of such evidence.

* * *

(d) Juvenile Adjudications. Evidence of juvenile adjudications is generally not admissible under this rule. The court may, however, in a criminal case allow evidence of a juvenile adjudication of a witness other than the accused if conviction of the offense would be admissible to attack the credibility of an adult and the court is satisfied that admission in evidence is necessary for a fair determination of the issue of guilt or innocence.

(e) Pendency of Appeal. The pendency of an appeal therefrom does not render evidence of a conviction inadmissible. Evidence of the pendency of an appeal is admissible.

42. *See* M. Graham, *Handbook of Federal Evidence* § 607.7 at 427 (St. Paul: West, 1981):

> Matters which may reasonably be expected to color the testimony of a witness or cause him to testify falsely are proper subjects of inquiry of any witness by any party. Emotions likely to be created under the influence of such matters, referred to collectively by Wigmore [3A Wigmore, *Evidence* § 945 at 782 (Chadbourn Rev. 1970)] as untrustworthy partiality, consist of:
>
> > Bias, in common acceptance, covers all varieties of hostility or prejudice against the opponent personally or of favor to the proponent personally.
> >
> > Interest signifies the specific inclination which is apt to be produced by the relation between the witness and the cause at issue in the litigation.
> >
> > Corruption is here to be understood as the conscious false intent which is inferrible from giving or taking a bribe or from expressions of a general unscrupulousness for the case in hand.
>
> In order to complete the definition of partiality, the inclusion of a fourth category is suggested: coercion, intended to include any form of mental, emotional, or physical duress or compulsion that overcomes a witness' duty to tell the truth.

43. *See* C. McCormick, *Evidence* § 47 at 97 (Cleary ed. 1972):

> Statements are elicited from Witness One, who has testified to a material story of an accident, crime, or other matters, to the effect that at the time he witnessed these matters the day was windy and cold and he, the witness, was wearing his green sweater. Let us suppose these latter statements about the day and the sweater to be "disproved." This may happen in several ways. Witness One on direct or cross-examination may acknowledge that he was in error. Or judicial notice may be taken that at the time and place it could not have been cold and windy, e.g., in Tucson in July. But commonly disproof or "contradiction" is attempted by calling Witness Two to testify to the contrary, i.e., that the day was warm and Witness One was in his shirt-sleeves.

44. Fed. R. Evid. 613 provides:

Prior Statements of Witnesses

(a) Examining Witness Concerning Prior Statement. In examining a witness concerning a prior statement made by him, whether written or not, the statement need not be shown nor its contents disclosed to him at that time, but on request the same shall be shown or disclosed to opposing counsel.

(b) Extrinsic Evidence of Prior Inconsistent Statement of Witness. Extrinsic evidence of a prior inconsistent statement by a witness is not admissible unless the witness is afforded an opportunity to explain or deny the same and the opposite party is afforded an opportunity to interrogate him thereon, or the interests of justice otherwise require. This provision does not apply to admissions of a party-opponent as defined in rule 801(d)(2).

45. Fed. R. Evid. 610 provides:

Religious Beliefs or Opinions

Evidence of the beliefs or opinions of a witness on matters of religion is not admissible for the purpose of showing that by reason of their nature his credibility is impaired or enhanced.

46. 448 U.S. 56 (1980).
47. *Id.* at 73:

In sum, we perceive no reason to resolve the reliability issue differently here than the Court did in [California v. Green]. "Since there was an adequate opportunity to cross-examine [the witness], and counsel . . . availed himself of that opportunity, the transcript . . . bore sufficient 'indicia of reliability' and afforded ' "the trier of fact a satisfactory basis for evaluating the truth of the prior statement." ' " 408 U.S. at 216, 92 S.Ct., at 2314.

48. Id. at 72:

Nor does it matter that, unlike *Green*, respondent had a different lawyer at trial from the one at the preliminary hearing. Although one might strain one's reading of *Green* to assign this factor some significance, respondent advances no reason of substance supporting the distinction. Indeed, if we were to accept this suggestion, *Green* would carry the seeds of its own demise; under a "same attorney" rule, a defendant could nullify the effect of *Green* by obtaining new counsel after the preliminary hearing was concluded.

49. *Id.* at 72-73:

Finally, we reject respondent's attempt to fall back on general principles of confrontation and his argument that this case falls among those in which the Court must undertake a particularized search for "indicia of reliability." Under this theory, the factors previously cited—absence of face-to-face contact at trial, presence of a new attorney, and the lack of classic cross-examination—combined with considerations uniquely tied to Anita to mandate exclusion of her statements. Anita, respondent says, had every reason to lie to avoid prosecution or parental reprobation. Her unknown whereabouts is explicable as an effort to avoid punishment, perjury, or self-incrimination. Given these facts, her prior testimony falls on the unreliable side, and should have been excluded.

In making this argument, respondent in effect asks us to disassociate preliminary hearing testimony previously subjected to cross-examination from previously cross-examined prior-trial testimony, which the Court has deemed generally immune from subsequent confrontation attack. Precedent requires us to decline this invitation. In *Green* the Court found guarantees of trustworthiness in the accounterments of the preliminary hearing itself; there was no mention of the inherent reliability or unreliability of Porter and his story. *See also* Mancusi v. Stubbs, 408 U.S., at 216.

50. On those occasions when the accused is available to be present and neither the identity of the witness, the content of the witness's testimony, nor delay is of critical concern, a deposition to perpetuate testimony is clearly a preferable alternative. Because the deposition to perpetuate testimony, unlike the preservation proceeding, assures admissibility of the witness's testimony as substantive evidence if the witness's testimony proves unavailable, the prosecution has substantial incentive to make use of the deposition procedure when circumstances permit.

51. Ill. R.S., c. 110A, § 412 (1983).

52. If the witness were to testify at trial when called by the government in a manner inconsistent with the testimony given during cross-examination, the prosecution could employ such inconsistent testimony to impeach and as substantive evidence, Rule 801(d)(1)(A).

53. Fed. R. Crim. P. 17 provides:

(a) For Attendance of Witnesses; Form; Issuance. A subpoena shall be issued by the clerk under seal of the court. It shall state the name of the court and the title, if any, of the proceeding, and shall command each person to whom it is directed to attend and give testimony at the time and place specified therein. The clerk shall issue a subpoena, signed and sealed but otherwise in blank to a party requesting it, who shall fill in the blanks before it is served. A subpoena shall be issued by a United States magistrate in a proceeding before him, but it need not be under the seal of the court.

* * *

(d) Service. A subpoena may be served by the marshall, by his deputy or by any other person who is not a party and who is not less than 18 years of age. Service of a subpoena shall be made by delivering a copy thereof to the person named and by tendering to him the fee for 1 day's attendance and the mileage allowed by law. Fees and mileage need not be tendered to the witness upon service of a subpoena issued in behalf of the United States or an officer or agency thereof.

* * *

(g) Contempt. Failure by any person without adequate excuse to obey a subpoena served upon him may be deemed by contempt of the court from which the subpoena issued or of the court for the district in which it issued if it was issued by a United States magistrate.

* * *

Service of a subpoena would be greatly facilitated by having subpoenas issued in blank to police officers to be filled out and served on occurrence witnesses at the scene. This would avoid the problem of having to relocate and serve the witness at some later time with a subpoena. By the time a subpoena would otherwise issue, the witness may already have decided that he or she will be hard to find. Moreover, in the unusual case, if standing procedures admit, the police officer could issue a subpoena for the immediate presence of the witness and accompany the witness to court.

54. *See* Fed. R. Crim. P. 15(d)(2).

55. It is uniformly agreed in similar contexts that objections about form of the question and those that can be obviated if raised must be made at the time of taking

or are waived. *See, e.g.*, Fed. R. Civ. P. 32(d)(3) relating to depositions.

56. Necessity of objecting on other grounds such as hearsay is not so easily handled. Florida Rule of Criminal Procedure 3.190(j) provides in connection with depositions to preserve testimony that the rules governing discovery in civil actions apply, that is, objections other than to form are preserved until trial. Uniform Rule of Criminal Procedure 431(i) in in accord. However Federal Rule of Criminal Procedure 15(f) states that "Objections to deposition testimony or evidence or parts thereof and the grounds for the objection shall be stated at the time of the taking of the deposition." 4 D. Louisell and C. Mueller, *Federal Evidence* § 487 at 1076-78 (Rochester: Lawyers Cooperative, 1980), favors the nonwaiver approach:

> First, Rule 804(b)(1) addresses only the hearsay issue. Thus a statement within the exception remains excludable on objection based upon some other ground if live testimony by the declarant of like effect would be excludable upon such objection. This principle is beyond reasonable dispute where the objecting party (or in civil cases his predecessor in interest) lacked an opportunity in the prior proceeding to assert the objection. The principle should apply, however, even though the objecting party (or in civil cases his predecessor in interest) did have an opportunity in the prior proceeding to object, but did not do so, except perhaps where privilege was the ground of objection and the failure to object amounts to a waiver of the privilege. An objection, however, to the form of the testimony, such as one which complains that the question was leading or the answer unresponsive or too much in the form of an opinion or conclusion, should not be permitted to block the receipt of a statement which otherwise qualifies as former testimony. These principles apply to depositions taken in civil actions, when offered in the trial of the very action in which they were taken, and should apply to former testimony in general.

It is improper to consider that an accused who is not present and did not select an attorney somehow waived anything. What is being suggested is that certain objections should be made at the preservation proceedings to make the determination of circumstantial guarantees of trustworthiness as accurate as possible. In this regard the presiding officer in the interests of justice should interject with respect to matters of form or obviable deficiencies if designated counsel fails to object.

57. The fact that the trial attorney for the accused will be different reduces the preparation effect of such cross-examination.

58. F. Bailey and H. Rothblatt, *Successful Techniques for Criminal Trials* § 25 at 26 (Rochester: Lawyers Cooperative, 1971).

59. Prosecutors prepare witnesses to respond to questions on cross-examination at trial by exploring such matters in advance with the witness, usually in the form of a mock cross-examination.

60. Coleman v. Alabama, 399 U.S. 1, 9 (1970) ("[T]he skilled interrogation of witnesses [at the preservation proceeding] by an experienced lawyer can fashon a vital impeachment tool for use in cross-examination of the State's witnesses at the trial.").

61. If the witness proves unavailable at trial and the witness's testimony at the preservation proceeding is admitted, matters bearing upon credibility, whether or not explored on cross-examination at the preservation proceeding, are admissible. Fed. R. Evid. 806 provides:

Attacking and Supporting Credibilty of Declarant

When a hearsay statement, or a statement defined in Rule 801(d)(2), (C), (D), or (E), has been admitted in evidence, the credibility of the declarant may be attacked, and if attacked may be supported, by any evidence which would be admissible for those purposes if declarant had testified as a witness. Evidence of a statement or conduct by the declarant at any time, inconsistent with his hearsay statement, is not subject to any requirement that he may have been afforded an opportunity to deny or explain. If the party against whom a hearsay statement has been admitted calls the declarant as a witness, the party is entitled to examine him on the statement as if under cross-examination.

62. Fed. R. Evid. 611(a) provides:

Mode and Order of Interrogation and Presentation

(a) Control by Court. The court shall exercise reasonable control over the mode and order of interrogating witnesses and presenting evidence so as to (1) make the interrogation and presentation effective for the ascertainment of the truth, (2) avoid needless consumption of time, and (3) protect witnesses from harassment or undue embarrassment.

63. Fed. R. Evid. 614 provides:

Calling and Interrogation of Witnesses by Court

(a) Calling by Court. The court may, on its own motion or at the suggestion of a party, call witnesses, and all parties are entitled to cross-examine witnesses thus called.

(b) Interrogation by Court. The court may interrogate witnesses, whether called by itself or by a party.

(c) Objections. Objections to the calling of witnesses by the court or to interrogation by it may be made at the time or at the next available opportunity when the jury is not present.

64. *See, e.g.*, United States v. Barbour, 420 F.2d 1319, 1320-21 (D.C. Cir. 1969) ("A trial judge is not a 'mere moderator'; his function extends to necessary assistance to 'the inexperienced laymen in the [jury] box in finding the truth in the confusing conflicts of contradictory evidence.' * * * Thus we have recognized 'the right of a trial judge to make proper inquiry of any witness when he deems that the end of justice may be served thereby.' "); United States v. Shursen, 649 F.2d 1250, 1254 (8th Cir. 1981) ("While it is true that the judge interrupted frequently and actively, he did so primarily because the witnesses gave vague, evasive or inconsistent testimony. 'It is the trial court's duty to clarify the testimony of a witness in order to avoid any misunderstanding of the testimony by the jury.' United States v. Cooper, 596 F.2d 327, 330 (8th Cir. 1979).").

In this context it does not appear essential that the presiding officer maintain an appearance of neutrality. In fact, it would probably assist the determination of trustworthiness if the officer maintained an appearance of skepticism. The preservation proceeding thus differs from the situation in which the court is inquiring of the witness before a jury where an appearance of neutrality must be maintained. *See, e.g.*, United States v. Marzano, 149 F.2d 923, 926 (2d Cir. 1945) (the court may question a witness but "he must not take on the role of a partisan; he must not enter the lists; he must not by his ardor induce the jury to join in a hue and cry against the accused. Prosecution and judgment are two quite separate functions in the administration of justice; they must not merge."); United States v. Wheeler, 444 F.2d 385, 390 (10th Cir. 1971) ("The trial judge is allowed to participate in a trial and ask questions of witnesses in order to ascertain the facts. He cannot show hostility toward one side or become an advocate for one side. The record here reveals that the judge's question to the witness was for the sole purpose of clarifying the facts. The question was within the realm of the judge's discretion. It did not prejudice the rights of the accused. It was a leading question asked to clarify a point important in the search for truth. The trial court may ask a leading question. Riley v. Goodman, 315 F.2d 232 (3rd Cir. 1963)."); United States v. Haro-Espinosa, 619 F.2d 789, 795 (9th Cir. 1980) ("It is entirely proper for the court to question witnesses in order to clarify questions and develop facts, so long as questions are nonprejudicial in form and tone, and the court does not become personally overinvolved. United States v. Landof, 591 F.2d 36, 39 (9th Cir. 1978). Here, the court questioned the witness only after redirect and recross-examinations had been conducted by counsel. The court's questions sought only to clarify the witness's confusing use of the terms 'possibility' and 'probability.' "); United States v. Bartlett, 633 F.2d 1184, 1188 (5th Cir. 1981) ("Following our common law heritage, a judge is not a mere moderator, and he has an obligation and duty to question witnesses and comment on the evidence when necessary. * * * In fact a trial judge may elicit facts not yet adduced or clarify those previously presented and he may maintain the pace of the trial by interrupting and curtailing counsel's examination as a matter of discretion. Only when the judge's conduct strays from neutrality is a defendant thereby denied a fair trial as required by the Constitution. *See* United States v. Middlebrooks, 618 F.2 272, 277 (5th Cir. 1980); United States v. Daniels, 572 F.2d 535, 541 (5th Cir. 1978).").

65. For example, the witness's record of arrests and convictions made available by the prosecution may be inconsistent with the witness's response. Other extrinsic evidence if particularly critical could be submitted in the form of an affidavit.

66. *See* Ilinois Supreme Court Rule 412(a)(i), *supra* and text accompanying note 51. *See also* People ex rel. Fisher v. Carey, 77 Ill.2d 259, 32 Ill.Dec. 904, 396 N.E. 2d 17 (1979) (a police report containing verbatim statements of a witness to be called at a preliminary hearing is subject to a subpoena duces tecum served on behalf of the defendant prior to a preliminary hearing but subsequent to charging of an accused, that is, when it becomes clear what offenses an accused will be finally charged with).

67. Fed. R. Crim. P. 26(b)(2):

> (2) Information Not Subject to Disclosure. Except as provided in paragraphs (A), (B), and (D) of subdivision (a)(1), this rule does not authorize the discovery or inspection of reports, memoranda, or other internal government documents made by the attorney for the government or other government agents in connection with the investigation or prosecution of the case, or of statements made by government witnesses or prospective government witnesses except as provided in 18 U.S.C. § 3500.

18 U.S.C. § 3500(a) states:

> (a) In any criminal prosecution brought by the United States, no statement or report in the possession of the United States which was made by a Government witness or prospective Government witness (other than the defendant) shall be the subject of subpoena, discovery, or inspection until said witness has testified on direct examination in the trial of the case.

68. Fed. R. Evid. 804(b)(1) provides:

> ***Former Testimony***
>
> (b) Hearsay Exceptions. The following are not excluded by the hearsay rule if the declarant is unavailable as a witness:
>
> (1) Former Testimony. Testimony given as a witness at another hearing of the same or a different proceeding, or in a deposition taken in compliance with law in the course of the same or another proceeding, if the party against whom the testimony is now offered, or, in a civil action or proceeding, a predecessor in interest, had an opportunity and similar motive to develop the testimony by direct, cross, or redirect examination.

69. The Report of the House Committee on the Judiciary states:

> Rule 804(b)(1) as submitted by the Court allowed prior testimony of an unavailable witness to be admissible if the party against whom it is offered or a person "with motive and interest similar" to his had an opportunity to examine the witness. The Committee considered that it is generally unfair to impose upon the party against whom the hearsay evidence is being offered responsibility for the manner in which the witness was previously handled by another party. The sole exception to this, in the Committee's view, is when a party's predecessor in interest in a civil action or proceeding had an opportunity and similar motive to examine the witness. The Committee amended the Rule to reflect these policy determinations.

70. *See* Ohio v. Roberts, 448 U.S. 56, 68-70 (1980):

> In [California v. Green, 399 U.S. 149 (1970)] at the preliminary hearing, a youth named Porter identified Green as a drug supplier. When called to the stand at Green's trial, however, Porter professed a lapse of memory. Frustrated in its attempt to adduce live testimony, the prosecution offered Porter's prior statements. The trial judge ruled the evidence admissible, and substantial portions of the preliminary hearing transcript were read to the jury. This Court found no error. . . . [T]he Court rejected Green's Confrontation Clause attack. It reasoned:
>
> > "Porter's statement at the preliminary hearing had already been given under circumstances closely approximating those that surround the typical trial. Porter was under oath; respondent was represented by counsel—the same counsel in fact who later represented him at the trial; respondent had every opportunity to cross-examine Porter as to his statement; and the proceedings were conducted before a judicial tribunal, equipped to provide a judicial record of the hearings." 399 U.S., at 165.

These factors, the Court concluded, provided all that the Sixth Amendment demands: "substantial compliance with the purposes behind the confrontation requirement." *Id.*, at 166.

This passage and others in the *Green* opinion suggest that the opportunity to cross-examine at the preliminary hearing—even absent actual cross-examination—satisfies the Confrontation Clause. Yet the record showed, and the Court recognized, that defense counsel in fact had cross-examined Porter at the earlier proceeding. *Id.*, at 151. Thus, Mr. Justice Brennan, writing in dissent, could conclude only that "[p]erhaps" "the mere opportunity for face-to-face encounter [is] sufficient." *Id.*, at 200, n.8.

* * *

We need not decide whether the Supreme Court of Ohio correctly dismissed statements in *Green* suggesting that the mere opportunity to cross-examine rendered the prior testimony admissible. . . . Nor need we decide whether de minimus questioning is sufficient, for defense counsel in this case tested Anita's testimony with the equivalent of significant cross-examination.

See also Chapter 4, Section B2 *supra.*

71. Mason v. United States, 408 F.2d 903, 906 (10th Cir. 1969) ("We consider, as did the trial court, that the important element is whether the *testimony* of the witness is sought and is available and not whether the witness's body is available.") (emphasis in original). *See also* McCormick, *Evidence* § 253 at 608 (Cleary ed. 1972) ("[W]hile the rather general practice is to speak loosely of unavailability of the witness, the critical factor is actually the unavailability of his testimony. . . . [T]he witness may be physically present in court but his testimony nevertheless unavailable.").

72. United States v. Lieberman, 637 F.2d 95, 103 (2d Cir. 1980) ("There is no question that Gaines was unavailable to testify. He was a defendant, and the government could not call him as a witness. *See* Fed. R. Evid. 804(a)(1)."). When the witness is also a codefendant, an express assertion of a Fifth Amendment privilege has not been required. United States v. Thomas, 571 F.2d 285 (5th Cir. 1978).

73. United States v. Elmore, 423 F.2d 775, 778 (4th Cir. 1970) ("The requirement that the declarant be unavailable to testify is satisfied by the fact that West successfully asserted his fifth amendment privilege against self-incrimination and declined to answer any questions about the matter."); United States v. Oropeza, 564 F.2d 316, 325 n.8 (9th Cir. 1977) ("[E]xpress claim of privilege and a ruling thereon should be made."). *See also* Advisory Committee's Note to Rule 804(a)(1) ("A ruling by the judge is required, which clearly implies that an actual claim of privilege must be made.").

74. United States v. Zappola, 646 F.2d 48, 54 (2d Cir. 1981) ("In United States v. Oliver, 626 F.2d 254 (2d Cir. 1980), this circuit held that an order from the court is an essential component in a declaration of unavailability under Rule 804(a)(2). *Id.* at 261. It is clear that in this case, the district court did not order Marano to testify. Instead, the district court relied on his assertion that he would refuse to testify even if ordered to by the court. The procedure that should have been followed by the court when faced with Marano's refusal to testify was (1) the issuance of an order, outside the presence of the jury, directing him to testify and (2) a warning the continued refusal to testify despite the court's order would be punishable by contempt.").

75. United States v. Mobley, 421 F.2d 354, 350-51 (5th Cir. 1970) ("Oliver's silence in reliance, albeit misplaced, upon Fifth Amendment rights, makes him no less unavailable than death or absence from the country or physical inability to speak.").

76. McDonnell v. United States, 472 F.2d 1153, 1155 (8th Cir. 1973) ("Since [the witness] testified to a lack of memory as to a material portion of the subject matter of his prior testimony, he would be 'unavailable' under Rule 804 and his former testimony on the subject would be admissible. Such a rule of evidence is supported by textwriters and case law. *See generally*, M. Ladd and R. Carlson, *Cases and Materials on Evidence*, 1001-1025 (1972); McCormick, *Evidence*, 611-12 (Cleary ed. 1972.").

77. A witness who has testified under oath at a preliminary hearing, before the grand jury, at a perpetuation deposition, at a preservation proceeding, or otherwise is more likely to claim lack of recollection if intimidated than to testify inconsistently with prior testimony for two reasons. First, lack of recollection, unlike inconsistent testimony, does not lead to automatic admissibility of the prior statement. *See* Rule 801(d)(1)(A) discussed in Chapter 4, Section C1 *supra*. Second, an inconsistent statement testified to at trial may lead to a perjury prosecution when the prior statement was also given under oath.

78. Mattox v. United States, 156 U.S. 237 (1895).

79. United States v. Hughes, 411 F.2d 461 (2d Cir. 1969) (supervening schizophrenia). *See also* C. McCormick, *Evidence* § 253 at 611 (Cleary ed. 1972) ("The decisions, in general terms, recognize insanity as a ground of unavailability. They do not discuss the question whether the derangement must be such that it disqualifies the person from testifying about the matter in question. Of course, not all insanity renders the witness so incompetent. Competency to testify requires only a minimum degree of ability to observe, remember and recount. If the person is proved to have become insane since the hearsay statement was made, it seems that the admission of the statement should depend not on whether the subsequent insanity has rendered the witness incompetent, but whether having in mind the witness's later loss of mental powers the previous statement is probably substantially more reliable than the present testimony of the insane person would be, a question upon which some discretion must be conceded to the trial court.").

80. United States v. Bell, 500 F.2d 1287 (2d Cir. 1974) (surgery incapacitating witness for two and one-half months).

81. United States v. Faison, 679 F.2d 292, 296-97 3d Cir. 1982):

> In this instance, the trial court decided that Mancuso, who was in the hospital suffering from a heart attack, was unavailable. The court therefore admitted Mancuso's earlier testimony and refused Faison's request for an adjournment so that Mancuso could be heard live. There is no question Mancuso was too sick to testify at the time of trial. That is not, however, dispositive. Our inquiry, instead, is whether the District Court properly exercised discretion in not adjourning the trial for a reasonable period to afford the witness enough time to recover from an illness which might be temporary, and thus to be available once more for live testimony.
>
> * * * On the date that the trial court made its determination not to adjourn, the court had before it information that Mancuso was about to undergo coronary

bypass surgery and would not be available to testify for at least four to five weeks after the surgery.

* * *

The trial judge's discretion on granting an adjournment for witnesses unavailable due to illness must be guided on the one hand by the policy of favoring live testimony and confrontation in the presence of the factfinder and, on the other, by the policy, manifested in the Speedy Trial Act, 18 U.S.C. § 3161 (1976), of prompt disposition of criminal trials. Moreover, since the witness availability affects the court's ability to manage its cases, the trial court's decision to refuse an adjournment and to admit prior testimony must be treated with respectful deference. In exercising discretion a trial judge must consider all relevant circumstances, including the importance of the absent witness for the case; the nature and extent of cross-examination in the earlier testimony; the nature of the illness; the expected time of recovery; the reliability of the evidence of the probable duration of the illness; any special circumstances counselling against delay. It is essential for appellate review that the district judge elaborate his considerations and explain his reasons for admitting prior testimony rather than granting a reasonable continuance. Such an analysis on the record would permit us to review the soundness of the District Court's exercise of discretion, and to insure that the relevant variables were considered.

Applying the above standards to this record, we hold that the District Court abused his discretion by not adjourning Faison's trial for a reasonable period. Here Mancuso was an important witness against defendant. The live cross-examination of such a witness before a jury, even if not constitutionally mandated, ought not to be lightly dispensed with. The fact that the first trial yielded a hung jury suggests that the evidence against defendant had weaknesses. The District Court should have been especially careful that the omission of live cross-examination of Mancuso before the new jury not tip the balance in a close case against defendant.

See also Peterson v. United States, 344 F.2d 419, 425 (5th Cir. 1965) ("In criminal prosecutions, according to the weight of authority, the mere temporary illness or disability of a witness is not sufficient to justify the reception of his former testimony."). *Compare* United States v. Amaya, 533 F.2d 188, 191 (5th Cir. 1976) ("Although the duration of an illness is a proper element of unavailability, the establishment of permanence as to the particular illness is not an absolute requirement. The duration of the illness need only be in probability long enough so that, with proper regard to the importance of the testimony, the trial cannot be postponed. 5 Wigmore, *Evidence* § 1406(a) (Chadbourn rev. 1974)."); United States v. Bell, 500 F.2d 1287, 1290 (2d Cir. 1974) ("We disagree with *Peterson supra,* if indeed it meant to imply that in every case where a witness is ill but will sometime recover, the prosecution must suffer a continuance [in this instance, one of several months . . .] or forego entirely the use of the evidence."). *See generally*, 4 *Weinstein's Evidence* ¶ 804(a)[01] at 804-40 (1979) ("In a civil case, or in a criminal case where defendant offers the hearsay statement, it is easier to find unavailability even when the disability is only temporary. In such a case, Wigmore's formula may be appropriate: 'The duration of the illness need only be in probability such that with regard to the importance of the testimony the trial cannot be postponed.' [5 Wigmore, *Evidence* §

1406(a) at 219 (Chadbourn Rev. 1974)]. This is a matter for the trial judge's discretion. In reaching his decision he may consider such factors as the nature of the disability and its expected duration, the length of time the case has been pending and whether delays, if any, are attributable to the proponent of the hearsay, the nature of the case, the significance of the disabled witness' testimony, the availability of other evidence on the same point, and whether the nature of the expected testimony and the subject of the hearsay statement is such that cross-examination would be expected to be particularly helpful.'').

82. United States v. Losada, 674 F.2d 167, 172 (2d Cir. 1982):

> Rule 804(a)(5) provides that prior testimony of a witness is admissible if he is absent ''and the proponent of his statement has been unable to procure his attendance . . . by process or other reasonable means.'' Lemos is a Colombian citizen living in Colombia and is not subject to compulsory process. The only issue, therefore, is whether the government used ''other reasonable means,'' such as a voluntary request, to obtain his attendance.
>
> We find that the government did make a reasonable attempt to obtain his attendance. The government submitted an affidavit and memorandum detailing its efforts to obtain Lemos' attendance. Judge Dooling properly accepted the government's representations and ruled that Lemos' prior testimony was admissible. Absent any showing whatsoever by Jesus that the government could have obtained the presence of Lemos at trial, or that it had cited in bad faith, there is no basis for disturbing Judge Dooling's ruling.;

United States v. Mann, 590 F.2d 361, 367 (1st Cir. 1978):

> Courts have consistently held that, pursuant to Rule 804(a)(5), the proponent must show at least a good faith effort to procure the witness' attendance. Even where the absent witness is beyond the court's jurisdiction, ''the government must show diligent effort on its part to secure the [witness] voluntary return to testify.'' Government of the Virgin Islands v. Acquino, 378 F2d 540, 551 (3d Cir. 1967). Furthermore, the effort must be ''genuine and bona fide.'' *Id.* at 552. *See also* United States v. Mathis, 550 F.2d 180 (4th Cir. 1976); United States v. Lynch, 163 U.S. App.D.C. 6, 18, 499 F.2d 1011, 1023 (1974). *Cf.* Phillips v. Wyrick, 558 F.2d 489, 494 (8th Cir. 1977) (requiring good faith effort as an aspect of the Sixth Amendment right to confrontation). In *Lynch* the court held that the admission of preliminary hearing testimony at trial was erroneous because the government had failed to show ''a search exercised both in good faith and with reasonable diligence and care.'' 163 U.S.App.D.C. at 18, 499 F.2d at 1023. After detailing the efforts the police had made to find the witnesses on the day she was to testify, the court said, ''It is difficult to believe that if the preliminary hearing testimony of this critical witness were not available, the prosecution would have abandoned its efforts at this point to locate [the witness] and concluded its case.'' *Id.* at 19, 499 F.2d at 1024.
>
> Here the witness is vital to the government's case. The government did not make as vigorous an attempt to secure the presence of the witness as it would have made if it did not have the prior recorded testimony. The language of Rule 804(a)(5) suggests that ''other reasonable means'' besides subpoenas must be tried before a witness can be found unavailable. This relatively high good faith

standard cannot be satisfied by perfunctory efforts, if the rule is not to sanction the government's procuring depositions of witnesses, especially shaky witnesses, but then discourage attempts to bring the witness to trial so long as the government is satisfied with what is in the transcript.

83. Fed. R. Crim. P. 17 states:

(e) Place of Service.

(1) In United States. A subpoena requiring the attendance of a witness at a hearing or trial may be served at any place within the United States.

(2) Abroad. A subpoena directed to a witness in a foreign country shall issue under the circumstances and in the manner and be served as provided in Title 28, U.S.C. § 1783.

28 U.S.C.A. § 1783 provides that a federal court may issue a subpoena to a United States national or resident present in a foreign country, "if the court finds that particular testimony . . . by him is necessary in the interest of justice, and, in other than a criminal action or proceeding, if the court finds, in addition that it is not possible to obtain his testimony in admissible form without his personal appearance."

84. "In all criminal prosecutions, the accused shall enjoy the right . . . to be confronted with the witnesses against him." United States Constitution, Amendment VI.

85. Barber v. Page, 390 U.S. 719, 723-25 (1968):

We start with the fact that the State made absolutely no effort to obtain the presence of Woods at trial other than to ascertain that he was in a federal prison outside Oklahoma. It must be acknowledged that various courts and commentators have heretofore assumed that the mere absence of a witness from the jurisdiction was sufficient ground for dispensing with confrontation on the theory that " it is impossible to compel his attendance, because the process of the trial Court is of no force without the jurisdiction, and the party desiring his testimony is therefore helpless." 5 Wigmore, *Evidence* § 1404 (3d ed. 1940).

Whatever may have been the accuracy of that theory at one time, it is clear that at the present time increased cooperation between the States and the Federal Government has largely deprived it of any continuing validity in the criminal law. For example, in the case of a prospective witness currently in federal custody, 28 U.S.C. § 2241(c)(5) gives federal courts the power to issue writs of habeas corpus *ad testificandum* at the request of state prosecutorial authorities. . . . In addition, it is the policy of the United States Bureau of Prisons to permit federal prisoners to testify in state court criminal proceedings pursuant to writs of habeas corpus *ad testificandum* issued out of state courts. . . . In short, a witness is not "unavailable" for purposes of the foregoing exception to the confrontation requirement unless the prosecutorial authorities have made a good-faith effort to obtain his presence at trial.;

Id. at 723-24 n.4 states:

For witnesses not in prison, the Uniform Act to Secure the Attendance of Witnesses from Without a State in Criminal Proceedings provides a means by which prosecuting authorities from one State can obtain an order from a court in the State where the witness is found directing the witness to appear in court in the first State to testify. The State seeking his appearance must pay the witness a specified sum as a travel allowance and compensation for his time. As of 1967 the Uniform Act was in force in 45 States, the District of Columbia, the Canal Zone, Puerto Rico, and the Virgin Islands. *See* 9 Uniform Laws Ann. 50 (1967 Supp.) For witnesses in prison, quite probably many state courts would utilize the common-law writ of habeas corpus *ad testificandum* at the request of prosecutorial authorities of a sister State upon a showing that adequate safeguards to keep the prisoner in custody would be maintained.;

Mancusi v. Stubbs, 408 U.S. 204, 212-13 (1972):

The Uniform Act to secure the attendance of witnesses from without a State, the availability of federal writs of habeas corpus *ad testificandum*, and the established practice of the United States Bureau of Prisons to honor state writs of habeas corpus *ad testificandum*, all supported the Court's conclusion in *Barber* that the State had not met its obligations to make a good-faith effort to obtain the presence of the witness merely by showing that he was beyond the boundaries of the prosecuting State. There have been, however, no corresponding developments in the area of obtaining witnesses between this country and foreign nations. Upon discovering that Holm resided in a foreign nation, the State of Tennessee so far as this record shows was powerless to compel his attendance at the second trial, either through its own process or through established procedures depending on the voluntary assistance of another government. . . . We therefore hold that the predicate of unavailability was sufficiently stronger here than in *Barber* that a federal habeas court was not warranted in upsetting the determination of the state trial court as to Holm's unavailability.

86. Ohio v. Roberts, 448 U.S. 56, 74-77 (1980):

The basic litmus of Sixth Amendment unavailability is established, "[A] witness is not 'unavailable' for purposes of . . . the exception to the confrontation requirement unless the prosecutorial authorities have made a *good-faith effort* to obtain his presence at trial." Barber v. Page, 390 U.S. at 724-25 (emphasis added). *Accord*, Mancusi v. Stubbs, *supra*; Green v. California, 399 U.S. at 161-162, 166, 167 n.16; Berger v. California, 393 U.S. 314 (1969).

Although it might be said that the Court's prior cases provide no further refinement of this statement of the rule, certain general propositions safely emerge. The law does not require the doing of a futile act. Thus, if no possibility of procuring the witness exists (as, for example, the witness' intervening death), "good faith" demands nothing of the prosecution. But if there is a possibility, albeit remote, that affirmative measures might produce the declarant, the obligation of good faith may demand their effectuation. "The lengths to which the prosecution must go to produce a witness . . . is a question of reasonableness." California v. Green, 399 U.S. at 189 n.22 (concurring opinion, citing Barber v. Page, *supra*). The ultimate question is whether the witness is unavailable despite good-faith efforts undertaken prior to trial to locate and present that witness. As with other evidentiary proponents, the prosecution bears the burden of establishing this predicate.

On the facts presented we hold that the trial court and the Supreme Court of Ohio correctly concluded that Anita's unavailability, in the constitutional sense, was established.

At the voir dire hearing, called for by the defense, it was shown that some four months prior to the trial the prosecutor was in touch with Amy Isaacs and discussed with her Anita's whereabouts. It may appropriately be inferred that Mrs. Isaacs told the prosecutor essentially the same facts to which she testified at voir dire: that the Isaacs had last heard from Anita during the preceding summer; that she was not then in San Francisco, but was traveling outside Ohio; and that the Isaacs and their other children knew of no way to reach Anita even in an emergency. This last fact takes on added significance when it is recalled that Anita's parents earlier had undertaken affirmative efforts to reach their daughter when the social worker's inquiry came in from San Francisco. This is not a case of parents abandoning all interest in an absent daughter.

The evidence of record demonstrates that the prosecutor issued a subpoena to Anita at her parents' home, not only once, but on five separate occasions over a period of several months. In addition, at the voir dire argument, the prosecutor stated to the court that respondent "witnessed that I have attempted to locate, I have subpoenaed, there has been a voir dire of the witness' parents, and they have not been able to locate her for over a year." App. 12.

Given these facts, the prosecution did not breach its duty of good-faith effort. To be sure, the prosecutor might have tried to locate by telephone the San Francisco social worker with whom Mrs. Isaacs had spoken many months before and have undertaken other steps in an effort to find Anita. One, in hindsight, may always think of other things. Nevertheless, the great improbability that such efforts would have resulted in locating the witness, and would have led to her production at trial, neutralizes any intimation that a concerpt of reasonableness required their execution. We accept as a general rule, of course, the proposition that "the possibility of a refusal is not the equivalent of asking and receiving a rebuff." Barber v. page, 390 U.S. at 724, quoting from the dissenting opinion in that case in the Court of Appeals (381 F.2d 479, 481 (C.A.10 1966). But the service and ineffectiveness of the five subpoenas and the conversation with Anita's mother were far more than mere reluctance to face the possibility of a refusal. It was investigation at the last-known real address, and it was conversation with a parent who was concerned about her daughter's whereabouts.

Barber and *Mancusi v. Stubbs, supra*, are the cases in which this Court has explored the issue of constitutional unavailability. Although each is factually distinguishable from this case, *Mancusi* provides significant support for a conclusion of good-faith effort here, and *Barber* has no contrary significance. Insofar as this record discloses no basis for concluding that Anita was abroad, the case is factually weaker than *Mancusi*; but it is stronger than *Mancusi* in the sense that the Ohio prosecutor, unlike the prosecutor in *Mancusi*, had no clear indication, if any at all, of Anita's whereabouts. In *Barber*, the court found an absence of good-faith effort where the prosecution made no attempt to secure the presence of a declarant incarcerated in a federal penitentiary in a neighboring State. There, the prosecution knew where the witness was, procedures existed whereby the witness could be brought to the trial, and the witness was not in a position to frustrate efforts to secure his production. Here, Anita's whereabouts were not known, and there was no assurance that she would be found in a place from which she could be forced to return to Ohio.

We conclude that the prosecution carried its burden of demonstrating that

Anita was constitutionally unavailable for purposes of respondent's trial.

87. United States v. Amaya, 533 F.2d 188 (5th Cir. 1976); United States v. Pelton, 578 F.2d 701 (8th Cir. 1978).

88. Motes v. United States, 178 U.S. 458, 474, (1900) (prior testimony excluded when the unavailability of the witness at trial was due to the "negligence" of the United States in removing him from custody before the trial and permitting him to stay in the custody of another government witness in a hotel room from which he escaped rather than in jail); United States v. Mathis, 550 F.2d 180, 181-82 (4th Cir. 1976) ("Karen Jones was not available to testify in person because she could not be located; inadvertently she had been released from a District of Columbia penal institution pursuant to a court order requiring the release of another prisoner bearing the same name. Jones' prior testimony was admissible under Rule 804 of the Federal Rules of Evidence if her attendance at the trial could not be procured by process or other reasonable means. Rule 804(a)(5). The record shows that reasonable efforts were made to find her, but to no avail. Motes v. United States, 178 U.S. 458, 20 S.Ct. 993, 44 L.Ed. 1150 (1900) is inapposite. In the instant case, unlike *Motes*, the disappearance of Jones was due to inadvertence, not reckless disregard of an obligation to produce her, and there is no evidence that the prison official who released her knew that she would be needed as a witness."); United States v. Rothbart, 653 F.2d 462, 466 (10th Cir. 1981) ("[T]he government in the case before us not only failed to make a good-faith effort to obtain Mitchell's presence at trial, but cleared existing obstacles to his journey outside the jurisdiction of the court by taking his deposition and releasing him from subpoena. Thus, Rothbart's constitutional right to be confronted by the witnesses against him was violated."); United States v. Puckett, 692 F.2d 6634, 670 (10th Cir. 1982) ("The trial court did not abuse its discretion by ruling that Krown's inability to procure the attendance of Messrs. Delman and Osserman was attributable to his attorney's tardiness to attempt to subpoena those witnesses until near the end of the second week of trial.").

89. *See* Fed. R. Evid. 806 set forth at note 61 *supra*.

90. *See* Chapter 4, Section I *supra*, discussing intimidation as a ground for deciding that the accused waived his objective to admission of an unavailable declarant's prior statement under both the hearsay rule and the Confrontation Clause. If intimidation alone can cause courts to declare a constitutional right to have been waived, it most certainly will be overvalued by the court in determining equivalent circumstantial guarantees of trustworthiness. The desire to punish one who has attempted to subvert the adjudicatory system is simply too strong—if considered, it will be controlling.

91. 448 U.S. 56, 66 (1980).

Chapter 8

Conclusion

Traditionally, the criminal justice system in this country has been offender oriented, focusing on the apprehension, prosecution, punishment, and rehabilitation of wrongdoers. Victims and witnesses have been considered only to the extent that they play a role in the identification and prosecution of offenders. Although the criminal justice system clearly understood it could not function without the assistance and cooperation of victims and witnesses, little if any effort was expended on their behalf. Victims of crime remained uncompensated by either the convicted defendant or the state for their losses. Only sporadic efforts were made to reduce the frustrations and economic sacrifices that involvement in criminal proceedings as a witness causes. Of more immediate concern, almost nothing was done to address the specific plight of the intimidated witness.

This attitude began to change a little more than a decade ago. During the last few years a strong national victim and witness assistance movement has had noticeable success in increasing the public's overall awareness of the problems and concerns of victims and witnesses. Today thousands of local assistance programs exist throughout the country to respond to the special needs of victims and witnesses. Special effort has been made to reduce the chance of a victim or witness being intimidated. Under the leadership of the National Organization for Victim Assistance, community organizations, church groups, bar associations, and service groups have been instrumental in bringing about this change in attitude and with it the beginnings of meaningful remedial action.

At the national level, the American Bar Association approved its recommendations on victim/witness intimidation in 1980. Congress enacted the Victim and Witness Protection Act of 1982. Later that same year the President's Task Force on Victims of Crime's final report was issued.

December 1983 saw the National Conference of the Judiciary on the Rights of Victims of Crime, held at the National Judicial College, Reno, Nevada, issue a similar call for action by all segments of our society involved in the criminal justice system. State legislatures have been active in responding to victim and witness needs as well.[1] Legislatures in 39 states have now enacted measures to provide compensation to victims of crime. Some states have enacted legislation encouraging courts to order criminal offenders to make restitution to their victims. States have also enacted legislation to assist victims and witnesses in understanding and participating in the criminal justice process. Twelve states have enacted comprehensive legislation recognizing a "bill of rights" for crime victims and witnesses.[2]

The American Bar Association recommendations, the Victims and Witnesses Protection Act of 1982, the Report of the President's Task Force on Victims of Crime, and the call to action by the National Conference on the Judiciary, National Judicial College, are definitely steps in the right direction for reducing witness intimidation. Since the Victims and Witness Protection Act of 1982 and attempts to implement recommendations set forth in the various reports are so recent, there has been very little review of such efforts by those concerned. The United States Department of Justice, Bureau of Justice Statistics has, however, issued a preliminary general assessment.[3] The bureau views the current state of affairs as merely a beginning and believes that "Further efforts are necessary, however, to ensure that the broad scope of victim/witness concerns are met in a comprehensive and effective manner in all jurisdictions."[4] The bureau indicates that new practices and procedures suggested in the various reports will impose substantial operating and financial demands on the criminal justice system and that technical, administrative and policy changes are critical to ensure that the objectives are met.[5] Thus it remains to be seen to what extent the current movement to address the plight of the crime victims will make a truly substantial contribution in obtaining fair treatment for victims and witnesses and in reducing the incidence of witness intimidation.[6]

At present, most out-of-court statements made by a witness to a crime are not admissible as substantive evidence at trial if the witness changes his or her testimony or proves unavailable by virtue of operation of the hearsay rule. Accordingly, there is substantial incentive on the part of criminal defendants to intimidate victims and witnesses and thus prevent the introduction of damaging testimony. Rather than subvert the principle that only trustworthy out-of-court statements be admitted as substantive evidence against the accused through efforts such as use of the waiver doctrine or impeachment in recognition that jurors disregard limiting instructions, procedures should be developed to preserve trustworthy out-of-court statements and admit them as substantive evidence at trial if the witness's testimony is lost by reason of intimidation.

Three specific recommendations are made. First, substantive admissibility of prior inconsistent statements should be expanded beyond that now provided in Rule 801(d)(1)(A) to include all statements possessing adequate assurance of certainty of making. In addition, a requirement of personal knowledge by the declarant about the subject matter of the statement should be imposed to eliminate those statements most subject to fabrication by the witness and most likely to be misapplied by the jury. Second, greater consideration should be given to taking advantage of those procedures that now provide for the perpetuation of testimony of witnesses following formal charge including production of the witness at a preliminary hearing or the taking of a deposition to perpetuate testimony. Unfortunately, practical considerations associated with the preliminary hearing make it less than likely that such increased consideration will result in significantly increased usage. With respect to the perpetuation deposition, the showing of "likelihood of unavailability" generally required by statute is difficult to establish in many cases since concern with potential intimidation is more often based upon experience coupled with hunch than on hard evidence admissible at a hearing. Delay associated with all currently available procedures detracts from their usefulness in combating witness intimidation as does the presence of the accused at the preliminary hearing or perpetuation deposition. Finally, a new proceeding denominated a preservation proceeding designed specifically to preserve the testimony of the witness is suggested. Statements taken at the preservation proceeding would be admissible as substantive evidence if the witness's testimony proves unavailable at trial only if the court finds that equivalent circumstantial guarantees of trustworthiness had been established as required by Rule 804(b)(5). Procedures applicable at the preservation proceeding are designed to increase drastically the probability that the testimony of the witness given at the preservation proceeding will be found to be sufficiently trustworthy.

Implementation of the foregoing proposals with respect to criminal trials in federal court would require amendment to Rule 801(d)(1)(A) and specific authorization to conduct a preservation proceeding. Implementation requirements for the proposals in state court will vary depending upon the particular position now adopted with respect to substantive admissibility of prior inconsistent statements, the availability of depositions to perpetuate testimony, and admissibility of hearsay statements under an exception for "other" trustworthy hearsay. In all instances in state court, specific authorization to conduct a preservation proceeding will be necessary.

Trustworthy testimony preserved and admitted as substantive evidence in accordance with one of the three methods previously discussed will often prevent a guilty defendant who successfully intimidates a witness from going free. In addition, it is hoped that a defendant knowledgeable that a witness's testimony will be admissible at trial even if the witness is intimidated to change his or her testimony or not testify at all will be less likely to intimidate the witness in the first place.

NOTES

1. National Judicial College, *Participant's Manual for Judges in the Rights of Victims and Witnesses* 3 (1984):

> From 1973 to 1983, the number of state-funded victim compensation programs grew from 9 to 39.
>
> From 1973 to 1983, the number of victims service programs soared from a handful of rape crisis centers, a few child abuse programs, and a few general victim assistance programs to literally thousands of program of all types throughout the country, along with state-assisted domestic violence programs in 40 states, state-aided sexual assault programs in over 15 states, and state-subsidized victim/witness programs in some 17 states.
>
> From 1973 to 1983, thought became father of the act as the "victim impact statement" changed from an idea in the mind of James Rowland, Chief Probation Officer of Fresno, California, to a mandatory procedure in 14 states and the Federal court system.
>
> And, from 1973 to 1983, a new form of justice emerged as rights for victims were statutorily defined in twelve states and in the Federal system, through the enactment of the Victim and Witness Protection Act of 1982.

2. The responsibility of the judiciary to respect the interests of victims and witnesses was acknowledged by Chief Justice Burger in *Morris v. Slappy*, ____U.S. ____, ____, 103 S. Ct. 1610, 1617, 75 L.Ed.2d 610, 623 (1983):

> Of course, inconvenience and embarrassment to witnesses cannot justify failing to enforce constitutional rights of an accused. . . . But in the administration of criminal justice, courts may not ignore the concerns of victims. Apart from all other factors, such a course would hardly encourage victims to report violations to the proper authorities; this is especially so when the crime is one calling for public testimony about a humiliating and degrading experience.

3. Bureau of Justice Statistics, U.S. Department of Justice, *Victim and Witness Assistance* 1-7 (May 1983).

4. *Id.* at 1.

5. *Id.* The Crime Victims Fund established by Congress on October 12, 1984, Pub. L. No. 98-473, is a step in the right direction.

6. No effort has been made in this book to evaluate each of the proposals comprising the current movement to address the plight of crime victims. Clearly, any problem with specific components of the basic package will be minor in comparison to the benefits full implementation will bring. There thus seems no point in risking curtailing the impetus the movement has obtained by detailed critical examination likely to be taken out of context. This is not to say that there are not some concerns to be addressed in the future. To name only two: first, it is hard to forsee how a victim's input into the sentencing process, if taken seriously, will always work smoothly in practice, especially in light of the victim's opportunity to receive restitution; second, saddling a financially poor defendant with the burden of making restitution payments over time may conflict with measures designed to convert the defendant from his criminal ways. *See generally*, A. Goldstein, *Defining the Role of the Victim in Criminal Prosecution*, 52 Miss. L. J. 515 (1982). See also, *The Unconstitutionality of the Victim and Witness Protection Act Under the Seventh Amendment*, 84 Colum. L. Rev. 1590 (1984) (relating to ordering restitution).

Bibliography

Abt Associates, Inc. *Compensating Victims of Crime: An Analysis of American Programs.* United States Department of Justice. Washington, D.C., 1982.

Advisory Committee Note on 1974 Amendment to Rule 15. 62 F.R.D. 271 (1974).

American Bar Association, Criminal Justice Section. *Bar Leadership on Victim/Witness Assistance.* Washington, D.C., 1980.

______. *Guidelines for Fair Treatment of Crime Victims and Witnesses.* Washington, D.C., 1983.

______. *Reducing Victim/Witness Intimidation: A Package.* Washington, D.C., 1981.

______. *Victim/Witness Legislation: Considerations for Policymakers.* Washington, D.C., 1981.

American Bar Association, Standards for Criminal Justice. *Discovery and Procedure Before Trial.* Washington, D.C., 1970.

The American Law Institute, *Code of Criminal Procedure* (March 1941).

Amsterdam, A., Segal, B., and Miller, M. *Trial Manual for the Defense of Criminal Cases.* Third Edition. Philadelphia: ALI-ABA, 1974.

Appendix to Compensating Crime Victims: Hearings on H.R. 4257 and Related Bills Before the Subcomm. on Criminal Justice of the Comm. on the Judiciary, 96th Cong., 1st Sess. (1979).

Ash, M. *On Witnesses: A Radical Critique of Criminal Court Procedures.* 48 Notre Dame Lawyer 386 (1972).

Bailey, F., and Rothblatt, H. *Successful Techniques for Criminal Trials.* Rochester: Lawyers Cooperative, 1971.

Bard, M., and Sangrey, D. *The Crime Victims Book.* New York: Basic Books, 1979.

Barnett, R. E., and Hagel, J. *Assessing the Criminal: Restitution, Retribution, and and the Legal Process.* Cambridge, Mass.: Ballinger, 1977.

Bein, F. *Prior Inconsistent Statements: The Hearsay Rule, 801(d)(1)(A) and 803(24).* 26 U.C.L.A. L. Rev. 967 (1979).

Blakey, W. *Substantive Use of Prior Inconsistent Statements Under the Federal Rules of Evidence.* 64 Ky. L. J. 3 (1976).

Bloom, M. *The Witness: Forgotten Men*. National Civil Review. October 1974.

Brennan, W. *The Criminal Prosecution: Sporting Event or Quest for Truth*. 1963 Wash. U. L. Q. 279.

Bureau of Justice Statistics, U.S. Department of Justice. *Victim and Witness Assistance*. May 1983.

Callow, W. C. *Crime and Consequences*. 20 The Judges Journal 34 (1981).

Cannavale, F., and Falcon, W. *Witness Cooperation*. Lexington, Mass.: D. C. Heath, 1976.

Carlson, R. *Jailing the Innocent: The Plight of the Material Witness*. 55 Iowa L. Rev. 1 (1969).

Carlson, R., and Voelpel, M. *Material Witness and Material Injustice*. 58 Wash. U. L. Q. 1 (1980).

Carrington, F. *Victim's Rights Litigation: A Wave of the Future?* 11 U. Rich. L. Rev. 447 (1977).

Childres, R. *Compensation for Criminally Inflicted Personal Injury*. 39 N.Y.U. L. Rev. 444 (1964).

Cleary, E. *Evidence as a Problem in Communicating*. 5 Vand. L. Rev. 277 (1952).

Compensation for Victims of Crime. 19 Vand. L. Rev. 220 (1965).

A Comprehensive Approach to Child Hearsay in Sex Abuse Cases. 83 Columbia L. Rev. 1745 (1983).

Confining Material Witnesses in Criminal Cases. 20 Wash. & Lee L. Rev. 164 (1963).

Connick, E. *Witness Intimidation: An Examination of the Criminal Justice System's Response to the Problem*. New York: Victim Services Agency, 1982.

Connick, E., and Davis, R. *Examining the Problem of Witness Intimidation*. 66 Judicature 439 (1983).

Criminal Defendant Has Sixth Amendment Right to Be Present at Videotaped Deposition. 1979 Wash. U. L. Q. 1106.

The Criminal Videotape Trail: Serious Constitutional Questions. 55 Oreg. L. Rev. 567 (1976).

Cutler, A. S. *Why the Good Citizen Avoids Testifying*. The Annals of the American Academy of Political and Social Science 103-9 (1953).

Davenport, D. *The Confrontation Clause and the Co-conspirator Exception in Criminal Prosecution: A Functional Analysis*. 85 Harv. L. Rev. 1378 (1972).

Davis, R., Russell, V., and Kunreuther, F. *The Role of the Complaining Witness in the Urban Criminal Court*. New York: Victim Services Agency and the Vera Institute of Justice, 1980.

Denroche, G. *Leading Questions*. 6 Crim. L. Q. 21 (1963).

Department of State, Justice, and Commerce, the Judiciary, and Related Agencies Appropriations for 1967: Hearings Before a Subcomm. of the House Comm. on Appropriations, 89th Cong., 2d Sess. (1966).

Dession, G. *The New Federal Rules of Criminal Procedure II*. 56 Yale L. J. 197 (1947).

Devitt, E., and Blackmar, C. *Federal Jury Practice and Instructions*. Third Edition. St. Paul: West, 1977.

Dow, D. *KLM v. Tuller: A New Approach to Admissibility of Prior Statements of a Witness*. 41 Neb. L. Rev. 598 (1962).

Evidence Act, 1938, 1 and 2 Geo. 6, C.28, § 1, repealed by Civil Evidence Act, 1968, C.64, § 20(2).

Exercise of the Privilege Against Self-Incrimination by Witness and Codefendants: The Effect Upon the Accused. 33 U. Chi. L. Rev. 151 (1965).

Falknor, J. *The Hearsay Rule and Its Exceptions.* 2 U.C.L.A. L. Rev. 43 (1954).

Federal Rules of Criminal Procedure Amendments Act of 1975: Hearings Before the Senate Comm. on the Judiciary, 94th Cong., 1st Sess. (1975).

Federal Rules of Criminal Procedure Amendment Act of 1975, Pub. L. No. 94-65, H.R. Rep. No. 247, 94th Cong., 1st Sess. (1975).

Federal Rules of Criminal Procedure Amendment Act of 1975, Senate Conference Rep. No. 94-336, July 28, 1975, to Accompany H.R. 6799, 94th Cong., 1st Sess. (1975).

Federal Rules of Evidence: Hearings on H.R. 5463 Before the House Subcomm. on Criminal Justice, 93d Cong., 1st Sess., Supp. (1973).

Federal Rules of Evidence. Report of House Comm. on the Judiciary, H.R. Rep. No. 650, 93rd Cong., 1st Sess. (1973).

Federal Rules of Evidence: Hearings on H.R. 5463 Before the Senate Comm. on the Judiciary, 93d Cong., 2d Sess. (1974).

Friedman, K. *Victims and Helpers: Reactions to Crime.* New York: Victim Services Agency, 1982.

Globe Newspaper Co. v. Superior Court: Right of Access to Criminal Trials After Richmond. 36 Ark. L. Rev. 688 (1983).

Goldstein, A. *Defining the Role of the Victim in Criminal Prosecution.* 52 Miss. L. J. 515 (1982).

Goldstock, R., and Coenen, D. *Controlling the Contemporary Loanshark: The Law of Illicit Lending and the Problem of Witness Fear.* 65 Cornell L. Rev. 127 (1980).

Gooderson, R. *Previous Consistent Statements.* 26 Cambridge, L. J. 64 (1968).

Graham, M. *The Confrontation Clause, the Hearsay Rule, and the Forgetful Witness.* 56 Tex. L. Rev. 151 (1978).

______. *Employing Inconsistent Statements for Impeachment and as Substantive Evidence: A Critical Review and Proposed Amendments of Federal Rules of Evidence 801(d)(1)(A), 613, and 607.* 75 Mich. L. Rev. 1565 (1977).

______. *Examination of a Party's Own Witness Under the Federal Rules of Evidence: A Promise Unfulfilled.* 54 Tex. L. Rev. 917 (1976).

______. *Handbook of Federal Evidence.* St. Paul: West, 1981.

______. *Prior Consistent Statements: Rule 801(d)(1)(B) of the Federal Rules of Evidence, Critique and Proposal.* 30 Hastings L. J. 575 (1979).

______. *The Relationship Among Federal Rules of Evidence 607, 801(d)(1)(A), and 403: A Reply to Weinstein's Evidence.* 55 Tex. L. Rev. 573 (1977).

Graham, P. *Treatment of Witnesses Laymen's Suggestions for Better Handling.* 34 A.B.A. J. 23 (1948).

Griswold, E. *The Due Process Resolution and Confrontation.* 119 U. Pa. L. Rev. 711 (1971).

Hale, W. *Impeachment of Witnesses by Prior Inconsistent Statements.* 10 S. Cal. L. Rev. 135 (1937).

Harland, A. T. *Monetary Remedies for the Victims of Crime: Assessing the Role of the Criminal Courts.* 30 U.C.L.A. L. Rev. 52 (1982).

Hearsay Under the Prepared Federal Rules: A Discretionary Approach. 15 Wayne L. Rev. 1077 (1969).

Hindelang, M. J., Gottfredson, M. R., and Garofalo, J. *Victims of Personal Crime: an Empirical Foundation for a Theory of Personal Victimization.* Cambridge, Mass.: Ballinger, 1978.

Illinois Supreme Court Committee on Evidence. *Majority Report on the Use of Prior Inconsistent Statements of Witnesses as Substantive Proof*, 1971.

The Impact of a Crime Wave: Perceptions, Fear, and Confidence in the Police. 17 Law and Society Rev. 319 (1983).

Impeaching One's Own Witness. 11 Ohio St. L. J. 364 (1950).

Impeachment of One's Own Witness: Present New York Law and Proposed Changes. 27 Cornell L. Q. 377 (1942).

Invasion of Privacy: Hearings Before the Subcomm. on Administrative Practice and Procedure of the Senate Comm. on the Judiciary, 89th Cong., 1st Sess. (1965).

The Jencks Legislation: Problems in Prospect. 67 Yale L. J. 674 (1958).

Judicial Control of Prosecutorial Discretion in Pretrial Diversion Programs. 31 Buffalo L. Rev. 909 (1982).

Kionka, E. *Torts in a Nutshell: Injuries to Persons and Property*. St. Paul: West, 1977.

Knudten, R. D. *Victims and Witnesses: Their Experiences with Crime and the Criminal Justice System.* Washington, D.C.: U.S. Government Printing Office, 1977.

Koessler, M. *Arrest as Material Witness.* 69 Case Com. 28 (March-April 1964).

Ladd, M. *Some Observations on Credibility: Impeachment of Witnesses.* 52 Cornell L. Q. 239 (1967).

______. *Impeachment of One's Own Witness—New Developments.* 4 U. Chi. L. Rev. 69 (1936).

Ladd, M., and Carlson, R. *Cases and Materials on Evidence.* Third Edition. Chicago: Callaghan, 1972.

Lamborn, L. *Toward a Victim Orientation in Crime.* 22 Rutgers L. Rev. 733 (1968).

Lawyers and Lineups. 77 Yale L. J. 390 (1967).

Libai, D. *The Protection of the Child Victim of a Sexual Offense in the Criminal Justice System.* 15 Wayne L. Rev. 177 (1969).

Louisell, D. *Criminal Discovery: Dilemma Real or Apparent.* 49 Calif. L. Rev. 56 (1961).

Louisell, D., and Mueller, C. *Federal Evidence.* Rochester: Lawyers Cooperative, 1977.

Maguire, J. *The Hearsay System: Around and Through the Thicket.* 14 Vand. L. Rev. 741 (1961).

Maguire, J., and Vincent, R. *Admissions Implied from Spoilations and Related Conduct.* 45 Yale L. J. 226 (1935).

Mass, S. *The Intimidated Witness.* 50 Fordham L. Rev. 582 (1982).

McCormick, C. *Handbook of the Law of Evidence.* St. Paul: West, 1954.

______. *Handbook of the Law of Evidence.* Second Edition. St. Paul: West, 1972.

______. *The Turncoat Witness: Previous Statements as Substantive Evidence.* 25 Tex. L. Rev. 573 (1947).

McDonald, W. F. *Criminal Justice and the Victim.* Beverly Hills, Calif.: Sage Publications, 1976.

McGillis, D., and Smith, P. *Compensation of Victims of Crime: Analysis of American Programs.* Washington, D.C.: National Institute of Justice, Department of Justice, 1983.

McInernay, J. *Proceedings Between Indictment and Trial.* 5 F.R.D. 156 (1945).

McIntyre, J. *Public Attitudes Toward Crime and Law Enforcement.* 6 American Crim. L. Q. 66 (1968).

Measures Relating to Organized Crime: Hearings on S.30, S.974, S.975, S.976, S.1623, S.1624, S.1861, S.2022, and S.2292 Before the Subcomm. on Criminal Laws and Procedures of the Senate Comm. on the Judiciary, 91st Cong., 1st Sess. (1969).

Moore's Federal Practice. Albany: Matthew Bender, 1975.

Morgan, E. *Basic Problems of Evidence.* Philadelphia: ALI-ABA, 1961.

______. *Hearsay Dangers and the Application of the Hearsay Concept.* 62 Harv. L. Rev. 177 (1948).

National Advisory Commission on Criminal Justice Standards and Goals. *A National Strategy to Reduce Crime.* Washington, D.C.: U.S. Government Printing Office, 1973.

National Organization for Victim Assistance. *The Victim Service System: A Guide to Action.* Washington, D.C., 1983.

Neubauer, D. W. *America's Courts and the Criminal Justice System,* North Scituate, Mass.: Duxbury Press, 1979.

Obstruction of Criminal Investigations, Senate Comm. on the Judiciary, S. Rep. No. 307, 90th Cong., 1st Sess. (1967).

The Omnibus Protection Act of 1982, S. Rep. No. 532, 97th Cong., 2d Sess. (1982).

Ordover, A. *That Damaging Turncoat Witness Is Still with Us: An Analysis of Federal Rules of Evidence 607, 801(d)(1)(A), and 403.* 5 Hofstra L. Rev. 65 (1976).

Orfield, L. *Criminal Procedure Under the Federal Rules.* Rochester: Lawyers Cooperative, 1966.

______. *Depositions in Federal Criminal Procedure.* 9 S.C. L. Rev. 376 (1957).

______. *The Federal Rules of Criminal Procedure.* 33 Calif. L. Rev. 543 (1945).

______. *The Preliminary Draft of the Federal Rules of Criminal Procedure.* 22 Tex. L. Rev. 37 (1944).

Organized Crime Control Act of 1969, Senate Comm. on the Judiciary, S. Rep. No. 617, 91st Cong., 1st Sess. (1969).

Organized Crime Control Act of 1970: Hearings on S.30 and Related Proposals Before Subcomm. No.5 of the House Comm. on the Judiciary, 91st Cong., 2d Sess. (1970).

Organized Crime Control Act of 1970, Pub. L. No. 91-452 §§ 501-4, 84 Stat. 922, 91st Cong., 2nd Sess. (1970).

Oversight of the Witness Protection Program: Hearings Before the Subcomm. on Administrative Practice and Procedure of the Senate Comm. on the Judiciary, 95th Cong., 1st Sess. (1979).

Parker, J. *The Child Witness Versus the Press: A Proposed Legislative Response to Globe v. Superior Court.* 47 Albany L. Rev. 408 (1983).

Participant's Manual for Judges on the Rights of Victims and Witnesses. Reno: National Judicial College, 1984.

Past Recollection Recorded. 28 Iowa L. Rev. 530 (1943).

Peeples, D. *Prior Inconsistent Statements and the Rule Against Impeachment of One's Own Witness: The Proposed Federal Rules.* 52 Tex. L. Rev. 1383 (1974).

The Plight of the Detained Material Witness. 7 Cath. U. L. Rev. 37 (1958).

President's Task Force on Victim's of Crime, *Final Report.* Washington, D.C., 1982.

Pretrial Detention of Witnesses. 117 U. Pa. L. Rev. 700 (1969).

Prior Inconsistent Statements as an Exception to the Hearsay Rule: An Analysis of People v. Johnson. 6 San Diego L. Rev. 92 (1969).

Proposed Amendments to the Federal Rules of Criminal Procedure. 14 Washburn L. J. 76 (1975).

Prosser, W. *Law of Torts*, Fourth Edition. St. Paul: West, 1971.

Rape Victim-Rape Crisis Counselor Communications: A New Testimonial Privilege. 86 Dickinson L. Rev. 539 (1982).

Read, F. *The New Confrontation Dilemma*. 45 S. Cal. L. Rev. 1 (1972).

Recent Developments, *Procedural Due Process and the Rules of Evidence—Federal Impeachment of the Voucher Rule*. 53 Wash. L. Rev. 319 (1978).

Rehabilitation of the Impeached Witness Through Prior Consistent Statements: An Analysis and Critique of a California Evidence Code Section 791. 50 S. Cal. L. Rev. 109 (1976).

Restatement (Second) of the Law of Torts. 1965.

Reutlinger, M. *Prior Inconsistent Statements: Presently Inconsistent Doctrine*. 26 Hastings L. J. 361 (1974).

Rosenthal, A. *Thirty-Eight Witnesses*. New York: McGraw-Hill, 1964.

Rothstein, P. *State Compensation for Criminally Inflicted Injuries*. 44 Tex. L. Rev. 38 (1965).

Semerjian, E. *The Right of Confrontation*. 55 A.B.A. J. 152 (1969).

Silbert, E. *Federal Rule of Evidence 801(d)(1)(A)*. 49 Temp. L. Q. 880 (1976).

Silverman, B. *Material Witnesses in Criminal Proceedings: Securing and Assuring Their Attendance*. 18 Mo. L. Rev. 38 (1953).

Smith, T. *The Hearsay Rule and the Docket Crises: The Futile Search for Paradise*. 54 A.B.A. J. 231 (1968).

Stalmack, J. *Prior Inconsistent Statement: Congress Takes a Compromising Step Backward in Enacting Rule 801(d)(1)(A)*. 8 Loy. U. Chi. L. J. 251 (1977).

Stern, L., and Gosh, D. *A Visit with Queen Caroline: Her Trial and Its Rule*. 6 Cap. U. L. Rev. 165 (1976).

Subin, H. *Criminal Justice in a Metropolitan Court*. Washington, D.C.: Office of Criminal Justice, United States Department of Justice, 1966.

Substantive Use of Extrajudicial Statements of Witnesses Under the Proposed Federal Rules of Evidence. 4 U. Rich. L. Rev. 110 (1969).

Thomas, R. *The Rule Against Impeaching One's Own Witness: A Reconsideration*. 31 Mo. L. Rev. 364 (1966).

Threats Inducing Emotional Reactions. 39 N.C. L. Rev. 74 (1960).

Trainer's Manual on the Rights of Victims and Witnesses. Reno: National Judicial College, 1984.

Traynor, R. *Ground Lost and Found in Criminal Discovery*. 39 N.Y.U. L. Rev. 228 (1964).

Underprivileged Communications: Extension of the Psychotherapist-Patient Privilege to Patients of Psychiatric Social Workers. 61 Calif. L. Rev. 1050 (1973).

Uniform Crime Victims Reparations Act. 11 U.L.A. 33 (1974).

United States Department of Justice. *Report of the Witness Security Program Review Committee*. Draft. 1978.

The Use of Prior Identification Evidence in Criminal Trials Under the Federal Rules of Evidence. 66 J. of Crim. Law and Criminology 240 (1975).

Victim Rights and Services: A Legislative Directory, 1983. Washington, D.C.: National Organization for Victims Assistance, 1983.

Victim and Witness Protection Act of 1982. Pub. L. No. 97-291, 96 Stat. 1248-58, 96th Cong., 1st Sess. (1982).

Weinstein, J. *Alternatives to the Present Hearsay Rule.* 44 F.R.D. 375 (1968).

Weinstein's Evidence. New York: Matthew Bender, 1982.

The Wetback as Material Witness: Pretrial Detention or Deposition. 7 Cal. W. L. Rev. 175 (1970).

Wigmore, J. *Evidence.* Third Edition. Boston: Little, Brown, 1940.

Witness Security Program: Hearings Before the Permanent Subcomm. on Investigations of the Senate Comm. on Governmental Affairs, 96th Cong., 2d Sess. (1980).

Witnesses—Imprisonment of the Material Witness for Failure to Give Bond. 40 Neb. L. Rev. 503 (1961).

Witnesses Under Article VI of the Proposed Federal Rules of Evidence. 15 Wayne L. Rev. 1236 (1969).

Wright, C. *Federal Practice and Procedure: Criminal.* Second Edition. St. Paul: West, 1982.

Wright, C., and Graham, K. *Federal Practice and Procedure.* Volumes 21-23. St. Paul: West, 1977.

Yarborough, R. *S. 2155 of the Eighty-Ninth Congress—The Criminal Injuries Compensation Act.* 50 Minn. L. Rev. 255 (1965).

Younger, I. *Confrontation and Hearsay: A Look Backward, a Peek Forward.* 1 Hofstra L. Rev. 32 (1975).

Index

Admissibility of prior statements. *See* Substantive admissibility of prior statements
Adopted testimony, 146
American Bar Association: recommendations on witness intimidation, 16-21, 303; Standards for Criminal Justice, 41, 50

Basic bill of rights for victims and witnesses, 23-24

Civil liability, 116-117
Community recommendations from ABA, 20
Confrontation Clause (Sixth Amendment), 61-65, 165-174
Context of intimidation, 5-8
Court recommendations from ABA, 19-20, 31-34
Court's witness doctrine, 232-233
Crime of intimidation. *See* Intimidation

Definition of witness intimidation. *See* Intimidation
Depositions to perpetuate testimony, 59-85, 259-263; and Amendment to Federal Rule of Criminal Procedure 15, 74-79; early statutory development, 65-67; and Federal Rule of Criminal Procedure 15, 67-72; and hearsay rule, 59-60; and Organized Crime Control Act of 1970 Title VI, 72, 74; and Sixth Amendment Confrontation Clause, 61-65; and Uniform Rules of Criminal Procedure, 79-82
Deterrent and remedial measures against intimidation: monetary recovery, 116-121; restraining order, 112-116
Discovery of prosecution witnesses: and Amended Federal Rule of Criminal Procedure 16, 39-41; and American Bar Association Standards, 41-44; common law and statutory development, 34-37; and Federal Rule of Criminal Procedure 16, 37-38, 46-50; in Jencks v. United States, 38-29; and Uniform Rules of Criminal Procedure, 44-47

Enforcers, 5
Examples of intimidation, 3-4, 73-74
Extent of problem of intimidation, 3-8

Family setting intimidation, 5-6
Federal Rule of Criminal Procedure 15, 67-72, 74-79

Federal Rule of Criminal Procedure 16, 37-41, 46-56
Federal Rule of Criminal Procedure 26.2, 39
Federal Rule of Evidence 803(24), 149-154
Federal Rule of Evidence 804(b)(5), 154-160, 276-280
Federal Rule of Evidence 403, 224-226
Forgetful witness, 143-144; feigned lack of recollection, 144-149; past recollection recorded, 164-165; true lack of recollection, 164-165
Former testimony, 127-133, 259
Forms of intimidation, 6-7

Hearings and depositions to perpetuate testimony, 259-263
Hearsay, 59-61, 125-127
Hearsay exception: past recollection recorded, 164-165; prior identification, 160-164; prior inconsistent statements, 133-149, 254-259; reliable hearsay, 149, 154; waiver of objection, 174-175
Hostile witnesses, 227-232

Impeachment: Court's witness doctrine, 232-233; and lack of recollection, 221; of own witness, 221; and prior inconsistent statements, 215-220; and voucher rule, 221-226
Inconsistency, requirement of, 140, 143
Inconsistent statement impeachment, 215-220
Intimidation: context of, 5-8; as a crime, 103-111; definition of, 4; deterrent and remedial measures against, 103-121; extent of problem, 3-8; in family setting, 5-6; forms of, 6-7; illustrations of, 3-4, 73-74; legislative response to, 8-11, 303-305; and Model Statute, 17, 103-111; and organized crime, 5; preventive measures against, 8-10, 16-89; in prison system, 6

Jencks Act, 38-39, 41, 52

Lack of recollection, 143, 226; feigned, 144-149; true, 164-165
Law enforcement recommendations from ABA, 17-18
Leading questions, 227-232

Material witness statutes, 56-59
Model Statute: Intimidation of Witnesses and Victims, 17, 103-111
Monetary recovery, 116-121

Names of witnesses, 34, 43, 44, 46, 51
National Conference of Commissioners on Uniform State Law, 44
National Judicial College recommendations, 30-34
National Organization for Victim Assistance, 303

Organized bar recommendations from ABA, 20-21
Organized Crime Control Act of 1970, 8, 72-74
Organized crime and intimidation, 5
Other reliable hearsay exception, 149, 154

Past recollection recorded, 164-165
Perpetuation of testimony, 59-85, 259-263
Preservation proceedings, 263-280
President's Task Force on Victims of Crime, 29-30; final report of, 303
Preventive initiatives, 8-11. *See also* American Bar Association, recommendations; Depositions to perpetuate testimony; Discovery of prosecution witnesses
Prior inconsistent statement impeachment, 215-221; and hostile witnesses, 227-232; and lack of recollection, 226-227; and leading questions, 227-232; prerequisites, 216-221; and the voucher rule, 222-226; and witness doctrine, 232-233
Prior inconsistent statements, proposal, 254-259

Prior statement of identification, 160-164
Prior statements, admissibility of. *See* Substantive admissibility of prior statements
Prison system intimidation, 6
Private sector recommendations from ABA, 20
Prosecution recommendations from ABA, 18-19

Refreshing recollection, 210-212
Reliable hearsay, 149-154
Responses to intimidation, 8-11
Restitution, 117-121
Restraining order, 112-116
Rights of victims and witnesses, 23-24

Second Act of Philip and Mary (1555), 56
Statements of witnesses, 43, 44
Statutory development regarding depositions and discovery, 35-37, 65-67
Substantive admissibility of statements, 125-127; and Confrontation Clause of Sixth Amendment, 165-174; expanding, 252-280; and Federal Rule of Evidence 803(24), 149-154; and Federal Rule of Evidence 804(b)(5), 154-160; and former testimony, 127-133; and past recollection, 164-165; and prior inconsistent statements, 133-149; and prior statement of identification, 160-161; and waiver doctrine, 174-181

Testimony: depositions to perpetuate, 59-85, 259-263; discovery of prosecution witnesses, 34-56
Tort liability, 116-117
Treatment of victims and witnesses, 16, 30, 31
True lack of recollection, 143-144

Unavailable declarant, 128-130, 168-173
Uniform Rules of Criminal Procedure, 44, 79-82

Victim and Witness Protection Act of 1982, 21-29, 102, 107, 303
Victim compensation programs, 121
Victim participation, 25, 32
Victim's bill of rights, 23-24
Victims Committee, 16
Voucher rule, 221-223

Waiver: hearsay objection, 174-181; right to confrontation, 174-181
Witness Protection Program, 85-89
Witness statements, 34, 44, 51

About the Author

MICHAEL H. GRAHAM, Professor in the School of Law at the University of Miami, is the author of *Tightening the Reins of Justice in America* (Greenwood Press, 1983), *Handbook of Federal Evidence*, and *Handbook of Illinois Evidence*.

www.ingramcontent.com/pod-product-compliance
Ingram Content Group UK Ltd.
Pitfield, Milton Keynes, MK11 3LW, UK
UKHW020239290926
15470UKWH00002B/620

9 780899 301044